The Hundred Glories of French Cooking

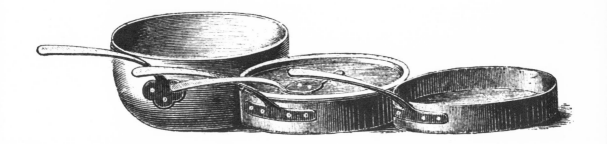

translated from the French by Derek Coltman

The Hundred Glories
of French Cooking

by ROBERT COURTINE

Farrar, Straus and Giroux, New York

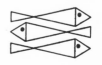

Originally published in France under the title:
Cent Merveilles de la cuisine française
Copyright © 1971 by R. J. Courtine
This translation © 1973 by Farrar, Straus and Giroux, Inc.
All rights reserved
First American printing, 1973
Published simultaneously in Canada by Doubleday Canada Ltd.,
Toronto
Library of Congress catalog card number: 73–85730
ISBN 0–374–17357–5
Printed in the United States of America
Designed by Kay Lee

Monsieur V. Azam

Dantan fit jadis la Caricature du Compositeur Pesarese
Aujourd'hui devenu Pianiste de la quatrième Classe il ne
s'oppose pas a ce qu'elle soit Publiée dans votre Journal

G. Rossini

Passy 28 Juin 1867

Contents

HORS D'OEUVRE   *10*

SOUPS   *15*

Soupe à l'Oignon   *17*   Soupe d'Orties   *29*

Soupe au Pistou   *23*   Potage Germiny   *33*

Bisque de Homard   *26*   Potage Queue de Boeuf   *39*

SHELLFISH   *43*

Homard à l'Américaine   *45*   Écrevisses à la Nage   *63*

Homard aux Légumes   *53*   Coquilles Saint-Jacques à la Nage   *69*

Huîtres Frites à la Villeroi   *57*   Escargots à la Suçarelle   *77*

FISH   *81*

Merlan Frit   83

Turbot Soufflé au Champagne   87

Truite de Mer Sauce Verte   93

Sole Normande   99

Cotriade   103

Sole Cubat   107

Estofinado   112

Terrine d'Anguilles   117

Friture   121

Brochet au Beurre Blanc   125

Truite au Bleu   129

Pochouse   133

Aïoli de Morue   137

Goujons à la Cascamèche   141

APPETIZERS AND EGG DISHES   *145*

Jambon Persillé   146

Gougères Bourguignonnes   150

Foie Gras   153

Gâteau de Foies Blonds de Volailles   157

Terrine de Canard Madeleine Decure   161

Andouillette   166

Les Petits Pâtés de Pézenas   169

Fricandeaux   173

Boudin à l'Auvergnate   177

Beuchelle Tourangelle   181

Oeufs Pochés à la Sauce Béchamelle   185

Oeufs en Meurette   191

Oeufs à la Toupinel   194

Omelette de la Mère Poulard   199

GAME AND POULTRY   *205*

Dindon Farci   206

Salmis de Faisan à la Laguipière   211

Lièvre à la Duchambais   217

Perdreaux en Chartreuse   221

Ortolans à la Robert Laporte   225

Poulet Marengo   228

Poulet Père Lathuile   231

Coq au Vin   235

Lapin en Gelée   240

Poule au Pot   245

Caneton aux Navets   250

Poussin Viroflay   254

Caneton Tour d'Argent   257

Poulet à la Crapaudine   261

Poulet Célestine   267

MEAT   *271*

Tournedos Rossini *273*	*Miroton* *325*
Potée Sarthoise *277*	*Tripes à la Mode de Caen* *333*
Navarin Printanier *283*	*Daube de Boeuf en Gelée* *337*
Ris de Veau Clamart *287*	*Pot-au-Feu* *343*
Boeuf à la Ficelle *291*	*Poitrine d'Agneau Farcie* *349*
Steack au Poivre *295*	*Blanquette de Veau* *353*
Côte de Veau Foyot *299*	*Jambon en Saupiquet* *359*
Choucroute *305*	*Côtes de Mouton Champvallon* *365*
Tête de Veau en Tortue *311*	*Côte de Boeuf Béarnaise* *371*
Cassoulet *317*	*Pieds de Porc à la Sainte-Ménehould* *375*
Gigot à la Sept Heures *321*	

VEGETABLES   *381*

Asperges à la Fontenelle *383*	*Gratin de Cèpes Farcis* *402*
Truffe en Feuilleté *387*	*Cardons à la Moelle* *406*
Pommes Soufflées *391*	*Timbale de Riz Roy Soleil* *411*
Timbale de Macaroni Financière *395*	*Morilles à la Crème* *415*
Caillettes *398*	*Salade de Lentilles* *419*

DESSERTS   *423*

Tarte Tatin *425*	*Crêpes Suzette* *442*
Baba au Rhum à la Chantilly *429*	*Pêche Melba* *449*
Melon de Schéhérazade *433*	*Soufflé Rothschild* *453*
Omelette Surprise Brésilienne *437*	*Fraises et Framboises Chantilly* *458*

Tarte Bourdaloue   463

Pithiviers   469

Raisiné de Courtenay   473

Riz à l'Impératrice   477

Beignets d'Ananas   482

Sorbets   487

POUSSE-CAFÉ   *491*

INDEX   *495*

Hors d'Oeuvre

The hundred glories? Perhaps I should have called it "my" hundred glories. Cooking is an art, and as we all know, judgment in such matters must always be subjective. So I hope none of my readers will be annoyed at encountering some dish he doesn't really care for, or become indignant over the omission of a personal favorite: there are far more than a hundred glories on the Kitchen Roll of Honor!

In other words, mine is an arbitrary selection, but a reasoned one. Is some culinary psychiatrist going to apply the old saying "Tell me what you eat and I'll tell you what you are," and then produce an imposing psychological portrait of the epicure I may—or may not—be? No matter. Though it is easy to see that I have tried to go beyond the purely practical boundaries of the kitchen.

For cooking is much more than just cooking. In the first place, it is a tradition, and like all traditions it has its origin in the infancy of a country's soil, or a certain ingredient, or a nation's customs. Geography, history, religion, manners, all have rocked its cradle to some extent.

Certainly all my hundred dishes have a history, even

the "unhistorical" ones, simply because they exist, because they all had a childhood somewhere (though it is sometimes shrouded in mystery, or just so ordinary that it's been forgotten), and also because they have survived, tucked away in the corners of menus, waiting for a chance meeting with an everyday appetite or the excitement of an extra-special celebration. So we must approach them with all this in mind, with respect, but also with a smile. We must lavish our time upon them without impatience. So I would like to suggest, if I may, that you treat each of these recipes as a game—just a little. But a game that is going to take all your intelligence, subtlety, poetry, and affection.

Jean-Louis Vaudoyer of the Academy once said: "The true epicure is not merely a man who has successfully educated and civilized his taste buds, who exercises his sense of taste with infallible precision: the true epicure is also an epicure in touching, in smelling, in seeing. Before it reaches the mind, a beautiful line of verse, a fine picture, or a noble symphony is perceived, just like a good dish, with the senses. The epicure who is an epicure only in front of a plate and a glass is an elementary epicure indeed."

How amply I should be repaid if, fork in hand, you were to rediscover, like a hidden watermark in the contents of your plate, all that the centuries have bequeathed to us through the simple truths and admirable symbols in even the humblest of these recipes! Delacroix was fond of saying: "One should have a relish for what one does." In cooking, you also have a relish for what others have done before you.

Yes, cooking is much more than just cooking. And that is why one should also talk about good food as one eats it. What better subject for a mealtime conversation than the meal? Balzac was particularly fond of spicing *La Comédie humaine* with such savory exchanges. And why not? Or rather: why no longer? Why should the age we live in—so difficult, to put it mildly—deprive us of enjoying this escape, this return to our beginnings, however fleetingly?

Recordier, the great French clown Auguste, said to me one day: "Going into the circus is like taking religious vows." And that, I feel, is the attitude we should adopt when we approach one of the glories of our epicurean traditions. What I wish you, then, is grace. And *bon appétit* too—of course!

AUTHOR'S NOTE

*In the Menus, an asterisk (*) preceding
an entry indicates
that a recipe for that dish
appears in this volume.*

*All the recipes are designed
to serve six to eight portions.*

SOUPS

Daumier: Soup

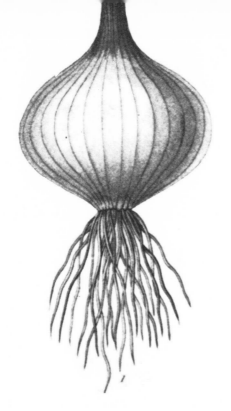

MENU

*Soupe à l'oignon
Assiette anglaise
(Coldcuts)
Salade de mâche
(Lamb's-lettuce salad)
Pommes bonne femme
(Baked apples)

Nothing to drink while you are eating onion soup. But what about afterward? Some may wish to fill the gap with a small glass of some spirit—marc brandy, kirsch, Calvados. Or, more simply, a first glass of the wine that is to accompany the cold meats. A Beaujolais for example.

Soupe à l'Oignon (Onion Soup)

Onion soup or *gratinée*, which should it be? The difference is a very slight one, and every onion soup, if it is to be truly succulent, must be more or less a *gratinée*. In culinary fact as well as in spirit.

In the whole of French cooking there is no more evocative dish, no dish better able to conjure up the sentimental, carefree feelings associated with unexpected nights of adventuring through the city streets.

There is no place for the *gratinée* on a well-ordered menu, simply because it *is* the menu, all on its own, even if it does happen to be followed by a dozen oysters or a plate of cold meat.

Though a daughter of the streets, your onion soup doesn't sit down to table with just anyone. She thumbs her nose derisively at *potage Soubise*, her bourgeois cousin, a different kind of onion soup altogether.

She gets up early and goes to bed late. Though in between she makes sure of a good siesta, for she adores the

city lights and the chiaroscuro of amorous emotions—like the true hooker she is. And you will find her hanging out around Les Halles because it provides her with the nourishing country smells that maintain her healthy complexion and robust constitution despite her wild life. She may sleep in the gutter, but her belly will be full. And her soul at peace. She cradles a whole world of bohemianism, of merrymaking, of fatigue and encroaching soberness in her sturdy matron's arms. She consoles, in those small hours, our sickness of heart and disillusions.

In her presence all castes dissolve. Rich and poor are equals in appetite. And from the subtle depths of all past ages the scent of the *gratinée* is the incense of haves and have-nots together in the dark, together because of the dark. The early-to-bed know nothing of her. They are the sons of error and she is certainty itself.

I had just got that far with my musings on the *gratinée* when a friend who hails from Lyons happened to stop by:

"So, if I understand you aright, you are saying that the *gratinée* is of Parisian origin?"

"Parisian? But of course! Quintessentially Parisian! Daughter of her blood, of her cobbles, of her revolutions and her barricades . . ."

"Well, perhaps. The *gratinée* perhaps. But *soupe à l'oignon*, no. That came beyond all doubt from Lyons."

And, documents in hand, he proceeded to establish the incontestable origin of the *soupe aux oignons*, reminding me that onions have always been the very foundation of all cookery in that region bounded by the Saône, the Rhône, and Beaujolais.

But I don't care.

This daughter of the night and night's pale dawns will always remain as elusive as those dawns themselves.

So now to the recipe. There are at least a hundred. There is only one. There must be onion in it, as its name indicates, and all the rest is relatively unimportant. Cheese? Yes, but the kind of cheese doesn't matter. Bread? Certainly, for those who are hungry. An aroma of wine, or a spirit? By all means, as long as it is merely as a supplement to the dominant "key," that of the onion in all its glory.

18

The goodhearted gastronome Gaston Derys, reminiscing about his bohemian days, told us once about a generous hostess at whose house he and his friends lingered on perhaps too often in merry argument, and about how she used to serve them onion soup in the early hours. But a dawn eventually came when the lady, tired perhaps of a tradition that was too greatly depleting her kitchen stocks, decided to make sure that her kitchen had neither stock nor Gruyère with which to keep it up. But she was forgetting the golden rule: only the onion is indispensable. Her shameless guests ran-

sacked her kitchen and discovered not only the onions but also some old Armagnac, a Camembert, a bottle of champagne, and some eggs. Whereupon they created a culinary masterpiece that reconciled hostess and guests forever.

And there is no doubt that the fortifying aspect of the onion soup will have been fortified itself by that champagne. How could that daughter of the night have failed to fall head over heels for the bubbling cavalier that accompanied so many warm and laughing nights?

A few years ago, on the radio program "Paris-Cocktail," a Parisian restaurant owner named Mme Louis offered her recipe: onions lightly gilded in butter, not browned or burned. Addition of a stock made from beef and chicken giblets. Individual earthenware terrines. A drop of grenache in the bottom of each and the stock poured in. On the surface, a slice of buttered toast with a generous covering of Gruyère, Comté, or Parmesan. Another drop of grenache, salt and pepper, then the whole thing popped into the oven.

Listeners wrote in to protest.

One of them said that she always made her *gratinée* with water because it was cheaper. Indeed it is. But stock is better! Others, however, always added white wine. And an Englishwoman waxed indignant in her letter about the barbarous custom of adding port to the soup. Why, in heaven's name? But perhaps Mme Louis's grenache, cooked at the bottom of the terrine, uncooked above, produces a yet more subtle aroma! Some add cognac or Armagnac. It's a question of taste.

The trickiest question of all, however, is to know whether the soup should be thick—a more or less solid broth—or somewhat more liquid. The discussion is still going on. Just as it is between those who bind the soup with egg yolks, those who make it with milk but without cheese, those who omit the cognac but add just a trickle of vinegar, those who employ Camembert, Brie, Roquefort, and so forth.

Soupe à l'oignon is a subject of eternal controversy. And that is a proof of its power, its personality.

20

Soupe à l'Oignon

½ lb large white onions
  4 tbs butter
4 tbs flour
  1½ qts beef or veal stock

1 cup milk
  salt and pepper
2 club rolls
  3 oz Gruyère or a similar cheese, grated

Peel the onions (under water to avoid tears) and slice them.

Place 4 tablespoons of the butter in a deep saucepan to melt but not brown. Toss in the sliced onions and keep turning with a wooden spoon until they are an all-over golden color. Dust with the flour. Continue stirring, and add the stock little by little.

Increase the heat as the stock is added. Go on stirring till the soup boils. Then turn down and leave to cook gently for 10 minutes.

Bring the milk to a boil and add to the onion soup, stirring it in well. Add salt and pepper to taste; then pour into a large pot or casserole that will go into your oven.

Cut the rolls into rounds one-eighth of an inch thick. Mix a pinch of pepper into the grated cheese. Melt the remaining butter in a saucepan. Set aside.

Arrange the rounds of bread on top of the soup. Sprinkle with the grated cheese. Pour the melted butter over. Then place in a hot oven and leave until the surface is bubbling and lightly browned, but not burned.

N O T E : You can use water instead of stock. You can use chicken stock instead of beef or veal stock. You can omit the milk. You can strain the onion soup before the last stage.

Basilicum Indicum macu, latum. Basilicum Medium.

A rosé, a "country retreat"
wine, is the only thing to go
with such a sun-drenched meal.
A rosé from Provence, a
Bandol, or a vin de Cassis.

Soupe au Pistou

(Vegetable Soup with Noodles and Basil)

The entire seacoast of Provence is enlivened by the aroma of
this *soupe au pistou*, but first of all we must reach some sort
of agreement on our definition of both the word and the
thing. Is the *pistou* simply the basil in the dish, or is it the paste
made with the basil? Opinion is divided. However, one thing
is clear: *pistou* is not just the same thing as basil.

The word probably derives from the action of pounding the garlic and basil together in the mortar. It was then
transferred from the action to the object, and the object
is simply this herb paste, the final ingredient in the soup (the
two first being the vegetables and the noodles). And since it
was this ingredient that gave the soup its whole character, its
"truth," its personality, it had of course to be incorporated
in the name of the dish. For this isn't any old vegetable-and-
noodle soup; it is the soup of soups, fragrant with pounded
garlic and basil—the *soupe au pistou*, what else?

Not that I wish to pass over the virtues of basil. In the
language of flowers, basil signifies "hate," but only because
there has at some point been an unfortunate confusion with
the basilisk, that malevolent reptile of legend. In fact, this

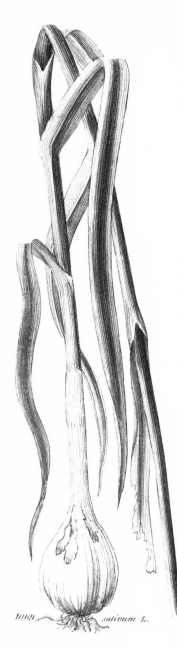

1069   *sativum L.*

pretty plant, a native of Asia and Africa, joins grace to utility. The Hindus look upon basil as a sacred plant and grow it on special pedestals in their temples.

Its stems and flowering tips, picked in summer and then dried, are an almost universal panacea in the folk pharmacopoeia. An infusion of them is a cure for general debility, for sluggish stomachs, for colic, for dizzy spells, and so forth. An infusion of its leaves will combat nervous conditions, hysteria, and epilepsy. Powdered, they will relieve migraines, head colds, and sinusitis. A decoction of them will provide a treatment for thrush. And oil of basil will halt the encroachment of baldness, keep away gout, and so forth.

A friend has pointed out to me that basil is an obligatory ingredient of the *olio*, "that appalling stew" that comes to us from Spain. By which he means the *olla podrida*, in which float ducks, pigeons, partridges, chicken, veal, lamb, unsalted bacon, and I know not what else, all cooked together with ginger, nutmeg, and pepper. And he then adds, being a historian of things epicurean: "Mme de Sévigné used only one sort of meat and bitter chicory instead of basil, which meant she never achieved a good *olio*. But Mme de Sévigné never had the reputation of being a good cook. Nor was she able to treat with any success the illness that carried her off. If she had used basil perhaps that would never have happened."

As we enjoy our *soupe au pistou* we may therefore muse on a suitable funeral oration for the letter-writing marquise, a brilliant lady but no great shakes as a gourmet.

As with all true dishes of the people, not codified by the chefs who created them but evolved by tradition, there is no one *soupe au pistou*. It is every man, and even more every woman, to his or her own taste. I remember reading one recipe that included bacon in the form of browned lardons, and another in which it was grated raw into the garlic-and-basil paste. Moreover, the choice of vegetables depends very much on both the season and the inspiration of the moment. If you don't happen to have any of the thick vermicelli referred to down in Provence as *méjanels*, then the usual kind will do almost as well. Because, when all is said and done, the important thing is the *pistou* itself, that intangible and triumphant alliance of garlic and basil.

I remember one *soupe au pistou* in particular, consumed one evening at a friend's home. All the guests enjoyed it, I may say. But for me it was something more. I had been up early that morning to go to Les Halles with the charming Provençale who was to make the *pistou*, and had then spent almost the whole day in the kitchen as her obedient potboy. For me it had been a day of shared enthusiasm and friendship and a great "lesson in *pistou*."

Soupe au Pistou

1 lb fresh lima beans or other fresh
white beans
   ½ lb fresh green stringbeans
2 carrots
   2 leeks
3 potatoes
   4 small zucchini, unpeeled
2 tomatoes
   1 large Spanish onion

3 qts boiling water
   salt and pepper
thyme, bayleaf, parsley
   3 cloves garlic
15 basil leaves
   4 to 6 tbs olive oil
2 oz grated Parmesan cheese
   2 oz grated Comté cheese
¼ lb thick vermicelli

Shell the lima beans, cut the stringbeans into short lengths, and the other vegetables into small dice; put them all into the boiling water with salt, pepper, a bayleaf, a sprig each of thyme and parsley, and simmer gently.

While the vegetables are simmering, pound the garlic and the basil in a mortar; then, drop by drop, add the olive oil and a little of each of the two kinds of grated cheese. Add only enough olive oil to pro-

duce a thick paste.

Fifteen minutes before the vegetable soup is completely cooked, remove the herbs and add the vermicelli. (It should simmer until vegetables are tender and the flavors well blended.)

Place the paste in the tureen. Pour the soup in on top of it.

Serve the rest of the grated cheese on the side.

MENU

*Bisque de homard
Faisan Souvarov
(Stuffed pheasant)
Bombe glacée
(Molded ice-cream shell,
    filled with mousse)

An "important" dinner (as the antique dealers say, "an important piece") from start to finish. Don't serve any wine with the bisque unless you intend to give your guests champagne throughout the meal (in which case you would of course begin serving it with the soup). Otherwise, a glass of water. Then, with the pheasant, a great Burgundy—a Richebourg, for example, from the Romanée-Conti estate.

Bisque de Homard (Lobster Bisque)

Ever since they started appearing in cans, hardly anyone seems to eat bisques. Not at formal dinners anyway. Is it because the ease with which they can be produced is a betrayal of their nature? Or rather is it the idea that people had of them as expensive, rich dishes—of something out of the ordinary?

Possibly. But perhaps there is another reason as well—the fact that the vulgarization of the word "bisque" has robbed it of all its poetry without making it in any way more explicable than before. For it is still swathed in mystery. So much so that its etymology is still unknown, and we aren't even certain of its gender.

Meslin de Saint-Gelais, the old chaplain of Francis I, wrote a punning poem on the dish, using the fact that *bisquer* also means to fly into a temper. But he wriggles out of giving it a gender. In any case, bisque in those days meant a kind of meat or game stew, very highly spiced.

It was not until the seventeenth century that the dish (usually made of quail, pigeons, or pheasants) had crayfish added to it, often crushed into a covering sauce. Later came croutons as a decoration. And in 1752, Vincent de la Chapelle

asserted that "a bisque with a good sauce is the most royal of royal dishes."

But what happened then—precisely because the best part of the dish was this sauce, this *coulis*—was that gradually everything other than the sauce began to disappear. Till finally, along with the strong seasoning and the croutons, that was all that remained, and the *coulis*, becoming a soup, abrogated the name of bisque entirely to itself.

So that a bisque—or, if you prefer, a bisque soup—has for almost two centuries now been a purée of shellfish (crayfish, prawns, crabs, crawfish, scampi, or lobster).

Bisque de Homard

⅓ cup carrots
 ¼ cup onions
2 tbs celery
 ⅓ cup butter
salt
 bayleaf
powdered thyme
 3½ lbs lobster (preferably made up of
 small lobsters of about ¾ lb each)

3 tbs cognac
 ¼ cup white wine
1 qt chicken stock
 3 oz long-grain rice
⅜ cup heavy cream
 cayenne
parsley

Dice the carrots, onions, and celery finely. Melt 2 tablespoons of the butter. Cook the vegetables gently in the melted butter, together with salt, bayleaf, and powdered thyme.

Split, devein, and cut up the lobsters. Drop the pieces into the cooked vegetables (in culinary terminology, a *mirepoix*) and toss over a hot flame. Pour on the cognac. Light the cognac; then add the white wine and reduce the result by two-thirds by boiling.

Pour in 1 cup of the chicken stock and cook for 10 minutes. Then remove the lobster tails and put them on one side.

Cook the rice in 2½ cups of chicken stock.

Pound the lobster pieces. Add the rice, the stock it was cooked in, and the stock the lobster was cooked in. Force the mixture through a sieve. Then put it back in a saucepan, add the remainder of the chicken stock, and boil for a few seconds. Put through a fine strainer and keep warm in a double boiler.

Dice the lobster tails finely.

Before serving add the remaining butter cut into small pieces, the cream (scalded but not boiled), a dash of cayenne, and the diced lobster tails, and garnish with parsley.

Martin Drolling: Rustic Interior

And to drink, the same kind of red wine that was used in the preparation of the peaches. It could be a Loire wine (a Chinon or a Bourgueil), but also one of the lesser Bordeaux reds (St.-Emilion). Chilled, of course.

Soupe d'Orties (Nettle Soup)

Man lived on a vegetable diet before he took to eating flesh, and he lost no time in discovering the merits of the innumerable plants that nature spread before him. Exercising his sense of taste, he selected the best among them. It was in the vegetable kingdom that gastronomy first took root, as it were.

Alas, since then man has become the overcivilized creature that we see today. He has forgotten the best of those herbs and plants without finding anything but synthetic and noxious replacements for them. No plant of general alimentary utility has been added to the world's diet since the beginning of written history. An account of the vegetables used in the twelfth century mentions celandine leaves, fumitory, cress and watercress, scurvy grass, wild horseradish, pennycress, shepherd's purse, sea kale, pepperwort, cow parsnip, borage, sow thistle, hop, wild sorrel, sweet rocket, goosefoot, wild salsify, samphire, plantain, couch grass, centaury, wild radish, clover, brome grass, dog's mercury, lamb's lettuce, stinging nettle, and others, all of which have returned today to the status of mere wild flowers or weeds.

It gladdens my heart to see the nettle figuring in that

eloquent list. The stinging nettle was a childhood companion of mine, not merely as an opponent in that age-old and painful battle between aggressive leaves and a child's calves, but also, in a way, as a guardian fairy of the hearth. For my grandmother, illiterate, yet how infinitely more learned than many present-day donkeys weighed down with their Sorbonne parchments, used it all the time in her cooking. With it she fed both my stomach and my young curiosity.

Her good taste was carrying on a tradition that already existed among the ancient Greeks, who, according to Aristophanes, harvested nettles before the arrival of the swallows and considered them a delicacy.

In the same way French peasants, once upon a time, were well aware of the plant's merits as a food for poultry. Chopped nettles are the best food you will find for fattening young turkeys. Nettles contain two and a half times as much protein as hay, five times more fat, and a third again more carbohydrate. The same peasants taught the medical profession that the leaves of the nettle have antiseptic properties, for there was a time, in the north particularly, when they wrapped meat in nettles to make it keep longer.

Today we know that the stinging nettle contains an antidiarrhetic and an antidiabetic and possesses a great many other virtues besides—virtues that my grandmother cultivated without even knowing it.

Their richness in chlorophyll makes nettles—or ought to make them—a particularly nutritious food. But the French are no different from the Americans in this respect (according to the National Research Council half the population of the United States never eats green vegetables!), and our planners will simply snicker at my praise of nettles. At moments one would like to whip such disbelievers with them. But no, on second thought it would be doing them too much of a favor, for in the nineteenth century scourging with nettles was a means of revivifying paralyzed limbs.

In the spring my grandmother made wonderful soups with nettle tops. She was of the "give us this day our daily soup" generation. Though admittedly she had lived too long in Paris to remain an adherent of the midday soup tradition. We had it only in the evening; but there was usually some left

over, and my grandfather never complained when it re-
appeared for his breakfast, steaming hot and thickened by a
thorough reheating. I myself, young idiot that I was, preferred *café au lait* (a genuine poison, as the medical profession
recognizes today). But the evening soup, served out of that
huge, steaming tureen, by lamplight, seemed to me wholly
worthy of our household gods. At school I was already flirt-
ing with Molière's handmaid and would have liked to be able
to say: "*Je vis de bonne soupe tant que de beau langage.*" ("I
live for good soup as much as for beautiful language.")

I remember those Thursdays and the garden shed. As
soon as the midday meal was over my grandmother would
tie on an apron faded with washing, take down a little osier
basket, arm herself with a small knife, and say to me: "Are
you coming to pick the soup with me?"

We went out. The garden was big, half carefully laid
out, half wild. The flowers grew every which way, always
on the run toward freedom, but the vegetables were all sown
in lines whose unwavering severity conjured up the "serious
things in life." A missing head of lettuce, devoured by slugs
or sapped by underground grubs, was like a frontal assault
on my grandfather's authority. He could not rest until the
affront had been repaired, like a man who knows the importance of order, a little autocrat of the well-kept garden.

So we went through the garden, my grandmother im-
provising her evening soup out loud as the various beds passed
before her eyes and the inspiration took her.

"Look there! That romaine will be bolting soon, let's
pick that, and then go over there to see if the round carrots
are ready to be pulled. Romaine in the soup must have carrot
with it."

Or else: "With the sautéed potatoes left over from lunch
we shall have a good soup tonight. We must have some spring
onions, and not just one or two! And a tomato for the color!"

And on such days, in the spring, as we approached the
wild corner of the garden—the tangle that grieved my grandfather's spirit so and aroused his angst at disorder to the quick,
the corner we had named "the hedgehog's corner"—if the
young nettles with their elegant feathered and frilled tops
happened to attract my grandmother's attention with their

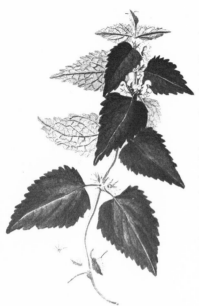

beautiful and tender green quintessence of vegetable innocence, she would murmur affectionately: "Three new potatoes and two white onions are what we need for nettles, but nettles must have coriander too, we must never forget that."

And trotting over to the other side of the garden, beyond the shed, I would reach the herb bed, its glassed-in frame propped open, and I would pick three, no more, of the little leaves from the top of the perennial she had asked for; delicate, narrow, pastel straps with an aroma so penetrating that it benumbed my buzzing senses as I stood beneath that sun so high in the sky.

And that evening we all lapped up our nettle soup.

Soupe d'Orties

1 lb stinging nettle tops
  1 qt boiling water
5 new potatoes
  2 white onions
salt

2 or 3 leaves fresh coriander
  2 tbs heavy cream
5 tsp butter
  pepper

Wash the nettle tops thoroughly; then throw them into the boiling water along with the potatoes and onions. Salt lightly. Add the coriander leaves.

Allow to boil gently until the potatoes are cooked. Put the soup through a mincer.

Replace in the saucepan with the cream and the butter, cut into small pieces. Heat, but do not allow to boil. Check seasoning and add salt to taste. Add pepper and serve.

A white wine, then a red. Two wines from Beaune (Burgundy), such as those from the Clos des Mouches.

Potage Germiny

(Cream of Sorrel Soup)

We live in an age of indifference and mediocrity, an age in which everything is a shade of gray. Who can tell me the name of the present governor of the Banque de France, for example? And what kind of man is he? A "Mister Average" of the ruling classes, whose very lack of features allows him to fit any post. A gray man in a black suit. What painter could possibly be interested in leaving such a man's features on record for posterity?

Perhaps in his Empire-style office this colorless creature sits beneath a portrait painted by a master. The subject, looking down on the banker below, is grave but distinguished; one senses that he is a man of quality. His side-whiskers are graying, and his barber has been in that morning to take care of the orderly perfection of his coiffure. The lips are slightly fleshy and indicate a sensuality that only adds to his social distinction: the sensuality of the gourmet. The eye is open, the gaze clear, with a sort of amused indulgence in the depths of the pupil. He is a man of figures, but not just a man of figures, and certainly not a man given to financial mounte-bankery. The subject of the portrait, looking down with

Giraud: Dining Room at Princess Mathilde's House

seeming irony on his successor, is named, or rather was named, Charles-Gabriel Le Bègue, Comte de Germiny.

I'm inventing it all, of course! Is there a portrait anywhere, I wonder, of this man who was Chief of Petitions for the Council of State, Collector of Taxes, prefect for the Seine et Marne, Minister of Finance, Governor of the Land Bank, Governor of the Banque de France, a senator, and Grand Officer of the Legion of Honor? But I am sure that if there is one then that is how it must be: the Count standing, three-quarter face, a beautiful, slightly plump hand on the back of a Louis XVI armchair, a desk at his back stamped with the mark of the famous cabinet-maker Riesener—perhaps a copy of Louis XV's own, still to be admired in the Louvre, scrolled all over in gold.

And all the riches of the Banque de France, in an age when our exchanges brimmed with gold and when the state, investing in sound policies, was reaping healthy finances—all those riches over which this amiable financier watched have sunk without a trace. Except for one very rich soup, one soup that remains as evidence of those past glories: *le potage Germiny*.

The difference between a *soupe* and a *potage* is quite clear, and it is really one of class. When a *soupe* moves up the social scale, it becomes a *potage*. It ceases to be either "sop"—the hunk of bread with which one soaked up one's broth—or that broth itself. And it is a long time since a *potage* was no more than the contents of a pot.

So that Carême, whose name symbolizes the ideal of perfect cooking, was able to write: "I have seen kings and emperors at table a thousand times, and all ate *potage* with relish."

Soupe warms our insides; it answers a need. *Potage* is a luxury, a peristyle for the edifice of an important meal. Think of a list of *soupes*. For example: *alsacienne, ardennaise, auvergnate, bûcheronne, fermière, flamande, laboureur, maraîchère, villageoise, normande, savoyarde, paysanne* . . . Now consider the following roster of *potages: Ambassadrice, Boieldieu, Bourbon, Bourdaloue, Castellane, Colbert, Demidoff, Diplomate, Dubarry, Grande Duchesse, Impératrice, Metternich, Montmorency, Nelson, Nesselrode, Princesse, Rossini, Souveraine, Windsor* . . . The difference isn't hard to see, is it?

And this *potage Germiny*, moreover, is to be found in the highest category of the *potages* themselves, among what the chefs call the *veloutés*. In company with those other *veloutés* named *Bagration, Cambacérès, Chevreuse, Condé, Conti, Joinville, La Vallière, Marie Stuart, Médicis*, and so forth.

We don't know who Charles-Gabriel Le Bègue's head cook was. But the supposition must be that this artist, happy to have such a gourmet for a master, dedicated this discovery to him in gratitude. And thanks to both inventor and godfather, the *potage Germiny* now figures in the gallery of the truly subtle dishes, those dishes that shine in menus of discreetest epicureanism, that perpetuate a tradition born in the little suppers of *la Régence*.

At one time the basis of the *potage Germiny* was what was called consommé "cubed." It was an age, one might say, of conspicuous reduction: a piece of beef was boiled in order to enrich a stock with its nutritive qualities. In this stock a second piece of beef was boiled, and the result of that was a stock "squared." And then, Lucullus having been invited to dine with Lucullus, in the twofold strength of that "squared" stock yet another piece of meat was boiled. Enriched with

such a generosity of juices, the "cubed" consommé certainly deserved a place in the thoughts of those who labored beneath the coffered ceilings of the Banque de France, whose stocks in those celebrated underground vaults were as strong, as secret, as unshakable, as powerful a foundation for the nation's investments as this stock "cubed" proved for a wise and thoughtful cook's rich new soup: the *Germiny*.

Today the rich themselves count their pennies, and the price of beef forbids such extravagances. The stock now is simply very strong stock. And yet even today, partly no doubt because it is still drawing interest from those past splendors, the *Germiny* remains as an example of what soups really were in their heyday.

It may be served hot or cold.

But need I add that cold is the way one should preferably make its acquaintance and learn to love it? True gastronomy centers on cold dishes, which are of a more uplifting subtlety and sensibility. You can't cheat with a cold dish. It is the final goal. The art of saucemaking, born of the marriage of fire and pot, finds its final flowering in this return to its sources, and the first cook who allowed her *boeuf-mode* to get cold was taking the culinary art another step forward—without knowing it perhaps, like Molière's M. Jourdain writing all that prose.

The *potage Germiny*, the creation of a chef, is really the province of none but the greatest of that profession. The *Germinys* of my life seem to have reflected in their opaque, green-tinged, and creamy mirror the nobly born head of that count and statesman, the distinguished, proud and secretly food-loving smile of Charles-Gabriel Le Bègue, guardian of France's fortune in an era of good fortune.

Potage Germiny

½ lb fresh sorrel
  1½ qts strong beef bouillon
3 cups heavy cream

9 egg yolks
  cayenne
  white pepper

Wash, dry, and trim the sorrel; then chop it up. Drop it into the boiling stock and allow to cook for 10 minutes. Let it cool.

In a big bowl mix the cream with the egg yolks, a pinch of cayenne, and a few twists of freshly ground white pepper. Dilute with a little stock.

Pour this mixture into the saucepan, stir well, and heat through gently. The soup should thicken without ever boiling. When it has reached the required consistency, pour it into a cold saucepan. Let it cool, stirring occasionally. Check the seasoning. When cool, place in refrigerator. Serve in cups.

MENU

*Potage queue de boeuf
    froid
*Sole normande
*Melon de Schéhérazade

A white wine with the sole: a great Burgundy, for example a Meursault Goutte d'Or.

Potage Queue de Boeuf

(Oxtail Soup)

Might one not say also of the bullock what has been said of the pig: "That vast walking meal waiting to be served"? So let us take our bullock, not by the horns but by the tail—its best, its tastiest, its most "tonic" portion. When I see those little tied-up bundles of chopped-up oxtail in the butcher's window, the dark-red flesh, the white vertebrae, I immediately envisage for them a lively escort of fresh garden herbs, that famous *bouquet garni* that is held out to the victor in contests of appetite, fragrant and plumed with tarragon instead of a laurel crown.

Oxtail is one of the dishes that come into the category of the *braisés*. Slow cooking means solidity of character, of appetite, of humor. And so this caudal extremity has ne'er a sting in it, and brings only the calming taste of certitude. To look at it you might well expect it to be eccentric, but on the contrary, it is, if not exactly down to earth, certainly elbows on the table. Waiting with a reassuring patience, with the "wait and see" attitude of the British.

And before seeing it softly nestling in its braising dish, surrounded by its intimate fragrance, we shall gladly wait

the necessary three or four hours that are worth their weight in gold. The time it takes to cook an oxtail is always a good investment for those who truly love good food. The blond shimmers with their shadings of red-brown on the surface of an oxtail stew, a *queue de boeuf en hochepot*, are the patina of time itself, the evidence of its patience and its victory. The Italians defiantly counter the Flemish *hochepot* with their *coda in vaccinara* and delight in it as much. I speak of the northern Italians, needless to say: there can be no Latin fantasy in a braised oxtail—quite the contrary. No useless ebullience if you please. Just calm certainty.

Yes, the British "wait and see." Yet curiously enough the British oxtail soup, such a favorite of gourmets on that side of the English Channel, was not originally a British dish. It was the French émigrés during the Revolution—alas, who am I to gainsay history?—who taught the islanders the virtues of this oxtail whose modesty could so easily pass for humility if one did not also sense in it, lurking beneath its silky surface, a legitimate and enduring pride.

But there is the same distance between an oxtail stew or *hochepot* and the proud oxtail soup as there is between a humble peasant cot and the palace of Versailles. The braised tail is a dish for a philosopher, the soup is a masque for a prince. Candide cultivated the first in his garden, Vatel pondered over the second for the prince whose life he ruled. The rays of the Sun King, melted down into pale gold, are almost palpable in a cup of oxtail. A garland of apprentice chefs participates in the austerely decorous, almost ritual ceremony— to an air by Lully. The ballet of chefs' hats and blue ribbons unfurls as if in the theater, in Molière's theater. As a prelude two violins tune up, and already Vatel is raising his sword to conduct the orchestra, before he impales himself on it over some odd rigmarole or other about the fish not arriving. A rigmarole that will be cleared up in time by that gossip of the age, that sly tittle-tattle the Marquise de Sévigné, upon whose pen Vatel is doomed to remain impaled till the end of time.

But all passes, and already some Chevalier d'Albignac (that triumphant salad-maker who in the 1790's ruled over so many émigré tables in London) is thinking that perhaps the sherry so dear to England's noble lords might well serve—

allegro ma non troppo—as the final modulation in a symphony of quintessentialized odors.

Alas, in these days when the impostor is triumphant in every field, what we are offered as oxtail soup is often no more than mere beef stock. And even then one feels thankful it didn't actually come out of a can.

For the genuine article is not a stock, nor even a concentrate. It is an elixir. Alchemy has gone into its making. The chef who makes it could justifiably exchange his white hat for a magician's cone, his saucepan for an alembic. That magical expression used in the old days to describe our alchemists—the "Dyers of the Moon"—seems to me perfectly suited also to the men who have sought, are seeking, will always continue to seek for the secret of the elixir of life to be derived from the tail of the ox, of that humble ruminant who stood by the manger, the peasant's familiar companion as he works his soil. As Epicurus is my witness.

Potage Queue de Boeuf

3½ lbs beef bones
3½ qts water
salt and pepper
¼ lb butter
3 onions
6 carrots
2⅓ lbs oxtail (cut up)

bouquet garni
1 lb lean beef
2 leeks (white part only)
1 white of egg
3 turnips
1 celery heart
2 tbs sherry

Cook the bones for the jelly for seven hours in three and a half quarts of water. Season. Strain.

Into an earthenware casserole, put half the butter, the sliced onions, 3 carrots, and the cut-up segments of oxtail. Add the *bouquet garni* (parsley, bayleaf, thyme, celery leaves). Season. Leave to brown over heat for a good quarter of an hour.

Pour the bone broth on top and leave to simmer very gently (no visible motion of broth) for four hours. Strain. Skim off fat.

Add the lean beef, minced, and the sliced leek bottoms beaten up with the white of egg. Cook for another hour. Strain through a cloth. Cut the other three carrots and the turnips into olive-shaped pieces. Dice the celery heart and heat the vegetables in the remaining butter.

Remove the meat from several sections of oxtail. Cut it into small dice.

Add the olive-shaped pieces of carrots and turnips, the dice of celery, and the diced oxtail to the soup. Check the seasoning. Finally add 2 tablespoons of sherry.

N O T E : This soup may be served hot or cold. When hot it can be accompanied with slivers of cheese.

42

SHELLFISH

Jan Davidsz de Heem: Lobster and Fruit

A white wine, of course, one that will be acceptable with the oysters, "keep going" with the lobster, and finally provide a suitable accompaniment to the almonds in the dessert. The choice is less difficult than you might think. It must be a great Burgundy, let's say a Corton-Charlemagne. A good year and about ten years old.

Homard à l'Américaine

(Lobster with Wine, Tomatoes, and Herbs)

It is a cruel fate that has left the lobster, that "knight in armor" of the seas, so vulnerable to so many enemies, among whom man, for all that he is the latest on the scene, is not the least cruel when he is wearing a tall white hat.

For there are many cookbooks that claim, quite heartlessly, that the lobster, if it is to be prepared *à l'américaine*, "requires to be cut up alive."

This is doubly untrue. In the first place, I have never heard any lobster requiring anything at all, and above all not that. Secondly, I am far from convinced that the dish is in any way improved by inflicting such a martyrdom on the poor beast. But what we can all agree on is that a grilled lobster is an excellent dish, even if you have been so softhearted as to toss it into boiling water before splitting it in two and subjecting it to the torments of your grill.

Moreover, this lobster that you picture to yourself as living savagely invulnerable in the depths of the sea, armed with its two asymmetrical claws—one called a shear claw, sharp as a razor; the other called a hammerclaw, massive, blunt, and intended to grasp and hold a prey often much larger than its owner—this lobster, this dauntless warrior, molts.

Yes, it is the strange fate of these crustaceans to be flabbergasted (in the words of M. Gwen-Aël Bolloré, in his amazing book *Destins tragiques du fond des mers*) at the sight of its own double—a useless carapace motionless beside it—and at suddenly feeling itself longer, fatter, but utterly soft and defenseless.

And a prey—until it has secreted the necessary calcium to harden that new, tissue-paper skin—to all its natural enemies: other crustaceans, such as crabs, rushing to attack such a tender quarry, dismembering it alive; the octopus, whose tentacles soon grip the defenseless lobster so that its hard beak can revel in that quivering flesh; the conger eel, whose monstrously toothed maw champs its victim to tiny bits.

And if by happy chance the lobster should escape its underwater enemies, then it may well end up in the fisherman's pots and find its way to our kitchens.

In a previous work by the author mentioned above, I was puzzled by the curious observation that "the Parisian has a sentimental affection for the crawfish or rock lobster."

Where the devil did this Breton get that idea? It's true that cold crawfish served with a mayonnaise is called *"langouste à la parisienne"* in the classic cookbooks, but *homard à l'américaine* was also created in Paris.

Lobster recipes are legion. There is a sort of simple-minded like-to-like tradition that makes chefs who are presented with a costly raw material start adding other rich and rare ingredients to it. So to the lobster, an exceptionally rich food in itself, they will add cream, truffles, and the best brandy. A twofold error that at once increases the cost of the dish and diminishes the pleasure of enjoying this crustacean in all its natural delicacy, its true "personality."

Which is why the best way of serving our *demoiselles de Cherbourg* (as they call the small English Channel lobsters weighing a little over half a pound and providing a good-sized portion for one) or those small Brittany lobsters that are so dark blue they are almost black (for the lobster does not become the "cardinal of the seas" until he's been cooked) is to cook them *à la nage*—in the very element they swim in.

The Champs-Elysées

Le café chantant.

This means that the lobster is cooked in a highly seasoned wine and sea-water *court-bouillon* and served still warm, with melted butter. Then it is a gift from Amphitrite herself, in all its primal purity.

If the lobster is larger, then serve it either Thermidor or *à l'américaine.*

Lobster Thermidor is an act of homage to the theater.

What a lover of the table was Victorien Sardou! It was Sardou who on Christmas day 1870, as he was leaving the French outposts around a besieged Paris, ravenously hungry, on his way to eat cat stew garnished with rats at Brébant's, was accosted by a mysterious basket-bearer:

"Monsieur Sardou, I've something for you here, if you're willing to pay my price."

"What is it?"

"Something for your Christmas dinner. A calf's head."

And, lifting the corner of a napkin, the man disclosed, on a bed of parsley, beautifully presented, a fresh, truly magnificent calf's head, with closed eyes, upright ears, and a truly admirable smell.

For sixty francs, basket included, Sardou set off back to Paris with his purchase. No sooner was he inside Brébant's

Banquet du *Figaro*, donné le jeudi 4 février, dans le salon du Restaurant du Passage des Princes (Péter's).

than he handed over his head to the waiter and entrusted him with the task of taking it out to the kitchens, with instructions to have it served up as a surprise that evening for a dinner of friends, including, I think I am right in saying, Edmond de Goncourt.

And so, later, at dinner:

The *maître d'hôtel* approached, with a smile, and very cautiously set down upon their table a great dish filled with a thick, yellowish, greasy liquid.

Sardou, his temper rising, cried: "And my head, wretch, where is my head?"

"There, monsieur."

Turned to liquid, melted—for, you see, it was a gelatine head, cleverly sculptured by a master hand, that the playwright had allowed to be palmed off on him.

Happily, however, as a consolation, after the success of his play *Thermidor*, he had the joy of tasting the new lobster dish that the chef of the Café de Paris dedicated to him on that occasion.

Lobster à l'américaine, on the other hand, is more by way of being a homage to truth. For despite all the claims of the culinary chauvinists, *homard à l'armoricaine* does not exist. *Homard à l'américaine* is the correct name of the dish.

It is an argument that went on for a long time though.

The supporters of *homard à l'armoricaine* put forward as their arguments the French "style" of the dish and the fact that the lobster is a Breton, or Armorican, product. The confusion arose, they explained, from an error in the transcription of a menu: "given a hasty pen, *armoricaine* can quickly become *américaine*."

Too true. But it happened the other way around, when a copyist, faced with someone else's bad writing—or handicapped by a slight hardness of hearing—turned *américaine* into *armoricaine*.

And in support of that statement there is the fact that no menu from any important restaurant, either in Paris or elsewhere, has ever been found with *armoricaine* antedating *américaine*. No, the latter has always preceded the former.

But in fact the origin of the dish was settled quite clearly a score or so years ago in a letter from an old Parisian gentleman to the noted gastronome Curnonsky in which he wrote: "As you so rightly say, the *homard à l'américaine* was created in Paris, and naturally enough by a Frenchman: Peters, born in Sète and in fact christened Pierre Fraisse. I knew Peters in about 1900 when he was seventy-eight, living quietly with his wife on the rue Germain Pilon. One evening when he was in a reminiscing mood he told me the story of that famous lobster dish."

From Pierre Fraisse's reminiscences and what was already known of him it is clear that this Frenchman from the South of France in fact began his career in the United States. Then, having returned to Paris, he took premises on the Passage des Princes and founded Peter's Restaurant around 1860.

Bought up later by a certain Noël, the restaurant then became Noël Peter's, but that is another story.

One architectural curiosity may be noted in passing: the main room of Noël Peter's was a copy of the Alhambra in Granada.

It was while he was running his own restaurant, the aforesaid Peter's, that Pierre Fraisse had the idea—and he was the first to have it—of planning his menus to include a par-

ticular dish that always recurred on a particular day of the
week. Here is his list taken from an old menu:

LUNCHEON DISHES OF THE DAY

MONDAY
Matelote marinière et oeufs à la tripe
(Fish stew and eggs in onion cream sauce)
TUESDAY
Boeuf salé à l'anglaise
(Salt beef, English style)
WEDNESDAY
* *Tripes à la mode de Caen*
THURSDAY
Aloyau à la hongroise
(Sirloin, Hungarian style)
FRIDAY
Bouillabaisse à la marseillaise
(Provençal fish soup)
SATURDAY
Selle de mouton à la boulangère
(Saddle of mutton with potatoes and onions)

And it was in the same restaurant that a party of Americans appeared late one evening, in a hurry, when there was almost nothing left except for some live lobsters awaiting next day's *court-bouillon*. Seized by inspiration, while the soup was being served, Fraisse created his new lobster dish.

The customers found it delicious.

"What is the name of this exquisite dish?"

And recalling that he had run a Café Américain in Chicago, that his present restaurant had an anglicized name, and that his customers were from over the Atlantic, Pierre Fraisse replied: "It's called *homard à l'américaine*."

To be truthful, the recipe is more Mediterranean than anything else, both in its conception and its ingredients. It recalls the crawfish *à la provençale* with which Escoffier launched his career, in Nice, at the restaurant Favre, in 1869. But that in no way implies that Fraisse was copying. Great minds do think alike, even in cooking.

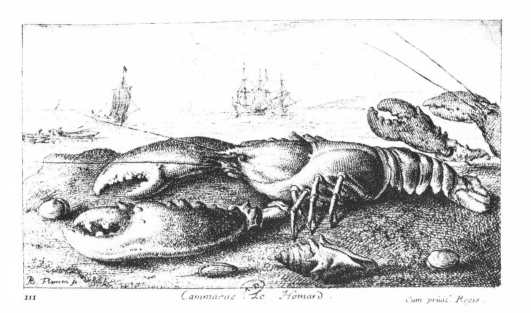

III   *Cammarue. Le Homard.*   *Cum priuil. Regis.*

Homard à l'Américaine

One lobster, about 2¾ lbs, or better
2 lobsters, each about 1½ or 1¾ lbs
   4 tbs oil
salt and pepper
   1 onion
2 shallots
   ¼ clove garlic
½ cup dry white wine

½ cup water
   4 tbs cognac
2 tomatoes
   tarragon
cayenne
   4 tbs butter
chervil
   parsley

Cut the claws off level with the body, cut up the tail into five or six rings, split the body in half lengthwise. Remove the bag from the head and throw away. Remove the creamy substance and the coral (if any) and keep them in a bowl.

Heat the oil in a skillet. When it is very hot, drop in the pieces of lobster. Add salt and pepper. Allow to brown till the shell is red. Remove lobster from pan and keep warm.

To the same oil add the onion, finely chopped, and cook it slowly, stirring it in the process. Then add the shallots, chopped, and the garlic, crushed. Drain off the oil.

Add the white wine, water, and 2 tablespoons of the cognac. Add the peeled, seeded flesh of the tomatoes, three sprigs of tarragon tied in a bunch, and a dash of cayenne. Place the lobster pieces on top, cover, and cook for 20 minutes.

Remove the lobster and arrange the pieces in your serving dish. Keep warm. Remove the tarragon and, over high heat, reduce the sauce in the pan by half.

Mash the creamy substance and the coral you have kept to one side with 2 tablespoons of the butter, a pinch of chopped chervil and a pinch of chopped tarragon. Bind the sauce with this mixture. The moment it begins to bubble again add the remaining butter and cognac. Pour the sauce over the lobster pieces and scatter finely chopped parsley on top.

Serve rice pilaff with the lobster.

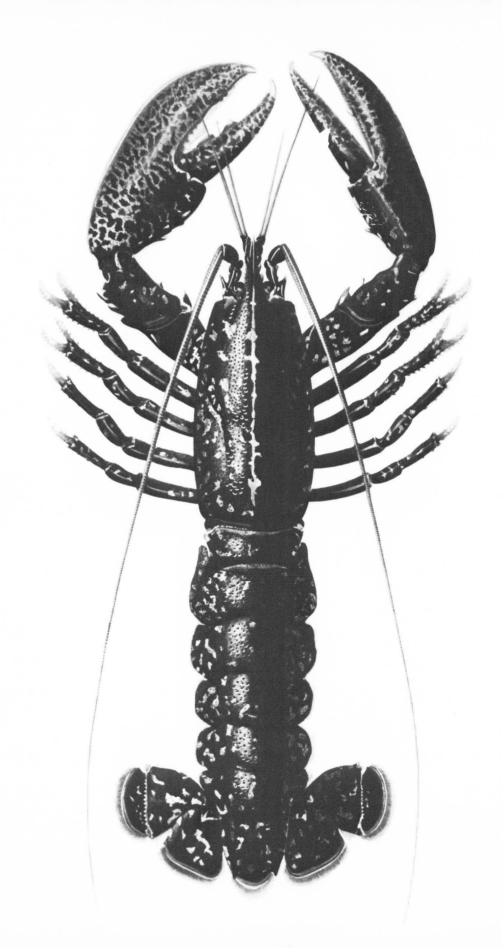

A champagne *nature* with the lobster. And then, away with orthodoxy say I, we'll continue it with the meat and the baba.

Homard aux Légumes

(Lobster with Vegetables)

For the gastronome, the lobster (*Homarus vulgaris* around the coasts of France) is incontestably the king of the crustaceans. This magnificent beast may attain two feet in length and weigh eight or nine pounds. Its color varies from a dark blue that is almost black to a purplish brown, broken with yellow patches. It goes gray as it ages, like man. And also like man it couples face to face—a position it shares, in the animal kingdom, only with whales, dogfish, sharks, seals, and hedgehogs.

As we have said, the small lobsters caught in the English Channel or the Atlantic, weighing a pound or less, are best in the best of lobster recipes: *homard à la nage*.

The *homard à l'américaine* has its partisans, of course. It is a recipe that presents you with the warm tones of a Provence landscape, with the spicy good humor of the Provence accent. Let us pass as quickly as possible over lobster Newburg, first known as Wenberg from the name of its creator, then in the disguised form of Newberg when he was disgraced, and finally, when he was forgotten, as Newburg. And as for grilled lobster, that is simply the desolation of desolation. As its flesh, oversealed, turns to perfectly vulcanized rubber, so the alcohol with which it is flambéed and the herbs with which its taste is killed combine to provide it with a sorry shroud perfectly in keeping with a third-class pauper's funeral.

No. Large lobsters may be cooked in a *court-bouillon* and served cold. Small lobsters should be cooked and served in a *court-bouillon* that is still warm.

I should add that the Royal Society for the Prevention of Cruelty to Animals in England has conducted a great deal of research into the most humane way of cooking lobsters. Dropped into boiling water, the average lobster will thresh about for perhaps a minute. Placed in warm water and slowly brought to the boil, it displays no signs of agitation whatever. So one of my English colleagues assures me anyway. Though the fact that the lobster doesn't struggle doesn't necessarily mean it's happy!

In an ancient and Balzacian house on the rue Chanoinesse, hard by the flank of Notre Dame, my friends Jackie and Gilbert have set up their Vieux Paris. It is an elegant and cheerful restaurant that true Parisians know and love. We like to imagine that here, at number 24, lived Mme de la Chanterie, of Balzac's *L'Envers de l'histoire contemporaine*, that this is the courtyard at the far side of which "blackly silhouetted rose a tall house flanked by an even taller square tower of remarkable age, and that the surrounding soil had little by little engulfed, to the point where what had originally been the ground floor was now the cellars."

Mme de la Chanterie kept a frugal table: a small turbot served with a white sauce, Balzac tells us, potatoes, a salad, and four dishes of fruit: peaches, grapes, strawberries, and fresh almonds; then, as hors d'oeuvre, honey in its comb the way they eat it in Switzerland, radishes and butter, cucumbers and sardines . . . In passing, let us pause to wonder at the "frugality" of those blessed times!

But at Jackie's you must order the *homard aux légumes*.

It is lobster *à la nage* of course, but with one new, original, yet almost stupidly obvious addition: the vegetables out of its own *court-bouillon*.

And this simple addition makes it into a dish of majesty.

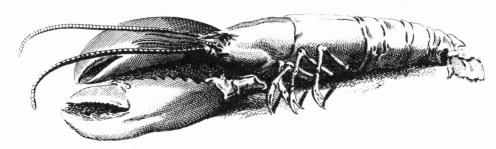

A Racinian dish. It is a term I tend to use a lot, and I have been blamed for it. But I do feel that it is possible to divide the world of cookery into two great currents: the Racinian current and the Cornelian current. Indeed, it is a classification you might well start by applying to men. I am a Corneliophobe because in everything to do with cooking I cannot find it in me to admire pomp and show, or mindless braggadocio, or overstatement, or the grandiose sentiments that produce mean little dishes.

And as the perfect antidote to them, here is the *homard aux légumes:* a great dish! Not great like the Cid's futile combat or Camille's imprecations, but like Phèdre's love.

Homard aux Légumes

4 carrots
   4 turnips
2 stalks celery
   2 large onions
whole cloves

bouquet garni (thyme and parsley)
   peppercorns
1 scant half cup sherry
   2 to 4 lobsters (about ¾ lb each)
½ lb stringbeans

● HOLLANDAISE SAUCE

lemon juice
   salt

3 egg yolks
   10 oz butter

Peel the carrots and turnips; then cut them lengthwise into large pieces. Slice the celery. Add the onions spiked with cloves plus a *bouquet garni* of thyme and parsley.

Put into water to cover with peppercorns and the sherry. Boil until the vegetables are cooked.

Add the lobsters and a little more boiling water, if necessary, and allow to simmer for 8 to 10 minutes.

Remove the lobsters, cut them in two, and break the claws.

Slice the stringbeans French style and cook in salted water.

Make a hollandaise sauce as follows: In a saucepan mix a tablespoon of lemon juice, a tablespoon of cold *court-bouillon* from the lobsters, and a little salt into 3 egg yolks. Put over hot water and work the sauce with a wooden spoon. As soon as the mixture begins to become light and frothy gradually add the butter, whisking all the while. As the sauce thickens add more *court-bouillon* to thin it. Check the seasoning for salt and pepper, especially the latter; then add a teaspoon of lemon juice.

In each hot dish make a bed of the vegetables from the *court-bouillon* (after discarding the onions and herbs) and the beans. Place the lobster on top. Spoon on a quantity of the hollandaise sauce.

N O T E : The sherry may be replaced with a dry white wine, but disadvantageously.

Huistres à l'Ecaille.

And for wine, a Domaine
de Chevalier (Graves blanc).

Huîtres Frites à la Villeroi

(Fried Oysters)

Let us begin by leafing through the history of this noblest
of all the shellfish.

The Romans, true gourmets that they were, appreciated
oysters. And their highest esteem was reserved for those
found in the English Channel, which during the winter
months they transported to Italy layered in snow, so tightly
compressed that they could not open. And this method of
packing oysters was still being used in the mid-nineteenth
century.

Theodore, who was king of Corsica for a time, when re-
tiring to England after his fall consoled himself with the
thought that at least he would now be able to eat as many
oysters as he liked. "My three passions," he said, "are love,
military glory, and the oyster!" Only the third was not taken
from him.

In his *Cris de Paris,* Mouilleron depicts the capital's
eighteenth-century oyster-women carrying their oysters on
their backs, in big baskets, and shouting, "Buy my shellfish!
Buy my shellfish!" so very loudly that an edict had to be
passed to silence them after 8 P.M.

It was Jean François de Troy, director of the French Academy at Rome, who painted the sumptuous oyster lunch attended by Crébillon *fils*, that most frivolous of storytellers. When asked how long he could go on eating them, Crébillon replied: "Forever!"

In those days there were no less than 365 different kinds of oysters on record—one for every day of the year in fact. And they were served up in more than thirty different ways. And there were several sorts of vinegar used to give them relish.

Louis XV ate them with tartar sauce.

Mirabeau, having swallowed 360 oysters, confessed that he had "almost died." Which is precisely what did happen, rather earlier, to the Roman Fabius Rutilius.

The nineteenth century was also a period of high oyster consumption. One day, when a publisher offered to buy him dinner, Balzac tipped down a whole hundred just for starters.

On February 17, 1863, returning home with Flaubert from a masked ball, Edmond de Goncourt saw literally cartloads of oyster shells being loaded and removed from the entrance to a restaurant.

An edict of the Paris Parliament promulgated on September 5, 1861, stated: "Oysters in the shell must be inspected by the licensed fish retailers. Merchants are required, upon arrival in Paris, to bear all oysters to the fish hall in Les Halles, where they may be examined prior to sale by the aforesaid licensed retailers."

Monsieur Schalouchine, whose sons became the bankers to the Tsar, was once a serf of Count Scheremetiev. Already the possessor of an enviable fortune amassed in the grain and sheep trades, he had on several occasions offered to buy his freedom, once even going as high as 250,000 rubles. But the Count had always refused. One day, feeling that the time was ripe for another attempt, Schalouchine went into St. Petersburg to visit his master, taking a barrel of oysters as a present. He arrived to find the Count in a wild rage with his butler because the unfortunate man had been unable to find a single oyster anywhere in the city for a luncheon the Count was giving:

"Ah, it's you, is it?" the Count said. "I suppose you've

come wanting your freedom again? Well you know you could have saved yourself the journey. I don't care a fig for all your rubles, and you know it. But just a moment, I'll tell you what. If you can find me some oysters for this lunch of mine, then I'll set you free."

Schalouchine called upon all those present to witness the Count's promise, then went out to fetch the barrel, which he had left in the antechamber. Count Scheremetiev kept his word. And then, turning to his ex-serf, he said:

"Monsieur Schalouchine, do please sit down and eat lunch with us."

In England, on every October 8, there once used to take place the great Colchester Oyster Fair, which was first established, by Royal Charter, in 1318.

In 1839, on the invitation of the mayor of Colchester, more than three thousand persons were invited to a banquet in celebration of the event, and together they consumed ten thousand dozen oysters while listening to speeches and drinking toasts.

Balzac's *Histoire des Treize* tells of a fat man who had an incredible passion for oysters.

"How many did he eat then?"

"Ten dozen every day."

"Without ill effects?"

"Absolutely none. Nature had ordered him to eat oysters; they were presumably essential to him."

It was in 1868 that the vessel *Morlaisien*, commanded by Captain Patoiseau out of Oléron, was driven off course by a storm while bringing a cargo of oysters from Portugal to Arcachon, and took refuge in the mouth of the Gironde. Supposing his cargo to be spoiled, the captain ordered the oysters thrown into the sea. But not all of them were dead. And the survivors thrived in their new home. Which is why we now have Portuguese oysters in abundance off La Rochelle, around the isle of Ré, in the mouth of the Charente, and creeping a little farther up toward Brittany year by year.

I could chat on about the oyster like this forever, though it might begin to seem somewhat tedious to contemporary readers, for whom the oyster is a food generally consumed *nature*, which is to say raw, sometimes with an unnecessary

Alexandre-François Desportes: The Meatless Luncheon

squeeze of lemon, sometimes with an absurd dash of shallot-flavored vinegar, and sometimes—much more to the point—with a quick twist of the pepper mill.

The cooked oyster has been allowed to fall into neglect; to such an extent that many people now take it to be a modern perversion, a misguided innovation. In fact, the habit of eating raw oysters is a recent one, and the old cookbooks are filled with various ways of preparing and serving oysters hot.

At the Tour d'Argent they serve oysters *à la Brolatti*, poached in their own juice and sprinkled with finely chopped shallots. The *Cuisinier royal* gives recipes for oysters *en atelets, au soleil, en marinade*, grilled, and stewed. And in other publications I have encountered oysters *bonne femme, à la daube, au parmesan, en hachis, à la bonhomme*, fried, in pies, as soup, and so forth. But my unhesitating choice is fried oysters *à la Villeroi*.

The Neufvilles, lords of Villeroi, take up a fair amount

of space in the reference books. The first famous one was Nicolas, Secretary of State under Marie de Médicis. His son, Charles, was governor of the Lyonnais, then ambassador to Rome in 1600. And Charles's son, another Nicolas, was marshal of France, guardian of the young Louis XIV, then created a Duke in 1663. And his son, François de Neufville, duc de Villeroi, a marshal of France apparently given to collecting defeats—the most famous being the one suffered at Ramillies at the hands of the Duke of Marlborough—guardian of Louis XV, and member of the Regency council, was probably the godfather of this recipe.

What subtle cook first dedicated a sauce to this noble patron, the sauce we know today as the Villeroi? There is no way of knowing. But once the sauce existed the oysters were bound to follow.

Huîtres Frites à la Villeroi

1 cup Villeroi sauce (or more, depending
on number served)
6 oysters per person
1 beaten egg
2 tbs oil

salt and pepper
white breadcrumbs browned in fat
frying fat
parsley

Make a Villeroi sauce by adding mushroom broth and egg yolks to very thick *velouté* sauce, made with fish broth. When reduced and bound with butter, it may be flavored with puréed onions or essence of truffles. Let it cool and thicken.

Filter the water of the oysters and poach them in it. Then trim them and sponge dry.

Dip each oyster in the Villeroi sauce so that it is thickly covered. Allow to cool completely.

Take up the oysters one by one. Dip them in the egg beaten up with a little oil, salt, and pepper, then in freshly browned breadcrumbs.

Fry quickly in hot fat.

Serve the oysters on napkins sprinkled with chopped parsley.

With the crayfish a glass or two of vodka, aquavit, gin, slivovitz, or a white wine (the one used for the *court-bouillon*). The same wine will serve for the rest of the meal.

Écrevisses à la Nage

(Freshwater Crayfish)

A refrain from the Belle Epoque sets the tone:

Nous mangerons des écrevisses
Au café des Ambassadeurs . . .

One can see it so clearly: the private room, a beautiful girl slyly smiling over the laborious task of stripping the little crustaceans of their shells, the champagne fizzing in the goblets to the distant rhythm of a violinist's strings; and the man, in evening dress, the spices of the *court-bouillon* titillating his veins, sounding those frills and furbelows with a languorous gaze.

Freshwater crayfish, in those days, were inseparable from lovers' feasts. Young clerks dreamed of them, shopgirls who couldn't say no murmured yes to them in advance, and mashers revived their sated appetites with them.

In those days they were still abundant in most streams and rivers throughout France and Navarre. Oh, you could no longer get Parisian crayfish like those that Gargantua and

his tutor Ponocrates went to fish for once a month at Gentilly, or Boulogne, or Montrouge, or the Pont de Charenton, or Vanves, or Saint-Cloud. Nevertheless, they were still coming into the capital from more or less all sides. From Alsace—for already in the time of Napoleon III Strasbourg crayfish as big as small lobsters were being peeled and munched in the taverns around Les Halles—from Normandy, from Burgundy, and so forth. And above all, and already, from abroad.

For the epidemics of the 1880s and succeeding years had seriously diminished the quantities available from French sources. In 1830 about 150,000 crayfish were consumed in Paris at an average price of three francs a hundred. Under the Second Empire more than 5 million were being sold yearly in Les Halles at between six and eight francs the hundred. In about 1888 the price for a hundred wavered between fifteen francs and twenty francs; but by 1902 the price had doubled, the quantity diminished, and almost all the crayfish sold had been imported from Russia and Silesia. During 1957 no more than 13,000 to 15,000 pounds came into Les Halles, but most of the import trade (amounting to from seventy to eighty tons, coming from Italy, Yugoslavia, Hungary, and above all Poland) was carried on directly between importers and retailers or restaurant owners. Prices fluctuated between seven and ten francs each.

"It's the inflationing that does it," as my concierge says.

This increase in prices is balanced by a steady decrease in the number of crayfish caught. In a very interesting little book on this crustacean, Marc André cites some of the many causes that have contributed to the diminishing distribution of the crayfish in Europe: dredging of ponds and canals, straightening of rivers, pollution of water by industrial effluents, and so forth. Doubtless the same things occur in Sweden too, but on a smaller scale presumably, and their August celebrations still include the *kräftor* marking the beginning of the crayfish season. It is an amusing, joyful, Rabelaisian sort of ceremony that has all the importance of a national holiday. Swedish holidays generally do, of course, tend to take concrete gastronomic forms. On November 11, the feast day of Martin Luther, they celebrate with a black soup made of goose or pig blood. On December 13, the gloomiest day of the year, they eat their *lussekatter*, which is bread made with saffron. And for the *kräftor* they produce pyramids of crayfish cooked in a dill-flavored broth which are demolished in an atmosphere of the most wonderful good humor, each claw sped on its way with a clink of glasses and a gulp of the local spirit.

Oh, happy Swedes! They are still able to serve their crayfish—that dish so diverting to eat—in vast tangles ("*en buisson*," French menus called it in the good old days), whereas we are reduced to selling them in ones!

Though perhaps, on the other hand, we could give them a point or two when it comes to preparing them. A list of the various French recipes, from *bisque* to *gratin*, from *velouté* to stew, is a sort of paean of praise to the imagination of our chefs.

For my own part there are three personal *kräftor* I look back on with nostalgia, three crayfish feasts as staggering then as they remain unforgettable now.

And when I do decide to order a portion of crayfish in a restaurant, six tiny, fragile, red things lost on their great dish, looking quite wretched, then these three crustacean galas unfailingly rise to fill my mind's eye.

One summer evening, in Sézanne-en-Champagne, in the dusk of the evening, listening to Curnonsky reminisce with anecdotes as spontaneous, as light, as merry as the palate-sharpening champagne in our glasses. And then someone brought in basins—what do I mean, basins? laundry tubs!—of crayfish in champagne. At which silence fell. And then, gradually, as the edge of appetite became blunted, as our hands continued their delicate work (and I think the pleasure that women take in eating crayfish is partly explained by the knowledge that they look so graceful doing so) and the minutes passed, so the conversation revived and wandered among us aimlessly, effortlessly. And still we nibbled away at those tasty crayfish, and still our glasses were refilled with that sparkling wine. Ah! What a night!

A lunch at Saint-Gérand-le-Puy, in Lucien Sarrassat's little restaurant. It is raining along the highway. It is raining in Vichy, which we have just left. The sky is gray, and so is the room, and so perhaps are our hearts. But suddenly everything is brightened by the sunshine of Sarrassat's crayfish, cooked *à la crème* in this case, as though swathed in a luminous mantle of bright silk. We dive into the dish. We daub our faces with that sauce. The little red claws explode and give up their treasures, the shells crack beneath our teeth, our tongues are in ecstasy at the fabric of interwoven seasonings haunting this utterly suave food.

Lyons. Inward unease, perhaps even a slight biliousness. Paul Bocuse, that young great chef, won't be at all pleased. But perhaps he had some inkling of it? At all events, without fanfare there arrived as a starter a salad of crayfish tails. The dewy freshness of the *fines herbes*, the slight tartness of an English sauce, the delicacy of freshwater crayfish meat, caught the evening before. A balm, that dish, a miracle of Comus's pharmacopoeia. An appetite-sharpener if ever there was one. I found myself asking: "Well, and what have you got for me now?"

Prepared thus, one would be only too glad to render the crayfish that "worship" demanded on their behalf by Brillat-Savarin.

Fish market section of Les Halles, Paris

Grandville: The Crayfish and Her Daughter

Ecrevisses à la Nage

24 crayfish
  1 qt dry white wine
1 qt water
  peppercorns
salt

1 onion, spiked with cloves
  thyme
bayleaf
  dill

It is wise to let the crayfish fast for a few days, keeping them hung in a net in a cool place. Before cooking, wash them in running water, then remove their intestines by giving a sharp twist to the central flap of the tail and then an equally sharp pull. (This latter operation is indispensable if the crayfish have not been fasting.)

Into a large earthenware casserole, three-quarters filled with the simmering water and dry white wine, put peppercorns, salt, a spiked onion, thyme, bayleaf, and a pinch of dill. Throw in the living crayfish and let them simmer for a good quarter of an hour. Leave them to cool slightly in the *court-bouillon;* then serve lukewarm.

N O T E : Dill is an aromatic plant resembling fennel slightly in taste as well as appearance (so that fennel is sometimes called "sweet dill"). Its strong anise flavor is such that confectioners often use it in place of anise. Dill was the symbol of joy and pleasure in antiquity, and the Romans wore crowns of dill at their banquets.

Let us drink our friend Violet's health in a Mâcon-Viré first; then in a Beaujolais.

Coquilles Saint-Jacques à la Nage *(Scallops)*

Legend has it that the wedding of the lord of Maya, in Galicia, was being celebrated on the very day that a boat was bringing back the body of St. James. Suddenly the groom's horse hurled itself into the sea and began swimming toward the jetty. Immediately both horseman and mount were covered in shells. Was it a miracle? The lord of Maya believed so and was converted. And the scallop, *Pecten maximus*, was christened *coquille Saint-Jacques*. And everyone was happy.

But in any case this mollusk certainly deserved to become the symbol of the pilgrims to Santiago de Compostela, since its shell makes a natural begging bowl in which to collect alms.

And often, gastronomically speaking, it is beggar's fare that caterers dispense when they sell us these same shells filled with a shapeless mixture covered in its turn with an appalling white sauce, so that the flesh of this precious bivalve, lost in the gluey mess, is less even than a memory.

Yet what a magical splendor it possesses, that flesh, unctuous and firm at the same time, meaty and delicately flavored in itself, but also a receptacle for all the riches of the sea, attaining its full perfection in those months when the pearly heart of this "fruit of the sea" is brightened by the blush of its own inner coral!

Yes, flesh so delicious that one must needs be a chef, which means wholly uncomprehending, or head of a soup kitchen, which means wholly unconcerned with your customers, to dare to serve them *à la provençale*, or in other words to massacre their purity with the tragically inappropriate fragrance of garlic.

And as an antidote to the idea of such a martyrdom for our St. James, let us sing a hymn of praise to its sincerest and also least elaborate sublimation: scallops *à la nage*. And let us remark, too, that the only man in Paris who dares to offer it in this way with an easy mind is a restaurateur from Lyons, whose restaurant serves only traditional Lyonnais fare.

Aux Lyonnais is the typical *bistro*. Or, to be more exact (since the word *bistro* has several meanings covering the various conceptions people have of the thing), the typical *petite-boîte*.

Walk into number 32 rue Saint-Marc and you will have entered a somewhat incongruous setting, with straw chairs and banquettes, fretted table legs, a hint of sawdust in the corners of the tiled floor, a counter in chaos, waitresses who treat you like one of the family—all things that are preconditions of the sort of place I am talking about. The *petite-boîte* depends on its regulars, so it can't be indifferent to newcomers: it either accepts them or rejects them wholeheartedly as it sees fit.

And it is those who have been rejected by Aux Lyonnais who dispute its primacy. They didn't even begin to understand! They didn't even speak the same language, for heaven's sake!

"The tedious part of it is the way the owner forces his own menu on you!"

How often have I heard that grating little complaint, intended as a savage indictment but always sounding simply foolish. Because, apart from anything else, it's just not true! Such people just haven't grasped that to get the owner to un-

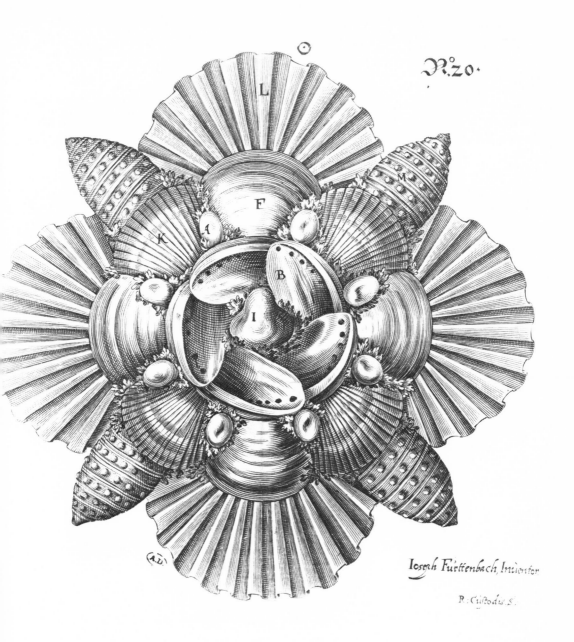

N.°20.

Ioseph Furttenbach, Inuentor

R. Custodis S.

derstand you, to get yourself accepted at Aux Lyonnais, you have to start by speaking the same language! And then you can eat what you like! Though it will still, of course, be what the owner likes, but since you talk his language you will always want just what he wants you to have! There's a subtle difference!

The owner's feelings toward you will be hearty. A hearty friendship or a hearty contempt, depending on you. Ah, how I pity those he despises because they don't deserve the life of friendship we lead at Aux Lyonnais, the friendly modus vivendi of Lyons itself.

Then there are also those who go there knowing in advance that they will be rebuffed. Mink-clad slummers of the table. Others would welcome them with inflated flattery and even more inflated prices! Daniel Violet, owner of Aux Lyonnais, just doubles his contempt. A real man!

I knew Violet the elder. Daniel, his son (already a grandfather, I think, but still young at heart), has the accent of their home town, that accent as songlike as the south, as slow as the north, and as solid as the center, the inimitable accent that makes Lyons the city of my choice. An accent that is a certainty!

Because Daniel is intransigence made flesh.

I have often shown his menu as an example to other restaurant owners—or people who think of themselves as such.

In the first place, inscribed with lapidary finality at the bottom (the menu never changes) is the following: "If a dish is occasionally absent from the menu, do not let this spoil your good humor. We are dependent upon the caprices of fishermen's catches, the state of the roads, and the seasons themselves. We apologize for that. Every day the owner brings back a new dish from the market for his regulars, and of course, if you telephone in advance there is always the *gratin dauphinois*."

With this necessary information given, the menu goes on to tell us that its contents are "all simple but delicious products of the Lyonnais region."

And then comes the discovery that it does not include *one single dish* that does not tempt me. And at this point it is

worth adding that there is one way of classifying restaurants that has never been used and perhaps ought to be. It would divide them into three categories:

1. The restaurants where, on reading the menu, you find there is not a single dish that tempts you. And they are, alas, too numerous.

2. The restaurants where you always find at least a few dishes to inspire your appetite.

3. The restaurants where *all* the dishes charm your expectations and fill you with desire.

In the third category I know only one: Aux Lyonnais!

But back to M. Violet's menu:

The chicken consommé is served with rusks and grated Gruyère.

The hot sausage is served as it is in most Lyonnais families: with its broth, butter, and boiled potatoes.

The cold bacon is served as it would be on a farm, with a green salad dressed with walnut oil.

Hans Baldung: Pilgrim to Santiago de Compostela

The beautifully white sheep's feet are served with a *rémoulade* sauce.

I must now leap over the other equally delicious entries in order to come to the incomparable *coquilles Saint-Jacques à la nage* (September to May, the menu informs us).

And then the *poule au pot* with its vegetables from the pot and its bowlful of rice, the roast duckling on its bed of fresh cabbage, and so forth. With game in season and cheeses, not forgetting the salad bowl of scallion-flavored cream cheese, which the locals in Lyons give a grosser name.

Coquilles Saint-Jacques à la Nage

24 scallops
  3 qts water
2 cups dry white wine
  2 cups milk

4 carrots
  2 onions spiked with whole cloves
bouquet garni
  1 bowl rémoulade *sauce*

Open the scallop shells, remove the inside, trim the foot and the coral, and wash carefully. Drain.

Prepare a *court-bouillon* with the water, white wine, and milk. Add 4 carrots in slices, two spiked onions, and a *bouquet garni*. Bring to a boil.

Drop the scallops into the boiling liquid. Leave them for five minutes. Drain them.

Serve them in a little of the *court-bouillon* accompanied with rounds of carrot and a cold *rémoulade* sauce containing mustard.

A *rémoulade* sauce is mayonnaise with the addition of chopped gherkins, capers, herbs, and a little anchovy paste. For the scallops, mustard is also added.

MENU

*Escargots à la suçarelle
Poulet froid salade
(Cold chicken salad)
*Tarte Bourdaloue

Exactly the moment for a rosé.
Choose a good one, though
they are rare. A Tavel,
full-bodied, fruity, and well
chilled, will do very well. It
won't be "killed" by the
sauce of the snails and will
continue to defend itself
admirably against the salad
(though make sure the
latter is not too vinegary!).

Escargots à la Suçarelle

(Snails in Sauce)

One could perhaps divide nations into two categories: the
snail-eaters and the ones who find that gastropod revolting to
the point of nausea.

And those who do enjoy eating it are quite fanatical on
the subject, delighting especially in the way the snail has inspired so many kinds of artists: architects (the spiral of its
shell is the origin of the spiral staircase), sculptors (the snail
was a symbol of resurrection right up till the Renaissance, and
is found carved in that role in the churches of Troyes, Lescar,
Saint-Rémy de Reims, and on St. Sebald's reliquary in Nur-
emberg), potters (Bernard Palissy, the originator of ceramics
in France, decorated his dishes with it), painters (Breughel,
Callot, and Salvador Dali), musicians and songwriters (Pré-
vert and Kosma among a host of others), writers (La Fontaine, Paul Fort, Charles Monselet, and the English poet
William Kean Seymour).

In France we have countless recipes for the preparation
of snails—and almost as many names for them.

But first of all we should state that officially snails are of
two sorts: *Helix pomatis Linnaeii* (commonly known as the

Burgundy snail) and *Helix aspersa Mullerii* (commonly known as the little gray).

Helix obviously refers to the spiraling shell. But how is it that neither of the French words for snail—*colimaçon* and *escargot*—is derived from the Latin *helix?* Well, *colimaçon* comes from the Latin *cocholimax*, the slug with a shell. But *escargot* seems a little more obscure. An engraving made in 1410 shows us a castle flanked with a bastion. And on top of that bastion there is a *tourelle*, a little tower, also known as an *escargaite*, with a snailshell roof. And the caption reads: "Struggle of soldiers and a woman against a slug." Does this mean, as Nizard thinks (according to his nineteenth-century *Grand Dictionnaire universel*), that the word *escargot* comes from the Old French *escargaite*, an advance guard and a sentry box?

Curnonsky

Along with Burgundy (extending into Alsace) and the Poitou-Vendée-Charente region (as far as Bordeaux), it is Provence and the Mediterranean part of the Languedoc that provide us with most snail recipes.

In the streets of Marseilles, once upon a time, they cried *"Limaçoun!"* (derived from the Latin *limax*) just as they might now cry "Roast chestnuts" or "Peanuts." And they organized *cacalausados* (meals consisting wholly of snail dishes) that drove their cooks to lyrical effusions: "When I bring the *cacalausado* to the table, the little creatures will swim in a bronze sauce that will make the whole hill smell good and will give the bread something worth soaking up!"

My own personal brand of poetry is more likely to be expended on a different recipe, and on a different cook: Coralie.

There was once a restaurant on the rue Sainte-Anne in Paris called Ugène & Coralie. Ugène was so exclusively concerned with his cellar that he died as a consequence. Coralie remained alone with her ovens. "Alone" is just a figure of speech. Her *habitueés* were more than mere customers; they were friends!

Coralie came, I believe, from down Arles way. She was also a royalist. Léon Daudet and Charles Maurras sometimes appeared to do justice to her *aïoli*, and she had special low

rates for royalist students and the young supporters of the royalist L'Action Française. Happy days! But wasted effort, some may say, since the Republic is still with us. And since the Fifth, in some ways, is the worst of them all. But at all events they were the days when, at one of Coralie's tables, I discovered *escargots à la suçarelle*.

Escargots à la Suçarelle

6 dozen little gray snails
  coarse salt
vinegar
  2 bouquets garnis (thyme, fennel, bayleaf, and rosemary)
¼ cup wine vinegar
  3 onions, spiked with whole cloves
3 whole carrots
  ¼ cup olive oil
2 onions, chopped
  4 tomatoes
1 garlic clove, crushed
  flour
spices
  salt and pepper
rind of 1 orange
  3 spinach leaves
3 sorrel leaves

Starve the snails (little grays) for a week, with coarse salt and vinegar.

Wash them with several changes of water.

Heat a good quantity of salted water with a *bouquet garni*. Add the wine vinegar, spiked onions, and carrots.

Drop in the snails and bring to the boil. Simmer for 3 hours. Drain.

Pierce the top of each shell.

In the olive oil brown 2 chopped onions. Add the tomatoes, peeled, seeded, and chopped, and the garlic clove.

Sprinkle lightly with flour. Pour in the white wine. Add spices to taste, salt and pepper, the orange rind, the spinach and sorrel leaves cut into strips, and another *bouquet garni*. Cook for 30 minutes.

Remove the *bouquet garni*, check the seasoning.

Add the snails and warm them through by continuing to cook this sauce, stirring often, for another 20 minutes.

Serve hot.

NOTE: One sucks out the snail and the juice with which it has become impregnated—through the little hole in its shell—at the same time. And it is because one sucks (*suce*) the snails —and one's fingers!—in this way that the dish is called *à la suçarelle*.

FISH

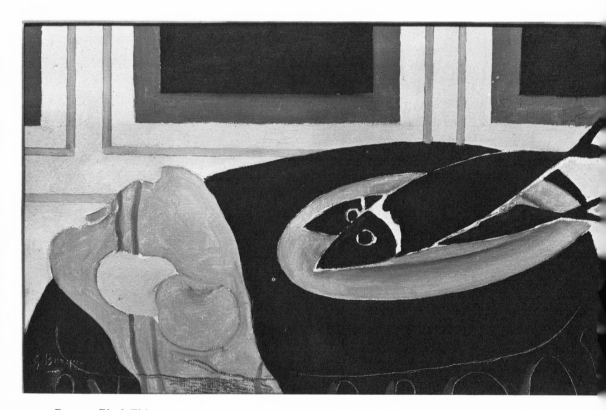

Braque: Black Fish

MENU

**Merlan en colère*
Champignons au gratin
(*Mushrooms with breadcrumb and cheese topping*)
Fromages
(*Cheeses*)
Fruits
(*Fresh fruit*)

A white wine such as a Montrachet (Burgundy) or a Hermitage (Côte du Rhône) would go well with the whole meal.

Merlan Frit (Fried Whiting)

"Her hair had been done by one of those hairdressers who look like whitings," Balzac writes somewhere or other. But you must not be too hasty and start imagining a hairdresser underwater, or with his feet stuck in his mouth. In the days of powdered wigs the hairdresser was always covered with his white rice powder the way a whiting is with flour before it's fried. The nineteenth-century man-in-the-street would have grasped our author's meaning immediately, you see. And the whiting, one might say, is the fish-in-the-street! Familiar and familial when fried, always welcome at the people's none-too-groaning boards, the friendly and everyday fish *par excellence*.

Its name in French, *merlan*, is derived from the Germanic *merleng*, a composite of *merle*, a thrush, and the suffix *-ing*. So our whiting is in fact a sea thrush. I wonder if Grimod de La Reynière was aware of that when he called the red mullet the "woodcock of the sea"?

Moreover, it is a member of the *gadidae*, and therefore related to the cod, the hake, the black and yellow pollacks, the ling, and the haddock. But of all these *gadidae* it is the smallest (eighteen inches long at the very most), and also, it must be said, the most immediately likable.

But take a look yourself: the long, slightly flattened body, the three dorsal fins it's so proud of, the two ventral fins, the two pectoral ones, and then those other two also under the belly, behind the anus. But it is above all its neat little scales and its gleaming whiteness (the back olive-green, the belly silvered to the tones of the sandy bottoms it lives above) that ensure its freedom from all feelings of inferiority. And another thing: it doesn't have that family barbel jutting out of its lower lip; the hairdresser must have tidied it up!

Though abundant in the North Sea and the Channel it is rarer in the Atlantic, and becomes increasingly so as you approach the south of Portugal, beyond which point it never goes; just as its numbers thin out as one moves north toward the coasts of Iceland. But are all these the same fish? The dictionary of the Académie des Gastronomes makes a distinction not only between the black whiting of the North Sea and the Channel and the gray or common whiting of the Atlantic, but also between these two and a gray Mediterranean whiting sometimes referred to as the *poutassou*.

It lives in fairly shallow water, feeding on worms, small crustaceans, and small fish. It lives in shoals, sometimes of considerable size, and is caught either in dragnets or with hooks.

It is excellent eating almost the whole year round if it is caught on a hook and glitters. But if it is soft and dull-scaled, either it has been crushed in the dragnet or it was about to spawn. The best fish are those taken in September and October around the Dogger Bank and those caught from July to October in the region of the Smalls.

Dietetically the whiting is the most easily digested of all fish, and very often the first solid food recommended in convalescence is poached whiting. Though poached whiting may be recommended for the sick, and although whiting fillets can be prepared in a score of ways (the flesh may also be pounded for use in fish stuffings and *mousses*), its natural destination is deep, hot fat, and fried whiting is part of our gastronomic folklore.

It must, however, be fried the right way. And there is a

Grandville: Waiting for a Guest

very specific technique: pans must be of tin-lined copper or thick cast iron, deep, and large enough so that they will not be more than half full when the groundnut oil is deep enough to cover the fish.

Yes, groundnut oil. Being so totally neutral, it is much better for fish frying than any other medium, whether tasty olive oil, magical goose fat, or the practical lard. The various stages of heated fat are well known: medium hot (parsley dropped into it will make it bubble), hot (it sizzles if whatever is plunged into it is slightly moist), and lastly very hot (it smokes and is pungent in the nose). It is in this very hot oil that fish should be fried. But take care: the hotter the oil the quicker the fish will turn from the lovely golden color you want to the brown tinge that means it's burnt. So it must be left in the fat as short a time as possible. And that is why your fried whiting in a restaurant is often insufficiently cooked, its flesh still pink along the spine.

For there is a trick that good chefs know but that their young assistants try to forget because they are in a hurry: you must spike the fish.

Here is your whiting, gutted and trimmed. With a pointed knife make deep incisions in the flesh all along the spine. Dip it in milk, then flour it. All that remains now is to toss it into the smoking oil.

But there is more than one sort of fried whiting, and you will meet it on menus described not only straightforwardly as *merlan frit* but also preciously as *merlan Colbert,* amusingly as *merlan en colère*, and fancifully as *merlan en lorgnette*. Here is what those three incarnations mean in practice:

Merlan en Colère

This is a whiting that you have made into a circle, fixing its tail between its jaws before you fry it. So that it looks as though it is in a fury with itself, angrily chasing its own tail in an elegant keep-fit exercise.

Merlan Colbert

Split the fish along the back so that you can remove the spine from the base of the neck to the base of the tail. Pull the two halves slightly apart in order to sprinkle with pepper, salt, and breadcrumbs before frying.

Merlan en Lorgnette

Same procedure as for *merlan Colbert*, but remove the tail along with the spine. Then, having covered the fish in breadcrumbs, you curl the two halves of the fish around on themselves to form two circles. Fix them in position with two small wooden skewers, one on each side of the head; then drop the fish into the oil.

The guinea hen makes two "important" dishes on the menu, so an "important" wine is what we're looking for. And since the turbot was braised in champagne we can be sure of not going far wrong with a Moët & Chandon Brut Impérial.

Turbot Soufflé au Champagne
(Stuffed Turbot Braised in Champagne)

The turbot, a fish that holds its mouth awry . . .

An urchin hanging around the fish stalls on the rue Lepic once described *Rhombus maximus* to me as "that fish as looks like it's been put through a wringer, head and all." It is a fish that is "all profile," as Proust said of Saint-Loup when he was surreptitiously entering a place of low repute.

Though the turbot, I hasten to add, frequents only places of the very highest repute—gastronomically speaking, at all events. Its flesh is so delicate, is possessed of such a delicious solidity and savor, that it cries out for royal treatment, and has its own particular utensil named and reserved for it: the *turbotière*, or turbot kettle.

Moreover, its renown dates back to antiquity. Juvenal praised it no less than the Emperor Domitian, and in the very same "Satire." For it was that emperor who called a meeting of the Senate so that they could decide what sauce he should serve with an enormous turbot that had been given him.

As I remember, though, the Senate dispersed without managing to come to a decision. Perhaps they were more interested in cooking the Emperor's goose. But never mind,

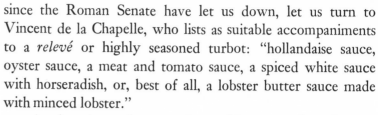

since the Roman Senate have let us down, let us turn to Vincent de la Chapelle, who lists as suitable accompaniments to a *relevé* or highly seasoned turbot: "hollandaise sauce, oyster sauce, a meat and tomato sauce, a spiced white sauce with horseradish, or, best of all, a lobster butter sauce made with minced lobster."

At that time, of course, he could not yet have known the sauce his colleague Duglèré was to invent for his customers at the Café Anglais—where he was the chef—and that connoisseurs of the Belle Epoque valued highly enough to immortalize with the name of its creator.

And so, throughout the centuries, in the hierarchy of the fish-eaters in the great oceanic popularity poll, the turbot has remained number one. It is the aristocrat of fish. Its legend is spiced with innumerable anecdotes that invariably redound to its credit, and it is Talleyrand who has by common consent been given (no doubt on the principle of "to those that have . . .") the benefit of the most famous—that of Chevet's two turbots.

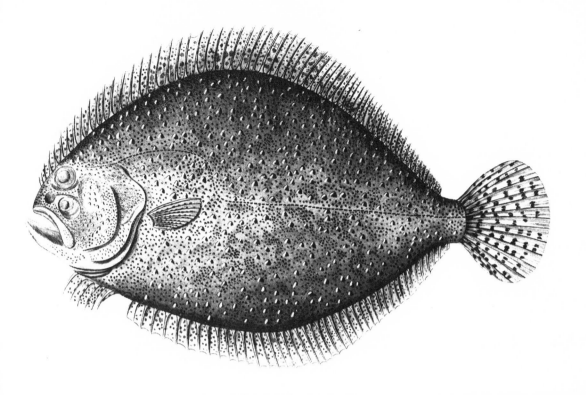

Chevet, the great caterer in the Palais Royal ("M. Chevet's dark little den—Palais Royal, number 220—is not empty for a moment from dawn till dusk," one reads in *La Table parisienne*. It was there Balzac went to order *pâté de foie gras*, lobster and sturgeon fillets, roast ham, plover *au gratin*, *grenadins de veau*, asparagus, pineapple *beignets*, and a basket of fruit). Chevet had made a present to the "Limping Devil," so the story goes, of two gigantic turbots, so huge that Paris had never seen their like.

Dilemma. Next day, it was quite true, Talleyrand had a dinner arranged at which the dozen guests were certainly of a caliber to appreciate both the exquisite flesh and the extraordinary size of his two fishes. But to serve them *two* such turbots —was that not somewhat vulgar, the ostentation of the *nouveau riche* financier rather than the munificence of the *grand seigneur?* And yet, and yet, the whole wonder of these marine giants lay in the very fact that there were two of them, both of equal dimensions. But already Talleyrand was smiling into his lace jabot. He had found his solution.

Next day, after the soups, his *maître d'hôtel* flung wide the double doors of the dining room to admit two footmen bearing in, on an enormous silver dish, the most prodigious turbot it had ever been given to diners to admire. Exclamations broke forth, admiration, compliments. Alas, the triumph ended in a cry of alarm. One of the footmen had slipped on the polished floor and the great fish was in ruins. Desolation filled the room.

But Talleyrand, impassive as always, merely ordered: "Bring in another."

And two more footmen, to even louder cries of admiration, duly carried in the second turbot.

Unfortunately history does not record how the chef (who might even, given the dates, have been Carême himself) cooked Chevet's two turbots. But for my part I shall certainly never forget a certain *turbot soufflé au champagne* that was served in honor of my dear Curnonsky, the Prince of Gastronomes, one evening in a salon on the rue Duphot. Not just a princely tribute but also a princely creation, it was a dish that provided a twofold pleasure.

Promeneurs.

Les promeneurs.

Turbot Soufflé au Champagne

10 oz mushrooms, finely chopped
  ½ lb butter
1 lemon
  2 whiting weighing ½ lb each
2 tbs béchamel *sauce*
  4 eggs, separated
2 cups heavy cream

salt
  cayenne
1 turbot weighing about 3¼ lbs
  pepper
3 shallots
  ½ bottle dry champagne

Cook the finely chopped mushrooms in a covered pan with a little salted water, a little of the butter, and the juice of the lemon. Fillet the raw whitings. Mash the fillets and the drained mushrooms, reserving the liquid. Mix the two together. Add the *béchamel* and 1 egg yolk. Put through a fine strainer.

To this filling add ¼ cup of the cream, whipped; then two stiffly beaten egg whites, salt, and cayenne pepper.

Clean and trim the turbot. Remove its head. Lay the fish on its gray side and make an incision down the middle of the white side. Lift the flesh away from the bone on either side of this cut, taking care not to pull it quite away. Sever the spine at head and tail. Salt and pepper inside the fish, then put in the filling or stuffing.

Generously butter your turbot kettle (which must have a grill). Sprinkle the chopped shallots over the bottom. Place the turbot on top. Pour the mushroom water and champagne over the fish. Cover with buttered paper and bring to a boil quickly. Thereafter, continue cooking in a medium oven for about 40 minutes.

Remove the grill and slide the turbot onto your heated serving dish. Leave the paper on to prevent the fish from drying out. Strain the stock.

Reduce the stock as quickly as possible in a saucepan. When it has been reduced by three-quarters, bind it with 3 egg yolks and the rest of the cream. Then, stirring gently, add the rest of the butter little by little. Whisk the sauce well and don't let it boil.

Remove the buttered paper, pour the sauce over the fish, and serve.

S. M. Napoléon III, revenant du bois.

Ledoyen's restaurant, on private-view day at the Salon

MENU

*Truite de mer sauce
   verte
Noisettes d'agneau aux
   pointes d'asperges
(Loin lamb chops with
   asparagus tips)
*Fraises et framboises
   Chantilly

For a great dish, a great wine:
with the trout a young
Puligny-Montrachet. With the
lamb a Bordeaux such as a
Château Léoville Las-Cases.

Truite de Mer Sauce Verte

(Salmon Trout with Green Sauce)

This *sauce verte*—or perhaps its sister—was already held in
high esteem in the fifteenth century. As early as the reign of
Louis XII the sauce-makers of Paris had formed themselves
into a company claiming the exclusive privilege of making
and selling sauces. Some sauce-makers became itinerant sauce-
sellers too, stimulating their prospective customers' gastric
juices with the following cry:

> Come now buy your green sauce!
> To eat with your carps and your sole
> Buy some and you'll please your boss
> Speak while the lid's off my bowl.

And Panurge, conqueror of King Anarche, was of a mind to
reduce his victim to the status of a "crier of green sauce."

This green sauce of the Middle Ages admittedly had
very little connection with what goes by the name of *sauce
verte* today. But, as you will have noted, it was already eaten
as an accompaniment to fish.

And what better fish can you find than the salmon trout?

This *salmo trutta*, which lives out in the open sea, though not too far from the estuaries that it enters in order to spawn in early winter, may reach ten or fifteen pounds in weight. Its flesh is a salmon-pink (because it feeds luxuriously on prawns) and it is one of the best and most delicate fish to come out of the sea.

In spring it is at the top of its form. In a back number of *Le Pot au feu* (May 1893 actually), I read: "It is now the season for the famous salmon trout *'sauce verte,'* which is traditionally served at Ledoyen's on the opening day of the Salon."

On the woody stretch of ground broken by swampy patches and a few small market gardens that, in the early seventeenth century, stretched beyond what is now the gate of the Tuileries, a number of open-air eating places gradually sprang up. It was after the Revolution that a certain Antoine-Nicolas Doyen, scion of a catering family, rented one of them from its original owner, Desmazures. It came to be known, naturally enough, as Chez Doyen, then Chez Ledoyen, then Ledoyen pure and simple.

Doyen used to send meals out too, even as far as the "country places" of some Directoire notables. Out toward Saint-Cloud, Madame Tallien, Marquise de Fontenay, and an amorous young creole who was about to be married off— with a view to curtailing her career—to a sallow, unkempt little soldier named Bonaparte, used often to share both the favors of Paul Barras and his delicate little suppers ordered from Doyen.

And to Doyen's restaurant itself the whole world flocked. A certain Dr. P. G. writes, on this subject: "Barras and the young General Bonaparte met there often, as did Robespierre, Saint-Just, and many others." However, Robespierre and Saint-Just had been guillotined a long while indeed by the time that Barras—having helped them on their way—had ceased to fear for his own life and recovered his appetite sufficiently to sample the fare at Doyen's.

But let it pass. And let us move on. In 1858, Ledoyen's was acquired by a certain Balvay. And by 1893, as we know from *Le Pot au feu,* Balvay's son-in-law had succeeded him and was then running the restaurant. This Balvay had been one of the Emperor's cooks—by which I mean the second Napoleon, Napoleon III—and we are told that it was at the imperial table in the Tuileries that he first served "his" *sauce verte.*

And this celebrated *sauce verte* then became a tradition, every May, on the opening day of the Salon.

The Salon, ancestor of all the many present-day "salons" of paintings, after becoming momentarily biennial in about 1853, had reverted to being an annual event by that time and was held, in the spring, at the nearby Grand Palais. The tradition of lunch at Ledoyen's before the opening was to be maintained for many years. In the Goncourts' *Journal* for May 1, 1882, we can read: "Today to the opening of the Salon and lunch chez Ledoyen with Daudet, Zola, Charpentier and wives. . . . Most of the painting world there, plus painters' wives causing stirs with their delayed entrances. . . . In one corner there was an old man with a model's head in the process of getting himself pickled in a very gesticulatory, Frédérick Lemaître manner. . . ."

I like to imagine that those annual lunches, the menus of which Alphonse Daudet used to stop by and arrange a few days in advance, paid tribute to our *sauce verte;* and that when I am enjoying a delicious *truite de mer sauce verte* at Ledoyen's—thanks to Gilbert Lejeune, the latest in line of Antoine-Nicolas Doyen's successors—I am still doing so in company with the aging Goncourt, the invalid Daudet, and that old grouser Zola.

But what was the *sauce verte* they ate? *Le Pot au feu* assures us that it was by no means just a simple mayonnaise with an admixture of herb juices. And that there were many "sophistications" involved. Which is why the journalist wrote: "On the Champs-Elysées, the sauce, though fairly thick, preserves a sort of lightness and fluidity unheard of in many establishments, where this sauce has a heavy, gluey appearance. The reason being that the mayonnaise must above all be made with an olive oil of irreproachable purity. Whereas the oil used is often adulterated, and every gourmet knows the insupportable taste of flour that inferior-quality oil imparts to a mayonnaise. Moreover, many chefs, thinking they are dealing with so-called gourmets most of whom ask no more of a *sauce verte* than that it should be well and truly green in color, content themselves with merely serving ordinary mayonnaise with the addition of some raw spinach juice or some green rouge, as it were. Since in the kitchen there is 'rouge' of every color in fact!"

And the author of the *Pot au feu* article, who signs himself Mazarin, then gives his recipe for *sauce verte*.

It is a more or less classic recipe, and I have never been able to find Balvay's own. It must have been similar. Like many cooks, he judged his success to be due to his knack. And why shouldn't he? But the truth is that great care and good ingredients are also necessary. In particular, a very high quality oil and a careful proportioning of the herbs.

But a poached salmon trout, removed from its broth, simply drained, still warm, with a well-chilled green sauce, is one of the great springtime dishes.

A still life that ought to inspire any painter worthy of his salt; indeed a fitting prologue to the Salon.

Truite de Mer Sauce Verte

1 fresh salmon trout	*1 champagne glass of champagne*
2 carrots	*peppercorns*
2 onions	*salt*
bouquet garni	*orange rind*

● GREEN SAUCE

olive oil	*tarragon*
white wine vinegar	*watercress*
eggs	*spinach leaves*
chervil	*scallion*
parsley	*capers*

Trim and gut a salmon trout. Simmer it in a well-flavored *court-bouillon* (carrots, onions, *bouquet garni*, a glass of champagne, peppercorns, salt, and a small piece of orange rind) and water to barely cover.

Drain the fish. Place it to cool on a dish. Trim it.

Make a mayonnaise with the best olive oil (cold), a fairly mild white wine vinegar, and very fresh eggs.

Blanch equal quantities of chervil, parsley, tarragon, and watercress in boiling water for one minute. Drain. Dry. Crush and strain out the juice. Add a little juice from some blanched and crushed spinach leaves.

Fold the juices into the mayonnaise, a little at a time, but very carefully, so that the mayonnaise doesn't curdle.

Chop a little chervil and a small scallion up very finely with a few capers. Add them to the sauce, which should remain fluid. Put it in a cold place (not the refrigerator) to get as cold as possible before serving, in a sauceboat, with the warm fish.

ROCHER DE CANCALE,

BORREL, *successeur de M.* **BALAINE**, *Restaurateur, rue Montorgueil, n° 61, et rue Mandar, n° 1.*

Nota. Sur simple demande, on envoie à Paris et dans les départemens du Poisson et des Huîtres de toute espèce en gros et en détail.

Les mets dont le prix n'est pas fixé manquent.

POTAGES.

	Fr. s.
A la julienne	12
Aux choux	12
Au vermicelle	12
Au riz	12
Consommé	12
Purée aux croutons à la Condé	15
Potage au lait	15
Potage au macaroni	
Potage en tortue	2 "

HUITRES.

	Fr. s.
Huîtres d'Ostende, la douzaine	1 10
Idem blanches, la douzaine	12
Idem vertes, la douzaine	16
Idem frites	2
Idem en coquille	2
Citron	8
Petit pain	5

HORS-D'ŒUVRES.

Beurre	4
Cornichons	6
Salade d'anchois	1
Thon	1
Olives	10
Œufs frais, deux	10
Saucisses, deux	8
Pied de cochon à la Sainte-Menehould	1
Idem farci aux truffes	1 15
Deux saucisses aux truffes	
Boudin noir	
Deux petits pains	

BŒUF.

Au naturel	10
A la sauce	12
A la sauce tomate	15
Bef-steak aux pommes de terre	1
Idem aux cornichons	1 5
Idem au beurre d'anchois	1 10
Idem sauté dans la glace	1 10
Idem sauté au vin de Madère	1 15
Idem aux truffes	2
Filet de bœuf piqué	1 5
Filet de bœuf braisé au vin de Madère	1 15

ENTRÉES DE VEAU.

Côtelette de veau au naturel ou panée	1
Idem en papillotte ou aux fines herbes	1 5
Nœ de veau piqué à l'oseille ou au jus	2 10
Idem à la chicorée	2 10
Idem à la sauce tomate	2 10
Idem à la financière	3 10
Idem à la financière aux truffes	4
Fricandeau à l'oseille	1
Idem au jus	1 5
Idem à la chicorée	1 5
Idem à la sauce tomate	1 5
Tête de veau au naturel	1
Idem en marinade	2 10
Idem en tortue	2 10
Cervelle de veau frite	1 5

	Fr. s.
Idem au beurre noir	1 5
Idem à la provençale	1 10

ENTRÉES DE MOUTON.

Deux côtelettes au naturel ou panées	18
Idem à la minute	1 5
Idem à la financière	3
Idem à la financière aux truffes	3 10
Filet de mouton sauté à la minute	1 5
Idem à la chicorée ou à la sauce tomate	1 5
Idem en chevreuil	1 10
Pieds de mouton à la poulette	1
Deux rognons à la brochette	18
Idem au vin de champagne	

ENTRÉES DE VOLAILLES.

Chapon au gros sel	2 10
La moitié	1 5
Idem, 5 fr. 10 s.; l'aile	3
Chapon au riz	2 10
La moitié	1 5
Fricassée de poulet	2
La moitié	1 10
Karis ou Pilau à l'indienne	4
La moitié	2
Poulet gras à la tartare	4
La moitié	2
Un Poulet à la Marengo aux truffes	4
La moitié	2
Salade de volaille	2
Cuisse de poulet en papillotte	1 5
Capilotade de volaille	1 10
Marinade en pâte de volaille	1 10
Blanquette de poularde	2
Idem aux truffes	3
Pigeon à la crapaudine	2 10
Ragoût mêlé à la financière	3 10
Idem aux truffes	3 10
Vol-au-vent à la financière	3
Idem aux truffes	
Coquille à la financière	2
Idem aux truffes	
Filets de volaille au suprême	3 10
Idem aux truffes	3

ENTRÉES DE GIBIER.

Un perdreau gris au salmis	
Idem aux truffes	
Un perdreau rouge au salmis	
Idem aux truffes	
Salmis de bécasse	
Idem aux truffes	
Une caille à la financière	
Idem à la financière aux truffes	
Purée de gibier à l'essence	

ENTRÉES DE POISSON.

Vol-au-vent de poisson	2 10
Matelotte d'anguille	2

	Fr. s.
Tronçon d'anguille à la tartare	1 15
Morue à la maître-d'hôtel	1 10
Idem à la provençale	1 10
Raie, sauce aux câpres	1 10
Idem au beurre noir	2
Turbot, sauce aux câpres	2
Idem à la hollandaise	2
Idem à la crème et au gratin	2
Idem à la provençale	2
Idem à l'huile	2
Idem aux huîtres	2
Idem aux homards	2
Sole au gratin, 2 f. 10 s.; 3 f., 4 f., 5 f. et	6
Carlet sur le plat, ou au gratin	
Idem à la provençale	1 15
Idem au matelotte normande	
Filets de carlets frits ou de soles	2
Idem à la provençale	2
Saumon grillé, sauce aux câpres ou au blanc	2
Idem à la hollandaise ou à la provençale	2
Idem à la génevoise	2
Truite saumonée au bleu ou à la genevoise	2
Idem à la hollandaise ou à la provençale	2
Cabillaud à la hollandaise	2
Idem à la maître-d'hôtel	2
Petite truite de rivière	1
Eperlans au gratin	1 15
Matelotte au gratin	1 15

POISSON FRIT.

Sole frite, 2, 3, 4 et	5
Carlet frit	2 10
Eperlans	
Goujons	1 5
Merlan	1 10

COQUILLAGES.

Ecrivisses	2 10
Homard, 2 f. 10 s., 3 f., 4 et	
Crevettes	1 10
Moule	1 5

ROTS DE VOLAILLE ET DE GIBIER.

Poulet à la reine	4
Poulet gras	6
Idem aux truffes	
Poulet normand	7
Idem aux truffes	
Perdreau gris	
Idem aux truffes	
Perdreau rouge	
Idem aux truffes	
Plovier doré	
Vanneau	
Bécassine	
Grive	
Trois mauviettes	
Canard sauvage	
Idem rouge de rivière	
Cercelle	
Pigeon de volière	
Caille	
Croupion de Bœuf	

VINS BLANCS.

	Fr. s.
Chablis	3
Idem première qualité	3 10
Idem de la comète	4
Meursault	4
Mont Rachet	8
Mont-Rachet 1802	8
Grave	3
Sauterne de madame Duroy	7
Sauterne 1802, de madame Duroy	8
Tisanne de Champagne	6
Champagne mousseux	7
Champagne rosé	7
Aï non mousseux	7
Sillery glacé	10
Vin du Rhin, 10 fr. et	
Vin du Rhin (1748)	20
Hermitage	6
Vin de Rognac	7

Porter, ou Bière anglaise	3
Eau de Seltz	2 10

VINS ROUGES.

	Fr. s.
Mâcon	3
Beaune	3 10
Beaune, première qualité	4
Pomard	4
Pomard, très-vieux	5
Volnay	5
Nuits	6
Chambertin	7 10
Chambertin, 1806	8
Clos Vougeot de MM. Tourton et Ravel	8 10
Bordeaux-Médoc	4
Bordeaux-Ségur	5
Bordeaux-Latour	6
Bordeaux Mouton-Laïtte	6
Bordeaux-Laîtte	6
Bordeaux-Laîtte, 1802	7
Porto	6
Champagne	7
Hermitage	7
Tavel très-vieux	4
Rancio de Couillœure	8

VINS D'ENTREMET ET LIQUEURS.

	Fr. s.
Madère sec	9
— la demi-bouteille, 5 fr.; le verre	10
Kérès, 8 fr.; le verre	15
Malvoisie de Madère, 15 fr.; le verre	15
Alicante	15
Rota, 8 fr.; le verre	15
Muscat de Frontignan et Lunel 6 f.; le ver.	15
Muscat de Rousillon, 7 fr.; le verre	15
Malaga, 8 fr.; le verre	15
Paille de Poligny la demi-bouteille	6
Tokai, la demi-bouteille	20
Constance, la demi-bouteille	20

LIQUEURS FINES.

Café, la demi-tasse	
Eau-de-vie	8
Idem d'Andaye	8
Anisette de Bordeaux	10
Fleur d'orange au vin de Champagne	10
Huile de rum	10
Huile de vanille	10
Scubac	10

	Fr. s.
Kirchwasser	10
Extrait d'absynthe	10
Genièvre d'Hollande	10
Noyau Sec	10
Crème d'absynthe	15
Eau-de-vie de Dantzick	15
Crème de Menthe	15
Crème de Cacheao	15
Elixir de Garus	15
Bonana bananin	15
Huile de kirchwasser	15
Crème de Créole	15
Anisette de Hollande	15
Marasquin	15
Curaçao d'Hollande	15
Gouttes de Malte	15
Mirobolant	15
Macaroni	15

Nota. Le public est prévenu que l'on ne fait pas de demi-bouteilles dans les Cabinets, et que le feu se paie à part.

ENTREMETS.

	Fr. s.
Haricots blancs	
Haricots verts	
Cardes	
Artichaut à la barigoule	1 10
Asperges en petits pois	
Truffes à l'italienne	5
Macédoine de légumes	
Champignons à la bordelaise	1 10
Croûte aux champignons	1 10
Chicorée	1
Pommes de terre à la maître-d'hôtel	
Epinards	1
Œufs pochés au jus	1
Idem à la chicorée	1
Œufs brouillés	1
Idem aux truffes	3
Omelette aux fines herbes	1
Idem au sucre	1
Idem aux confitures	1 5
Idem soufflée	
Petit pot de crème	1
Charlotte de pomme et d'abricots	2
Beignets de pommes	
Gelée de liqueur	2 10
Soufflé de pommes de terre	1 10
Macaroni	1 10
Salade de différentes espèces	

DESSERTS.

Raisin de Fontainebleau	
Pêche et sucre	
Poire	
Pomme	
Marrons de Lyon	
Mandians	
Compotte de différentes espèces	1 5
Confiture de cerise	
Gelée de groseille	
Idem de pommes ou de coings	
Marmelade d'abricots	5
Pâte d'abricots	
Groseilles de Bar, rouges et blanches, la tasse	5
Chinoise	
Meringue aux confitures	
Idem à la crème	15
Biscuit en caisse	10
Macarons	10
Fromage de Gruyère et Brie	10
Idem de Neufchâtel	10
Idem de Parmesan	15
Idem de Roquefort	15
Idem de Chester	10
Deux prunes à l'eau-de-vie	10
Cerises à l'eau-de-vie	15
Pêche à l'eau-de-vie	10

Tony Johannot: Hugo, Dumas, and Balzac

For a very important dish
indeed a very important wine: a
white Burgundy. For example
a Puligny-Montrachet. If
you feel it would be an
imposition on such a wine to
continue it with the Brie
(though it would not worry me
personally), then you can
follow the white Burgundy
with a red.

Sole Normande (Filet of Sole with Shellfish and Mushrooms)

The *sole normande* is a "monument" of the French *grande cuisine*, a rich, sumptuous, aristocratic, and also no doubt slightly precious dish. But what is its history? Its true history, that is. Because I am not absolutely certain that we were right, in 1937, when we celebrated the centenary of its creation—in 1837—by Langlais, the chef of Le Rocher de Cancale.

Le Rocher de Cancale was situated on the rue Montorgueil. It was there that Brillat-Savarin came once a week to savor a *turbot à la broche*. It was there that Grimod de La Reynière had presided over the well-known (but less than wholly serious) *Jury Gourmand*. Other frequent visitors were Dumas the elder, Hugo, Musset, and Balzac, many of whose characters gave dinners and generally made whoopee there with their mistresses and what we should now, in a charitable mood, call "starlets." And again it was at Le Rocher de Cancale that the Duc d'Orléans, after the taking of Anvers, gave a dinner to all his officers that cost eighty francs a head—a record at that time.

This restaurant, run first by Balaine then by Borel, made

a particular specialty of fish and shellfish, and carried the following notice at the foot of its menus: "Customers are asked to note that half-bottles are not served in private rooms and that fires are not inclusive."

And it was in 1837, so the story goes, that the chef Langlais created this recipe in the Rocher's kitchens.

Except that Gouffé, who supplied this information, seems himself to have contradicted it a little further on. Here is what he says: "The recipe I give . . . I believe to be completely authentic and was given it by the inventor, M. Langlais, *chef de cuisine* at Le Rocher de Cancale at the time of its great vogue. He was kind enough to explain his method to me." And further on: "This dish has never been described in any work. It is only a few years as yet since it first came into existence and we first saw it served in Hanneveu's establishment, Le Cadran Bleu."

That was written in 1843. And it doesn't make it clear how Gouffé could possibly have seen *sole normande* "first served" at Le Cadran Bleu yet also claim that it was invented by Langlais, in 1837, at Le Rocher de Cancale. Because Le Rocher de Cancale still existed in 1843, and even if Langlais had left it for the kitchens of Le Cadran Bleu, the restaurant where he had invented it would still have continued to serve his sole!

So the facts of gastronomic history are just as difficult to pin down as those of history with a capital H. Was Langlais ever chef at Le Cadran Bleu? No one is in a position to be certain one way or the other, and the writer quoted above, though he had been given the recipe for this *sole normande* by Langlais himself, never thought to ask him. Rather surprising, to say the least!

Moreover if we go to the *Larousse gastronomique* we learn that some writers claim the *sole normande* to have been the invention of one Philippe, owner of a restaurant on the rue Montorgueil early in the nineteenth century.

Except that Philippe's restaurant wasn't on the rue Montorgueil!

The establishment he opened in 1804 was on the rue des Petits-Carreaux. Though it is true that the rue des Petits-Carreaux is a continuation of the rue Montorgueil, running

Le Rocher de Cancale, Paris

along the same route, outside the old walls, as what was called in the sixteenth century the Chemin de la Marée (that is, the road by which the fish train—in the old sense—came into Paris), which incidentally explains the number of restaurants specializing in fish dishes along the route.

In 1864, Pascal, the former cook at the Jockey Club, took over the restaurant Philippe. Goncourt used to dine there sometimes (see the *Journal*, April 1866–October 1867) and the banquets of the Dîner Bixio and the Club des Grands Estomacs were also held there.

But let us turn to the recipe: it is basically a sole poached in a concentrated broth or *fumet* made with fish and white wine, then served with a garnish of mussels, oysters, prawns, mushrooms, crayfish, and so forth.

But did Langlais really invent it?

Because in Carême's *L'Art de la cuisine française au dix-neuvième siècle*, published in 1835, there is already a stew, or *ragoût de matelote normande*, to be found that includes two soles and a plaice cooked with mushrooms and sauternes, and the sauce of which (obtained by adding to the broth of the flat fish the broth of mussels, *sauce allemande*, sauternes, meat jelly, butter, and lemon juice) was enriched with mussels, oysters, smelts, soft roe of carp, prawn tails, and croutons.

Replace the soft roe of carp with crayfish and you have something that may not be exactly *sole normande* but certainly approximates it.

Sole Normande

4 oysters
12 mussels
white wine
4 crayfish
court-bouillon
1 onion
1 carrot
bouquet garni
pepper
24 small mushroom caps

1 sole (about 1 lb)
¼ lb butter
1 tbs flour
2 egg yolks
5 tbs heavy cream
2 oz shelled prawn tails
1 small truffle, cooked in champagne
breadcrumbs
4 smelts
4 crescents golden puff pastry

Poach the oysters in water. Drain and trim them, and reserve the broth.

Open the mussels. Clean them well and cook them in white wine. Drain them. Filter the broth.

Cook the crayfish in a highly seasoned *court-bouillon*. Set aside.

Make a *fumet* (a strong, well-reduced fish stock) from the trimmings of the fish boiled in a mixture of equal parts of water and white wine, together with an onion, a carrot cut into rounds, a *bouquet garni*, and pepper.

Add to this *fumet* the filtered broth of the mussels and oysters as well as the broth of the mushrooms cooked in white wine. Trim a good sole. Make an incision, gently lift the fillets away from the spine on the side from which you have removed the skin, then break the spine in three places: neck, belly, and tail.

Poach the sole in the *fumet* to which you have added the other broths.

Drain it, pat it dry, remove the spine and set the sole on a long, heated dish. Arrange the oysters, mussels, and mushrooms around it, and keep warm.

With 1¾ ounces of butter and 1 tablespoon of flour make a blond *roux*. Add some of the *fumet* and cook at a gentle simmer for an hour. Strain through a sieve.

To ½ cup of this sauce add the same quantity of the broth the sole has been cooked in. Mix 2 egg yolks well into 2 tablespoons of cream. Add them to the sauce. Turn the heat up. Cook till your sauce has been reduced by a third. Then finish off with the remaining butter and cream and strain through a sieve.

Add 2 ounces of shelled prawn tails.

Pour this *sauce normande* over the sole and its garnish.

Cut a small truffle cooked in champagne into 6 slices. Arrange them around the sole.

Fry 4 generously breadcrumbed smelts with their mouths biting their tails. Truss your crayfish. Arrange smelts and crayfish alternately around the dish.

Lastly, add the crescents of golden puff pastry as decoration.

Why not hard cider? Or else
a very young Muscadet.

Cotriade (Fisherman's Stew)

The day the members of the French Academy elected Jonnard in preference to Maurras, the historian André Bellessort began his lecture thus: "Gentlemen, the Académie Française has just elected M. Jonnard to join it. I shall now talk to you about Charles Maurras . . ."

In rather the same way I could begin this chapter by saying: "Readers, everyone is talking about *bouillabaisse*. I am going to tell you about the *cotriade!*"

And for several reasons.

The *bouillabaisse*, Georges Simenon has written somewhere, is the dish that has produced more idiotic remarks than any other. And I wouldn't want to add to their number.

Also, and above all, I can't really count it as being one of the glories of French cooking! Not even of Mediterranean French cooking!

The *bouillabaisse* is an entertainment. Genuinely traditional perhaps, but turned into sickening tourist fodder like the *farandole* and the *tutu-panpan*. It has emerged from the fisherman's boat, where it was simply the simplest dish to be made from the ingredients to hand, and pushed its way onto every snob's table.

But being a fisherman's dish the *bouillabaisse* in fact belongs to all seas and all coasts. So much so that the Flemish *waterzoïï* resembles it not only in culinary principle but also in name, since both mean "boiling water." The Basque *ttoro*, the *chaudrée* from Saintonge, the *marmite* from Dieppe, and the Breton *cotriade* are all *bouillabaisses* too. But—I hope I shall be forgiven for saying—civilized *bouillabaisses* that make no use of those aggressive ingredients: garlic, saffron, and an excess of herbs. Yes, it's a question of latitude, I agree. But also a question of one's attitude toward life, toward the appetite, toward what one thinks of as "the nature of things."

And I have chosen the *cotriade* from among all the other non-meridional *bouillabaisses* because it is in fact the anti-*bouillabaisse*.

Since it is Breton, and in a sense separatist. All Frenchmen, from no matter what region, if they love their native land must also be Breton separatists. For Brittany is their second homeland.

Because the fish of Brittany are the king of fish. Neptune's private stable as it were.

Because in that heavenly scented casserole, like distinctive watermarks, we can perceive not only the Breton reefs and spray, not only the solid, honest, massive silhouettes of the oil-skinned fishermen, but also the gorse of the dunes, the crushing weight of the menhirs, the disturbing beauty of the sprites that haunt them, the secrets of the Druids, the eternal Celtic hope, and a sigh from Mélusine, the fairy from the legends of Poitou.

And since, like the *bouillabaisse* of Provence, the *cotriade* is a fisherman's dish, it is also a simple dish. It would be ridiculous to put lobster or crayfish in the sunny *bouillabaisse*; but in the *cotriade* of which I give the recipe here, one of the ingredients is, in fact, lobster.

So I feel something of a cheat. But then I tell myself that the lobster, in this case, represents the reward of effort, that in the rough, calloused hands of the Breton fisherman that costly jewel the blue lobster, that precious stone of the sea, is not ridiculous.

And that anyway I am eating my *cotriade* in Paris.

For here is another important factor: the *bouillabaisse* in Paris is absurd. The *cotriade* isn't at all. The *bouillabaisse* seems to be in fancy dress. Its beautiful sunny accent grates on our ears like bad grammar and on our appetite like an error of taste. It is a loud-mouthed dame trying to make us believe she is perfectly at home as a society hostess—and failing utterly! The *cotriade*, on the other hand, can make the transition from fishing boat to the gray tones of Paris and its night world without any difficulty at all. Outside, the rain seems to take on a slightly salty taste. A gust of wind blows in through the open door bearing a whiff of seaweed and cider:

"*Kenavo*," the maid of the old farmhouse greets you in Breton.

"Good day," I am greeted by Jacqueline Libois, the owner of a farmhouse restaurant much frequented by Parisian gourmets.

And the heart behind the words is the same, because the copper pots in the hearth have been simmering that fish soup since the beginning of time to greet the hungry traveler. And because, as elsewhere they keep a ham hanging in the cupboard against the unexpected visit, or the smoked goose in its

pot, or the truffles in their goose fat, or as they will run out to the hen run to pick up the newly laid eggs for you, so here they run out to the tank, to the wicker pot, to fetch the lobster brought in that morning so that they can add it to the *cotriade* in honor of the unexpected guest.

The lobster is a special addition. A guest of honor for a guest of honor. Jacqueline, Yannick, Mélanie, or Maryvonne already has the preparation of the lobster well in hand as her man goes out to fetch in a bottle of their best hard cider.

Kenavo! A greeting and a promise of feasting!

Cotriade

4 onions
  2 oz salt butter
2 lbs potatoes
  1 wineglass hard cider
4 cups fumet
  4 lbs white fish steaks such as bass or halibut

2 small lobsters (about ½ lb each) or 1 large one
  1 tbs heavy cream
fried croutons
  1 bowl shallot vinaigrette sauce

Peel, slice and chop the onions. Brown them lightly in the butter; then add the potatoes, peeled, and cut into thick slices. Allow to brown for 5 minutes.

Pour in the hard cider.

Make the *fumet* (concentrated fish broth) with fish heads, a few sliced carrots and onions, and a *bouquet garni*.

Strain this *fumet* and pour it over the potatoes. Bring to the boil. Add the fish steaks. Add pepper. Allow to simmer.

Poach the lobster separately in a fish *fumet*.

Serve the fish and the lobster on top of the potatoes in a hot dish.

Serve the broth separately, strained, then thickened with the heavy cream. Top with fried croutons.

Also separately, serve a highly seasoned shallot vinaigrette sauce.

Only one wine need be served throughout. A white Graves, for example. Or a Monbazillac.

Sole Cubat

(Sole with Mushroom Sauce)

It is found rarely on menus, and usually misspelled "Cuba" even then. That is how easily chefs forget their own kind. In this case Pierre Cubat, who was nevertheless renowned in his lifetime.

He had been a student of Dugléré at the Café Anglais (and of course Dugléré also gave his name to a recipe for sole) before going on to take charge of the kitchens of Tsar Alexander II. In the palace of that northern Caesar they did not soon forget the dinner of the Knights of St. George: eight hundred covers served in the Winter Palace of St. Petersburg, and a glittering success. Back in France, Cubat opened premises, after the 1870 war, on the Champs-Elysées.

And here I must digress.

A country without courtesans is a country in which civilization is moving backward. France today is living proof of that. Our *grand cuisine* existed solely on account of our courtesans and vanished with the Belle Epoque itself, killed off by a few thoughtless bullets, at Sarajevo, in the spring of 1914.

And I perceive a clear symbol of these truths in the fact

that the building in which Cubat opened his establishment was the former town house of La Païva, who had also, in her day, come to us from Russia.

Thérèse Lachman was the daughter of a humble Muscovite tailor, endowed with a startling beauty in the Judeo-Oriental mode, as well as considerable intelligence, and very much aware even at the time of her first marriage—when she was sixteen—that her body was to be her open-sesame to fame and fortune.

In 1856 she undertook the construction of her town house on the Champs-Elysées, on the site of an old shack. She had just married the Marquis de Païva, who was crippled with debts but possessed of an authentic title, while her lover was the Count Guido Henckel of Donnersmarck, who was unimaginably rich. This happy conjunction of circumstances enabled her to hire the architect Manguin and give him a free hand in the construction of this mini-palace of Renaissance inspiration in which only the rarest of materials were to be used.

La Païva's house still exists, as number 25, Champs-Elysées, squashed between two appalling new buildings. A miracle! The demolition contractors haven't got their hands on it yet. The furniture has all gone, but the Travellers' Club,

which now occupies the premises, has preserved the great onyx staircase decorated with its statues of Virgil, Petrarch, and Dante. The engraved gold bed has vanished, but the onyx bathtub with its gold-plated taps remains. The marquetry floors, the flagstones in alternate colors, the coffered ceilings, the carved doors, the chimney pieces with their lapis lazuli decorations endure as witnesses of that Byzantine world of luxury, and the ceiling of the great drawing room, decorated with a Baudry painting entitled "Day Driving Out Night," still preserves the opulent curves of its mistress in this house for whose greater glory she had herself painted nude.

There is a famous anecdote of the outside steps: during the construction of the house, in which she was to receive Liszt, Wagner, Théophile Gautier, Mérimée, Girardin, and many other notables, La Païva asked all these gentlemen to provide her with a motto to be carved in letters of gold over the short staircase outside the house. And one of them, irreverently, suggested the famous line from *Phèdre:* "Vice, like virtue, has its steps." But what virtue, tell me that, could ever have built this charming souvenir of stone?

After the Franco-Prussian War the troubles began. Accused of spying, the Comtesse de Donnersmarck (for, having obtained a divorce from Rome, La Païva had succeeded in making a husband of her last love—to whom, in all, she was faithful for thirty years: a lease that many an honest woman would find very long!) and her husband were asked to leave France. The house on the Champs-Elysées was sold for 1,430,000 francs.

And that was where Pierre Cubat opened up shop.

The writer Arsène Houssaye, a regular at La Païva's receptions and later at the restaurant's tables, wrote to him at the time:

"A thousand and one compliments, *mon chef* Monsieur Cubat, now we know what real Imperial cooking is. The ghost of the Marquise de Païva must often appear to you and whisper: 'I'm so pleased with you!' . . . I dined with her two or three hundred times, but never better than in your establishment."

The old Goncourt, who wrote at length in his *Journal* about the courtesan with whom he occasionally dined, notes

on May 9, 1895: "Today I was dining for my twelve francs at Voisin's when I heard tell of lunches costing thirty or fifty francs a head at the restaurant that has been opened in La Païva's house; and when I ask what one can possibly eat there that's so extraordinary, the only answer I ever get out of people is: 'Oh! a caviar . . . a caviar such as you just can't find anywhere else!' Thank you very much, but I'm afraid I prefer just my simple French grub."

But at all events, despite its high prices, the restaurant Cubat did not prosper. So when the Tsar chanced to visit Paris, Pierre Cubat, who had once been the head cook of the Imperial kitchens, sent his former master a beautiful ikon he had found in an antique shop. Touched, the Tsar came to visit Cubat, who asked if he could come back to the Imperial court. He was given an affirmative answer, and he closed up shop. The courtesan had taken her revenge, you might say.

I had better admit right away that the *sole Cubat* is not one of my favorite dishes. The chef—and the chef with a taste for the complicated and the grandiose—is too much apparent in it. The sole, that fish so elegant and rich in itself, has no need of so much flattery. If you want to say it's raining, just say "it's raining," Boileau advises. One longs to whisper to the chef: "If you want to serve a sole, just cook it, as simply as you can!" But after all, behind Cubat there is the Court of the Northern Emperor, there is Duglèré and the Café Anglais, there is La Païva and her adventures, as well as her dinners, which were, according to Goncourt, "good but lacking any element of astonishment for the stomach such as one expects at a courtesan's," and it is permissible, just once in a while, to enjoy a meal less on account of the dish one is eating than on account of what that dish represents.

Sole Cubat

1 lb fresh mushrooms
¼ cup heavy cream
1 cup béchamel *sauce*
salt and pepper
nutmeg
½ lb butter

4 soles, ½ lb each
2 small truffles
2 tbs fumet
1 oz Parmesan, grated
1 oz Gruyère, grated

Clean the mushrooms, mince and then force them through a sieve. Put the resulting purée into a saucepan over high heat, stirring until all the water has evaporated.

Combine the cream and ½ cup of *béchamel* sauce. Reduce by a third over high heat, stirring all the while.

Add this mixture to the mushrooms. Add also a pinch of salt, two pinches of pepper, and a little grated nutmeg. Stir over the heat for a few minutes. Remove from heat, add half the butter and mix well in.

Trim the soles. Poach them in a buttered dish with a little mushroom broth.

Take up the soles and lay them on a long dish. Cover them with the mushroom purée.

Place four slices of truffle on each fish.

To the remaining *béchamel* sauce add the *fumet* and reduce over gentle heat. Add the Parmesan and Gruyère, and allow to melt, stirring meanwhile. Remove from heat and add the rest of the butter.

Cover the soles with this sauce and put the dish in the oven to brown it.

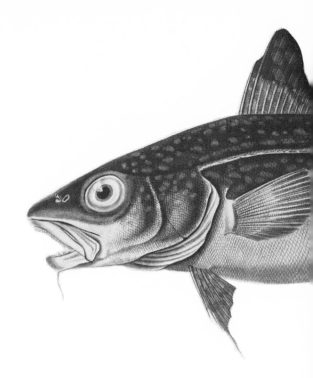

MENU

Friture des éperlans
(*Fried smelts*)
*Estofinado
Blanc-manger
(*Custard*)

A single white wine, say a little Chablis, with the two fish dishes. But with the *blanc-manger* I can't really see anything but a champagne, whether *nature* or not. If it is a *blanc de blancs nature*, then you could savor its delights throughout the meal.

Estofinado

(Cod with Potatoes and Eggs)

For centuries now the fishermen of Europe have been throwing out their lines, then their nets, to catch the *Gadus morrhua*, called cod in English and *cabillaud* in French until it is salted or dried, whereupon it becomes *morue*.

A hundred years before Columbus' discovery of America the fishermen of the Basque country were already familiar with Newfoundland, where the female of the cod, prodigiously prolific, lays up to five million eggs at a time on the sea bed close inshore.

Meanwhile the fishermen of Scandinavia were exploring the coasts of Iceland, and from the English Channel and the North Sea, from Norway to Scotland, from the Faroes to Greenland, the manna from the sea continued to enrich and nourish the folks back home.

And it is still from the north that our dried cod, our *morue*, comes even today. For, curiously, this fish when dried is primarily eaten in the south; not only the south of France but also in Portugal, in Spain, and in Italy. Doubtless the reason is that, being dried or salted, it keeps and can therefore travel without deterioration. But also because, being a food of

112

seagoing men, it tends to be imported by countries with long coastlines. And lastly because it is such a bargain, because in proportion to its volume it is dietetically extremely rich.

When simply salted the codfish is called *morue verte;* dried rapidly, then salted, it is *morue blanche;* dried slowly, it is *morue noire;* dried, cut open, and flattened, it is called *morue plate* or stockfish.

Oddly enough, the English word "stockfish" somehow got borrowed as the name of a French dish made with it, and after the dialect concerned had got through with it, the result was *estofinado.* The *estofinado* is highly thought of in the coal-mining region of the Aveyron. A native of the region has given me the following explanation of this fact: When at the duke's instigation the metal industry first set up factories in Decazeville and the first furnaces were lit, the iron ore smelted there came from Spain. It came by ship to Bordeaux and was there unloaded onto barges, which brought it up to Decazeville via the river Lot. And in those days Bordeaux was France's principal marketing center for dried and salt cod.

At the Bègles warehouses the Bordeaux boatmen and bargees used to buy this same stockfish (the least expensive variety of *morue*), which needs at least eight days' soaking in fresh running water before it becomes edible. Eight days? Exactly the length of time it took the barges to get from Bordeaux to Capdenac, and we are assured that the bargees tied the stockfish to the sterns of their barges so that when they arrived at their destination, without having to give the matter another moment's thought, they had on hand a goodly

supply of desalted cod, which they used to make a sort of warm salad (after they'd cooked it, of course) together with potatoes, sliced hard-boiled eggs, crushed garlic, parsley, and walnut oil.

The whole of Provence enjoys its dried cod (in particular in the form of the celebrated *brandade* which is in fact a sort of *aïoli de morue*). Italy has innumerable recipes for preparing its *baccalà*, all of them more or less similar to those of the French Midi. In Spain the *bacalao* is eaten in every province, but especially in the Basque country. In Portugal the *bacalhau* is cooked according to almost identical recipes.

But in France its two most typical incarnations, spiritually so uplifting in their savor and gastronomically quite remarkable, are the *brandade* and the *estofinado*.

The Rouergue (now Aveyron) is a "savory" province. Its limestone plateaus alternate with the lush pastures of the Larzac, where the sheep's milk produces Roquefort, one of the best cheeses in the world. The people here relish their solid *pot-au-feu* cooked with saffron, the "divine" products of their pork butchers, their famous tripe dishes, their *pascades* (crêpes made with eggs and walnut oil), and lastly, and above all, the *estofinado*.

The sight of this triumphant dish may well set one wondering at the strange journey of the stockfish. How this salted cod from the northern ocean has made its way south to such a

114

victory in the very heart of inland France. How many sailors, how many captains (yes, it is an epic worthy of Victor Hugo himself), and how many tempests braved to bring it to the dark little shop of the village storekeeper who herself has never been beyond the nearest town, a mile or so up the road? The sole local contribution to the recipe is its walnut oil. For the potato, you remember, also comes from beyond the seas, from that "New World" which has so totally outstripped Columbus' expectations. And the egg belongs everywhere. However, it is precisely the walnut oil, so wonderfully rustic and patrician at the same time, that gives the *estofinado* such a distinctive note: the dash of local color, the exalted and un-rivaled solidity. And that makes the dish into a sort of "sacred monster"—as we say in the theater of our indisputably great but rather self-indulgent and melodramatic old actors.

I am glad that we can still find the *estofinado* on the menu of a few Parisian bistros, places whose owners are de-termined to keep the tradition alive. Guy Nouyrigat's restau-rant for example, where by virtue of his *estofinado*—hardly to be expected so close to the Comédie Française and the Palais Royal—a winter Friday may sometimes be irradiated with the joy and almost the sunlight itself of the south.

Estofinado

4 lbs stockfish (*dried and split cod*)
  1 lb potatoes
1 clove garlic
  parsley

pepper
  10 eggs
1 cup walnut oil

Have the stockfish sawed into pieces. Soak the salt out of it for a week or so. (In the country, in memory of those bargees of yesteryear, the best way is to put the pieces in a sieve and leave it in a stream.)

When the cod is soft, put it in an earthen-ware casserole. Cover with water and bring to a boil. Let it simmer 20 minutes. Allow to cool in its broth. Drain. Reserve the broth. Break the fish up into flakes, remov-ing and discarding all bones and skin.

Peel the potatoes and boil them in some of the cod broth. Drain them. Mash them roughly with a fork and mix the flakes of cod into them. Put this mixture together with the garlic, crushed, and a lot of chopped parsley into a top-of-the-stove casserole. Add pepper to taste. Hard-boil 5 of the eggs, shell them, slice them into rounds, and add them to the casserole.

Beat the remaining eggs and pour them over the mixture.

Heat about a cup of very fresh walnut oil in a pan. Just before it boils, pour it over the fish and potatoes. Stir over a high flame for a few minutes; then serve.

A single red wine will suffice:
Bourgueil, or Chinon, or
Beaujolais. Or, if you
prefer, a Muscadet with the eel
and with the veal.

Terrine d'Anguilles *(Baked Eel)*

The astounding saga of the eel family is well known: how they swim out from Europe every year, how they journey across thousands of miles of ocean, how they eventually foregather in the wide Sargasso Sea—close to Bermuda—in order to reproduce their kind. When the eggs hatch, the elvers that appear are less than an inch long, and they put in a hard two years getting back to our shores. By that time they are about three inches long. These young eels are referred to along the Loire as *civelles*, and along the Adour as *piballes*. Billions of eels-to-be appear every spring in this form in our estuaries.

The males will not be able to reproduce until they are ten years old; the females until they are twenty.

Billions? And yet almost no one in France eats eel these days.

The *matelote* is the typical eel dish. Sometimes it's referred to as *matelote du marinier*, which might perhaps seem a little redundant, since *matelote* comes from *matelot*, which in turn means much the same as *marinier*. Anyway, what is implied is a wine sauce. It is also a simple, easy, somewhat coarse-natured dish. A dish that carries with it an aroma of open-air restaurants on river banks, of meals beneath arbors while a waltz moans with pleasure in an accordion's pleated grip.

In the Vendée, where eels are still found in profusion, they make a local version of the *matelote* called a *bouilleture* or *bouilliture*.

In Provence there is the *catigot*, which Maurras placed in the very first rank of Mistral-country dishes.

But all that doesn't exactly decimate our eel population, and certainly much less so than in the past.

In Skania (southern Sweden), long before the Vikings, the "Eel Guild" used to meet during the first dark nights of fall for a massacre of these . . . are they fish? I suppose so. And in France, during the Middle Ages, the eel was a much-sought-after dish. Charlemagne had eel tanks built especially for his own private use.

And that was the age of pies. In the dismantling of those bastions of pastry crust and cooked meat—giving even the least of meals a Pantagruelish dimension—the eel pie played a major role. Its recipe is to be found in the very first cookbook. But later on, in a dictionary of cooking, I find the following: "The flesh of the eel is both delicate and nourishing; but by its nature, and even more on account of the quantity of oily fat it contains, it is of difficult digestion for those who have cold and weak stomachs, sluggish digestive juices, and who lead a sedentary life. When we remove a large proportion of its fat, by our means of preparing it, and add strong-tasting seasonings to it, then it becomes easier to digest."

Without wishing to reject the *matelote*, which seems to have taken its color from the background to Renoir's boaters and its kindly vulgarity from Maupassant's stories; without wishing to distress the supporters of smoked eel (which is nonetheless inferior to smoked salmon), it is in the form of the pie that I personally like to renew my acquaintance with our ancestors' relish for the eel. Except that since the days of the village feast are no longer with us, and appetites have become less gigantic, the pie has lost its battlemented crust and become the terrine.

You will find a *terrine d'anguilles* on the menu at Lasserre's. And also on that of a little bistro on the rue de Verveuil called Les Copains.

Ah, what a wonderful confrontation between two such modern versions of eel pie! How one would like to order both for a comparison, and invite all those gourmets for whom cooking is still poetry, science, music, and architecture all in one!

At first glance one would tend to assume that the settings tell all there is to be told—that Lasserre's terrine will be all refinement and elegance and the one from Les Copains a creation of simple rusticity. And there is some justice in that reaction; though it's by no means all there is to it. Let us look further, let us delve, let us dissect. No, the terrine of our friend M. Forgerit (Les Copains) is not so simple! It is the outcome of a long, empirical expedition through time, heavy still with the carved splendors of another age. Though disencumbered of its buttresses, its ramparts, and its bastions of pastry, this terrine is still a piece of fine workmanship, finely wrought, in the sense that a Cellini dagger is, with its delicate chasings. Whereas the delicacy of Lasserre's dish is derived from a blander, more unctuous love of good food—the prevailing sin of virtuous monks. The chasing is still there, but the dagger is now a prelate's jewel.

A great deal more could be said on the subject of this comparison, but I shall content myself with giving you M. Forgerit's Les Copains recipe. It is totally classical in its form and owes a great deal to the pies of the old days.

Terrine d'Anguilles

1 large pike
  salt
pepper
  quatre épices (*a blend of pepper, nutmeg,
  cloves, and cinnamon or ginger*)
5 oz anchovy butter
  5 eggs, separated
5 tbs heavy cream

4 lbs eel
  2 tbs port
2 tbs brandy
  sliced bacon
shallot-flavored butter
  parsley
lemon slices

Gut the pike. Remove the spine and smaller bones and use a filleting knife to remove all the skin. (Never use a pike's eggs or soft roe. They are poisonous and can, at the very least, produce unpleasant intestinal upsets.)

Force the flesh through a fine sieve until you have obtained an oily paste.

Put the bowl containing the pike flesh on ice. Add salt, pepper, the *quatre épices*, and a little of the anchovy butter. Work with a wooden spoon. Add the egg yolks and work those in too.

Spoonful by spoonful add the cream until the mixture is very light and fluffy—the consistency of a *mousse*. Leave on ice for an hour.

Skin the gutted, cleaned, and thoroughly washed eels. Cut into sections. Flatten the sections into steaks and spread them thinly with the rest of the anchovy butter. Put them to steep for one and a half hours in a mixture of the port and brandy.

Line a terrine mold with bacon slices.

Drain the eel pieces and "stiffen" them in hot, shallot-flavored butter. Beat the egg whites to a stiff consistency and fold them into the pike *mousse*.

Place a layer of this *mousse* over the bacon lining the terrine. Then some eel pieces, then a second layer of *mousse*. Then the rest of the eel and a last layer of *mousse*.

Cover with thinly sliced bacon.

Pour the port and cognac mixture over the top.

Bake in a covered casserole in a hot oven for an hour and a half.

N O T E : In the Middle Ages eel pie was eaten hot. But it is probably
           better to serve this terrine cold, with chopped parsley and
           lemon slices on the side.

Anguilla L'Anguille.

MENU

*Friture de petits poissons
Entrecôte à l'échalote
(Rib steak with shallots)
Tarte aux prunes
(Plum tart)

And a *vin rosé* as fresh as
dew on roses.

Friture (Fried Freshwater Fish)

Leafing through a guide to the fish of France is like saying
a rosary of our rivers and listening to the litany of their wood-
land poetry. And the very essence of that poetry is the *friture*,
the dish of small fried river fish.

Why should I think immediately of the bleak, when our
fishermen are just as likely to be baiting their hooks for the
barbel and the bream, the chub and the carp, the gudgeon
and the perch, the rudd and the trout, even for the eel, the
pike, the lamprey, the minnow, the dace, the black bass, the
sewin, and the catfish, according to their local conditions and
their whim of the moment? Because the bleak seems somehow
to me a symbol. The symbol of the average fisherman.

Socially as well as sociologically, the fisherman is a being
apart. He is a wisdom-fighter—as we say freedom-fighter. A
good-natured, almost a simple-minded familiar of nature, he
settles himself down, monolithic and serene, in his chosen setting. And the setting builds itself around him, in accordance
with the highest laws—the laws of nature, of course.

It does not take long to realize that the presence of the
fish in all this is merely a detail. The important things are the

shade, the silence, the gentle ripples on the river, forever passing yet forever there, and the existential totality they form. And let us add, to crown this picture of natural wisdom, a drowsy pipe and a bottle cooling in the water.

The solitary fisherman is relaxing without knowing it, and fishermen as a whole, that vast and pacific army, exemplify the "stream of consciousness" in its sanest state. How admirable, in our bustling, thunderous age, that the fisherman today, his bottom resting so good-temperedly on his canvas stool, can still follow the slow downstream progress of his float with the same placid gaze that his Cro-Magnon ancestor must have employed to keep watch on his primitive tackle!

And what better fish to symbolize that quiet wisdom, that calm store of spiritual wealth, that small and unpretentious paradise on so human a scale, that good honest citizen's heaven typified by the tranquil fisherman, than the silver glinting bleak?

And to say bleak to a Frenchman is to say *friture*.

For his day's catch fried is the fisherman's link with the everyday world of all the nonfishermen. Or rather, through that *friture* thousands of other humans—even though they may not be aware of it—are permitted to enter into the fisherman's secret world.

122

Through the *friture* and in particular through the fried bleak.

The bleak, that weasel among freshwater fish. And *friture*, that common, that rapscallion dish. As one says, affectionately, "you young rapscallion."

Scattered lives, fleeting loves, oaths sworn without malice, and scents of country taverns hover among the golden, interlacing bodies of a *friture* from the Marne. And perhaps, indeed, all such *fritures* were born in the misty past from peals of light laughter and moist kisses beneath the lindens?

An old story, the *friture?*

Are we on the brink of a new world? Of a synthetic world, planned and joyless? Is the oil already boiling for the last *friture?* Let us hope not.

To your bleak you may add gudgeons, small perch, roach, not to mention all the little saltwater fishes if you happen to be by the sea—smelts and sand eels. And you will have a *friture* that is not just a treat but a delightful game. One in which everyone will have a winning hand, for your *friture* must be eaten with the fingers, if possible in the open air, with one or two—or several—bottles of white wine standing coolly by in a pail. I can almost hear a bee buzzing around the plum tart. A white butterfly bumps clumsily into its own shadow. The conversation is desultory but spiced with irony—just a dash. I can see you around your table. I wish I could be with you. *Bon appétit* to all those who know how a *friture* ought to be enjoyed.

"Be off with you and find some then, with your d--n face like a bleak!"
"Don't bite my head off!"

Friture

The small fish for a *friture* are not generally gutted. However, you can rid them of their air bladders and intestines by squeezing a thumb along their abdomens.

Don't wash them. Just wipe them carefully with a dry cloth.

Dip the fish in milk or in beer before rolling them in flour. The flour can be corn flour if you like.

The fat for a *friture* must never smoke. Better results can be obtained by frying the fish twice. The first time with the fat barely hot (so that they take on a yellow tint), the second time with the fat very hot (so that they become crisp).

Drain them on paper to absorb any superfluous fat.

Serve the fish with lemon and sorrel fritters (slices of lemon and sorrel leaves dipped in batter and fried separately). They provide complementary vitamins.

The *beurre blanc* comes from the Loire, so let us serve it with its natural companion: a Muscadet. A Sèvres et Maine Muscadet, that dry white wine with its taste of gun flint, will raise this divine sauce to heights still more celestial. And after that, let us have the courage of our regionalism and drink a red Chinon with the mutton.

Brochet au Beurre Blanc

(Pike with Shallot-Vinegar-Butter Sauce)

The *beurre blanc* is primarily a gift. It cannot be learned, it can only be summoned up by ancestral divinations and secret formulas, like an alchemical process hidden within the bosom of the bountiful earth itself. For a true *beurre blanc* carries within it, like a watermark, the green pastures of the Charentes. It is on the same scale as, and the scale by which we measure, a whole province, or rather that province's river: the Loire.

The *beurre blanc* is also a challenge.

It appears at first sight, or at least its recipe does, so ridiculously simple that a child could make it: butter, vinegar, shallots. You see? What could be simpler than that? Nothing! It's true, isn't it? Nothing! And yet nothing can prove more difficult, more tricky, more maliciously elusive.

This queen of sauces ennobles many dishes, or rather many fishes. For your lobster *au beurre blanc*, your scallops *au beurre blanc*, these are merely things devised by chefs in the mood to show off. But of all the fishes that are served with it—the bass, the brill, the turbot, the trout—it is the pike that was particularly destined for it from the beginning of time.

Someone once referred to the pike as "that freshwater Attila," but a learned work informs me that its nicknames are in fact legion. No need to list them. They all seem to revolve around one particular point: the pike is not a lovable fish. Even though that savage head with its all too well-furnished jaws is a delectable sight to the skilled and patient fisherman. For the pike is a worthy quarry and a worthy catch.

In the first place, the pike has long, forked, and acutely vicious bones. The learned work I mentioned assures us that they are "easy to locate." Hmmm! . . . Easy to swallow too. And it is indeed the sole justification for the *quenelle*—in other contexts an unsubstantial and gastronomically overrated thing —that it can present the pike in a less perilously assimilable form. But I shall return to that subject later, thereby unleashing upon my head the full fury of the cooks of Lyons, a city where the *quenelle* is almost an object of worship to the so many devotees of the saucepan whose skill in clothing it with their divine sauces I herewith salute.

But back to our pike. In the second place, some will accuse it, if it comes from a lake, of tasting of mud. This, it seems, is the result of its swallowing all the smaller fish in the lake that have in their turn been eating the vegetation in it. Much of this muddy taste can be eliminated by having the fish starve for several hours in a tub of fresh water. If it is still alive, that is. Because you must remember that pike tend to go bad rather quickly. So buy yours alive; or if you caught it yourself, eat it immediately.

In the old days the pike was widely enjoyed wrapped in vine leaves and cooked on a spit. Simpler still—especially with several small pike—is to braise the fish in the oven with white wine and cream. I also know a recipe for pike stew that would be delicious if only those accursed bones weren't lurking in it to ruin the pleasure. Lastly, the commonest method of cooking is still in a *court-bouillon*. If eaten cold, the fish should be served with a seasoned sauce (mustard, mayonnaise, or an herb sauce); if eaten hot, with *beurre blanc*.

Pike and *beurre blanc*. It isn't just a love match, like that of the duckling and spring turnips, for example. It is something more, and something better. It is the justification of their whole existence. As if this conjunction had been decided upon in heaven, at the very beginning, as a gift to us all from Comus himself. Without the pike the *beurre blanc* would be merely *beurre blanc*. Without *beurre blanc* the pike would be nothing. I know impatient gourmets who indulge in *beurre blanc* with turbot, with brill, even with trout. And in that way they evade the terrible trap of the pike's forked bones. But they are also losing something very rare: the chance to enjoy a perfect match, a pre-established and even, I am not afraid to claim, a supernatural harmony, a harmony that is, as it were, the reflection of a world beyond this one, where all is sweetest music and a wonder of melting colors.

Brochet au Beurre Blanc

6 tsp chopped shallots
  2 tbs wine vinegar
1¼ lbs sweet butter

salt
  pepper

Put the very finely chopped shallots in a pan with the vinegar. Reduce over gentle heat till almost dry. Leave to cool.

Cut the butter into small lumps. Return the shallots to the heat and add the butter lump by lump, whisking all the time, so that a creamy sauce is produced. Add the salt and pepper and pour over the fish, which you have poached, trimmed, and kept hot.

NOTE: It is the temperature at which you work the sauce that is the most critical factor: too hot or not hot enough and your *beurre blanc* will turn to oil.

Nignon: The Gourmets' "Heptameron"

MENU

*Truite au bleu
Épaulé d'agneau farcie
(Stuffed shoulder of lamb)
Pêches au vin
(Peaches in wine)

Serve a white wine. And a dry white wine, I mean. For the associations, a Rhine wine would be delightful. But a Muscadet would do quite well. And a young red Bordeaux with the lamb.

Truite au Bleu (Blue Trout)

I have no wish, heaven knows, to offend the memory of our poet-epicure, but I personally would rather not have the trout that Grimod de La Reynière called the "partridge of brook and stream"; I would much rather have it served up to me *au bleu*—the *Forelle blau!*

You will excuse me, I hope, for calling it by its German name. Not as a tribute to Schubert so much as in homage to the poetry of the word itself. *Forelle!* One pictures some young nymph of a sparkling stream, a freshwater mermaid scattering the pearls of a cascade with fresh and festive laughter. There is something winged in that name. The quicksilver of the free and leaping trout sets a seal on the flick of the fisherman's wrist with its glinting, airborne flourish. The contest has been a fair one. The victor is vanquished by his prize, by a sort of melodious tenderness welling up from the depths of time and the pellucid stream. The water sparkles and leaps, the *Forelle* leaps too—into the waiting *court-bouillon*.

But there is also the sad fact that we're not allowed to eat them any more in France—these *truites au bleu*. Not in restaurants at least. Since the French fisherman is forbidden by law to sell our native European trout (*Trutta fario*), the French diner is thereby forbidden, in practice, to eat it.

The rainbow trout (*Salmo irideus*), which comes to us from America and provides the vast majority of the trout commercially available, even when well raised is no more than an ersatz thing with cottony flesh. It tastes like "a damp dressing," as Curnonsky put it.

The rainbow trout presents the gastronomic conscience with a problem, one famous gourmet once said to me.

But I can't see that it even does that.

How can such a no-thing be a problem? Except insofar as it aids and abets that insanity the *truite aux amandes* that chefs today want us to accept as a genuine epicurean discovery.

Though it's true, of course, that the rainbow trout can be either more or less unpleasing according to the way it is reared. Some are just fed on spoiled flour, some on fish mash. Even so, no one is going to persuade me that they are going to be improved by living in those tanks of chlorinated water in our restaurants! Ah, little *Forellen* of the brooks, twisting and darting as you pursue the tiny freshwater shrimps that "pink" your flesh,* that lend it that fleeting, almost evanescent hint of rosiness that is a tender testimony to your free way of life, little *Forellen* that we must henceforth go and search out in Germany if we are to taste you *blau*, how we miss you, how we look back to the days when you lent your shimmering beauty to meals beside vacation highways as we drove south.

It is the mucus protecting the fish's skin, suddenly set by the vinegary *court-bouillon*, which produces that shimmering, uncertain blue tint, and one is reminded of those ancient Roman sybarites watching their surmullets cooking alive on the table in a crystal vase, so that the changing colors of their death agonies should be clearly visible.

But here, take comfort, the trout is killed with a swift blow before it is cooked, and the prized "blue" is not a product of barbarity. But read the recipe for yourself:

* Commercially raised trout are "pinked" artificially by the addition of carotene extract to their mash.

130

Truite au Bleu

vinegar
  2 or 3 onions
2 carrots
  peppercorns
salt
  bouquet garni

*1 trout per person (they should be caught
in a net and transported in a container of
river water)*
  fresh parsley
lemon
  melted butter

First make a *court-bouillon* from water, a liberal amount of vinegar, 2 or 3 onions cut in quarters, 2 sliced carrots, peppercorns, salt, and a *bouquet garni*. Bring to a boil.

Remove the trout from their water, kill them with a sharp blow on the head, gut them, sprinkle them with vinegar, throw them into the *court-bouillon*, and let them simmer (17 minutes for a trout weighing about 6 ounces).

Serve on a napkin decorated with fresh parsley and halves of lemon, with melted butter on the side.

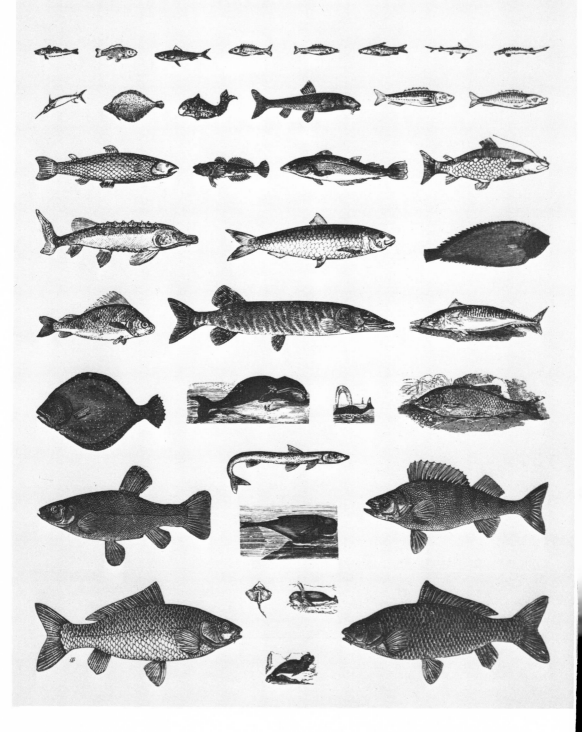

The most suitable wine is the
same one you used to make
the dish, which is to say
a white Burgundy, a
Mâcon-Viré, a Pouilly-Fuissé,
even a Muscadet.

Pochouse *(Fish Stew)*

Your humble servant is, and has been for many years now, a
Chevalier de la Pochouse. True, I don't often wear it around
my neck, the yellow and blue ribbon with its pendant bronze
medallion assuring the world that "I am big eater, and swim-
mer too," but that's not to say I'm not very proud of it. And
of being, as it were, an adopted son of Verdun in consequence.

But let's get this quite straight. I mean Verdun-sur-le-
Doubs, in the department of Saône-et-Loire, with its ancient
ramparts, the city where, eminent historiographers assure us,
the Treaty of Verdun was signed in 843 despite the *Petit Larousse*'s claim that it was the Verdun on the Meuse. But what
matter? I have no wish to get mixed up in polemics over these
backstage bickerings of history, and the *pochouse* itself is a
more than ample subject of discussion for me. For a start
there's its spelling. Some claim we should spell it *pauchouse*,
others *panchouse*. And others still write it as I do but with a
circumflex over the *o: pôchouse*.

Does the word come from *poche*, meaning a sort of river
fisherman's bag or holding net? Some say so. I will accept
that, though I refuse to refer to it as a *matelote*. Freshwater

bouillabaisse would be nearer the mark. But why don't we just say *pochouse* and leave it at that—except for sampling it of course, if possible in its cradle as it were, at the confluence of the Saône and the Doubs.

The fish that go into it? They are four in number: pike, perch, tench, and eel. But just a moment! I can hear a purist rejecting my pike and refusing to accept anything in its place but the extremely rare river burbot. And a good lady trying to find a place, just this once, for the trout and the barbel. No. The burbot—yes, I think we can make an exception for that; it is so rare that we can accept it as we do one of those fabulous people who lend, by their very presence, a mystery to things. But that is the limit.

So there it is: pike, perch, tench, eel. And none of them can be left out either. It is the mixture of all four, in equal proportions, that *is* the essence of this divine dish.

You also need white wine. And not just any white wine. A white wine such as the one that used once to be harvested in this part of the country, very dry, very tart, and even perhaps somewhat unfitted for daily consumption. That's what one is told by the old fishermen and the honest country housewives. Otherwise, a Mâcon-Viré will do very well. But whatever happens, no red wine. As a connoisseur in the matter has written: "The cream and the white wine lend the *pochouse* a very individual physical appearance." Moreover, and this is why it is not so very wild to talk of *bouillabaisse,* the *pochouse* must contain garlic. A considerable amount of garlic too for such a northern region. And that is not the least astonishing thing about the dish.

A dish of the people, the dish of the fishermen on the barges that used once to navigate on the Saône and the Doubs. But what about the cream? you may ask. Was that usual in such floating kitchens? Undoubtedly not. It must be an addition of latter-day cooks, and of riverbank housewives before them. But it does nothing to conceal the *pochouse*'s rustic origins.

You will observe that the fish concerned are not the most elegant in the world. The pike and perch both have treacherous bones. The tench is very hard to kill and goes on jumping or twitching even when cut into pieces. And the eel I don't have to tell you about. None of these reefs should deter the cook. In the fairly long list of fish stews (*bouillabaisse, ttoro, chaudrée, cotriade, waterzoïi,* without leaving the coast, to say nothing of the *matelote* of our rustic suburban arbors), the *pochouse* has its own very individual place. Its personality.

Pochouse

1 lb each of the four fish (pike, perch, tench, and eel)
  thyme
bayleaf
  parsley
3 yellow onions
  2 cloves garlic
¼ lb lean bacon

5 cups dry white wine
  3½ tbs butter
2 tbs flour
  24 small white onions
garlic
  ¼ cup heavy cream
fried croutons

Trim and wash the fish and cut them into slabs.

Put the heads of the fish and some thyme, bayleaf, and parsley, the onions and garlic in a pan with 2 cups of the white wine. Cook. Put through a fine strainer. Make a white *roux* with the butter and flour (that is, don't brown the mixture of butter and flour); mix into it a little of the fish broth and cook it. Add the white onions, the bacon, blanched, and cut into pieces, and some finely chopped garlic (the exact quantity is a matter of taste, but you need a fair amount). Allow to cook for about an hour.

Make a *court-bouillon* with 3 cups of the dry wine and some of the broth as above. Poach the slabs of fish in it.

Add the cream to this composition, whisking as you do so. Pour over the fish which you have kept hot in a dish. Decorate with croutons rubbed with garlic.

Illustration for Zola's *Le Ventre de Paris*

MENU

Aïoli de morue
Yaourt
(*Yogurt*)
Salade de fruits
(*Fruit salad*)

And a bottle of young
rouge de Cassis.

Aïoli de Morue

(Garlic Mayonnaise with Cod)

I have a reputation for not liking garlic because I will not accept its changing the taste of things that I like for themselves. But there are certain dishes that demand garlic, I am then peremptorily informed. Such as leg of lamb, mushrooms, frogs' legs, scallops, and eggplant. I beg my censors' pardon, but I prefer my scallops grilled just as they are, my frogs' legs *meunière*, my mushrooms cooked with shallots, my eggplant with garlic, and my leg of lamb just stroked with it.

"Let the garlic be there," that great chef Alexandre Dumaine said to me once, apropos of a dish of leaf spinach prepared as only he could prepare it. "Let the garlic be there—but let the nose not detect it."

"Then you don't like garlic?"

"What? Indeed I do! In fact, I make a dish composed of nothing else."

"How do you mean?"

"I mean the *aïoli*, which is a cream made of garlic. Yes, the *aïoli*, that sauce that you put in every other sauce; well, I enjoy it just as it is, spread on bread."

"Ah, yes, *aïoli*. Of course."

It is a quintessence. Almost a medicament. Among the peoples living around the Mediterranean coasts, the use of garlic dates back to the very beginning of cooking itself. But as Léon Daudet observed, with the *aïoli* it attained its peak of perfection, "the very highest degree of those truly civilized customs and habits that unite health with well-being."

So that we need feel no astonishment at learning that when the poet Mistral founded a Provençal newspaper (this was in 1891), he called it *L'Aïoli*. The sauce had become a symbol. And he wrote of it with justice: "It concentrates all the warmth, the strength, the sun-loving gaiety of Provence in its essence, but it also has a particular virtue: it keeps flies away. Those who don't like it, those whose stomachs rise at the thought of our oil, won't come buzzing around us wasting our time. There'll be just the family."

And elsewhere again: "The *aïoli* goes slightly to the head, impregnates the body with its warmth, and bathes the soul with its enthusiasm. Where are the men from Provence, tell me this, who won't feel themselves brothers around a truly fragrant *aïoli?*"

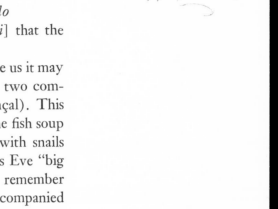

There are those who like to believe that garlic makes a man amorous, but I myself am more inclined to the more level-headed conclusion of the dictionary of the Académie des Gastronomes that "this magnificent dish nevertheless tends to predispose one to sleep."

Venis, dis, lou li faguè tant dur
Qu'au mourtié lou trissoun tenié testo levado

(Venus made it so thick for him [God's *aïoli*] that the pestle stood upright in the mortar.)

The *aïoli* (and not *ailloli* as some try to persuade us it may also be written) is a word formed from the dish's two components: garlic (*ail*) and olive oil (*oli* in Provençal). This solid sauce is served with fish, with the *bourride* (the fish soup of Provence), with hard-boiled eggs, with salad, with snails (snails *à l'aïoli* are part of the traditional Christmas Eve "big supper" in Provence), even with meat, and in Aix I remember being served generous slices of cold leg of lamb accompanied by this unguent paste.

The *aïoli*, I must repeat, is the paste, the sauce, but because it is so often served with dried cod it is this dish that tends to come to mind first—together with the water in one's mouth—when the magic word is uttered.

The *aïoli de morue* is eaten more particularly on Fridays in Provence. Which reminds me of an incident that occurred a few years ago, during the rice festival in Arles. There were several of us there, being marched around pitilessly from banquet to banquet by the organizers, who thought they were delighting our palates with their stuffed soles and saddles of veal *bouquetière* and *bombes glacées*. Of regional dishes not even the shadow. It couldn't go on. A few of us went into a huddle and decided to play truant for a while and organize our own eating pleasure. Alas, not a single hotel or restaurant had an *aïoli* on its menu. It wasn't Friday. And by the time Friday came we would all be far away. It was just at this point that someone suggested a man who, perhaps . . . It was a run-of-the-mill brasserie, but I had an open-sesame: my sheer enthusiasm. The owner was not immune to it:

"All right then, will tomorrow evening do? How many will there be of you?"

"Let's say five."

"I'll make you the *grand aïoli* for six, that should do it."

Ah, my lords, the *grand aïoli* is an *aïoli* to the tenth power. It is an *aïoli* for Gargantua. It is a legend from the past such as you scarcely ever meet in these thin days. Imagine the *aïoli* of which I give the recipe below, already majestic in content, as Brillat-Savarin would say; then add beef and mutton from a *pot-au-feu* together with their vegetables, and also a tureenful of chick peas.

We attacked the dish with brilliance. Perhaps with excessive brilliance, but our hearts were in it. At the halfway mark some of us were already slowing our pace. At the three-quarters mark we were almost ready to give up. But that old devil of a restaurateur had put the word around. We were surrounded by a local audience, scarcely bothering to veil in irony their anticipated delight at seeing these Parisians defeated. It was pride that drove us on to the finish. The last glass of rosé helped down the last mouthful of cod and *aïoli*. And, believe me or not, the spectators applauded.

Aïoli de Morue

2 lbs dried salted cod	3 dozen snails
1 lb beets	5 oz garlic
1 lb carrots	4 egg yolks
1 lb stringbeans	2 tsp coarse salt
1 small cauliflower	1 cup olive oil
2 lbs potatoes	lemon juice
6 hard-boiled eggs	

Soak the cod for twenty-four hours. Then poach it. Drain it, trim it, and leave it to cool slightly on a dish.

Boil all the vegetables separately (beets, carrots, beans, cauliflower—the last in two lots of water) and arrange them on the dish around the cod. Cook the potatoes in their jackets, keep two aside, peel the rest, and add them to the other vegetables.

Peel the hard-boiled eggs, cut them in two, arrange them on the dish.

Cook the snails in water, replace them in their shells, and arrange them on the dish.

Peel the garlic and pound it in a mortar with the salt. Add the egg yolks and the two potatoes. Continue pounding and adding olive oil, as with an ordinary mayonnaise. Just before the end add a squeeze of lemon juice.

N O T E : An *aïoli* can go wrong just like a mayonnaise, in which case all the oil will start coming to the surface. If this happens, empty the mortar and wash it. Pound a fresh clove of garlic with a little salt and begin the operation again, adding the curdled *aïoli* little by little.

MENU

*Goujons à la cascamèche
*Poitrine d'agneau farcie
*Fraises et framboises
    Chantilly

A white wine, naturally, from either Pouilly or Sancerre. It will go with the stuffed breast too, unless you decide to honor it with a rare but amazing red Sancerre.

Goujons à la Cascamèche

(Marinated Gudgeons)

I have already sung the praises of the fisherman in our chapter on the *friture*. The true fisherman. The wise fisherman. For whom fishing is not a sport but a method of repose.

I have sung the praises of the *friture* too. And of them all, perhaps the best, certainly the most distinguished gastronomically speaking, is that composed of gudgeons.

Yet in his book *Les Poissons*, Roby accords them no more than a few disdainful lines. And Larousse is scarcely more affectionate: "Gudgeon: bony river fish very common in France."

And it's not even true, I feel. If I am to believe the fishermen themselves, it is more often bleak, or roach, or even bitter minnows that they catch with the worms they have collected from river mud or bank.

You must stir up the sandy river bottom, muddy the water, before the cunning gudgeon will rise to take the hook you trail along that bottom. But I remember, in my youth, going out with the other kids of Précy-sous-Tille to catch gudgeons in jam jars. On other days, instead of going down to the stream we climbed up into the hills, up as far as the feudal castle of which there can hardly be more than a crumbling wall or two remaining now. My companions would start playing some warlike game or other; but I would stretch out in the grass, in the shade of one of the remaining arrow-slitted walls, and reconstruct the castle in my mind as it must have been in the Middle Ages. I brought it to life with pale and beauteous ladies wearing wimples, ferocious liege lords, pages with lace at their sleeves, ruddy-faced retainers cowering in corners, chambermaids being immoderately manhandled in the shadows of dark alcoves, hieratic greyhounds. I furnished it with animal skins and tapestries, with stuffed birds of paradise and wild boars' heads, and of course with men in armor.

And furnish is the right word too. I had little interest in the men inside—only in the armor. Constructions of iron standing rigidly upright in the watchtowers and along the long stone corridors, beneath the tall, pointed arches. The sunlight reflected from a sliver of stone up on the crenelated keep—no longer ascendable because there were too many steps missing from the stone stairs—reached my eyes as the glint of a halberd or an arquebus in the hand of some warlike watcher up there on the tower, a sentry looking down and seeing "only the dust on the road, only the leaves waving on the trees," as in *Bluebeard*. (You will gather that I tended to confuse my settings and my genres a little!)

And in the midst of the warlike accouterments caparisoning those iron men—plume, kneepieces, gauntlets, breastplate, helmet, thigh armor, and steel shoes—there glittered the resplendent *cascamèche!*

Yes, it's true: that word—spoken heaven knows when or how in my presence—had mysteriously found its way in my mind into the category of knightly accouterments. *Cascamèche!* Ah, what a heroic ring!

I had no idea what the word really meant. And I am still by no means sure today. It doesn't occur in Littré's *Dictionnaire de la langue française*, or in Larousse, or in Robert's dictionary. It seems to have been born simply by chance one fine day, to be no more than a vague evocation of the secret pomps of some glorious yesteryear: *cascamèche!*

It was not until much later that I met that mystery-charged word again; this time in a book of recipes, and in the title *Goujons de Loire à la cascamèche.*

But before giving you this recipe I ought to tell you that this pleasant hors d'oeuvre, as stimulating to the appetite as to the imagination, is very like the fish *à l'escabèche* that they serve in Spain.

And for *à l'escabèche* there is a straightforward explanation. It refers to fish that have had their heads (*cabezas*) cut off. So to prepare fish *à l'escabèche* means quite simply to cut their heads off before cooking them. In North Africa this has become *à la scabetche* in the colonial patois. And in Belgium, harking back to a time when the Lowlands were occupied by a Spanish army, they say *à l'escavèche*.

Yes, I agree it's still a long way from *cascamèche*. But since there are no other explanations forthcoming, I see no harm in construing it as another corruption of the same thing. Of the word *scabetche*, for example, heard by zouaves in Algeria. Why not? They brought back the word *mazagran*, for example. And that developed from meaning the cold coffee itself to the container that held it—thanks to the porcelain factory in Bourges. And that's not very far from Nevers and the Nivernais—which is the country of origin of our *goujons à la cascamèche*, a recipe that could also fit without any doubt whatever into the category *poisson à l'escabèche*, *à la scabetche*, or *à l'escavèche* according to the number of degrees north.

Ah, my beautiful casque of days gone by, my shining suit of armor. Lost forever now. Gone with my vacations down Précy-sous-Tille way, where the gudgeons that I caught were fried for me as a simple *friture*.

But never mind. Have you seen Nevers? With its steeples

it is a "pointy" town as children say, rather like the acid dressing we used to sprinkle over that *friture*, over the gudgeons that no one fishes for any more at the foot of the bridge over the Loire. And Nevers always gave her visitors a generous welcome, was always ready to use her fishing tackle in their service. In 1403, Louis d'Orléans was presented with two barrels of "wine full red to the value twelve gold crowns"; in 1409, Comte Philippe received "capons, small birds and chickens, beefs, fat muttons and six quarts of wine" as an offering; and Isabelle de Coucy also received gifts: "a salmon, four carps, four pikelets, four perch, a bream, a trout"; in 1560, the Count of Charolais was honored with "twelve quarts of wine, four of cream, a basket of cherries, a basket of pears, and a great cheese"; lastly, in 1730 the Intendant of the province was offered thirty-six bottles of wine, two carps, an eel, two pikes, nine woodcocks, five partridges, four leverets, four rabbits, and six ducks.

Not a sign in all those lists of any gudgeons. Doubtless they were too small a prize for such nobilities.

And they would certainly not have been cooked *à la cascamèche*, since the recipe can't, at the very outside, be more than a century and a half old. Nor is it of French origin. Never mind. We will consider it naturalized. By adoption. We will claim it as one of ours because we can be sure that "they" haven't any Loire gudgeons down there in Saragossa, or in the Scheldt, or around Boumedienne!

Goujons à la Cascamèche

Take the best gudgeons you can, gut them, cut off their heads, and wipe them without washing them.

Mix a little flour with some milk in a dish. Turn the fish in the mixture; then toss them into very hot fat. Drain them.

In a bowl with a cover make a bed of chopped onions mixed with a crushed shallot and a crushed garlic clove, parsley sprigs, a few peppercorns, two pinches of powdered thyme, and a crushed bayleaf.

Arrange the still hot gudgeons on the top. Salt lightly.

Heat some wine vinegar. When it boils pour it generously over the fish. Stir quickly. Cover. Leave for three days in a cool place to marinate, stirring occasionally.

When you serve the gudgeons—on an hors d'oeuvre dish—add a trickle of olive oil.

APPETIZERS AND
EGG DISHES

A red Burgundy, the one used
to make the *meurette* sauce.
It could be a Mercurey.

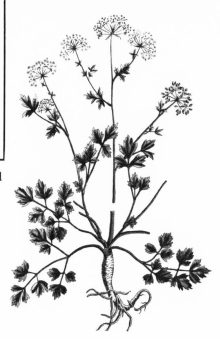

Jambon Persillé (Parsleyed Ham)

"Happy Burgundy!" Erasmus exclaimed. "Because of its milk, it may well be called the mother of men."

This Burgundian milk, its wine, seems to have conditioned an entire school of cooking. A school of cooking that is both rich and solid at the same time. Food of merchant princes rather than of aesthetes. Have you ever seen the Palace of the Dukes in Dijon? At its heart you will find a prodigious concept. Others have built fireplaces in their kitchens, but the Dukes of Burgundy decided to build a kitchen inside fireplaces! The four walls of the immense vaulted room simply constitute an enormous machine for cooking, for roasting, for boiling, for grilling, for saucemaking, for frying . . .

And somewhere in that great cooking complex, there is no gainsaying, in some small corner, room must be found for the humble and magical ham.

The ham is the very ecstasy of pork. Ham is with us all our lives in one form or another. It garlands our days. It appears everywhere, in countless forms, from the dry and dusty sandwich of railroad buffets and night bistros, companion of the tragic hard-boiled egg, to the tables of princes, pink and

Market at Quimper, Brittany

plump beneath its ceremonial crust. It is at home in so many forms, so many different sorts of dishes, so many cities—Bayonne or Prague, Parma or Mainz—that it has the air of a polyglot traveler. Too polyglot, to be quite honest, whereas it is in fact honesty itself! In Paris there is even a Ham Fair, old as old Paris itself, in which the hams for which it was once famous are now no more than a memory. But then a good ham stays a long while in a good gourmet's memory.

But the only truly Burgundian ham dish is this *jambon persillé*. Yet it does not seem to have been accorded the place it deserves in the great roster of ham dishes. Or so I feel.

Perhaps because it is deceptive, because it does not have the outward form of the quintessential ham: that magical mandolin we welcome from Parma, that gourd of *vin rosé* from Bayonne, those portly and prosperous bagpipes from York. No, the *jambon persillé* conceals itself within a round terrine, very domestic, very simple. But don't think that I mean the word "simple" in the sense of half-witted! Our terrine of parsleyed ham is all sharp knowingness. Everything, down to that aftertaste of parsley-flavored white wine hovering still on the palate, combines to lend it an acidity full of an almost coarse gaiety that has nothing academic in it at all. It

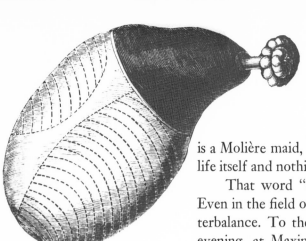

is a Molière maid, a snappy retort always at the ready, full of life itself and nothing else.

That word "coarse" might upset some people, I know. Even in the field of cooking. I see it more as a necessary counterbalance. To the lady at the table next to mine the other evening, at Maxim's, dissecting her *sole soufflé* with disillusioned fork, it would clearly have been merely an expression of disdain. For her, *moules marinières* would have been coarse. They would have contaminated even the fingerbowl with their baseness.

And fingerbowl reminds me of a favorite anecdote.

The scene of it, again, is Maxim's, just after World War II. A shopkeeper couple, having made a fortune on the black market, are eating there for the first time. They have ordered asparagus, and naturally when the asparagus is served they are brought fingerbowls at the same time.

"What's this for?" the man asks the wife.

"Bless me, I have no idea," she confesses.

"I'll ask them," the husband said.

"Are you mad? We shall look like absolute fools," the woman tells him. "Wait!"

So they wait. Keeping a sharp lookout on the nearby tables. If the waiters would only bring one of those little crystal bowls, with its three rose petals floating in water, to just one of the other diners, then perhaps they will be able to watch. But, alas, no one else near them has ordered a dish necessitating a fingerbowl. And they have finished their asparagus. And the *maître d'hôtel* is coming over.

"Oh, well," the man said. "Here goes. I'll just have to ask him!"

The *maître d'hôtel*, very obliging, explains what the fingerbowls are and how to use them.

To the utter stupefaction of the couple.

And the woman, very bitter, furious at the man's disclosure of their ignorance, blurts out: "You see! Ask a silly question and you get a silly answer!"

But back to our *jambon persillé*. Its slightly acid, piquant taste makes it a dish to sharpen the appetite. Though appetite is not a thing usually lacking in Burgundy, and as long as you've got your appetite going, why then you've got everything going, and in particular your wine-appreciating faculties. And just as the *gougère* is the best spur to red-wine tasting, so, it seems to me, is your *jambon persillé* the perfect foil for the whites.

The *jambon persillé* dates back to the mists of gastronomic antiquity, by which I mean the Middle Ages. Why, as I pronounce its magic name, do I see a dark room behind a merchant's store, lit solely by the reflection of flames on copper, on brass, on the polished wood of the sturdy furniture? A cloth merchant with comfortably rounded belly, his old, dried-up wife, gray and bent, his daughter all pink and gold and still a virgin, the clerks silent, the servant girl tossing her head, a pug at the master's feet. He has just come back from Flanders and his affairs have prospered there. The *Grandes Compagnies* haven't got their hands on his money bags, he is sated with beer and *waterzoïi*, he has kept good cheer with his colleagues in Ghent, but he is glad to be home again.

"Well, my dearest, tell me the news."

And the old woman launches into her parish gossip. But he isn't listening to her, he is sniffing the air, he is quivering with anticipation and delight: Nanon is bringing in the terrine of *jambon persillé*.

Jambon Persillé

2 cups white Mâcon wine
  3¾ qts water
1 onion spiked with a clove
  bouquet garni
3 cloves garlic

5 black peppercorns
  5½ lbs slightly salted ham
parsley
  white wine vinegar

Make a *court-bouillon* with the white wine and water, the onion spiked with a clove, the *bouquet garni*, garlic, and peppercorns.

In this *court-bouillon* bake the ham for an hour and a half.

When the ham is cooked, drain it, and cut into small pieces.

Place a layer of ham in a salad bowl, or mold, then a layer of vinegared parsley (finely chopped parsley steeped in white wine vinegar). Continue making layers until the ham and parsley are used up. Press down hard. Put a plate or a board over the ham with a weight on top to keep it pressed down, and leave in a cool place for several hours.

Turn out.

NOTE: Some people pour a little aspic over the ham before pressing down so that it seeps down between the layers.

Gougères Bourguignonnes

(Cheese Tarts)

In our wineries, when cheese crackers are served as an accompaniment to wine tasting; at very British dining tables, after the ladies have departed, when the men begin their cigars and start to pass around a port whose reflections, in the refracting facets of its decanter, are mingled purple and old gold, and the cheese biscuits in silver bowls are served to accompany that wine traditionally picked up as a ballast back across the Bay of Biscay; when we less formal folk entertain our friends and offer them an apéritif and accompany it with a cheese cracker—do any of us realize that we are in fact keeping up a tradition that goes back to the Middle Ages?

For the Burgundian *gougère* and the Flemish *goyère* are both sisters of that medieval cheese tart the *flammiche*, from Dinant, the favorite dessert of the canons of Liège who prized it because the cheese in it sharpened their palates so delightfully for the enjoyment of the great Burgundies in their cellars.

Cheese is, in fact, the drinker's spur. Perhaps excessively so. By which I mean that its taste sometimes can be too strong to permit us to judge a wine properly, and at other times can improve its taste excessively. How many times, in the cellars of some wine-making château near Bordeaux, nibbling at a slice of *étuvé*—that Dutch cheese so dry that it almost crumbles in the hand—I have waxed enthusiastic over a wine that next day, drunk with some meat or other, has seemed to me far less good? But the *gougère* is cheese that has been tamed a little, and hence the wine-taster's ideal.

Its patent of nobility dates back to Jehan Froissart, who used to enjoy it with the passing minstrels he entertained when vicar of Les Estinnes. And to François Villon, who included *goyères*, along with pheasants, tarts, and flans, as suitable fare for midnight celebrations. And, indeed, the word *goyère* is supposed to come from *goguer*: to make good cheer.

So three cheers still for the cheer of *goyères* and *gougères* both. Not forgetting—though I almost did—the *talmouse*, which is a first cousin of those not forgotten medieval beauties. The word comes from the Old French *talemose* (*talemelier*, "baker"), and it is simply a little puff pastry case with a cheese filling made with cream and eggs. Those made in Saint-Denis were once famed far and wide. Villon bequeathed one in his testament to his friend Jehan Régnier, and Balzac, in *Un Début dans la vie*, has Pierrotin's stagecoach stop outside the door of the innkeeper in Saint-Denis "who sells the famous *talmouses* for which all the travelers stop," so that Georges Marest can buy *talmouses* and Alicante wine for all his traveling companions.

The Flemish *goyère* is made of *brisé* pastry, cream cheese, eggs, milk, and Maroillers, the cheese with the high yet delicate taste that was a favorite of Charles V.

As for the *gougère*, there are a number of recipes for it of varying richness. Here is a version for the true epicure that I extracted one day from a winegrower's wife in Mercurey, after having tasted the wines in that Burgundian village's cellars.

Gougères Bourguignonnes

2 cups milk
  salt and pepper
8 tbs butter
  ½ lb flour

8 eggs
  6 oz. Gruyère
2 tbs cream

Pour the milk into a saucepan. Add salt, pepper and the butter; then bring to a boil.

Remove from heat and stir in the flour with a spatula. Replace on heat for one minute, stirring all the time.

Remove from heat again, add 7 of the eggs, one by one, and 4 ounces of the Gruyère, finely diced, stirring all the time. Lastly fold in the cream.

Place this mixture in small muffin tins, half-filling each one. Beat the remaining egg and brush it over the tops. Then push tiny pieces of cheese into them and bake in a medium oven. Serve hot.

All wines—white, red, or rosé—are suitable to drink with these spurs to bacchic enjoyment. If you really want to enjoy yourselves, have several ready to taste—and to argue about!

MENU

*Foie gras
Turbot poché au beurre
*   blanc*
(Poached turbot in
*   vinegar-shallot-butter*
*   sauce)*
Brie
Sorbet au champagne
(Champagne sherbet)

The great question of what goes best with *foie gras* will never be settled. Everyone has his opinion, conditioned by personal taste and regional pride. People from Bordeaux will suggest a Sauternes (an iced Yquem, with *foie gras*, is the very last word in perfection in Montaigne country!) and Alsatians a Tokay.

There are those I know who prefer a very old port, others a red wine, and others still—myself among them—who would opt for a champagne *nature*. Moreover a champagne will go very well with the rest of the meal, even with the cheese—perfectly in fact.

Foie Gras (Goose-liver Pâté)

Late in December the time comes around once more for the first fresh *foie gras* of the year. One of the Parisian chefs who know how to treat it with the respect it deserves, with the love that alone will serve, Guy Nouyrigat, or Pierre Olivier, or one of the others, will call me up: "Come and taste the first *foie gras*."

Smooth as marble in its dish, it has the glints and the nobility of that classical stone as well.

It is matter at its richest, its most living, and it is shot through with evanescent tints of sublime death agonies: one thinks of those Romans who used to cook their surmullets alive at the table, in crystal containers, in order to watch the changing colors that came upon them with death.

And this broad, thick slab, an unreal pink or a broken yellow in color, this rainbow of matter, this poem of shadings, this block of suavity speaks eloquently of the long history of that organ so early raised to divine status by human *gourmandise*. Raised so high indeed as to have acquired a new name.

For this internal organ, reddish in color, containing a

bile-secreting gland common to man and mammals, was the Latin *jecur*. And this *jecur* in the goose, when fattened with a diet of figs, was to become, as we know from the epicurean Apicius, a great delicacy. Roman lovers of good food came to revel in "goose liver fattened with figs," in *jecum ficatum*. And as that culinary term gradually ousted the original noun *jecur*, so the organ from which we sometimes suffer acquired a new name derived from the fig, and over the centuries *ficatum* became the French word *foie*.

The goose, "that walking *foie gras* factory," was the first bird domesticated by man. Long before the cock crew thrice —as the frescoes in the tomb of Princess Atet bear witness— the Egyptians (following the Persians and the Assyrians, no doubt) already knew how to breed—and even to force-feed, as the bas-reliefs in another tomb near Memphis make quite clear—the goose.

From Boethos of Chalcedon's "Child with a Goose" to Penelope's dream comparing her suitors to the geese in the royal farmyard; from Cato's *De re rustica* to the dinner given by Nasidienus at which Horace saw "boys bringing in a vast dish containing the carved-up limbs of a male crane, lightly dusted with salt and garnished with pastry; the liver of a female white goose made fat with rich figs; shoulders of hare; thrushes with burned breasts; and pigeons without parsons' noses"—the goose itself has figured less on the gourmet's table than one might suppose, considering the high regard in which its overdeveloped liver has been held.

The making of the fatted liver of geese into *pâtés* is a more recent development. And also, to the displeasure of its more ardent advocates, of lesser interest. For the Romans, with Apicius, were right in believing that the goose's liver deserves to be prepared whole and savored for its own sake, plain and unadorned.

In a cookbook published in Frankfurt in 1581 (Rumpolt's *Kockbuch*) we can read: "I roasted the liver of a goose fattened by the Jews of Bohemia that weighed somewhat more than three pounds. It can also be made into a paste."

Here we can see the Strasbourg *foie gras* beginning to take shape, whereas the Périgord *pâté de foie gras* was not mentioned until the *Dictionnaire des aliments* by *M.C.D.*,

Head of the Kitchens of Monsieur le Prince de . . . , dating
from 1750.

But even then we must let a little more time pass.

It was not until late in the eighteenth century that the
chef to the Maréchal de Contades, at that time military governor of Alsace, a fellow by the name of Close or Clause or
Claude (historians are less than unanimous on the point), had
the notion of what he called the *pâté à la Contades: foie gras*
served in a pastry crust. Louis XVI tasted it on the eve of the
Revolution and paid twenty-five *pistoles* to Clause (let us
settle for that spelling), who shortly afterward married a
young widow, a Strasbourg pastrycook, Marie-Anne Maring.
His *pâté* made her shop's fortune.

It has been said that it was another chef, Doyen, from
Bordeaux, who "added the embellishment of the truffle" to
Clause's *pâté*. I put the phrase in quotation marks because I
personally can't agree that the truffle is an embellishment to
it, and even less—according to another fine phrase—that this
addition to *foie gras* "gave it a soul."

But at all events it was between 1808 and 1820, at the

other end of France, that the *pâté de foie gras* industry developed in Périgueux. And there too the *pâtés* generally included truffles.

Why am I not an advocate of the truffle in fresh *foie gras?* Because the nuances of its natural flavor can only suffer by juxtaposition with the more powerful flavor of the truffle. And also because combining two rich ingredients does not necessarily improve either of them. Because *foie gras* with truffles is merely an awful *nouveau riche* creature with too many rings on his fingers.

Which is why I wish to treat my generous slice of fresh *foie gras*, heralding winter and the massacre of so many liverish geese, according to its true quality, as a princess. I want to have it served up at the beginning of my meal, as the most prestigious first course of them all. I want it spared all vulgar contact with anything but my fork, served without any unnecessary lettuce leaf, without the insult of gherkins or any other pickle, without anything at all, I repeat, except perhaps a slice of toast, not too thick, not too well done, and warm.

Foie Gras

1 goose liver
　salt and pepper
quatre épices
　thyme

bayleaf
　1 wineglass Madeira
1 liqueur glass Armagnac
　sliced bacon

Separate the two lobes of the raw liver. Split them lengthwise with a long, pointed knife in several places and carefully remove all the blood vessels. Remove the skin covering the liver.

Sprinkle both lobes with a mixture of salt, pepper, and *quatre épices*. Place them in a terrine with a sprig of thyme and half a bayleaf. Squash down. Pour over the Madeira and the Armagnac; then cover and leave to marinate for 24 hours.

Remove the liver from the marinade. Pour the latter into a bowl. Line the terrine with bacon slices; then replace the liver and press it down. Pour in a little of the marinade. Fold the tops of the bacon over on top of the liver. Cover with greaseproof paper folded in quarters, then with the lid.

Cook the terrine in a steamer in a low oven for 1¼ hours. Allow to cool before turning out.

NOTE: You can use duck liver instead. I'd forgotten to mention it but fresh *foie gras* made from duck liver is also, at more or less the same time of year, a thing of moment. A little higher in flavor, a little stronger. And if you do use duck liver then it would be better to use port instead of Madeira.

156

It is perhaps not orthodox
but I would enjoy a red Arbois
with both the liver *gâteau*
and the cold lamb.

Gâteau de Foies Blonds de Volailles (Blond Chicken-liver Cake)

First a factual observation. This dish is in fact a cake (*gâteau*) of chicken livers. You may find it on a menu, or in a cookbook, referred to as *gâteau de foies de volailles*. But such a designation is incorrect because it is incomplete.

It is incomplete because it does not tell you that just any chickens—and therefore just any chickens' livers—won't do. And if I insist here that it be termed *gâteau de foies blonds*, it is precisely because the livers used in this dish are no ordinary livers and must come from creatures quite other than the common run of fowl you meet with just anywhere.

It is a dish from the Bresse district. And it is a shy dish too. It doesn't like travel and has never so much as crossed the frontiers of La Bresse and its annex, Le Bugey. And even in La Bresse, the very cradle of its being, partly from modesty but partly from pride too, it doesn't frequent many restaurants or turn up on many menus, but prefers to hide like Cinderella beside the ranges of that province's old, wise housewives and cooks.

I can imagine the old women and the *gâteaux* talking to one another in low voices, exchanging joyous memories and sad regrets, philosophers in their own way.

Brillat-Savarin

The old woman says: "Do you remember, we first met at my first communion? My father was very proud of your mother who had just won a medal at the poultry fair in Bourg. You looked put out because the course that preceded you in the meal was an *oreiller de la Belle Aurore*, and after such a lordly creation you were worried about cutting a sorry figure."

And the *gâteau* replies: "Ah, that *oreiller de la Belle Aurore!* I knew her of course, being so much older than you. The Belle Aurore it was named after, Brillat-Savarin's mother. And I once did service on the table of Lucien Tendret too, that poet of the kitchen. An amazing man. A Christian who stayed home from Mass on Sundays to stuff the tomatoes for his guests because, he said, 'preparing the good things the Lord provides, if we prepare them with love, is a higher method of praising Him.'"

So the magic dialogue would go in that dark, rustic kitchen on a farm in deepest Bresse.

I can just see the farm. A square of low farm buildings surrounding a snow-covered yard. Sharply sloping roofs covered in Roman tiles. A big well in the middle of the yard. Bunches of golden corn heads hanging to dry from the beams jutting out in front of the hearth. And because the Bresse farmer likes to live in proud and solitary splendor on his own domain, everything except for the salt and the coffee is produced there.

This traditional "folk dish" requires "blond" chicken livers, the unique livers to be found in the poultry of this province, the famous hens, capons, chickens of Bresse. And as I suggested earlier, the *gâteau de foies blonds de volailles* is

a woman's dish, the dish of a rustic vestal, the dish of genius unaware of its own existence.

But let us begin at the beginning—by which I mean with the birds themselves. Louhans blacks, Bourg whites, Bény grays, they all have blue claws, juicy and jolly meat, and blond livers, a characteristic that they owe perhaps to the corn that is used to feed them but certainly to their patrician origin. Blond as the caress of Venus's hand. Blond as the tenderness of love.

And this *gâteau* (and note that we don't call it a terrine, or a *pâté*, or a loaf, as one says *terrine de foie gras*, or *pâté d'alouette*, or *pain de brochet*), so discreet and even secretive, helps us to be intelligent!

Here it is! It appears clothed in a *coulis*, or sauce, of crayfish, for Bresse and Bugey are among those happy provinces blessed with exceptional natural resources where one can still find "real" crayfish, with red claws, with meaty and delicate flesh. More humbly, a housewife on some day when potluck has failed her may content herself with a *coulis* made of tomatoes. You think that sounds like a disaster? I can assure you it isn't. The *gâteau de foies blonds* is a dish that provides food for thought as well as for the stomach but does not thrust itself forward. Yet for all its shyness it won't stand being trifled with either. It is what it is. As though its mother province, the cradle of Brillat-Savarin, had in return been irradiated forever with the wisdom of the author of *Physiologie du goût*. For they are inseparable from one another. A chef—may the profession forgive me!—could only be an intruder here, with his big knife, his great white hat, his self-confidence, and his stubbornness.

Centuries of true epicurean aristocracy, of nobility of taste, of housewifely science have gone into the elaboration of this wonder never to be found in cookbooks and forever absent from our menus—as though, when they come to Paris, the poultry of Bresse are always doomed to leave their livers as well as their hearts at home!

Gâteau de Foies Blonds de Volailles

garlic
  6 blond Bresse poultry livers
2 tbs beef marrow, poached
  1 cup meat juice
2 cups milk (approx.)

3 eggs
  3 egg yolks
salt and pepper
  crayfish-tail sauce

Rub the bottom and sides of a mortar very gently with a little garlic. No more than a breath, if you please.

Pound the blond livers in the mortar with the poached beef marrow.

Add the meat juice and enough of the milk to produce a very liquid paste. Mix in the 3 whole eggs and the 3 egg yolks. Salt and pepper. Strain.

Generously oil, then drain, a wrought-iron mold. On the bottom of it fit a circle of greaseproof paper. Pour the liver paste into the mold, which it should not entirely fill.

Set the mold in a saucepan of cold water but don't let the bottom of the mold touch the bottom of the saucepan. Heat the water, but don't let it boil. Allow to cook just below boiling for 1½ hours.

Remove the mold, wipe it, turn the *gâteau* out into a dish.

Cover with a sauce of crayfish tails.

160

A dry white wine, a Chablis of the last vintage; then with the terrine whichever wine you used to make it. It could have been a Châteauneuf-du-Pape, for example. Nothing with the chestnuts and cream, unless it be a glass of iced water.

Terrine de Canard Madeleine Decure (Pâté of Jellied Duck)

"*Que grand tu as!*" Pantagruel exclaimed, flabbergasted at the sight of his newborn son. And that was the christening of Gargantua, the symbol of a love of food verging on wildest gluttony. But perhaps it is only in our wretched age that the son of Rabelais has been reduced to the status of symbol? The other day I was reading a menu from the reign of Louis XIV. Oh, Lord, the appetite of that age!

All those people must have been able to recite the litanies of that poet son of Cahors, Clément Marot:

> From small dinner and bad cooking
> From no supper and no sleeping
> From wine lees and wine acidulous
>   Good Lord deliver us!

The big eaters and the big drinkers are vanishing. In his *Mémoires*, Galtier-Boissière relates the end—a good and noble one, everything considered—of the restaurateur Talboutier. He was enormous, and suffered a stroke. At the hospital, he was unable to speak and could express himself only by indicating the letters of a large, printed alphabet with a limp hand.

"What is there we can do for you?" his friends asked.

The numbed fingers slowly pointed: C . . . H . . . A . . .

"Champagne," one of them guessed with delight.

Happy at having been understood, Talboutier smiled, formed a word on his lips, and died.

Isn't that like a noble Roman death?

An ironic voice murmurs in my ear that we are little better than sissies and softies nowadays. *Mauviettes* in French. And it is an opportune voice too, because *mauviettes* in their other sense are what I want to talk about next. Apart from meaning sissy or softy, *mauviette* also means a lark in the eating season. As the first autumn mists begin to drift us into the dusk of the year, so *alouettes* become *mauviettes* and begin arriving in France in vast numbers. Thatch, thickets, underbrush all lend them the plumpness so beloved of gourmets and so at variance with the other, pejorative sense of the word *mauviette;* for a *mauviette* in the bird kingdom is certainly no wilting creature. Quite the contrary. Just ask the lark-catchers who go out hunting them, from October to March, with their regulation nets, meticulous observers of the law that restricts such activities strictly to the *arrondissement* of Pithiviers.

And what delicious pies they make!

The famous pies of Pithiviers have been its glory ever since Charles IX. That gentle king was on his way home through the forest of Orléans. He had just left his lady, the tender Marie Touchet, at the Château du Hallier. And having been parted from his followers, he fell into an ambush set for him by the Huguenots. The enemy was preparing for a feast. They invited their prize, from whom they hoped to extract a rich ransom (they had not recognized him as the king). A pie keeping warm near the embers was served. Charles IX drove in his blade to carve it. A subtle aroma of spices and herbs rose from the crust, while set in a truffled filling he beheld two dozen plump birds which proved to be of exceptional tastiness. When his escort finally caught up with the king he pardoned his captors on condition they tell him the name of the cook who made such good pies. They told him

the pie had come from Margeolet, known as Provenchère, rue du Cygne, in Pithiviers.

The Provenchère family maintained that tradition for three centuries, and in the reign of Louis-Philippe the original pie-maker's descendants were still enjoying the privilege of a royal patent. *Alouettes, gentilles alouettes*, you made the fortune of your celebrated murderer Margeolet. And he prepared your pastry coffin as for a siege, as though it were the fortification of a town to be taken by assault. Pastry towers quivered at explosions of martial laughter, the great keep fell, and the entire garrison surrendered to the conquerors: whole birds, generous slices of ham, bacon, minced meat, herb fragrances. What a feast of victory! Yes, in those days towns and pies were sacked in the same joyous fashion. Hunger, like war, makes a man thirsty.

Ah, let us pity our little pies of today, whether modest confections of veal and ham or richly filled with *foie gras* and delicate game; their slightly dry crust gives up its nourishment too quickly, their aromatic heart seduces us all too swiftly, and we must perforce move on to sterner battles without delay.

Often we even suppress the crust. And the pie becomes a terrine. This lightening of the pie's gastronomic burden would have made d'Artagnan smile and Porthos wax indignant. But we are no longer made of the same stuff as those revelers of old, at home in forest and brake, for whom the recipe of a

APPETIZERS AND EGG DISHES **163**

Provenchère pie was worth a king's ransom. All good things come to an end.

But here, at the happy halfway mark between rustic simplicity and grandiose palace fare, is a recipe for a duck terrine.

Terrine de Canard Madeleine Decure

1 duck
   1 tbs wine vinegar
2 cups red wine
   5 oz tongue
1½ lbs fat bacon
   5 oz chicken livers
2 tbs butter
   1 tbs chopped shallots
½ lb lean pork
   3 eggs

2 tbs brandy
   1 truffle
salt and pepper
   ½ lb bacon slices
thyme
   bayleaf
spices
   4 cups jellied consommé
ham
   chervil

When killing the duck put aside the blood, adding the wine vinegar and a little of the red wine to it. Then pluck and gut the bird and leave it to stand till next day.

Next day: singe the duck, wipe it with a cloth, open it up down the back and bone it, taking care to keep the skin intact. Cut the meat of the stomach up into strips. Cut up the tongue and about 5¼ ounces of the fat bacon into similar strips. Put all the strips of meat between two plates.

Quickly firm the duck's liver and the sliced chicken livers in hot butter with the chopped shallots. Allow to cool; then mash.

Chop up the rest of the duck meat, legs, wings, meat off the carcass, the lean pork, and the rest of the fat bacon. Add the mashed livers to the chopped meat. Mix it all together, gradually adding 3 whole eggs, 1 tablespoonful of brandy, the duck's blood, and the trimmed truffle. Salt and pepper.

Spread out the duck's skin on a napkin. Spread a layer of your mixture on it, followed by the strips of duck, tongue, and fat bacon, then put the rest of the mixture on top. Pull the edges of the skin in to the center so that it holds the contents together.

Line an oval terrine mold with bacon slices. Put the galantine on top. Cover it with another layer of bacon slices, on top of which put the thyme, bayleaf, salt, and spices. Pour in the remainder of the brandy and red wine. Cover. Seal on the lid of the terrine with flour and water paste. Cook in a steamer in a hot oven for 2 hours. When you remove it from the oven take off the lid and replace with a flat piece of wood with weights (4 to 6 pounds) on top and leave to cool overnight.

Next day turn out. Remove the bacon slices. Trim the galantine. Wash the terrine. Melt the jellied consommé and clarify it, then allow to cool until it is still just fluid. Pour about ½ inch into the bottom of the terrine. Arrange stars cut out of ham on the layer, scatter chopped chervil over it, then put the galantine back in. Pour over the remainder of the jelly. Put into refrigerator.

To serve, run a knife around the wall of the terrine then turn the molded mixture out onto its serving dish.

Jean-Baptiste Oudry: The White Duck

MENU

Portugaises vertes
(*Raw Portuguese oysters*)
*Andouillette à la purée
de haricots rouges
Fromage de chèvres
(*Goat cheese*)
*Sorbet

A single white wine could very well go with the whole meal, from oysters right through to and including the cheese. I would suggest a Sancerre or a Pouilly-Fuissé. Otherwise, Muscadet with the oysters and Beaujolais with the chitterling sausage.

Andouillette (Chitterling Sausage)

The other evening I was rereading Balzac's *La Peau de chagrin*. Suddenly I encountered the following sentence, obscure in more ways than one: "He uttered the great French swear word without dressing it up in any of the Jesuitical hesitations of the Abbess des Andouillettes."

The Abbess des Andouillettes! You may well imagine that for someone not merely a passionate eater of chitterling sausages but actually the founder and general secretary of the A.A.A.A. (Association Amicale des Amateurs d'Andouillettes Authentiques) the words must have rung out like the summons of fate. Who was this Abbess, and what her origin? The only connection between pork sausages and religion I was aware of at that time was the *andouillette de Lourdes*, which, as every lover of good food knows, is a sausage twisted into a sort of rosary.

A friend who has an answer for everything explained the connection. The Abbess des Andouillettes is a character from Sterne's *Life and Opinions of Tristram Shandy*, a book that Balzac was very fond of (and alludes to on several other occasions too). In Chapter XX of this book, then, we meet

166

Pieter Brueghel
the Elder:
Les Gras

the Abbess des Andouillettes, who in the company of a novice
from her convent is leaving her Abbey des Andouillettes, situated among the hills on the frontiers of Burgundy and Savoy,
for the warm waters of Bourbon.

I shall not here bore you with the story of how the convent gardener, promoted to the rank of muleteer and coach-
man, was tempted by a thirst-quenching grape-arbor and
came to abandon the old coach lined with green frieze in
which the two holy women had taken their places; or how,
in order to escape the possible perils of the night and get the
mules to set off again, the two employed a certain stratagem
to utter the two swear words (for despite Balzac's referring
to only one, two in fact there were) that alone will make
mules budge but that also put the souls of nuns in jeopardy. I
am sure you will be glad to know, however, that this point of
history has been satisfactorily settled, and duly salted away in
the *andouillette* file.

Next point: the *andouillette* or chitterling sausage seems
to me to have been rather neglected by gourmets, despite its
widespread occurrence—North, Midi, East, and West—and its
diverse but evident merits.

We of the A.A.A.A., having hunted the beast assidu-
ously in every corner of France, have definitely established
the claims of the chitterling sausage of Arras and Cambrai,
that of Troyes, that of Brittany and that of Vouvray, that
of Jargeau and the incomparable one produced in Châtillon-
sur-Loire, that of Fleurie-en-Beaujolais, and that of Lourdes
(which was a revelation), that of Aubagne, which is made

Gustave Doré: Gargamelle and Grandgousier

with herbs, that of Paris, that of Ebreuil, and a score or more besides.

There are two classic ways of preparing it for the table: grilling, or frying and then braising in white wine. More fantastical are: *andouillette en chemise* (inside a *crêpe*), *andouillette flambée* (using either brandy or whisky). But the braised *andouillette* itself also gives rise to two possibilities: grill it first, then braise it, or just braise it (which softens it).

But the great argument concerns what one should serve with it. The purists of the A.A.A.A. insist that it should simply be grilled and served with nothing else but strong mustard. One thing is certain: serving it with French fries is an appalling error. Fat on fat should always be banned. Similarly, herring fillets should no more be asked to contend with *pommes à l'huile* (potatoes in oil) than should hot sausage (which the inhabitants of Lyons, food-loving but wise, have the good sense to serve with boiled potatoes). But back to the *andouillette*, to our patron lady the *andouillette*, whom we would like to see escorted by less mundane vegetables. If potatoes it simply has to be, then let them be creamed, let them be *en purée*. Though purée for purée, a *purée soubise* (onions), a purée of *haricots rouge* (red kidney beans), or lentils, or celery, or split peas, or stringbeans would all be better.

We have tried raw red cabbage, very finely sliced, then lightly flavored with vinegar and mustard. That wasn't bad. Nor were fried onions. Or Chinese artichokes. And I was forgetting salsify! You can see that the choice is wide, and yet there are probably some I have omitted. Anyone who has any brainwaves on the subject will be doing all of us in the A.A.A.A. a good turn by passing them on.

A dry, cool white wine
seems the best bet to me. What
about a Pouilly-Fumé?

Les Petits Pâtés de Pézenas

(The Little Pies of Pézenas)

Pies are an important element in the British diet. They are dishes of meat or vegetables (sometimes both together), or fruit cooked inside a pastry crust, either in the oven or in steam—in which case they are, technically, puddings.

Among what we would call the desserts we must count apple pie, lemon pie, and all kinds of fruit pies.

Among the main dishes we must include steak-and-kidney pie (filled with alternate layers of beef and kidney), sheep's-tail pie (served with mint sauce), shepherd's pie (chopped mutton with a mashed-potato top instead of pastry), and chicken pie. In Cornwall there even exists a star-gazy pie, which is made with whole herrings wrapped in a pastry so that their heads stick out.

But to the French the most amazing pies of all are the mince pies that the English eat as a pudding, but whose composition, combining as it does the suet of kidneys with dried fruit, makes it in the Frenchman's eyes into something oddly hybrid, bizarre, astounding.

But the only reason why such a mixture of salt and sugar and these sugared meats amaze us is that we have forgotten

PEZENAS.

the recipes of the medieval world. I am inclined to term these mince pies "Gothic cooking," as indeed is all British cooking in a way, for boiled leg of lamb too is a sort of survival from an age when all roasts were boiled before they were roasted.

And so true is this that our forefathers in the Languedoc were less surprised than merely charmed, two centuries ago, to be introduced to these little pies of Pézenas. Their memories were obviously less short than ours in such matters.

Pézenas is an eighteenth-century town now frozen in its own glorious past. "One word of mockery from the mouth of a Molière or a La Fontaine was enough," it has been written, "to turn any small provincial town into a synonym for absurdity: such was the fate of Landerneau and Quimper-Corentin, as well as Pézenas."

And it is indeed true that Molière wrote his *Précieuses ridicules* there; but that does not mean that his heroine, the Marquise d'Escarbagnas, was necessarily a figure from this particular region of the Languedoc—for which he performed his first plays in 1650 and continued to perform them until 1657.

This meal is really magnificent, each is drinking with his lady;
but it makes me sad—I'd rather have more leftovers

In the next century Pézenas was the Riviera of the tourists and a center for the ailing travelers who had come to consult the members of the faculty of the famous medical university at Montpellier. Which explains how Clive of India, toward the end of his life (he died in 1774), came to take a rest cure there for a while. He lived in grand style, and entertained all the aristocratic families of the district in his château near Larzac, in the valley of the Peyne. Was Lord Clive's cook an Indian? Opinion remains divided on the point. But one thing is certain: he cooked magically. And one of his specialties was a somewhat individualistic version of the mince pie, one that his master doted on and that the whole town was soon clamoring to become acquainted with.

With his master's permission the cook gave the recipe for his pies to several of the great families in the Pézenas district. Then a Piscenois pastrycook with a shop on the rue des Chevaliers-Saint-Jean, one Roucairol, also began making Lord Clive's "little Scottish pies." Now they are baked as far afield as Béziers.

A year or so ago I spent a long time wandering through

Ce repas est fort magnifique
On y boit avec sa Philis

Mais il me rend melancolique
j'aimerois mieux un beau debris.

Pézenas, which a halfhearted town council now allows to remain a quiet backwater far from the tourist tide. What an amazing counterblast to Molière's irony, and how one would love to live in this city that once bore a coat of arms awarded to it by Charles VII as a reward for having victoriously resisted the assaults of the English. But how glad I am that in later times it failed to resist the blandishments of English cooking, and that Clive of India's pies have become *les petits pâtés de Pézenas*.

I mused for a long while on such matters in front of the Hôtel de Grasset and its noble steps, outside the Hôtel de Conti and that same Hôtel d'Alfonce where Molière and his troupe gave a performance on the evening of November 8, 1654; outside the Golden Griffon and the Silver Packsaddle that once gave shelter to travelers in days gone by, and in which one can imagine Molière himself staying, with his companion Dassoucy, sitting up late, stirring up the embers in the hearth, and telling one another stories. Then I ate my lunch outside the house of the barber Gély, friend and host of the author of *Le Misanthrope*, a lunch consisting of the little pies, bought not far away, from a pastrycook who was perhaps a descendant of Roucairol.

Les Petits Pâtés de Pézenas

flaky pastry
  ½ lb leg of mutton
¾ lb kidney suet
  ¼ lb mixed candied citron, lemon, and orange peel

rind of 2 fresh lemons
  1 lb brown sugar
egg yolk

Make your flaky pastry. Refrigerate it for an hour; then roll it out and cut circles from it 2½ inches in diameter. Form them into little baskets. Cut out covers for each basket.

Finely chop the leg of mutton from which all the fat has been removed.

Finely chop the kidney suet (preferably from a sheep or calf), and mix it with the chopped mutton.

Chop up the candied peels and the lemon rind.

Add this mixture to the meat and suet, and blend well. Lastly add the brown sugar and keep this filling in a cool place for 48 hours.

Put a little of your filling into each pastry basket. Then wet the rims of the baskets, add the covers and pinch them to seal well. Prick two or three holes in the top of each little pie. Leave overnight.

Next day, brush with egg yolk and bake in the oven on an oiled baking sheet.

172

MENU
Asperges à la Fontenelle
Fricandeaux
Jambon persillé
Salade de laitue
(Lettuce salad)
Clafoutis
(Cherry cake)

Why not a Madiran, that warm and scented wine from Gascony? If you don't feel like a glass of water after the asparagus, why not a glass of Vouvray? Then you can finish the bottle with the *clafoutis*.

Fricandeaux (Larded Meatballs)

The mere sight of the word brings an old vaudeville air to mind:

> A table! A table! A table!
> Mangeons ce fricandeau
> Qui serait détestable
> S'il n'était mangé chaud . . .

Which immediately tells us one thing at all events, if the authors are right: that a *fricandeau* is not edible if allowed to get cold.

But precisely what *fricandeau* are we talking about?

The one whose recipe is given by the classic cookbooks and of which the dictionary of the Académie des Gastronomes says: "Culinary preparation of the same (and obscure) etymological derivation as *fricasser*. The *fricandeau* is a slice of veal—or of a fish such as sturgeon, salmon, or tuna—larded with bacon, braised, and served on a bed of sorrel and chicory."

It is to a veal *fricandeau* of this sort that the verse quoted refers.

Le Patiſſier.

The culinographer Joseph Favre gave the following recipe for it:

"Remove the central portion from a leg of veal, cut it in two lengthwise (in the same direction as the fibers), trim the two pieces, and lard them generously with bacon.

"Line a stewpan with bacon, sliced onions, and the trimmings of the veal; place the *fricandeau* (that is, the prepared and larded pieces of meat) in the pan and seal it in a hot oven or over the heat. When the onions are a good brown color season with peppercorns, salt, and a clove of garlic, pour water or veal stock (not beef) over the *fricandeau*, put the stewpan in the oven and baste often, taking care to pour the juice through a perforated spoon or small strainer so as not to drop any bits of onion or veal onto the meat.

"When the *fricandeau* is three-quarters cooked, place it in a deep, narrow saucepan and strain the juice from the stewpan over it so that it is covered. Keep basting until the juice is reduced to a glaze and the *fricandeau* is thoroughly cooked.

"Cut up the *fricandeau* and then reassemble the pieces as they were before. Cover them with some of the glaze from the saucepan, serving the rest separately in a sauceboat. Serve the accompanying vegetable—*macédoine, petits pois*, sorrel, or spinach—in a separate vegetable dish.

"Remarks: Whatever the *fricandeau* you are dealing with, it must be remembered that the stock used to moisten it must be derived from the same meat; that basting must be frequent;

174

that the cooking juices must be allowed to reduce to a glaze, which means that the *fricandeau* will be very well done. Some cookbooks tell one to 'cover the *fricandeau* with stock.' Such a procedure is unworthy of the art of French cooking. It simply boils away all the meat's taste and juices."

As you can see, Joseph Favre didn't treat the *fricandeau* lightly.

Simenon's Madame Maigret often has a *fricandeau à l'oseille* reducing away in the oven for her husband the Inspector. It is a recipe *à la bourgeoise*, as they would have said in the nineteenth century, implying an unfancy solidity, an absence of pretension: the thick slice of rolled veal or thick end of the loin, generously larded, is braised in veal stock until the broth is reduced to a thick sauce. And it is served with a sorrel purée because sorrel is, of its very essence, the calf's childhood friend.

Only, only . . . is it true?

I know that the dictionary of the Académie des Gastronomes goes on: "This dish comes to us from the Orient, where it is served on their wedding eve to young newlyweds, who find in it, apparently, a promise, a spur, and a comfort."

That sounds more to me like the fantasy life of a lot of randy old gastronomers than any kind of genuine historical research. Veal is no more Oriental in origin than salmon is.

Moreover, in *Le Cuisinier françois* (1651), La Varenne gives the following recipe for *fricandeau*: "To make it, take veal, cut it in small slices and beat them well with the handle of a knife. Chop all kinds of herbs together with fat of beef or mutton and a little bacon. The meat being well seasoned with all this and bound with raw eggs, set it to cook in a pie plate or terrine. When the meat is cooked, serve it with its own sauce."

This three-hundred-year-old recipe seems to me to be the "mother" of all the true *fricandeaux*, including the *fricandeau* of Aveyron, which may not contain any veal—an expensive and rare meat in that poor district—but nevertheless derives from the same principle: a fricassée of chopped meats bound with egg.

That the *fricandeau* should have gradually become ennobled in our towns until it consisted exclusively of veal—and

moreover exclusively of fillet of veal, the most expensive cut!
—is possible. That it should have been found necessary, in
order to counter the insipidity of the meat, to accompany it
with sorrel is more than likely.

And yet there is a part of me, an earthy, peasant part of
which I am proud, that doesn't really see anything noble in the
fricandeau of veal and yet does perceive something really and
more deeply noble in the *fricandeau* from the Auvergne.

In the first place it is companionable. It is there, in the
larder, modestly and contentedly waiting on our appetites. It
is always available, that's what I'm trying to say. You feel a
tiny, unseasonable pang of hunger, and lo and behold the
remedy is there as close to hand as the knife in your pocket:
you pull out the knife, you cut off a hunk of bread, and you
spread on a little *fricandeau*. It is the workman's breakfast, the
noon snack, the four-o'clock tea, and the evening meal, with a
quickly dispatched salad. No need to make a great fuss of it,
for it's just one of the family. But quick as a flash, if an unexpected guest should appear, a garland of parsley will make it
into something worth offering, for it is a willing helper as well
as a good companion.

And those Oriental newlyweds? Pooh! Our own married
couples have other things to sustain them on that day, during
that night. Though I think the *fricandeau* might justifiably be
involved in a young man's choice of bride: "If she makes a
fricandeau as well as her mother, why then she will bear me
children just as fine and will be a good wife to me indeed!"

Fricandeaux

2 lbs pork throat
1 lb pig's liver
salt and pepper

1½ tsp cornstarch
1 cup milk
caul

Coarsely chop the pork and pig's liver. Salt
and pepper. Add the cornstarch and mix the
milk in.

Make the result into 3 equal-sized balls
and wrap them in a caul.

Place on a dish and cook gently for 1½
hours in the oven.

MENU

Plateau de fruits de mer
(Assorted shellfish)
*Boudin à l'Auvergnate
*Omelette surprise
brésilienne

And for wine, a Chateaugay.

Boudin à l'Auvergnate

(Blood Sausage, Auvergne Style)

The "invention" of the *boudin,* or blood sausage, has been
attributed to the Greek cook Aphtonetes. Was he really the
first to think of introducing a paste made with a basis of blood
into a length of intestine? Others think that intestine-stuffing
was known among the Assyrians and Phoenicians, and certainly there were preparations based on blood already in
existence before Aphtonetes, such as the Spartans' black
broth, the *myma* of Epaenetes, and the recipe given by the
cook Erasistrates for a certain *hyposphagma,* which was a
cooked mixture of blood, honey, cheese, salt, caraway, and
silphium.

The word's etymology is even more uncertain still. Is it
related perhaps to the Old French *boudine* (big belly, swelling)? The Spanish call the dish *embutinos.* The English *black
pudding.* Which came first, "pudding" or *boudin?* The word
"pudding" on its own does not imply the use of blood, you
may say. But isn't the making of *boudin* simply the art of
inserting extremely various kinds of comestibles into intestines? You can make *boudin* with rabbit, with crayfish, with
meat and game, even with bread. And some "white" *boudins*

APPETIZERS AND EGG DISHES **177**

are no more than what the French think of as "pudding" stuffed into an intestine.

Though it is true that *boudin* to the gourmet is first and foremost black *boudin*—which is to say a sausage made of pork blood. Its capital is Nancy, and its kingdom stretches from Flanders to the Lyonnais, even though Paris has adopted it to such an extent that the capital alone now consumes more than the rest of the country put together.

The *boudin* was for a long while one of the indispensable concomitants of Christmas feasts. Here is a recipe for the yuletide *boudin* in verse:

> Chop onions fine, and on flame not high
> With equal parts of bacon fry.
> Toss till onion is a golden color
> And kitchen filled with sweet aroma.
> Mix with the blood and season well
> With pepper, salt, and spice as well.
> A glass of brandy add, then fill
> A pig's intestine, though not until
> One end's been tied. When all your paste
> Is safely in, and both ends laced,
> Cook twenty minutes, or thereabout,
> In simmering water, then hoist out.
>> Now by the yule log's crackling blaze
>> Inviting you to stretch and laze
>> Reap the reward of all your toil
>> And watch your *boudins* gently broil.

The proportions of the classic *boudin* are: to one quart of blood add one pound of onions, one pound of finely chopped fresh pork fat, a cup of cream, a handful of breadcrumbs, salt, pepper, fennel, and chopped parsley.

But there are as many varieties of *boudin* as there are good pork butchers—or almost.

In Poitou they add spinach cooked in salted boiling water, then strained and chopped, in lieu of the onions (14 ounces of spinach to replace one pound of onions) and they also add creamed eggs.

In Lyons they omit the cream and the breadcrumbs. They also put in less pork fat and onions for the same amount of blood and add a little red pepper.

LA BOUDINIÈRE

I also know of a recipe for *boudin au rhum*. You simply add one small glass of Demerara rum and a pinch of sugar to the classic ingredients.

But the best *boudin* of all is in fact the simplest: that of the "*Tua*," as they call the annual pig-killing in those country districts where they also refer to the pig himself, with great respect, as "Monsieur." And the death of Monsieur is at once a ritual celebration and an act of grace toward the dispenser of all food.

The literature of folklore is full of fine pages on this December death, the prelude to the celebration of the Nativity. In the crib, we read, He lay between the ox and the ass. But where was the pig, that encyclopedic animal, that divine gift to man's appetite? Without a pig the crib is empty!

The Auvergne remains true to its mission as the land of men at once rugged and wise, as well as passionately and powerfully in love with life. A friend, alas no longer with us, used to tell how his grandmother gave her granddaughter this advice: "Mark my words, my pet, the trouble always starts with dining rooms. If ever you become a great rich lady, then make sure you spend plenty of time in your kitchen. Your children will be healthy and your husband will be wealthy, that I can tell you now." And it's true enough, of course, that the dining room is a modern invention.

In the countryside of the Auvergne, killing the pig is called *faire mongougne*, and the woman who comes in to help the farmer's wife, the farmer's daughter, and his servants to make the sausages and *boudins* is called *la mongougnière*. And the children, having learned their catechisms, all know full well that the greatest feast of the year is not Christmas, or Corpus Christi, or Easter, but "the day we kill Monsieur." It is the man's job to hang up the bacon. It is a rite. He has checked all the hooks to make sure they are still firm. The household holds its breath, even the pendulum in the old cherrywood clock pauses in its swing: the bacon is good, the family will not go hungry this winter!

But making the *boudin* is the woman's task.

Boudin à l'Auvergnate

intestines
  salt
spices
  10 large leeks
6 qts pig's blood
  6 white onions
2 lbs pork neck
  ¼ lb fat, unsalted bacon

spinach leaves
  parsley
2 cups heavy cream
  6 eggs
pepper
  apples
2 tsp prepared mustard

Wash the intestines thoroughly and put to steep in a crock with salt, spices, and the leeks split in two.

Collect the pig's blood in another crock. Stir for a moment; then stand in a cool place.

Boil the onions.

Cook the pork neck and the bacon, diced, in a *cocotte*, without salting. Add 2 handfuls of spinach leaves and parsley previously blanched in boiling water. Cook very thoroughly. Allow to cool, then chop finely.

To the finely chopped contents of the *cocotte* add the puréed onions, the eggs, and enough of the cream to make a paste, and stir well. Salt, pepper, and spice generously.

Mix all this with the blood. Fill the lengths of intestine with the resulting mixture, tying up one end first and also leaving enough empty space at the end you fill from so that it can be easily tied.

Stack the *boudins* in a cauldron. Cover with cold water, bring to a gentle simmer, and cook without allowing the water to boil.

When you can prick the *boudins* with a steel fork and no blood comes out, then they are sufficiently cooked. Take off the heat and allow to cool.

Cut off lengths of cold *boudin*. Broil them on an oiled rack with the grill as hot as possible, until the skin becomes crackly and caramelized.

Sauté thick slices of apple in a pan with some unsalted bacon.

When the apple slices are well browned and cooked, pepper them, and add the mustard and 2 tablespoons of cream.

Serve the *boudins* on a bed of these apples.

MENU

*Beuchelle tourangelle
Côtes d'agneau grillées
(Broiled lamb chops)
Haricots verts
(Stringbeans)
Salade de fruits
(Fruit salad)

We need a great wine but a light one that won't swamp the delicacy of this exquisite dish and can also be drunk with the lamb. Let us say a Médoc, not too young but not too old. A Château Calon-Ségur would do perfectly in my opinion.

Beuchelle Tourangelle

(Kidneys, Sweetbreads, and Mushrooms)

To write of this unusual dish is to write before all else of Nignon. And to write of Edouard Nignon is in a sense to repair an injustice. For this chef, the greatest since Carême perhaps, is unknown even to many professional cooks, whereas names like those of Montagné and Escoffier are famous—and justifiably famous—among even the general public.

"This man," Sacha Guitry wrote of the person he referred to respectfully as "Monsieur Nignon," "spent two-thirds of his life either all in black or all in white. Head cook to Tsar Nicholas II of Russia, then to Emperor Franz Josef of Austria, for twenty years he wore the white garments and the high hat, like a well-risen brioche, whose brightness and whiteness so calms the mind when glimpsed beyond a swinging door. At the age of forty he exchanged his white apparel for a frockcoat, and from then until the age of sixty he lived his life all in black. Moving from table to table, advising the choice of a sole, recommending a partridge, suggesting a dessert, salting this, sweetening that, he could truly say that anyone who was anyone in Paris had been seen dining at his tables."

He was born in Nantes. As was Charles Monselet, the poet of the table. And one day on a return visit to his native town the writer said to the young apprentice cook: "Cherish your art, young man, cherish it well. It is the noblest of them all!" And his words did not go unheeded.

In 1880 the young Nignon began his Parisian apprenticeship; at Potel et Chabot's first, then at the Maison Dorée, then the Café Anglais, Chez Voisin, the Restaurant Bignon, and others. These great names of yesterday, now vanished, are still full of memories for a lover of good food, despite the settling dust of time. Potel et Chabot was the famous catering firm that served the Banquet of the Mayors in 1900 to more than twenty thousand guests. The Maison Dorée was the temple where Casimir Moisson was serving the Prince of Wales and his latest conquest when the spurned husband appeared, stick in hand, and belabored the royal shoulders. The Café Anglais and its private dining room, the Grand 16, was celebrated by Offenbach in *La Vie Parisienne*. And it was Voisin, during the siege of 1870, who served up the elephant and the bears from the zoo.

But back to Nignon. He felt the urge to travel—just as

Carême had. He went first to the Trianon in Vienna, a favorite haunt of Franz Josef and his court, and he was in Moscow, at the Hermitage, with 120 white hats under him, when he decided to exchange his own white hat for a black frockcoat and return to Paris to manage the restaurant Larue.

In his *Eloges de la cuisine française*, a precious and incomparable book, a sort of prose poem to the glory of that *haute cuisine* that is still our most effective ambassador to the world, Nignon shares his memories of several celebrated gourmets. He served many noted men of letters, among them Marcel Proust and Edmond Rostand, Anatole France and Alfred Capus, Maurice Barrès and Robert de Flers. And that Marquis de Rougé who would arrive for his solitary repast, order a Rouen duck *à la presse*, a bottle of Musigny 1858, and ask "to be left alone for his communion."

But let us come to the *beuchelle*.

It was in Vienna that Nignon made the acquaintance of that local, homebody dish known as the *beuschell*. It was a poor man's dish, cooked very slowly and made with the cheapest kinds of calf's offal: membranes, tongue, etc. Nignon, however, had the notion of using the nobler cuts of offal: kidneys and sweetbreads. To this stew he added truffles, fresh morels, and christened the result *la beuchelle*.

Perhaps for the sake of the rhyme, he gave this new dish a pseudo-home in the Loire Valley, and called it the *beuchelle tourangelle*. Perhaps—for he was a Breton himself—there was a hint of malice in it. Or perhaps—and most likely of all—the richness, the moderation, the patrician balance of the dish evoked for him, as indeed for us, that quietly contented countryside, its harmonious châteaux, and the soft, pure sky above the Loire. It is an explanation that certainly satisfies me.

But Nignon's recipe was then forgotten, by chefs and gourmets alike. Perhaps it would have remained no more than a memory had it not been for another chef, also a great one, our contemporary M. Pointaire.

Pointaire has a lofty, uncompromising, and quite wonderful conception of his trade. When he quits his piano (the professional's term for his stove) it is for his library. He has Nignon's *Eloges* in it. And he has studied it. His attention was caught by this *beuchelle*, then riveted by it. And now it appears every day on his menu, in that tucked-away Levallois-Perret street, not far from Paris.

Only those in the know make their way through into Pointaire's own tiny dining room to savor his *beuchelle*. As though in secret. They speak of it almost in whispers. It has become their password. They guard it jealously. Their *beuchelle* is their communion, one might almost dare to say.

And when it is time for the coffee, for the cigars, for the old Armagnac and conversation between old friends, then Pointaire comes in to join his guests and talk to them, still, of Edouard Nignon, the unknown genius who thought up this great unknown dish.

Beuchelle Tourangelle

3 calf's kidneys
3 generous tbs butter
cognac (the best you have)
3 calf's sweetbreads

1 cup heavy fresh cream
¼ lb fresh morels
2 average-size truffles

Cut the kidneys into thin slices and toss them in hot butter, using half the butter. Flambé them in the cognac. Put to one side.

Blanch the sweetbreads in boiling water. Trim, slice, and flambé them; then bind them with half the cream.

Sauté the well-washed morels and the thinly sliced truffles in the remainder of the butter; then bind them with the remainder of the cream.

Put all these prepared ingredients together in a heavy pan and mix together gently but thoroughly.

Serve in a silver dish.

NOTE: You can use dried morels (1¾ ounces will be enough). You can substitute fresh mushrooms for truffles if they are in season. You can serve your *beuchelle* in a *vol au vent* crust straight from the oven.

Purists will tell you that you mustn't drink wine with eggs. So tell the purists you'll remember not to invite them whenever you have eggs, and having enjoyed a glass of sherry with your melon and Parma ham (it goes excellently well), serve the wine with your eggs that you will continue to drink with the Camembert. Let it be a goodhearted kind of a red. I am thinking of a Bouzy, for example (a red wine from Champagne), or an Arbois.

Oeufs Pochés à la Sauce Béchamelle

(Poached Eggs in Béchamel Sauce)

"Béchameil had done very well in business while keeping a good reputation, insofar as financiers who become rich are able to preserve such a thing. . . . He was a man of wit, very good at his job, enjoying delicate and choice fare both at his table and in the company he kept, and accustomed to seeing in his house the best society that town and Court had to offer. His taste in paintings, stones, furniture, architecture, and gardens was exquisite, and it was he who was responsible for all the beauties of Saint-Cloud."

Thus wrote Saint-Simon.

But a little further on, in recounting the following anecdote, he demonstrates that Béchameil was also vain and rather stupid.

"He was of handsome figure and face and entertained the belief that he resembled the Duc de Gramont in appearance. One day, seeing him walking in the Tuileries, the Comte de Gramont said to those with him: 'Who will wager with me that I cannot give this Béchameil a good kick in the behind and then make him as grateful for it as a spaniel?' Whereupon he walked over and delivered the kick. Béchameil, very

LE SUPERBE REPAS PRESENTÉ AU ROY ET AUX PRINCES DE SA COUR

Dinner given for the King and his Court at the Town Hall, Paris,
by the Aldermen and the Merchants' Guild

astonished, turned around; the Comte de Gramont apologized
profusely, explaining that he had taken Béchameil for his
nephew the duke. Béchameil was delighted, and those who
witnessed the incident even more so."

An epicurean in many fields, and rich to boot, Béchameil
employed many of the best cooks of his time, and it was one
of these, wishing to honor his master, who dedicated to him
a sauce that was to become *sauce à la Béchameil*, then *à la
Béchamel*, then *sauce Béchamelle*.

But was it a true creation? The old Duc d'Escars is on
record as having made this disillusioned comment: "He's a
lucky fellow, that little Béchameil. I was having minced
chicken served in a cream sauce twenty years before he was
born, but I've never had the good fortune to give my name
to even the least among sauces." And it seems likely that this
tribute from a chef for whom Béchameil had just bought the
office of Royal Maître d'Hôtel was no more than an improvement upon quite an old recipe.

Moreover, it is a recipe that has nothing whatever to do
with all the so-called *béchamel* sauces that you find pretty
well everywhere and that would be much better called by
their other name: white sauce. They are family sauces, quickly
made, nourishing, cheap. Whereas the *Béchameil* was a financier's sauce, rich, subtle, and expensive.

As such it has earned a place among what Carême termed
the "mother sauces." And it is certainly true that the *Béchameil* sauce has provided the basis for a number of other sauces,
the best known of which is the *Nantua* (arrived at by adding
shrimp butter). Just as by adding grated cheese to a white
sauce we arrive at *sauce Mornay*.

Contrary to an old proverb invented, I should imagine,
by a bad cook, the sauce does not disguise the fish. Or less-
than-fresh ingredients either. I am more inclined to agree with
the idea that a sauce "ought to continue and draw out the
taste of a dish, never mask or distort it."

The sauce dedicated to Monsieur de Béchameil, which
one might justifiably term "the old" *béchamel* as opposed to
the white sauce that also goes by that name, is of an indisputable succulence and would in itself suffice to lend the
simplest dish of boiled carrots nobility. We have already heard

that the Duc d'Escars used to have minced chicken served in it. It also goes miraculously with asparagus. But it is as an accompaniment to poached eggs that it earns my top mark for gustatory bliss.

Oeufs Pochés à la Sauce Béchamelle

1 qt chicken stock
1 qt heavy cream

salt and pepper
12 eggs

Mix the stock and cream in a saucepan. Bring to a boil and allow to cook very gently for 1 hour, stirring from time to time with a wooden spoon. The sauce should by then have been reduced by half. Salt and pepper. Pass through a fine sieve.

Poach the eggs in slightly salted boiling water. Drain them. Trim them. Arrange them on a warm dish and pour the sauce over them.

N O T E : Grated nutmeg may be included in the seasoning. The dish may also be sprinkled with grated cheese and browned in the oven, but that destroys its "purity."

Dürer: A Peasant at Market

The wine used for the *meurette* sauce will be welcome throughout the meal. May I advise, for a delightful change, a Loire wine: Bourgueil?

Oeufs en Meurette

(Poached Eggs with Meurette Sauce)

Talleyrand, you may remember, was appalled by England's lack of sauces. France, he claimed, had four hundred sauces, whereas the only thing the English seemed to have four hundred of was religious sects. Well, the *meurette* is one of those four hundred sauces. It is one of the many peasant sauces, as opposed to the chefs' sauces that make up the other half of the family tree. The chefs' sauces are the product of subtle calculations; the peasant sauces seem to have sprung already constructed from the soil itself. And the *meurette* is, moreover, a regional sauce, a sort of farmer's wife's sauce. Burgundy was its cradle, and the word *meurette* itself is of Burgundian origin. But this sauce—made with red wine—did not take long to cross the Burgundian frontiers: you will meet it too in Berry, in the Nivernais, and in Champagne. And where white wine is master, then the sauce *meurette* has known how to yield to its supremacy with good sense and fortunate results.

Consequently, though there is doubtless only one real recipe for sauce *meurette*, there are twenty variations on it.

And this sauce is not an end in itself. It is strictly an ac-

Dürer: The Tavern Keeper and Her Cook

companiment sauce. Depending on where you meet it, it can accompany fish, truffles (though I'm not sure that it's up to that honor), meat even, and lastly hard-boiled or poached eggs.

And it is with those same poached eggs that it goes best. So much so that this particular marriage has little by little come to be known as *la meurette*, as though the part had become the whole, as if in the sunset red of that sauce a fleeting flash of gold, an egg yolk pierced by an anticipatory fork, had splashed and filled the whole culinary horizon.

These eggs *meurette* in their little individual ramekins, or in the little earthenware dishes some Parisian restaurants use, have an almost sentimental, certainly a poetic value for me. The reader may perhaps smile, but surely forgive me. I once knew a young lady, a lover of good food like myself, who made a belated discovery of eggs *meurette* while in my company. The name on the menu had intrigued her, and she determined to try them. It was in a restaurant, moreover, where the eggs *meurette* weren't, if one was strict, exactly *meurette*. The red-wine sauce had been so lengthily, so lovingly simmered that it had lost its original color and arrived at those warm browns you find in the Italian Renaissance masters. And also, atop the egg itself, the chef had added diced pieces of beef marrow quivering like cubes of antique ivory. But those eggs in wine sauce, *meurette* or not, were—and still are—exquisite. My companion waxed enthusiastic, and so we decided on a tour of the capital's various eggs *meurette*.

I introduced her first to eggs *au Bouzy* (the red wine from Champagne, lending its refinements to a sauce as unctuous as cream). But unfortunately in that restaurant the eggs had been carelessly poached, badly trimmed, so that there were deep, unpleasantly gaping folds in the egg white, filled with a scarlet seepage.

She also made the acquaintance of eggs in a sauce made from the white wine of the Nivernais, more "smooth-tongued," tawny ocher in color, but highlighted with the pink tints of bacon pieces and a sprightly scattering of parsley.

She was introduced to the genuine eggs *à la bourguignonne* in their thick, almost solid sauce, dark as the purple lees of wine and sometimes almost as dark as chocolate.

And so, from one color or savor to the next, we continued our pilgrimage to the sources of the sauce *meurette* and its relationship with the egg, that closed and still relatively unexplored world.

And what does it matter if I did not again see my companion in those experiments and discoveries after they were over? With every egg *meurette* I eat, a little of her lovely presence reappears in memory, suspended in that sauce in which I seek a very present, epicurean pleasure as well as a little of my past.

But enough of sentiment. Whether cook's dish or chef's dish (and there are many differences that could be investigated between the two), the egg in wine sauce remains a typical dish of a type of French cooking sprung from the same soil as the vine itself. It should be accompanied by the wine that has given it its bouquet. It should be drunk as much as eaten, and through it one should be paying homage to the winegrower's labors and the lineage of his stock.

Oeufs en Meurette

1 qt wine
   thyme, bayleaf
clove of garlic
   6 eggs
5 oz lean bacon

8 tbs butter
   ¼ lb large mushrooms
5 oz small white onions
   3 slices soft bread
pinch of flour

Pour the wine (it should be young and of good quality) into a saucepan with a sprig of thyme, a bayleaf, and a clove of garlic. Bring to the boil.

The eggs must be very fresh, so that the white will solidify immediately on contact with the liquid. Break the shell of the egg, open it just above the wine, just at the spot where the boiling bubbles are rising (there are also practical utensils available for poaching eggs). When you have broken all the eggs into the wine, bring it to a lively simmer and let the eggs poach from 3 to 3½ minutes. Remove the eggs with a slotted spoon, dip them into cold water to halt the cooking process; then trim off any untidy edges of white with scissors. Keep them to one side in warm salted water.

Reduce the wine very quickly. Meanwhile cut the bacon into small pieces and blanch them in boiling water; then sauté them in some of the butter over high heat. Cut the mushrooms into quarters and sauté them in the same pan. Brown the onions in more of the butter in a separate pan. Cut the three slices of bread into triangular halves and fry them in butter.

Arrange the triangles of fried bread on a warm dish with a poached egg on top of each. Strain the reduced wine, thicken it with a little flour; then add the bacon pieces, the mushrooms, and the onions. Pour this sauce, making sure it is still very hot, over the eggs.

NOTE: The pieces of fried bread may be lightly rubbed with garlic.

Despite the purists, if you
take my tip you'll drink
a well-chilled dry Vouvray
throughout the meal.

Oeufs à la Toupinel

(Poached Eggs in Baked Potatoes)

When Francis Amunategui (in his *Art des mets*) classified
poached eggs *à la Toupinel* under "dishes with histories," I
don't think he realized how far he was understating the case.

According to him: "Early in this century, or very late in
the last one, a nearby theater—the Renaissance perhaps—was
opening a new vaudeville show: *Feu Toupinel*. The Restaurant Maire, hoping topicality would mean publicity, launched
its *oeufs Toupinel*. And delicious they are."

But the vaudeville show in question, Alexandre Bisson's
Feu Toupinel, first performed February 27, 1890, was at the
Vaudeville Theater on the boulevard des Italiens—replaced in
1925 by the present Paramount cinema.

So it was rather a long way from the *Feu Toupinel* theater to the Restaurant Maire, which occupied the corner site at
the junction of the boulevard Saint-Denis and the boulevard
de Strasbourg.

But was it there that eggs *à la Toupinel* was in fact created? Apart from Amunategui's statement I can find not a
scrap of evidence one way or the other.

"The Restaurant Maire enjoyed a great reputation," he

194

goes on, "and I can remember it being spoken of with great respect at home, when I was still very young. I even remember having been taken there once. The dining rooms were upstairs on the second floor, as I recall. The decorations impressed me a great deal, but the whole thing is very vague in my memory and in any case totally devoid of interest."

But that's just it, it isn't!

For one has to go even further back than that to place the Maire. In 1867, on the occasion of the Exposition Universelle, there appeared a publication entitled *Paris-Guide*. In it, a certain August Luchet provided a panorama of the capital's great kitchens and cellars. Of the Restaurant Maire, this *Paris-Guide* said: "This is a good tavern that once had a better reputation than it does now, but is still to be recommended for its Mercurey, its *entrecôte bordelaise*, and its *macaroni Périgueux*."

Héron de Villefosse, writing later in his *Histoire et géographie gourmande de Paris*, quotes Luchet, then adds that he himself has never tasted *macaroni Périgueux*, and that in 1867 the chef at the Maire had not yet invented the lobster Thermidor that was to owe its name to Sardou's play of that name.

But alas for M. de Villefosse, though lobster Thermidor was certainly dedicated to the playwright he mentions, it was not by the chef of the Restaurant Maire, but by Tony Girod, head of the kitchens at the Café de Paris.

So where Héron de Villefosse has slipped up, where Amunategui seems a trifle hesitant, it would be at the least unwise to claim certain knowledge.

Whatever the truth, however, the Restaurant Maire certainly continued to prosper. Though even so, in Adolphe Joanne's *Paris illustré* of 1875 it is listed only among the second-class establishments (along with the Boeuf à la Mode, Père Lathuile, and Ledoyen's), though with the added comment that its wines were quite remarkable. Goncourt dined there (see the *Journal*) on October 19, 1855, and in the following year, on August 1, was there again, this time with the poet Banville, known as a gourmet, as his guest. He notes: "Banville, even before the Chambertin, a delightful talker displaying the finest irony, the most amusingly malicious barbs."

In November of the same year the Goncourts dined "with the crayfish boiled in herbs and resembling a plaster for Macbeth's witches to put on the bruises they'd got on the way to a sabbath." The devil they were! That puts a very different complexion on things! What is the explanation? We find it a little further on in the famous *Journal:* "Ah, that Restaurant Maire! In about 1850, in the days when it was just a wine merchant's and there was just one tiny room beyond the zinc-topped counter that could just about hold six people if they squeezed together. And there old Père Maire himself used to serve people of whose culinary taste he had a high opinion with a mutton stew *aux morilles*, or an indescribably magnificent *macaroni aux truffes*, using real silver plate, and producing several bottles of those pretty little Burgundies from King Louis-Philippe's cellar, which he had bought up almost in its entirety."

So there you are: the Mercurey and the *macaroni à la Périgueux* of the *Paris-Guide* obviously. But the Goncourts, as we know, had somewhat higher standards than Parisian journalists!

And none of that is any proof at all that by 1890, having changed owners or chefs, the Restaurant Maire had not become one of the great restaurants again.

Which is why, since we lack any further information, we must accept that it was the birthplace of poached eggs *à la Toupinel*—the dish that provoked this discourse, a dish that ranks among the very best I know, a dish that you will almost never find on a restaurant menu.

Oeufs à la Toupinel

8 potatoes	8 tsp lean minced ham
1 tbs butter	8 poached eggs
2 tbs heavy cream	breadcrumbs
salt	Parmesan
nutmeg	melted butter
1 scant cup Mornay sauce	

Select large, well-shaped potatoes. Bake them in the oven. With the point of a sharp knife cut a hole in each of them and keep the piece of skin you have removed. Remove two-thirds of the inside of each potato with a spoon, then mash it in a bowl with the butter, cream, a pinch of fine salt, and a pinch of grated nutmeg. Replace this mashed potato in the skins, leaving a cavity in the center into which you then place in each potato:

1. 1 teaspoon of Mornay sauce
2. 1 teaspoon of lean minced ham
3. A warm and well-drained poached egg
4. Over the egg a tablespoon of Mornay sauce
5. Over the sauce a scattering of fine breadcrumbs and grated Parmesan in equal proportions
6. A few drops of melted butter

Place in a hot oven to brown.

Mont Saint-Michel

MENU

*Omelette de la Mère
    Poulard
Gigot rôti
(Roast leg of lamb)
Tarte aux pommes
(Apple tart)

And since we are in Normandy,
why not a bottle of hard
cider with it?

Omelette de la Mère Poulard

(Mother Poulard's Omelet)

The egg and us . . .

Dr. Bécard, that eminent cardiologist and gourmet with
the winning tableside manner, has given a great deal of study
to that closed world, that miracle food, the egg. He, after all,
was the man who invented a spit that would enable us to cook
eggs in their shells without putting them in noxious water that
will seep through their porous shells.

The things that appear simplest at first glance are often
the most difficult in practice.

It was from Dr. Bécard—one spring evening, in the tiny
garden of his house on the boulevard Berthier—that I learned
the secret of a good omelet.

One of the secrets of success, he told me, is to use a
good enough frying pan, which is to say a thick pan, one
with a strictly flat bottom, in no way concave, convex, or
any mixture of the two, so that the butter will be evenly
spread and the eggs prevented from sticking to any bumps not
coated with fat.

And he added: "Don't stint when you're buying your
pan. It should cost a lot of money but last you all your life."

Lastly, he added the following two axioms:

1. The pan should never be used for anything but omelets.

2. The pan should never be washed.

He was being excessive, I admit, because you can use the same pan for *crêpes*. But nothing else. And you must clean your pan with a pad of newspaper while it's still hot. With a little coarse salt to rub away any egg that has stuck to the sides. Lastly you must oil it so that it doesn't rust and wrap it in paper till you want to use it again.

The good Dr. Bécard also said: "It is easier to make two omelets of three or four eggs than one of six or eight."

Finally, he advised me to fold it in three, like a napkin, in order to close it completely.

The omelet is, as it were, the egg in its sublime state. Whites and yolks beaten separately, then mixed together (*oeufs meslette*, from *mesler*, "to mix," is how the word "omelet" began life) and projected into the sky of appetite to form a permanent constellation. To this egg omelet (and please don't smile at that expression: my grandmother, to amuse me, used to stuff a delightfully runny one with roundels of hard-boiled egg, as though piling Pelion on Ossa), many things may be and are added, until the egg itself is sometimes nothing more than a forgotten memory.

But let us avoid such niggard confections, such as the one in which Parmentier (who developed potato culture in France)—as though using some lark *pâté* as a model—invites us to balance two pounds of potatoes against a single egg.

You would like a few omelets?

Aux fines herbes (parsley, chives, tarragon, chervil, and so forth), it is a song of spring in the kitchen garden.

Aux champignons (which includes various kinds of mushrooms), it is enriched with the hidden aromas of the woods.

Aux truffes, it becomes an aristocrat.

Au fromage (Parmesan, Gruyère, Comté, even Roquefort or Camembert), it becomes rustic, an apple-cheeked farmer's wife with an earthy laugh on her lips.

Aux croûtons (tiny squares of fried bread), it is a *divertissement*.

Candling eggs at Les Halles, Paris, at the turn of the century

Aux rognons (beef, veal, or sheep's kidneys previously roasted and diced), it becomes citified—and very much on the right side of the tracks.

Au macaroni (cooked *al dente* and cut up into small pieces with grated cheese), it is showing off.

With bacon, or ham, or sausage, or black pudding, it resembles the burning halo of St. Anthony himself.

A l'oignon (the onion first gently cooked in butter), it has a hint of the rather bored lady-about-town reviving her spirits in the early hours.

With asparagus tips or *petits pois*, it is a *Vogue* model wandering in a kitchen garden.

A l'italienne (stuffed with a paste of garlic, anchovies, and capers crushed in olive oil and tomato sauce), it is a Mediterranean adventure.

With shellfish (oysters, mussels, cockles, or scallops previously blanched), it is a pact signed with Amphitrite.

With chicken livers, it is the quintessence of the hen run's true glory.

With spinach and ham, it is called Viroflay.

And what about that dish of such interest to Brillat-Savarin, the *omelette du curé*, which mingles in its eggy

womb the soft roe of carps and fresh tuna fish? And all the dessert omelets, with sugar, with fruit, with jam? Richly stuffed with the gifts of Pomona, they are often set aflame with alcohol, as though being offered up as sacrifices to the god of good eating—though there are times when such things can be taken too far. A mere drop of liqueur should suffice to impart a fragrance, and in the sweet-tooth department it is perhaps the *omelette de printemps,* enriched with a few chopped acacia flowers and a drop of kirsch, that is the perfect model.

For the omelet is first, is foremost, is above all the egg.

And that is why the *omelette au naturel* always has my true preference.

Someone wrote once: "Mother Poulard's omelet has attracted more tourists to the Mont Saint-Michel than the famous Gothic church on top of it or the dramatic sight of the inrushing tide." Though he was quite wrong, since without the site there would have been no omelet, because there would have been no Mother Poulard: one doesn't open a tavern in the middle of nowhere.

This prodigious architectural and natural whole, unique in the world, arrowing upward from the sands of that vast Breton bay, the flaming choir of the abbey, those solid ramparts and those delicate terraced gardens, that spire like a cry of hope directed up to heaven, all have as their culinary but terrestrially pure symbol, however carnal, Mother Poulard's omelet.

But who was she, this Mother Poulard? She sold her business in 1904, I am told, and died on May 7, 1931, still in retirement and at a great age. At the beginning of the century she was charging two francs for an omelet, ham, a fried sole, cutlets of salt-meadow lamb, chicken roasted over a wood fire, a salad and desserts (cheese in those days counted as part of the desserts), with cider and butter on the tables included.

All dishes of a simplicity verging on austerity. A menu in profound harmony both with the celebrated omelet and the setting.

Omelette de la Mère Poulard

10 eggs
¼ lb butter

2 tbs heavy cream
salt and pepper

Break the eggs. Separate the yolks from the whites. Beat them separately.

Melt the butter in your omelet pan over high heat. Don't let the butter darken. Pour in the beaten yolks. As soon as the yolks begin to solidify pour on the cream, then the whites, shaking the pan all the while.

GAME AND POULTRY

A fairly full-bodied wine, such as a Châteauneuf-du-Pape, should go perfectly with this dish.

Dindon Farci *(Roast Stuffed Turkey)*

"Nay, it is true, or else I am a Turk," Othello cried. By which he meant, of course, that a Turk was the last thing he was. And that, I am afraid, is also true of the turkey, which in fact came to us from Mexico.

It was discovered there by the Spaniards; and the Jesuits domesticated it on their New World farms. It was they who later imported it into France. Or so the legend has it; and for a long time, in certain regions—and we have Brillat-Savarin's evidence that it was so in his day—turkeys were in fact usually referred to as *jésuites*.

Alexandre Dumas is alone in claiming that our turkey was known to the Greeks. It was brought into that country by Meleager, king of Macedonia, he tells us, where they were called *meleagrides*, and Sophocles, in one of his lost tragedies, introduced a chorus of turkeys lamenting Meleager's death. But despite the description in Pliny it seems likely that these Greek turkeys were in fact no more than guinea fowl.

Dumas also says that the ships of the rich merchant Jacques Coeur brought back the first Indian turkeys from that country to the court of Charles VII in 1432. But Dumas was

Boilly: The Gourmand

never stinting with his imaginative powers, as we all know to our delight, so let us leave him for a moment and make a note of the following—absolutely reliable—date: November 26, 1570.

On that day, at Mézières, King Charles IX was married to Elisabeth, daughter of the Emperor Maximilian II. And at the wedding feast they served the very first turkeys ever to be seen in France. Moreover, we know that the young bride found them so succulent that two courtiers, the lords of Mesmes and Biron, declared that the raising of such birds ought to be encouraged in France.

Shortly afterward the Jesuits—yes, those Jesuits again—succeeded in introducing a breeding stock of the birds at Bourges; and soon its products were infiltrating the whole of France. Apropos of which, here is another comment from Dumas: "Some people with a poor sense of humor have got into the habit of referring to turkeys as Jesuits. No wonder turkeys always seem to be in such a temper."

From Mexico the turkey also spread northward into the United States, where Brillat-Savarin encountered it during his exile. It was love at first sight. "It is the finest gift the New World has to offer the Old," he was to say. And he gives us an account of a turkey shoot "among the Illinois." Or so Dumas would have it. In fact, the shoot took place in Connecticut.

At this point I must make a confession: relations between the turkey and myself leave something to be desired. I even wrote one day—Comus forgive me!—that its flesh has a taste of old legionnaires, which is a terrible insult to the memory—fading now—of our legionnaires and also, to boot, totally unjustified, since I have never eaten one. Only an old desert lion has the right to make such a remark. Nevertheless, the fact remains: I am not a *dindonophile*, as Brillat-Savarin puts it, and I am less than wild with enthusiasm over the fact that the turkey—still according to the same authority—"enjoys the unique advantage of uniting all classes of society around it."

But to continue: it was during his stay in Hartford, in October of 1794, where he was the guest of a gentleman farmer named Bulow, that Brillat-Savarin shot several gray partridges, a few squirrels, and a magnificent tom turkey. He carried it proudly back to the house and had it served up as a roast. It was "a delight to the eye, titillating to the nose, and delicious to the taste." And much good all its qualities did the poor bird.

There is one thing about the turkey, however: one need never go short of anecdotes about it.

For example, there is the story about Grimod de La Reynière, the financier, father of the famous epicure. One evening, during one of his whirlwind journeys across France, he entered a village inn, utterly famished.

"Alas!" the host informed him. "I have nothing to give Monsieur for supper."

Through the doorway Grimod could see the flames of a gigantic fire burning in the kitchen. He walked through. There were seven turkeys turning together on a spit.

"What about those?" Grimod asked.

"Ah, monsieur," the innkeeper sighed, "I'm afraid all those have already been reserved by a traveler who arrived just before you."

"And he is traveling alone, this gentleman?"

Grandville: A Banker

"Oh yes, quite alone."

"Heavens, what kind of a man is he then? Gargantua?"

"I'm afraid I can't say, monsieur."

Grimod had himself shown up to the other traveler's room in order to ask if he might share his feast. And what did he find?

"What? So it's you, my son!"

"Yes, Father."

"And you have seven turkeys roasting on that spit down there for your supper?"

"Yes, Father. It's terrible, I know, but the innkeeper didn't have any chickens or pheasants."

"That's not what I mean. Why *seven* turkeys?"

"Oh, Father, I only intended to eat the pope's noses."

Selecting only the best, is that not a sort of duty?

At any rate, you will have gathered that young Grimod was less enamored of this fowl than a certain President of the Court in Avignon who is on record as saying: "We have just eaten a superb turkey. It was excellent. Stuffed to the beak with truffles, tender as a capon, plump as an ortolan, tasty as a thrush. And we left not a scrap uneaten, not a thing but its bones."

"And how many were you at table?" a curious lawyer inquired.

"Oh, just the two of us, sir," came the answer. "The turkey and myself."

But we must call a halt there. There are just too many such stories. All of them untrue, quite probably. For how are we to accept, as Dumas claims to, the story that the reason why Boileau became a satirical rather than a lyric poet was that an angry turkey, in the writer's childhood, had somewhat mangled an important part of his person? The testiness of the bird is certainly not in doubt, or its phobia for the color red, or its idiotic vanity, but all the same . . .

Dindon Farci

1 turkey, 8 to 10 lbs
  1 cup chopped onions
½ lb butter
  2 apples
5 oz mushrooms
  3 slices fresh pineapple
2 oz raisins
  5 cups white breadcrumbs
milk
  salt and pepper
paprika
  sage
parsley
  ½ cup stock made from the giblets
cranberry sauce

Sauté the onion in some of the butter. Dice the apples finely, chop up the mushrooms and the pineapple. Soak the raisins in water and the breadcrumbs in milk. Add the sage and parsley.

Make a stuffing with all the above ingredients plus the turkey's liver sautéed in butter and mashed. Add salt and pepper and a little paprika. Add enough of the giblet stock to make the mixture workable. Stuff the bird with it.

Butter the carcass generously on the outside and place in the oven. Roast it at 325° F. for 4 to 4½ hours. Serve with cranberry sauce on the side.

MENU

Huîtres
(Oysters)
**Salmis de faisan à la Laguipière*
**Babas au rhum*

After a white Burgundy with the oysters, a red Burgundy with the pheasant. A Corton *blanc*, then a Corton *rouge*.

Salmis de Faisan à la Laguipière (Ragout of Pheasant)

The pheasant originated in Colchis, and loves grain above all other kinds of food. The Creator has endowed the male of the species with the most varied, the most silkily seductive of the colors on his palette; and I have only recently learned, from the pen of a female colleague, one further detail that I find enchanting: "The cock, although polygamous, is extremely jealous."

The cock, moreover, is what you put at the top of the "bag," the huntsman's gift. You give it to a pretty lady, who opens her eyes wide with wonder; or to a snob who knows no better and will be enchanted by it. But for the gourmet—and that of course means yourself!—you keep the hen pheasant, with her humble plumage but her much finer, tenderer, "shorter" flesh.

The pheasant can live to a considerable age but ought to be eaten in its first year, whatever the particular species: golden, silver, Amherst's, Argus, grouse, tufted grouse, or pero. The requisite youth can be recognized by a bright eye, slender claws, supple flight feathers and breastbone, and short, rounded spurs. The months of November and December are

those when its defeat leads to its greatest triumphs—in your saucepan.

I write saucepan because I feel that even the hen pheasant, when spit-roasted, is still a trifle dry of flesh. In this matter I am a Voltairian, and the three lines of the patriarch of Ferney remain my law:

"The woodcock, the grouse, and the bird from the Phasis,
  Of twenty rich stews the savory basis,
  Nose, eyes, and palate will ever enchant."

But, alas, Voltaire says *ragoût* and my recipe is called a *salmis*—I am seized suddenly by fearful vertigo. Am I about to unleash another war such as the one that tore the Kingdom of Gastronomy asunder only a few years or so ago? For when Simon Arbellot defined the *salmis* as "a *ragoût* made with wine," Charles Barrier, a great chef of the Touraine, became wroth, and summoned to his aid the authority of Urbain Dubois, author of *La Cuisine classique*.

"The game meat used in a *salmis* should at no point have boiled," was Dubois' opinion. But why should the "authority" of Urbain Dubois be more authoritative than any other? That is the problem. Why, for example, should it outweigh that of Alex Humbert—that prince of saucemakers, who seems to hedge slightly over the question—or that of chef Raymond Oliver, who quite unhesitatingly identifies the *salmis* "in practice" as "a sort of *civet*," while Littré adds (authoritatively I need hardly say) that *civet* means *ragoût*.

But where does this word *salmis* come from? From pre-classical cookery, Escoffier tells us. Rather vague, isn't it? Littré is mute on the point. The Larousse. on the other hand, is quite definite: "A *salmis* is a *ragoût* made with items of game previously cooked on a spit." And it adds that the word is an abbreviation of *salmigondis*, though without offering a

definition of that word. The dictionary of the Académie des Gastronomes, on the other hand, serves the *salmigondis* up as a *ragoût* of leftovers, and the *salmis*, its derivative, as a careful preparation of game that has previously been incompletely roasted.

Well, with a smokescreen like that I can afford to make a fool of myself! Who's to say I'm right or wrong?

But it is time we returned to the pheasant himself, to the cockbird with that bearing so full of nobility, that tail so proudly, almost nonchalantly draped behind him as he goose-steps on in slow and arrogant motion. He makes me think of Jacques Brel's song: "For an hour, one little hour, to be handsome as a god, and dumb!" Because the pheasant is stupid. The Creator, so Emile-Louis Blanchet, a great hunter and gourmet, tells us, "forgot to finish off his brain." Some of the compartments are still empty. In mist it will lose itself with an amazing facility, rushing wildly out into the open plain instead of taking shelter in the wood where it lives. And as a final proof of its stupidity—and it often does prove final—this proud dandy will start singing just when he ought to be keeping his beak shut: in the evening, just underneath the tree where he's decided to roost. An invitation to bright, night-seeing eyes and watering mouths.

But let us not leave our huntsman without a last word of advice. A number 5 or 6 cartridge is best, but be warned: the pheasant goes up very quickly from the ground, so stick to the rule: tail, head, fire! Otherwise you will miss him. Or blow off his tail and perhaps even his feet. In which case your bird will continue its motorcycle noise, and his frightened "coc, coc, coc" will disappear over the hedge and leave you standing there frustrated and sad of heart.

The French word *faisandage*, meaning the "hanging" of game generally, obviously derives from *faisan*, the word for pheasant. Not surprisingly perhaps. But it is a subject that

merits going into a little. When absolutely fresh, the flesh of the pheasant—and in that I include the flesh of the hen pheasant too—is, I must repeat quite plainly, tough and rather tasteless. But this flesh will grow tender and tasty in the course of its mortification.

Mortification, however, is not the same thing as putrefaction. If the bird has been killed by just one or two pieces of shot, not ripped about by the complete contents of a cartridge, then its carcass will be gradually permeated by non-toxic microbes, spreading outward from its own intestines, that will partially break down its muscle fibers while at the same time impregnating them with a certain scent. This is the scent of true *faisandage;* and because it is so distinctive in the pheasant, this bird has lent its name to the process in general. But if, on the other hand, the bird has been badly damaged by your gunshot, then the torn muscles will be infected by toxic microbes from outside, and the putrefaction that will then ensue is both dangerous and malodorous.

Having no wish—unlike Brillat-Savarin—to wait for the "breakdown into the ultimate savor," we shall leave our pheasant to hang for a few days only. Three at least, six at the most.

And *ragoût* or not, we shall prepare it according to this recipe devised by Laguipière.

Unrepentantly, moreover, since Carême himself wrote of that great cook that he knew how "to add a dash of genius to his sauces."

Salmis de Faisan à la Laguipière

1 pheasant	*½ cup bouillon*
thin bacon slices	*4 tbs meat gravy*
salt and pepper	*½ lb mushrooms*
¼ lb fat bacon	*3½ tbs butter*
3 onions	*oil*
1 cup red wine	*toast*
½ cup Madeira	

Remove the bird's liver and put it on one side.

Trim the pheasant and tie it up in strips of bacon. Salt and pepper. Place in the oven and roast for 10 minutes.

Remove from oven. Cut string and remove bacon. Carve off the four limbs and cut up the carcass into small pieces. Then grind these pieces in a mortar, taking care to crush the bones well.

Dice the fat bacon and put the pieces in a cast-iron casserole with the chopped onions. Sauté for 5 minutes. Add the red wine, Madeira, bouillon, meat gravy, and the ground-up pieces of carcass. Cook gently for 45 minutes.

Remove the bacon dice and strain the rest. Put the strained sauce back into the casserole. Add the mushrooms cut into pieces and the four limbs of the pheasant, also cut into pieces. Cook for 15 minutes at a moderate heat.

Heat butter and oil in a frying pan over a hot flame. Add the cut-up liver and mash it with a fork. Pour the result into the casserole. Salt and pepper to taste. Stir well.

Make some slices of toast. Spoon the pieces of pheasant onto the toast. Pour the sauce over the top.

Dürer: Young Hare

A good Burgundy from the Côte des Nuits would be best. But since the recipe hails from the Bourbonnais, why not a simple wine from the Allier—a red Saint-Pourçain?

Lièvre à la Duchambais

(Hare in Cream Sauce)

This, beyond dispute, is a recipe from the Bourbonnais, even though it does not figure as such in Austin de Croze and Curnonsky's *Trésor gastronomique de la France*.

In his little book *La Vraie Cuisine du Bourbonnais*, Roger Lallemand writes: "It is appropriate to give here the recipe for *sauce Duchambais*, a typically Bourbonnais preparation that may be served with all kinds of roasts: beef, veal, pork, poultry, and so forth:

"Brown a little lean bacon together with some chopped shallots (and if you have any meat leftovers, then add those and brown them too). Add a little flour, some parsley, chervil, thyme, and bayleaf. When this mixture is well browned pour onto it a liqueur glass of vinegar and a quart of stock. Cook for an hour and a half. Strain off the sauce and add to it a generous glass of cream. Allow to boil until the sauce is rich and thick."

And a little further on Lallemand also gives us his recipe for duck *à la Duchambais:* "Cut a duck into pieces, brown them in an iron casserole with some bacon and chopped shallot. Deglaze with half a glass of vinegar; add a little flour; place in the oven for a few minutes. Wet with stock. Cook in the oven with the lid on after having adjusted the seasoning. Before serving add a generous ladleful of cream."

But note that some people add the vinegar just before serving; that the stock may be replaced by the local red wine (Saint-Pourçain); that this way of employing flour, not incorporated in a *roux* but toasted in the oven, is a traditional medieval procedure.

But something else that should be noted is that Lallemand later gives another recipe for making a Duchambais sauce, one sent to him by a lady gourmet in Montluçon and handed down from generation to generation, we are told, for more than 150 years (which would take us back to 1817, let it also be noted, since it may prove of interest later on). And this second recipe is particularly suitable as an accompaniment to saddle of hare, rabbit, and venison.

It is extremely complicated, and also, I feel bound to add, too "artistic" in my opinion to be an authentically traditional recipe. For instance, it involves port for the deglazing, calf's liver mashed in a mortar with red wine and mustard for mixing into the sauce, and a *roux* mixed with a marinade made of olive oil (olive oil in the Bourbonnais in 1817? Come now!).

Finally, Lallemand concludes: "The name Duchambais is apparently that of a pre-Revolution parish priest."

We have since had this author-cook on the TV program *Cuisine à quatre mains*. Raymond Oliver cooked Lallemand's duck *à la Duchambais* for him, in his presence and following his recipe. It was excellent. But Lallemand didn't seem to be entirely sure about the origin of the sauce, so we appealed to the viewers.

We received a great many replies (demonstrating, incidentally, how fascinating those interested in cooking find such niceties) of varying value. The more serious among them made reference to an alternative spelling—*sauce à la Du Chambet*—which was supposed to be the name of a family and of a château in the Bourbonnais not far from Lapalisse.

And at almost the same time, by coincidence, I happened to receive a letter from Mme Lucien Lamoureux, a knowledgeable cook if ever there was one, telling me that the "*lièvre à la Du Chambet* is named after a nobleman from the Bourbonnais who made the recipe popular. And he had originally been given it by some Austrian or Bavarian soldiers who camped for several weeks near his château in 1815. I have always heard of it as a hare recipe rather than a duck one, but perhaps it was adapted in another part of the Bourbonnais."

1815! The recipe that M. du Chambet learned from his occupying troops could very well have been transplanted from Lapalisse to Montluçon. For this "authentic" recipe, as you will see, has much more the feeling of an "authentic" recipe than the other, being simpler yet at the same time more original, owing nothing, in short, to the fanciful folderols of a chef. And that this Du Chambet sauce for a hare could then have been adapted to make a sauce for various kinds of roast meat, that its spelling could well have become distorted— through ignorance of a perhaps extinct family and of a forgotten château—into the familiar Duchambais, there is nothing impossible or even very farfetched in all that.

But whatever the truth of the matter, here is the hare *à la Du Chambet* as sent to me by Mme Lucien Lamoureux.

Lièvre à la Duchambais

1 tsp pepper
  ¼ cup wine vinegar
4 cups thick cream
  shallots

1 hare
  salt and pepper
butter

Mix 1 teaspoonful of pepper and the wine vinegar into the very fresh, thick cream. Salt. Add a handful of finely chopped shallots and mix them in.

Skin the hare, then salt and pepper it on both sides. Place some pieces of butter at the bottom of the cast-iron Dutch oven in which the hare is to be cooked, then the hare itself on top of them, followed by more butter. Then pour half the sauce over it. Cover. Put very hot burning charcoal underneath the pot and cook the whole very slowly. The hare must be basted constantly with the sauce and turned from time to time so that it doesn't stick.

After about 2 hours the sauce will have been completely reduced. Nothing will be left but the melted butter on top. Skim this off carefully with a spoon.

Take out the hare and carve it into pieces. Wipe the pan with a cloth, put the pieces of hare back into it, then pour over the remaining sauce. Put the pan back on the heat for 15 minutes, stirring with a wooden spoon till the sauce becomes thick.

Take out the pieces of hare. Arrange them on a very hot dish, pour the sauce over them, and serve.

Willem van Mieris: The Cook

MENU

Salade de coques
(*Cockle salad*)
*Perdreaux en chartreuse
*Tarte Tatin

After a Muscadet with the
cockles, a trip back to
Burgundy: a wine from the
Côte de Nuits will assume
its fullest meaning with a dish of
partridges and cabbage.

Perdreaux en Chartreuse

(Young Partridges with Vegetables)

The expression *chartreuse de perdreau* on a menu seems to
me improper. It would be better to say *perdreau en chartreuse*,
though the term *en chartreuse* did once apply to many other
similarly prepared dishes, the common denominator of which
was the serving of the principal ingredient in a smooth mold
(round or oval) whose walls had first been lined with vegetables or other ingredients in superimposed rows, all of which
were of course on the outside when the dish was turned out
of the mold.

Here is what Carême says of the matter in his *Traité des
entrées chaudes:* "The *chartreuse* is assuredly the queen of
all the entrées one can serve; it is composed of vegetables and
root vegetables, but it is at its perfection only in the months
of May, June, July, and August, that laughing and propitious
season of the year when everything in nature is springing to
new life and seems to be urging us to even greater care than
ever in our operations, in view of the tenderness of its excellent products."

So why *en chartreuse?* Because the principal ingredient
(the partridge, for example) appears buried beneath a dome

of vegetables, like a monk in his cell. Though in fact, in the particular case we are dealing with here, the *chartreuse de perdreau*—or *perdreau en chartreuse*—is usually nothing more, despite its elegant title, than a *perdrix aux choux* (partridge with cabbage).

Though don't think that I consider the *perdrix aux choux* as anything but delectable. Quite the contrary! Especially when it becomes a distillation of itself. By which I mean when the cabbage is cooked along with some old partridges that give up all their savor to it and is then served, unctuously fragrant from that gift, with a young roast partridge!

There are several kinds of partridge: the gray partridge, the red-legged partridge, and in France the rare *bartavelle*. But the important thing to remember is that a young partridge can be considered as such only from the time it ceases to be a fledgling until it is twelve months old. After that it is a grown bird (*perdrix* as opposed to *perdreau*). And from then on, according to that great hunter and gourmet M. Blanchet, "they will be much less tender and sometimes very tough, and they should be cooked *aux choux* or in a *salmis*."

Which brings us back to our *chartreuse*, even though in the best restaurants, as I have said, they will serve you roasted young birds with cabbage that has been lovingly braised in the company of some much older ones. And in the company also of slices of bacon, *chipolatas* (small sausages), sliced carrots, and—why not?—boiled potatoes. And for two pins I am inclined to add that it is the cabbage that makes it all worthwhile, and I could quite easily do without the roast partridge, however young. The cell is worth more than the monk in this instance.

Hunters will tell you that the red-legged partridge perches, whereas the gray partridge doesn't. The gray partridge scours the plains on foot; the red-legged partridge is cunning, will run when you expect it to fly, twist and turn, and vanish into the woods.

Pheasant is also served *aux choux*, or, as the chefs will have it, *en chartreuse*.

The pheasant is a dry-fleshed and to my mind much overrated beast. And the best way to counter its deficiencies is therefore to suggest having it cooked with cabbage and bacon that will soften and enrich it. It is to counteract its dryness of flesh that housewives stuff it with *petit suisse* sausages before roasting it, and also cover it with bacon rashers.

Perdreaux en Chartreuse

1 adult partridge
  fat for browning
1 large cabbage
  ½ lb piece of lean bacon, including rind
1 carrot
  1 onion
1 bouquet garni
  1 raw garlic sausage, about 5 oz
2 tbs chicken fat
  stock for deglazing

2 or 3 young partridges
  ¼ lb young turnips
¼ lb carrots
  5 oz stringbeans
½ cup small peas
  butter
¼ lb veal forcemeat
  cream
chipolatas (*small sausages*)

Brown the adult partridge in fat in a *cocotte* or Dutch oven for 8 minutes. Remove the partridge, but leave the browned fat in the *cocotte*.

Cut up the cabbage, wash the leaves, and boil them in a deep saucepan for 15 minutes with the piece of lean bacon. Remove the bacon. Drain the cabbage leaves, refresh them with cold water, then drain them again.

Line the bottom of the saucepan with the rind of the bacon piece, then put in one-third of the cabbage, the partridge, carrot, onion, *bouquet garni*, another third of the cabbage, the bacon, the garlic sausage, chicken fat, and the last third of the cabbage. Bring to a boil.

Deglaze the browning off the bottom of the *cocotte* with some stock; then pour that into the saucepan too.

Cut a circle of greaseproof paper a little larger than the saucepan, put it over the saucepan, then put the cover on the saucepan, and allow the contents to cook for 2 hours over a very low heat. But remove the bacon and the sausage after three-quarters of an hour of this braising process.

Roast two or three tender young partridges.

Cook separately, in a little stock, the turnips, the carrots cut into sticks, the string-beans cut into pieces the same length as the carrot sticks (about 1½ inches) and cooked in salted water, and the peas.

Butter a charlotte mold with plenty of butter.

Starting at the edge, arrange the turnip and carrot sticks alternately to form a pattern on the bottom. At the outer edge of the mold place a pea between each vegetable stick, and in the center put slices of sausage.

Decorate the sides of the mold, beginning from the bottom, with the sticks of turnip and carrot, the peas, and the beans. Bind them all together with a thin layer of the veal forcemeat mixed with cream, then fill the mold with the drained cabbage, quarters of the young roast partridge, bacon cut into rectangles, more cabbage, and the rest of the sausage. Press well down. Finish off with a layer of veal forcemeat.

Place the mold in a saucepan three-quarters full of boiling water and steam gently for 40 minutes. Allow to stand, then turn out the mold onto the serving dish.

Garnish with *chipolatas* cooked separately in a frying pan.

What about the old partridge, you ask? Bah, we've squeezed all the taste out of it, why not just throw it away? Or else slice up the meat and put it in a soup.

Joachim Beuckelaer: The Poultry Seller

MENU

*Coquilles Saint-Jacques
   à la nage
*Ortolans à la Robert
   Laporte
*Pithiviers

No need to stray further than
the Bordeaux region for our
wines: a white Graves
to start with, a Château d'Yquem
to end with, and with the
ortolans a Médoc.

Ortolans à la Robert Laporte

(European Buntings)

The ortolan was for many years the symbol of Epicurean richness. It was, in Grimod de La Reynière's words, "a bird whose name is ordinarily used to designate that roast reputed the most exquisite of them all."

It has since been replaced as a symbol by other dishes—caviar, for example.

Was this because it fell out of favor with gourmets? Or because the bird itself became so rare? I think the second explanation is the more likely. In the southwest, where enthusiasts deify them, these charming migratory creatures have been driven away by sonic booms. An admirable symbol this time! Modern beastliness, ignoble "progress" threatening one of the last joys of living. Ah, to go back to the Middle Ages when they burned scientists as witches!

But I digress. These little birds fly across the southwest of France twice a year (May and October), and are there trapped with lures, fattened for forty days on millet, then drowned in Armagnac before being handed over to the cook.

The little ball of fat flesh then becomes the object of what can only be called a cult, and I admit a slightly exagger-

ated one. Though I have no wish to dispute the subtlety of its light, tender flesh, which Grimod openly admitted has more delicacy than actual taste, and of which he wrote that it is "too cloying for one to eat a great deal of it." And he also added: "Its fat, though emollient, resolvent, and demulcent, does not suit all stomachs."

But this fat is also the source of the bird's merits. And the great error is to cook them on a spit, since all the fat runs out. On the other hand, the suggestion I once came across in an old cookbook that one should wrap them in bacon seems to me quite absurd. Adding the relatively coarse fat of bacon to that of the ortolan makes no sense whatever, even if one were then to add the juice of an orange, as Grimod de la Reynière suggests.

No, it is the last century that set the best example by extolling the *ortolan en caissette* as the dish most fit to serve a king.

And from Toulouse to Villeneuve-de-Marsan, from Bordeaux to Biarritz, the ortolan may be heard chirruping in its own fat in this way, in the little box of corrugated paper referred to as a *caisse* or *caissette*. But it was in Biarritz that I encountered the ortolan in its most mouth-watering form of all.

Biarritz is a seaside resort that deserves a better title. On a gastronomade it could be the central point of a radiant series of trips to savor the Basque, the Béarnais, and the Landais cuisines, all of which are so varied and contrasted with one another, a series of expeditions that would take in ortolans and *foie gras, piperade* and *ttoro, garbure* and smoked goose. And literature of course didn't wait for the Empress Eugénie to discover this toe of the Pyrenees dangling in the Bay of Biscay: Victor Hugo, Prosper Mérimée, Alexandre Dumas, Gustave Flaubert all had their affairs with Biarritz before novelist Valéry Larbaud, Louis Bromfield, Ernest Hemingway, or even Rudyard Kipling went there.

But if Biarritz is a place of fellowship, a place whose name and fare lie so sweetly on the tongue, that is largely due to the Laporte family—Robert Laporte, the father, and Pierre Laporte, the son. It was in the Café de Paris, in Biarritz, in a cultured setting recalling the Café de Paris in Paris as the last of the *boulevardiers* must have known it, that we relived Robert Laporte's "childhood in the kitchen" with him.

"In those days," he told us, "a chicken cost forty sous. You used ten to make a chicken *velouté* and there was no need of any flour to thicken it!"

And M. Laporte might also have added that he has trained his son so well that today still, in the kitchens of the Biarritz Café de Paris, not a speck of flour ever goes into the sauces. Now that is cooking!

But why are the Laportes' *ortolans en caissettes* different from anyone else's? Why, in the presence of this dish, did I imagine a "free-liver" of the Belle Epoque, nostrils aquiver, majestically fleshed, eyes asparkle, hand all indulgence, allowing his whole being to be irradiated as though by a simultaneous blaze of all the senses and intelligence together? Difficult to say. Or rather, it can't be said at all, it can't be written. It can only be felt, fork in hand.

Ortolans à la Robert Laporte

ortolans
  salt and pepper
slices of toast

goose fat
  Roquefort cheese

Salt and pepper (using freshly ground pepper) the outside of each ortolan; then place it in its little corrugated paper box (*caissette*).

Place the paper boxes, on a sheet of oiled paper, on a hotplate on your stove and allow the little birds to cook until their melted fat is sizzling (about 25 minutes).

Fry the slices of toast in goose fat. Spread with Roquefort cheese.

Take an ortolan by the head and pop it into your mouth. Pour the fat from the *caissette* over the Roquefort toast and chew toast and bird together slowly.

GAME AND POULTRY **227**

The slightly "common" side to this fricassée, its slight acidity (from the tomatoes), and lastly the eggs, which affect the taste of wine, mean that we must not go looking for a great wine or any particularly noble vintage. I would pick a Côtes du Rhône rosé—a Tavel—chilled.

Poulet Marengo (Chicken Marengo)

The time: evening of June 14, 1800. Scene: the battlefield of Marengo.

In the fading din of a battle without precedent in history, the victors are pitching camp. Their heroic charges have smashed the Austrian infantry's squares, General Louis Desaix de Veygoux has met his death, but the thoughts of the survivors are all on the life that fate has allowed them to keep. And they are hungry. . . .

Napoleon at the dinner table. An unusual picture. Of course he was still only Bonaparte then, but already the demanding, perpetually hurried leader of men was in evidence, always eating quickly and badly. He was already the figure of whom Brillat-Savarin was to say: "The irregularity of his eating habits was just another expression of the absolute will that he exercised in all things. As soon as the appetite was felt, it had to be satisfied, and his household was organized in such a way that no matter where he was or what the hour of day he had but to speak one word in order to be presented with a chicken, cutlets, and coffee."

What a contrast with Barras, the great eater; with Talley-

FÊTE DONNÉE AUX GRENADIERS RUSSES PAR LES GRENADIERS DE LA GRANDE ARMÉE

rand, the great gourmet! Napoleon was one of those who eat to live and yet never have the time to live. At the Tuileries he was almost always to lunch alone, on the corner of some occasional table, off some very simple, unseasoned dish. And he would drink a glass of Chambertin, his favorite wine, but generously diluted with water. A great deal of coffee. Was that the cause of the terrible stomach pains that were so soon to assail him—sometimes even leading to vomiting—preludes to the ulcer that was eventually to carry him off?

But today, on this battlefield, outside the tiny village of Marengo, Napoleon is still only Bonaparte. He summons his generals and orders his meal to be served while he works out the profits and losses of his victory and sketches out tomorrow's operations.

Alas! Though Dunan is there, close beside him, he is alone. Dunan is the great chief's great chef, Bonaparte's cook. He is a clever, methodical Swiss, never disconcerted. His supply system is well organized and foolproof. Several wagons follow the army wherever it goes, and inside them chickens are constantly being roasted to satisfy the master's impatience without a moment's delay.

But today the wagons aren't there.

They've got lost, somewhere in the rear, and in his own carriage Dunan has little more than a drum of oil and a flask of brandy. But Dunan is a cook with a wise head on his shoulders and a lot of imagination. He sends off a few horsemen toward Marengo, whose thatched roofs are still asmoke, half burned down by the shells. Soon his horsemen are galloping back with a few chickens from a farm plus some tomatoes and garlic from its garden. Another appears with eggs. Victory! In the twinkling of an eye the birds are plucked. They are cut up with a saber and set to brown in some oil while the garlic is being crushed between two stones and the tomatoes thrown into the frying pan without even being peeled. A spurt of brandy flavors the sauce. And the victorious general was served as befits a leader condescending to gratify his palate. The *poulet Marengo* was born, attended by a ring of fried eggs and full military honors.

Later on, crawfish were to be added. In the Jura and the French Alps they serve a *poulet aux écrevisses* less summarily dispatched and served than Dunan's but something like it. The most interesting thing, however, is that when the news of the victory reached Paris, the owner of the Grâce de Dieu restaurant on the rue Montmartre christened a veal stew he had made his specialty Marengo. And the two recipes are very much alike!

Poulet Marengo

1 large chicken
  salt and pepper
1 tbs flour
  3 tbs olive oil
1 liqueur glass brandy
  1 wineglass white wine
6 tomatoes

bouquet garni
  2 cloves garlic
6 rounds bread
  oil for frying bread and eggs
parsley
  6 eggs

Cut the raw chicken into six pieces. Season them with salt and pepper, lightly flour them, and brown them in the warmed oil in a saucepan.

Pour in the brandy and light it. Add the white wine, the peeled and seeded tomatoes cut into quarters, additional salt and pepper to taste, and the *bouquet garni*. Simmer for 40 minutes with the cover on.

Crush the garlic in a mortar. Cut six small rounds of bread and fry them in oil. Chop the parsley. Fry the eggs, also in oil.

Remove the *bouquet garni* and skim the excess fat from the chicken broth. Add the crushed garlic and mix in well.

Arrange the pieces of fried bread all around a warm serving dish with the fried eggs on top. Pour the chicken and its sauce in the center. Sprinkle with the parsley.

NOTE: You can add mushrooms to the chicken at the same time as the tomatoes. You can use shallots instead of garlic.

MENU

*Crevettes
(Prawns)*
**Poulet père Lathuile
Savarin
(Yeast cake with rum
syrup)*

A Provence rosé would go with
the whole meal. Otherwise,
after the white with the
prawns, choose a
fairly coarse-grained red to
go with the onion flavor of the
chicken: a Moulin-à-Vent,
for example.

Poulet Père Lathuile

(Chicken with Potatoes and Artichokes)

To anyone walking through the Place Clichy today it must
seem highly improbable that only one hundred and fifty years
ago there were cows grazing there on the grass of Batignolles
common. Nevertheless, on the site of the present number 7,
avenue de Clichy, there used to be a farm whose sixty or so
cows provided some of the Parisians' daily milk. The farmer,
Père Lathuile, later added a tavern, which in 1814 came under
a certain amount of fire.

Let us try to imagine the scene.

March 28, 1814. A flood of countryfolk, of peasants, flee-
ing the invading Cossack army, comes streaming through the
Clichy gate with its cattle, and camps in the streets. On the
night of March 29–30, Maréchal Moncey, who with the
Garde Nationale and the students of the Polytechnique had
set up a line of defense at the gate, made the tavern his head-
quarters. Bloody engagements then ensued. The Cossacks
were under the command of the Comte de Langeron.

Here opinions differ as to the exact role of Père Lathuile.
Did he fight side by side with the Garde Nationale? Was he
mentioned in dispatches by Moncey for his heroism? Or did

he merely distribute wine and victuals to the troops, spurred on to even greater generosity by the knowledge that what they didn't consume the enemy would loot in a day or two's time? We cannot say. A cover of the magazine *La Cuisine des familles* in 1907 shows under the caption "Defense of the Clichy Gate" a picture of the famous sign *"Au bon poulet sauté—chez le père Lathuile,"* which must have been hit by more than one bullet during those brave days.

But in 1907 the restaurant had already ceased to exist, having shut its doors the previous year.

In 1831 Lathuile's son became Père Lathuile in his turn. Then the trees, shrubs, and arbors of the historic open-air tavern began to spread their greenery. Banquets were held there and wedding feasts. Artists and writers began to frequent it. Dumas *père* was to be seen there, and the poet Béranger; then, later, Zola and Cézanne, Manet, Renoir, Degas, Monet. In 1890, in his *Journal,* a disillusioned Goncourt wrote: "Lunch at le père Lathuile's. Ah, what a decrepit old tavern it is, with its fossil waiters and its lunches that look like stage-property meals."

And indeed, it is a violently literary dish, if not actually a theatrical one, the famous *poulet père Lathuile.* It is brought in already heavily laden with memories culled from the history of art and literature. It has been painted once and for all in our little personal museum of epicurean memories, and stands out as brightly on the canvas of days gone by as a boldly outlined Manet. And indeed somewhere (I think in the Musée de Tournai) there is a Manet painting actually entitled *Chez le père Lathuile.* Our present dish does not figure in it, but the lovers at the tables have just consumed it, I fancy, even though they are now engaged in other than culinary delights, and in the background there is a waiter, old if not actually a fossil, who may well have waited on Goncourt the day before.

This chicken dish—one more in the long list of fricassées —started with the great advantage of being a farm chicken, a free-range chicken. A thing of disturbing rarity today, in our age of battery breeding, the farm chicken in those days, tasting of what it was, held the promise of a simple feast in its plump flesh, half rustic and half bourgeois, but unequaled in sheer flavor.

I ate my first chicken cooked according to the Lathuile recipe ten or fifteen years ago, in a suburb farther out than that original Clichy yet less truly rustic all the same, and in an elegantly appointed hostelry. And prepared by Raymond Oliver! It was a revelation. And something of a disappointment too, because it was too well presented, too Parisian, too much the "poor artist who's made it."

It is perhaps the weight of memories it carries with it that prevents its appearance on restaurant menus, for one never sees it there. Or perhaps its simplicity causes it to be scorned

Père Lathuile distributing provisions to the defenders of the Clichy Gate

by the gourmets, or those who think themselves gourmets. But perhaps, also, it is because good chickens are now so rare.

Poulet Père Lathuile

⅓ cup butter
1 chicken
salt and pepper
½ lb potatoes

⅓ cup artichoke hearts
3 large onions
fat for frying onions
parsley

Heat two-thirds of the butter in a frying pan.

Cut the raw chicken into a dozen pieces, season with salt and pepper, and place them in the frying pan. Cut the potatoes into thin slices and the artichoke hearts into small dice. Add them to the chicken and press down with a fork.

When you think the bottom is sufficiently brown, turn the contents of the pan out whole onto a plate; then slide it back into the pan to cook on the other side. The whole process should take about 1 hour at the most.

Cut the onions into rings and fry them. Serve the chicken by tipping out onto a dish. Pour the remainder of the butter (melted) over it, sprinkle with chopped parsley, and surround with fried onions.

MENU

*Consommé froid à la
    tomate
(Cold tomato consommé)*
*Coq au vin blanc
Fromage de Comté
(Comté cheese)
Ananas au rhum ambré
(Pineapple with dark
    rum)*

One should drink the same
wine used for cooking
the rooster. In this instance,
an Alsatian dry white. Let's say
a Traminer. It won't quarrel
with the Comté cheese
either.

Coq au Vin   *(Rooster in Wine)*

A few years ago, at the Great Gastronomic Parliament in Dijon, a worthy—albeit slightly irresponsible—assembly of chefs undertook to codify the recipe for *coq au vin.*

As if there were only one *coq au vin!* As if, like Aesop's tongue, it did not contain within itself the possibility of proving either the best or—all too often—the worst of dishes!

The origins of the *coq au vin* are distant and doubtful. The Auvergne claims that the original ancestor was made with its Chanturgue wine. Burgundy claims its invention as one of the province's glories and local traditions. But the very fact that it is the most basic of all dishes based on wine makes every vineyard in the land its home and place of origin in practice. I must insist on this: a *coq au vin* from Saint-Emilion in the Bordeaux region, or made with red Bouzy from Champagne, or with a Bourgueil from the Touraine, all these have just as much claim to seniority. Or at the very least can justifiably claim to be no less ancient than the wines themselves.

And we also find *coq au vin* made with white wines: with Vouvray around Tours, with Riesling in Alsace, with Pouilly in the Nièvre. Not forgetting, needless to say, the *coq*

NE' POUR LA PEINE

Reueille matin de Campagne

But
des gens
de Campagne
Tailles payee'

Collecteur

L'ABEILLE ou
mouche à miel

Chacun a part à
ses trauaux

LA VACHE

par son moyen l'on boit et mange

LE COCHON

Il est meprise' et necessaire

et des animaux

du paysan

LA POULE

sa journée est d'un petit prix

attributs

l'acquisition

qui ne nourrit rien n'a rien

N. Guerard inv et fecit

au champagne (whose bubbles give the sauce a sort of effervescence in the imagination and an indisputable lightness in physical fact). And I was almost forgetting—up in that north so deprived by nature in a vinicultural sense—the *coq à la bière*. Made with the beer that existed among our Gaulish ancestors long before the wine from the first vines brought by the Phoenicians of Phocaea. So that if we go far enough back through time and men's appetites, the *coq à la bière* is perhaps the "authentic" ancestor of all the *coqs au vin*.

At this point I become suddenly aware of many shameful omissions: I have not mentioned the *coq au vin d'Arbois*, or the *coq au muscadin* from Anjou, or the *coq au rosé de Provence*, or the *coq à l'irrouléguy* from the Basque country. As for the *coq au Chambertin*, that, I'm afraid, may be no more than a legend. Oh, I know that it appears on many a menu. And it looks quite impressive—not to say pretentious! For such culinary pomp seems to me indicative of a certain *folie de grandeur*. We know that you need an honest-to-goodness, goodhearted wine to use in the kitchen. But there is no need to use a *grand cru:* its delicacy will certainly not survive the cooking process.

A gourmet friend of mine—despite being fundamentally disapproving of this too often questionable dish—likes to imagine sometimes that the *coq au Chambertin* was the last meal of Charles the Bold before "a simpleton of a lord from Lorraine, ignorant of all good manners, killed him out of sheer carelessness." But that historic tableau in no way prevents far too many dishes proclaimed as *coq au Chambertin* being made with good old red wine, and being also—I unashamedly add—none the worse for it. I have my iconoclastic moments too, you see.

But back to my gourmet friend. His theory of the *coq au vin* goes roughly like this: "Poverty rather than excess of sauce. No flambé-ing and even less cream. As few mushrooms as possible but an abundance of bacon pieces and tiny onions. And lastly, the cock itself must really be a cock, and a tender, tasty, white-fleshed one."

In all of which I recognize the rigor of the gastronomer as opposed to the happy-go-lucky attitude of the chef. If he is just a little doubtful about a chicken, the restaurant keeper

says to himself: "Ah well, it will do for a *coq au vin.*" Whereas the opposite is really the truth, and many a fowl of humble origins or inadequate breeding will prove possible steamed, or roasted, eaten cold, but could never prove worthy of the true purple, of glorious death in the service of Bacchus.

Of all the *coqs au vin* milestoning a fairly long career as a sampler of such delights, it is a "literary" *coq* that has most charmed my senses—that of Mme Maigret. The wife of Simenon's famous detective was of course originally from Alsace. And so the *coq au vin* that she cooks, simmers with love, for the world-famous inspector, is a *coq au vin blanc.* (And I should like to slip in an aside here: the *coq au vin blanc* is more digestible, more ethereal, less heavy than those made with red wine.) And, moreover, a white wine from Alsace.

But even so, Mme Pardon, her friend, confesses to her one day that she detects in Mme Maigret's *coq au vin* an intangible something different, a subtle and flavorsome nuance in its taste.

"Ah," Mme Maigret replies with celestial placidity, "that's because I flavor my sauce with a drop of sloe gin."

I have tried the recipe. And flavorsome indeed it is.

Mme Maigret's Coq au Vin Blanc

½ lb lean bacon
1 tbs butter
1 tbs oil
4 large mushrooms
24 small white onions
1 fine rooster
flour

½ clove garlic
salt and pepper
2 cups dry white wine
2 tsp sloe gin
6 small rounds of fried bread
oil for frying bread
chopped parsley

Cut the bacon into middling sized dice and brown it in a saucepan in a mixture of butter and oil. Add the peeled, blanched, quartered mushrooms and the onions. Let them brown slightly. Remove them with a slotted spoon and keep them warm.

Cut the raw bird into 8 pieces. Brown them in the same saucepan. Dust in some flour as you stir and allow that to brown slightly. Then put the pieces of bacon, the mushrooms, and the onions back in. Add the half clove of garlic crushed. Salt and pepper. Pour in the white wine. Cover and let simmer for 1½ to 2 hours.

15 minutes before serving (the flesh must fall easily away from the bones) add the sloe gin. Check the seasoning and finish cooking with the lid off.

Fry the rounds of bread in oil. Arrange them around the dish. Sprinkle with chopped parsley.

NOTE: Obviously a chicken can be used but the taste of a rooster is better. The garlic is optional, but it does give the dish a lift. Steamed potatoes may be served with the *coq au vin*.

Since the *pithiviers*, an almond
cake, goes extremely well
with a fragrant white wine
(such as the Sancerre Sauvignon
wines), and since such a wine
will also not disagree with
the mussels, you can
serve one wine throughout the
meal. If you wish to drink a
red wine all the same, then
choose a light one, a
Beaujolais or a Loire wine.

Lapin en Gelée (Jellied Rabbit)

What a curious beast the rabbit is—in a saucepan!

In his hutch he is sweet, amusing, endearing. One is always happy to go and pay him a visit, to smile at the way he
wrinkles his nose, at the way he sometimes seems to lose con-
trol of those long ears. One feels one wants to stroke him, and
one pities him—a little—this household servant who seems to be
nibbling away at his bonds with such patience.

One wanders away with tender murmurs of: "Poor animals. And to think people eat them!" Except that people
never do eat them.

You won't find them on the menu in a restaurant. One
can only suppose that the chef would be too ashamed! In the
home it remains merely the occasional dish, product of a sudden whim, but certainly not one that you would think of
carefully preparing for a guest. The lady of the house would
really never stoop so low!

But, in heaven's name, why? Is it because the rabbit
makes us think, first and foremost, of the rabbit stew, the
gibelotte?

For the *gibelotte* is a concierge's dish. In the older streets

Grandville: "Ah, I've got you, my rabbit!"

of Paris, those tunnel entrances and those sticky stairways are sometimes enriched by slightly vulgar but nevertheless rare aromas. It is the hour of the casserole, the stew, the *civet*, the rich concoction of leftovers, as Balzac, the poet of such things, more or less put it. The *gibelotte* is at home in such places. Mme Cibot, the concierge in Balzac's *Cousin Pons*, was a past-mistress of it. In Paris, the tame rabbit, the rabbit from the hutch in the yard, is the poor man's game. But even there its sway is already weakening: modern concierges' lodges are bright and airy, and the grill is replacing the casserole.

Faced with these inroads, the *gibelotte* withdrew a little to the outdoor taverns on the outskirts, Paris's countryside. There it found suitable companions in light white wine and merry airs played on the accordion. For young girls just in bloom, feeding themselves on French fries and strawberries and cream, it was served with—of course—French fries and a salad. The iron tables beneath the spring leaves were dappled with golden money. The *gibelotte* beside the Marne, beside the Seine, beside the Oise, made no attempt to conceal its hand: onions, mushrooms, diced bacon, and that slightly acid

flavor of cooked white wine. But even there the *gibelotte* is now in eclipse, and the girls consume the fashionable grill.

In ten years of culinary prospecting, hunting the chitterling sausage and the *navarin* (mutton stew) in every corner of the capital, I came across rabbit once. No, twice. Not in a *gibelotte*, needless to say! Only the back meat was served. In the first place it was cooked *à la moutarde*, and very simply and well. In the second it was roasted with herbs, and faced with that enormous lump of dry, tough, stringy flesh, I wondered whether I had perhaps been served one of those fabled giant rabbits, the terror of every Australian farmer.

And that reminded me of the remark once made by one of my colleagues in the pursuit of the pleasures of the table: "In Australia they abhor the rabbit, in America they despise it, everywhere else they blithely ignore it. It needs the air, the grass, the sky of *la belle France*, those little hutches built out in the yard between the laundry boiler and the thrown-out bed, to make a really fine rabbit with truly tender white flesh."

Perhaps, dear colleague, perhaps, and yet I am rather afraid that the cult of the rabbit is dying out here too. Except perhaps as regards the so-called rabbit terrines. But how is one ever to know just what exactly has gone into a terrine?

All the same, it is certainly true that *lapin en gelée* is a tasty dish. In an epicurean topography of Paris it has its clearly defined area. It begins to emerge on the first slopes of Montmartre—something else that is now no more than a shadow of its former self—and comes into full bloom on the Butte itself, beneath the last pleached eating arbors where, naturally, more Beaujolais is now drunk than Argenteuil or Suresnes, those merry wines of yesteryear.

Older Parisians will remember the *lapin en gelée* of Mère Adrienne, on the rue Sainte-Rustique. Ah, what a coincidence of names there! For if ever there was a delicately rustic dish, is it not this one? But Adrienne's recipe was a little complicated, and I am fairly certain that it took three rabbits to serve up one, so that, like the celebrated duck at the Tour d'Argent, it is a little excessive for our less lavish age.

I prefer to give you a simpler recipe. And to ask you, to beg you, to go down on my bended knees to you, not to turn up your nose at it. With a salad from the garden sprinkled with fresh chopped tarragon, and a cool wine from a bottle in a pail of cold water, the *terrine de lapin en gelée* is worthy of anyone's respectful attention. Believe me.

Lapin en Gelée

1 rabbit
  salt and pepper
1 whole clove
  1 clove garlic
2 onions
  2 carrots

parsley sprigs
  thyme
1 qt dry white wine
  3 egg whites
1 tsp beef extract
  1 tbs Calvados

Skin, gut, and cut up the rabbit. Put the pieces, including the head, into an earthenware casserole with salt, pepper, the clove, the crushed garlic, the sliced onions and carrots, the parsley sprigs and the thyme. Pour on the white wine and leave to marinate with the lid on for 48 hours.

Remove the rabbit pieces but leave the head in the marinade. Add to the liquid three beaten whites of eggs and a spoonful of beef extract. Bring to a boil. Check the seasoning and strain through a fine strainer.

Arrange the rabbit pieces in an earthenware casserole. Pour the Calvados over them. Pour in the strained marinade, which should more or less cover the meat. Cover with the lid and seal it on with a flour and water paste. Cook in a slow oven in a steamer for 3 hours. Remove the lid and allow to cool before placing in the refrigerator to jell.

Henri IV at the home of the miller of Lieusaint

The "native" wine of the
poule au pot from the Béarn is
the Jurançon. If that is not
available, choose another red
wine. But not a great wine.
A full-bodied but light
one would be best (a Cahors, or
a Beaujolais of the
Moulin-à-Vent type).

Poule au Pot (Chicken in the Pot)

The good King Henri IV wanted a France in which every
family would have a chicken every Sunday to put in its pot.

To tell the truth, he himself preferred the delights of
garlic soup, but we must suppose that princes enjoy Graces
of State—for Henri's heady breath did not displease the beauties of the age.

The *poule au pot* dated from long before that age of
course. Back to the day when the first caveman found out
how to make vessels he could boil water in. The spit is the
first tottering step of the culinary art. Then the broth; then
the first sauce. In the Middle Ages all meats were boiled in
the first place; then prepared for the table afterward, either
grilled or dressed with a sauce.

Thus boiled meat—and therefore naturally enough the
broth obtained by boiling meat—was already a traditional dish
in town and country alike. One had a pot and into it one put
whatever came to hand and whatever one's means permitted:
beef, pork, poultry, or all three. Or simply vegetables with a
little bacon. In picking the *poule au pot* as a fitting Sunday
dinner, Henri IV was simply wishing the poorest in his realm
enjoyment of the middle-class dish *par excellence*.

Years ago now, in the kitchen book of a food-loving lady from the Béarn—who had inherited it in turn from her great-grandmother—I remember finding an extremely full recipe for the "genuine" *poule au pot*. There are no doubt hundreds of different recipes, all "genuine," from every province in the fair realm of France. Nevertheless, this one's simplicity spoke loudly in its favor.

"Take," the book said, "a chicken neither too young nor too old (about two years old), a quantity of fairly fat bacon with which to cover it, 200 grams of raw Bayonne ham, and all the other necessary ingredients . . ."

I must confess that I find this mixture of precision and wanton vagueness very fetching. Further on, when it came to singeing the bird, the forthright old lady insisted on the exclusive use of spirits of wine because, she said, one should "beware of spirits sold for burning whose excessively low price betrays the presence of wood alcohol, which, smoking as it does, exposes you to the same risks as using paper for your singeing."

The broth had to be served on sops (slices of bread), and the bird itself, disencumbered of its covering of bacon, surrounded by its vegetables and with coarse salt.

With it you were required to drink red Jurançon, the wine with which the Henri IV-to-be had been baptized.

Our chefs have naturally embellished this humble but priceless recipe. In a stuffing worthy of the name simple breadcrumbs have been replaced by truffle, ham by *foie gras*. Perhaps that was how the *poularde demi-deuil* came into being—so called because its flesh, swollen with generous slices of truffle in many places, has taken on a tint of ivory inlaid with ebony by the time it emerges from the pot.

But it was women, France's cooks, the "Holy Mothers" of Lyons, who nevertheless brought this flavorsome dish to its peak of perfection. And one of my friends from the Lyonnais once told me how, as a child, he was taken by his father to eat in a humble bistro whose shutters bore the legend: "Fillioux, Wine Merchant."

In the dining room old Madame Fillioux herself appeared, he said, "brandishing her legendary little knife, merry as a grig, nimble, allowing no customer to feel left out, holding

sovereign sway among her staff. She carved our bird and deposited on my place a portion that would have made a hungry trooper blench."

And the old lady was only too glad to tell you her secret: "The important thing is to put a minimum of twenty birds to cook all at the same time—carefully selected ones, of course, and they must be from Bresse, nowhere else!—so that their different aromas all mix together and soak into one another."

And Alexandre Dumaine, that great chef of Saulieu, extrapolated, if I may so express it, from this postulate of Mère Fillioux's. He too used to cook several fowl at the same time, thereby producing a fragrant broth. And that broth, concentrated to the nth degree, then served him in the cooking of another, single fowl, on red-letter days. It was not cooked vulgarly *in* the liquid though. Oh, no! For this sacred bird Dumaine had invented a sort of tripod that stood inside his copper casserole. And on that sacred tripod the truffled stuffed bird would be reverentially set. The broth was brought to the boil, and the vapor it gave off, its very essence, rose to caress the succulent flesh before encountering the hermetically sealed lid of the vessel, gathering there, and falling once more in suave and redolent tears. Imagine the quintessence of the morning's fowl impregnating the new victim, cooking now in the grandeur of its solitude, in that transmuting mist. How could the result be anything other than perfection?

Basically, of course—the prosaic among us remark at this point—the result is simply a poached fowl—simply the old-fashioned *poule au pot* of yesteryear.

Of course! And the recipes are infinite—or almost. You only have to open the nearest cookbook to find recipes for chicken *à l'allemande* (poached, then covered in a *sauce allemande* with the addition of some of the reduced broth), *à l'aurore* (served with a *sauce aurore*), *à la Chivry* (covered in *sauce Chivry*), *à l'estragon* (covered in a tarragon sauce thickened with arrowroot), *aux huîtres* (covered in a *sauce suprême* containing poached oysters), *à l'indienne* (covered in *sauce indienne*), *à la Nantua* (covered in Nantua sauce), *à l'anglaise* (poached, surrounded with cooked tongue and boiled vegetables, and covered in *béchamel* sauce), Renaissance (served with a Renaissance garnish and covered with a *sauce suprême* flavored with mushroom essence), Stanley (covered with sauce Stanley), and so forth.

But ought we not to see it as precisely the wonder of this age-old family dish that it has in fact given rise to so many variants. The art of cookery has taken this *poule au pot* that a goodhearted king wished all his subjects might enjoy and embroidered on the theme a thousand rich inventions.

Poule au Pot

1 fowl
½ lb raw ham
3 eggs
  salt and pepper
grated nutmeg
  1 tbs shallots
1 clove garlic
  parsley
tarragon

1 tbs breadcrumbs
  3 tbs milk
sliced bacon
  5 oz carrots
¼ lb turnips
  1½ tbs the white part of a leek
1 onion spiked with a clove
  1 stalk celery

Pluck, singe, and gut the bird.

Chop the liver of the bird and the ham into small pieces.

Break three fresh eggs into a small bowl, beat them lightly with a fork, add a little salt and pepper, and a pinch of grated nutmeg.

Peel the shallots and garlic and chop them finely with the parsley and the tarragon.

Soak the breadcrumbs in cold milk.

Mix in a bowl the beaten eggs, the bread soaked in milk, the chopped liver and ham and the chopped herbs. Mix together well.

Stuff the bird with the result. Truss the bird and cover with bacon.

Pour 3 quarts of water into a tall pan and add to it the claws and the cleaned gizzard of the bird. Bring to a boil. As the water boils add the bird, then wait for boiling to recommence. Skim. Salt moderately and simmer for 1 hour with the lid on but not sealed.

After this hour of simmering add the carrots, the turnips, the white of leek, the spiked onion, and the celery. Continue to cook for another 1½ hours.

N O T E : If you wish to add potatoes to the vegetables, boil them separately.

MENU

Salade niçoise
(Salad Niçoise)
*Caneton aux navets
Tarte aux cerises
(Cherry tart)

And just one wine, a light
Bordeaux, a red wine of
Provence, or a Loire
wine (Chinon, Bourgueil).

Caneton aux Navets

(Duckling with New Turnips)

A hypercritical friend has taken me to task for having praised
the asparagus at the expense of the turnip, and even for having
been unjustly dismissive about the latter. "There are fairies to
watch over this humbler vegetable too," he assures me, "and
in particular over its true 'love match' with the duckling."

And I am only too glad to yield him his point.

Alexandre Dumas assures us that there is an aristocracy
among vegetables. And he added that the three best kinds of
turnip were those named Cressy, Belle-Isle-en-Mer, and
Meaux, even though most of those eaten in Paris came from
either Freneuse or Vaugirard.

Happy age! The only turnips you see in Montparnasse
these days are on canvas, either in picture galleries or painters'
studios. And even painting is now deserting that neighborhood, which once offered nothing but market gardens to the
gaze of the creator of *The Three Musketeers* as he made his
way out toward the Barrière du Maine (to eat at old Mère
Saguet's tavern with the young Hugo, Musset, and Béranger.

Belittle the turnip? Me? Far be any such thought from
my mind! And yet, in truth, what a strange vegetable this tur-

nip is! Ten months of the year it is no more than the humblest of private soldiers in the vegetable army, an extra, a spear-carrier, as they say in the theater of those whose names are all huddled together at the end of the cast list. It "walks on" with the other vegetables from the pot and stands around the throne of the boiling chicken or the piece of top ribs of beef. Its slightly insipid, sweetish flavor blends in imperceptibly with those of all the others. Its pallor sets off the green of the leek or the orange of the carrot like the white background of a flag. If it were not there we should miss it perhaps; but we don't really notice its presence.

And then, quite suddenly, lent a new grace by the spring, so round, so fresh, so suave in its youthfully fragrant fragility, the turnip accedes to glory at exactly the same time as the duckling, in the farmyard, is losing its down and graduating from the role of bird-child to that of victim. The turnip is no longer just a vegetable: it is *the* vegetable.

Fleeting apotheosis of this round-rooted brassica whose name, in France, has come to be a scornful synonym of everything failed and misbegotten.

It was seeing Curius Dentatus preparing his turnips for his humble supper, in the cottage to which he had withdrawn with the laurels of victory still fresh on his brow, that the Samnites realized at last how useless the bait of gold would be to tempt such frugality.

You may tell me that the vegetable Curius was cooking wasn't strictly a turnip. Theophrastus and Pliny have both already said the same thing. But I'm still not convinced.

Dumas—and I am always happy to return to Dumas—in his *Dictionnaire de cuisine* gives the recipe for turnips *à la d'Esclignac*. What can have earned this unknown the honor of lending his name to a turnip dish? I don't know and Dumas doesn't attempt to enlighten us. He merely passes on the recipe, which is, all in all, a rather ordinary one: Cut some long turnips in quarters, blanch them, drain them, put them in a saucepan with butter and sugar, pour over some stock and cook with the lid on. When they are cooked, check the seasoning, remove the turnips, deglaze the saucepan with a little meat gravy, add a little butter, and pour over the turnips.

Any statistician will tell you that there are more marriages in May than in any other month. That between duckling and spring turnips is both a love match and a marriage of reason. A classic instance. One can imagine the sages, all down the centuries, offering them as an example of the durable union. Both parties from the same rustic background, both endowed with the same freshness of soul and sweet nature. Ah, I can already hear the ironists dismissing them as bourgeois simpletons! And indeed, the duckling and turnip marriage is one of the peaks of bourgeois French cooking.

Curnonsky, who was wisdom itself and liked everything to taste of what it is, rated no dish higher than the *caneton aux navets*. Though there is no reason why one should not sometimes wish for less well-matched unions, for somewhat more tumultuous matches. Ones in which the agreement of the partners is arrived at only after violent confrontations, after conflicts that eventually melt into happy reconciliations. To connoisseurs of such conjugal storms I recommend the *canard aux cerises* (duck with cherries), another ambassador of spring. They are a somewhat Bohemian couple. Other families tend to talk about them rather. Not unkindly, though. It

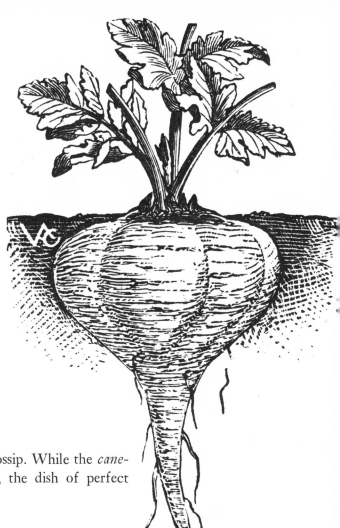

is a dish that's always good for a little gossip. While the *caneton aux navets* remains, imperturbably, the dish of perfect wedded bliss.

Caneton aux Navets

1½ oz fat bacon
1 duckling
1 lb new turnips
   pinch powdered sugar

1 onion
1 tbs flour
2 cups bouillon
   salt and pepper

Chop the bacon finely. Render it in a heavy saucepan. When it is hot and melting, brown the duckling in it over moderate heat. In 15 minutes the duckling should be a uniform golden brown all over. Remove it and keep it hot.

Into the same fat put the turnips, trimmed into olive-shaped pieces. Shake until they are browned all over, add a pinch of sugar, and continue to sauté them for a few minutes. Drain the fat from them and keep them in a strainer.

Still using the same fat, sauté the chopped onion. Add the flour and cook it brown, stirring with a wooden spoon. Pour in the bouillon. Bring to a full boil while continu-ing to stir. Then allow to boil gently for 10 minutes, skimming any fat and scum from the surface. Strain.

Having rinsed the pan in hot water, pour the strained sauce back into it and bring back to a boil. Add the duckling and the turnips. Cover the duckling with buttered paper; then put the lid on the pan. Cook over gentle heat for 45 minutes.

Remove the duckling, drain it, and put it on a serving dish. Remove the turnips with a slotted spoon and arrange them around the duckling. Keep warm. Skim any fat off the sauce, reduce if necessary, and add salt and pepper to taste. Pour over the bird and turnips.

Another "important" dinner, so we must think of wines to match. A red Bordeaux of the Graves type, say a Château Haut-Brion, or more simply a Domaine de Chevalier, would seem to be a good accompaniment to the chicken and cheeses. Nothing to drink with the lobster cocktail. And the peach Melba cries out for champagne.

Poussin Viroflay

(Squab-Chicken with Spinach)

The discovery of a new dish does more for the happiness of the human race than the discovery of a new star.

What does it matter that Brillat-Savarin's ninth aphorism was no more than an adaptation of a formula already dear to Henrion de Pansey, first to conceive the notion of an Académie de Gastronomes, "whose gaiety and wit defied the advancing ice of age"? It doesn't. The important thing was that those two eighteenth-century all-rounders should have dared to proclaim their beliefs.

It is even said that Henrion de Pansey went so far as to add, addressing the scientists Laplace, Chaptal, and Berthollet, "There are always enough stars to be seen."

And how true that observation remains today, when sheer gall is creating them at the turn of a disk and the science of death is adding its artificial satellites to our already violated skies.

But have we any new dishes?

Certainly they are rare. And even before World War I a young and revolutionary chef was saying: "The art of cooking is still centered on the same dozen or so pitifully over-

254

worked recipes. The same dishes continue to make the rounds of our tables and are merely christened and rechristened time and again with high-sounding names that we hope will disguise their mediocre uniformity. For three centuries now, no truly new dish has been presented to the world."

His name was Jules Maincave. He was killed in World War I, but not before producing the outline for a theory of mixtures and spices that had already led to the creation of a *boeuf au kummel*, a chicken cooked with lily-of-the-valley, a *noix de veau* in absinthe, and sole fillets in rum. Since then, no one has taken up the torch or attempted to lead us out of our all too beaten tracks.

For my own part, the only real inventions I have encountered in the realm of cooking in three or four decades have been a lobster *à l'orange*, a *Bresse-bleu* sauce, and this present recipe: *poussin Viroflay*.

We owe it to the researches of René Lasserre, a man who in a very few years has succeeded in raising his restaurant to a place among the circle of the truly great: it is the meeting place of the renowned Club de la Casserole and a chosen venue for the most fashionable of Paris society's galas.

Poussin, in the kitchen, means a spring chicken or squab weighing about a pound. Though the term is also applied to a strain of very small chickens, the best of which is the *poussin de Hambourg.* These have slightly insipid but very delicate flesh.

René Lasserre's recipe can be employed equally well with either kind of *poussin.* The term *Viroflay* indicates that the dish involves the addition of spinach. Viroflay, not far from Paris, was in fact as famous for its spinach at one time as Argenteuil still is for its asparagus.

Poussin Viroflay

3 squab-chickens
   1 slice stale white bread
¼ lb fat bacon
   thyme flowers
parsley
   savory
3 egg yolks

¼ lb spinach
   salt and pepper
2½ oz goose fat
   3 onions
3 carrots
   1 wineglass dry white wine
3 tbs veal gravy

Gut and singe the chickens. Split them down the back and bone them, leaving in only the drumsticks.

Pound the livers with the slice of bread. Scald the bacon, then chop it into the liver and bread mixture, adding a sprig of parsley, some thyme flowers, and 2 leaves of savory. Bind this stuffing with the egg yolks.

Cook the spinach leaves whole in salted water. Shake them dry and mix them into the stuffing. Salt and pepper it. Stuff the chickens so that they resume their original shape.

Grease the bottom of a cast-iron casserole with the goose fat. Arrange the onions and sliced carrots in it, also a few stalks of parsley. Place the chickens on top and bake in a medium oven for 35 minutes.

When the chickens and vegetables are tender, place the chickens in a heated dish. Set the casserole over high heat and pour the white wine and veal gravy into it. Bring to a boil. Adjust the seasoning and pour this gravy over the chickens.

N O T E : Puff-pastry tartlets containing asparagus tips have been suggested as an accompaniment to the dish.

MENU

*Potage Germiny
*Caneton Tour d'Argent
*Pommes soufflées
*Crêpes Suzette

Burgundy or Bordeaux? Opinion
is divided on the matter. The
fillets in the sauce cry out
for Burgundy, the grilled legs
would be better with a
Bordeaux, but . . . However,
don't be downhearted. Why not
pick a Chambertin, Napoleon's
favorite wine? You will have
no cause to lament.

Caneton Tour d'Argent

(Duckling, Tour d'Argent)

From 1582 to 1890, the bank of the Seine opposite Notre-
Dame was both the stage and the wings of history.

From the Tour d'Argent itself—built in 1582 of stone
brought down by barge from the chalky quarries of the
Champagne, stone so pale that the sunlight playing on it
seemed to turn it to silver—to the original and humble Tour
d'Argent restaurant with its wooden frame—outside the door
of which, in 1887, the new owner Frédéric had himself photo-
graphed in his intellectual's pince-nez and his heavy Victorian father style mane and beard—history with a capital H was
consistently paralleled by the history of the table.

It was hereabouts, for a start, that the fork first entered
our daily lives, in the time of Henri III, of the Italian ballets
at the Louvre, of doublets with slashed and ballooning sleeves.

And from then on, figure after figure springs to brief life:
La Grande Mademoiselle, Anne Marie Louise d'Orleáns, ordering the cannons of the Bastille fired to the greater glory of
le Grand Siècle, in the reign of Louis XIV, and the *canard au
sang* that was to oust the favorite *poule au pot* of Henri IV's
reign. Then the court gossip, Mme de Sévigné, discovering hot

chocolate for the first time, served in tiny cups that she was to look back on in later life with such nostalgia. Then the Regency, then the Court abbés and enlightened philosophers speeding toward the brink of '89. The Romantic movement explodes. Balzac comes probing and noting. Dumas brings his camellia-wearing daughter-in-law here on his arm. No, no, the man with the goatee isn't a bank clerk on the spree; it's M. France, you must know that. Anatole! That terrifying roar? The actor Mounet-Sully. That tempest? Sarah Bernhardt. And meanwhile, Frédéric, looking rather like a moral tutor, is trussing his ducklings and rising to the realm of fame, with three centuries of memories in tow.

Daudet describes him in his memoirs "with his pince-nez, his graying side-whiskers, and his unshakable gravity, cutting up his plump, already trussed and singed quackquack, dropping the pieces into a pan, making his sauce, salting and peppering the way Claude Monet painted, with the objectivity of perfect instinct and a mathematician's precision, opening up for one in advance with that infallible hand all the vistas of the palate."

For Frédéric had made over that perennial recipe for *canard au sang* and found a new way of cooking and serving it: "He has made it into a double dish, the *canard au sang* first, followed by an equally exquisite grill."

When did he first get the idea of numbering his ducklings? In 1890, very probably. And it is also probable that he entered his own name in the original Log Book—which has since vanished, alas!—as the consumer of number *one*.

Several months after that, the Prince of Wales, the future Edward VII, was devouring duckling number 328.

A quarter of a century later, in 1914, Alphonse XIII was having duckling number 40,362 dismembered for him.

I can imagine a statistician enthusiastically plotting the future probabilities of this progression of ducklings at the Tour d'Argent. But first let us skip another quarter of a century. We are in 1938, and duckling number 147,888 is being served up to the Duke of Windsor.

Which means that whereas the first twenty-five years spelt doom to a mere 40,000 ducklings, the next twenty-five involved the massacre of 100,000. Let us jump another twenty-five years, and we have reached 1963 and duckling number

15, Quai de la Tournelle   PARIS

324,047, which means 175,000 suffocated ducklings in that one quarter of a century. And in between, I note, the young Princess Elizabeth and the Duke of Edinburgh (in 1948) had devoured numbers 185,397 and 185,398. A royal appetite! And your humble servant, not very long ago, ate number 388,065.

At the present rate, an expert has calculated, the first year of the next century may well see the breathless death, on the Quai de la Tournelle, of duckling number 750,000.

Last century, the Marquis Lauzières de Thémines, a frequenter of the muses as well as of the great Frédéric's restaurant, put this recipe into verse of a kind. The result could be

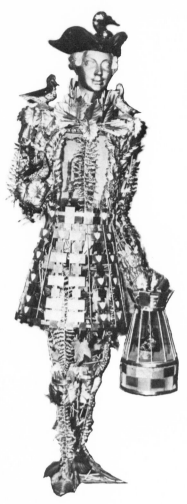

sung, he affirmed, to the tune of the popular song "La Corde sensible." The tune has been forgotten, and M. le marquis as well, but the Tour d'Argent lives on, and . . .

> ". . . There, of a duckling the carcass remaining
> By visible means they crush and reduce;
> An engine descends, and then, by straining,
> They extract a rich and delectable juice.
> And many plump slices once carved from the breast,
> They strip off the skin, serve the legs on their own
> Then far from discarding the ribs and the rest,
> The carcass is used to the very last bone. . . .

So now you can even *recite* the *canard à la presse*. Which is as it should be, since it is a very theatrical dish. So much so that a theater has now been placed in the upstairs room of the present Tour d'Argent, overlooking the Seine and Notre-Dame. Or, to be more exact, a scale model of the Paris Opéra, in which, in the backdrop, you can see the "duck-pressers" at work in a Jordaens lighting. And this spectacle, "opening up in advance all the vistas of the palate," can even make you forget Notre-Dame outside, silhouetted against the gray sky.

I have been told, and do in part believe, that in Frédéric's day it took three ducklings for every one that was served up. The recipe that follows, needless to say, has been adapted to the exigencies of our own day and age. It remains peerless nonetheless.

Caneton Tour d'Argent

1 duckling
1 cup port
1 liqueur glass cognac

1 cup consommé
salt and pepper

The duckling (6 to 8 weeks old at the most, and specially fattened during the last two) must have been killed by asphyxiation so that it will not have lost any blood. Roast it for 20 minutes or so.

Chop up the raw liver. Place it in a pot with the port and the cognac over high heat. Carve the duckling. Grill the legs. Cut the meat from the body into thin slices.

Crush what's left of the carcass in a duck press and collect all the blood. Add to it the consommé (which should ideally be made from the carcass of another duckling, and highly seasoned). Add this liquid to the liver mixture and beat for 25 minutes till it thickens.

Add the slices of duck to the sauce in order to heat them up. Serve with *pommes soufflées*. The grilled legs are then served as a third course with a salad.

MENU

Omelette fines herbes
(*Omelet with herbs*)
**Poulet à la crapaudine*
Fromage à la crème
(*Cream cheese*)

A springtime menu. Countrified, rustic, almost bucolic! You might almost think yourself under Mère Saguet's arbors. So let us try to recapture that village wine with its charming color of red currants. Try a light Beaujolais-Villages.

Poulet à la Crapaudine

(Grilled Chicken)

Isn't there something charming in the fact that in a Paris where the streets are perpetually being rechristened as soon as you turn your back—with the ephemeral names of heroes made famous by no less ephemeral events—that there still exists a rue du Moulin-de-Beurre?

And in being still able to picture for ourselves, where number seven rue du Moulin-de-Beurre used to be, the old cabaret or tavern where Mère Saguet, that simple cook of literary fame, was wont to ply her tasty trade?

We can still see the wall of her modest tavern, depicted in an 1830 lithograph, painted red and bearing this inscription:

AU RANDE VOUS
DES ROMANT [IQUES]
SAGUET
Md. de VIN TRAI[EUR]
Bon vin à 15 [sous]

And there Mère Saguet cooked away, without suspecting for a moment, in all probability, that she was fated to go

down to posterity sung by Béranger (under the name of Mme Grégoire) and painted by Courbet (in a picture to be seen in a Chicago museum).

One of her most frequent customers was Nicolas Charlet, the portraitist of Napoleon's veterans. Possibly because Mère Saguet's husband had himself served under the Emperor —indeed, had lost a leg in one battle or another, and was by this time a pensioner at the Hôtel des Invalides.

Be that as it may, one Sunday when he had been out for cakes and ale at Butter Mill farm, young Abel Hugo heard laughter and singing on his way home. He walked into Mère Saguet's cabaret, struck up an acquaintance with Charlet and his cronies, had dinner with them, and was so delighted by the place that he came back again bringing his brother Victor with him.

And then Victor Hugo brought his friends too. A sort of artists' club took to gathering there: the sculptor David d'Angers, Delacroix, Gavarni, Alexandre Dumas, Musset, and also Gérard de Nerval, Béranger, even the historian Adolphe Thiers, and Marc-Antoine Désaugiers, who was not too proud to sing for them there.

A chronicler records that Mère Saguet's cooking was "not of the most complicated: vegetables from the kitchen garden, the produce of her little farmyard, eggs, fricassées of rabbit, and chickens that she accorded only the most summary culinary treatment."

Victor Hugo has left an account of the meals his brother Abel gave there, the gigantic omelets and the chicken *à la crapaudine* that Mère Saguet hacked in two, then grilled before serving them with a piquant sauce. "And with it as much cheese and white wine as you could get through; the fare was such that we could remain at table from six till ten and leave it radiant with satisfaction."

Mère Saguet retired shortly after the revolution of 1830, leaving the business to her son-in-law, one Bolay. But not, apparently, for long, since in 1845 there was a sign over the entrance on the rue du Moulin-de-Beurre that read: "Bourdon, successor to the Widow Saguet, food and drink served."

But even if she did retire, we know that on her birthday, regular as clockwork every year until her death, she came back to "give the saucepan a stir" and to rustle up omelets and chickens *à la crapaudine* for the survivors of that merry band of yore.

> "Oft to her inn when I was twenty
> I hied to laugh and drink and sing . . ."

Béranger was to write. And the Goncourts noted in their *Journal*: "We drank a great deal of that village wine that has such a charming red-currant color."

But what exactly is this *poulet à la crapaudine?*

It is an old recipe, a traditional way of preparing small chickens or pigeons by splitting them in two, then flattening them out so that they will cook more quickly.

Treated in this way, with its limbs pressed flat, the bird assumes the shape of a toad (*crapaud*), and that is the basic derivation of the name.

There is an acrobat's trick called the *crapaudine*—also by analogy with the toad, obviously enough—in which the performer folds both legs behind his or her neck. And there was a torture once by the same name, an unpleasantness that took the form of roping the victim's limbs into much the same position.

Etymology aside, however, I have a technical culinary work here that informs me: "This method of preparation gives excellent results because it 'balls' the bird and helps to concentrate all its juices without drying the flesh up."

Grilled chicken *à la diable* differs solely in that it has been brushed with mustard before being grilled. And grilled chicken *à l'américaine* is also in fact a form of chicken *à la crapaudine*. They are simple dishes, admirably suited to the free and easy atmosphere of open-air eating and barbecues; sprightly dishes that will spur your appetites; food for merry-making.

And while you are eating them, there is nothing to stop you thinking that you are, for a moment, the familiar of Monsieur Hugo (Abel will do if you daren't aspire to Victor), Béranger's table companion, a friend of Gavarni, and a customer, in short, of our dear old Mère Saguet in her cabaret on the rue du Moulin-de-Beurre.

Poulet à la Crapaudine

1 chicken
⅓ cup butter

salt and pepper
pickle slices

Cut the chicken in half horizontally, from pope's nose to neck. Pull the two halves apart. Crush them till they remain slightly flattened. Brush with melted butter. Season with salt and pepper, then grill fairly slowly on both sides, basting once or twice with more butter in the process.

Serve with a garnish of pickle slices and a *sauce diable*.

Sauce Diable (Deviled Sauce)

2 tbs chopped shallot
¼ cup white wine
¼ cup white wine vinegar
2 tbs butter
2 tbs flour

½ cup bouillon
pepper
chervil
tarragon

Simmer the chopped shallot in the wine and vinegar till they have been reduced by three-quarters.

Make a brown *roux* of the flour, the butter, and the bouillon. Add it to the shallot purée. Boil 5 minutes. Strain. Pepper generously. Remove from heat and add the chopped chervil and tarragon.

Picasso: Still-life with Cock and Knife

I should like just one wine
with this menu: a red Arbois
with its strong taste of
humus and the earth that
produced it. Or more simply a
Saint-Amour (Beaujolais),
because its name goes so
well with the dish.

Poulet Célestine

(Chicken and Mushrooms)

The year 1860. Amalgamation of Nice and Savoy into
France. Beginnings of the liberal Empire. Abraham Lincoln
elected to the presidency of the United States. Victor Hugo
was finishing *Les Misérables*. Death of Désirée Clary, queen
of Sweden. The Jardin d'Acclimatation was opened to the
public. Labiche's *Le Voyage de M. Perrichon* opened. Baude-
laire published *Les Paradis artificiels*.

One could go on, listing anecdote after anecdote, recalling that on July 18, 1860, there was a total eclipse of the
sun, that in September Liszt made his will, that the Solférino
Bridge was being built over the Seine, and that Rigolboche
was making his début at the Théâtre des Délassements Com-
iques.

And in Lyons?

In Lyons, where the *Gazette* had received a governmental
warning on June 29, and was closed down four months later
on account of its excessive allegiance to the Vatican, on the
square that is today named after Maréchal Lyautey but was
then the Place Louis XVI, on the second story of a well-to-do
apartment house, the Cercle des Amis had just opened its
doors.

A group of young middle-class men ("in the wind," as Félix Benoit, a big eater of that town and Grand Chancelier of the Ordre du Clou put it) used to meet there. And then, since a restaurant had also opened its doors on the ground floor—and had naturally enough taken the name Restaurant du Cercle—they took to frequenting it.

The Restaurant du Cercle was owned and run by a woman, a young and pretty widow in her prime: Mme Célestine Blanchard. And its kitchen was run by a cook of considerable talent just two years her junior at twenty-eight: one Jacques Rousselot. Each was one of the prime causes of the restaurant's success.

For a love of good eating need not (I hope you will agree) cause us to stop using our eyes. And the beautiful Célestine knew only too well how to ration out her glances, how to set a heart aflame like one of her succulent *omelettes au rhum*.

But, alas, her chef himself also succumbed to those forbidden but constantly evident charms. He sighed over his saucepans and generally played the part of the lovelorn peasant in love with a princess. But the beautiful Célestine still persisted in keeping her melting looks and her heartbreaking smiles solely for the gilded youth that came to swell her businesswoman's coffers.

A sad story of despised love. And an unpleasant situation for young Rousselot, snorting with impatience and indignation on the wrong side of the kitchen hatch, peering out at his employer and Dulcinea simpering in front of her callow customers. He began to lose weight. He chewed the cud of rancor. He meditated the necessity for some decisive and dazzling feat. For the fact that one is a chef does not mean one is not also a man!

And one day, just before the restaurant was to open for luncheon, as Célestine herself was preparing to eat her noon meal, beside her till, he screwed up his courage.

Bursting from his kitchen, white hat freshly laundered and ironed, preceded by two unknowing scullery boys, he advanced majestically, and setting down a silver dish before his employer he announced: "*le poulet Célestine!*"

Eccentricity is not looked upon very kindly in the restaurant business. The Olympian brown eyebrow (why do I imagine that the widowed Célestine Blanchard must have been a brunette? Perhaps because widows always look so well in brown?) frowned in somewhat anxious indignation. In kitchens, as in barracks, the "wait for orders" principle is what makes for smooth running and quiet days. However, a pleasant aroma was by now rising from the dish. Mme Célestine took a sniff, took a helping, raised a mouthful to her sternly pursed lips and . . . married her chef!

In reality it didn't perhaps come about quite so quickly.

In reality it must be admitted that a hint of self-interest may have entered into the affair: when one has a good chef it is important to keep him, and how better to keep a chef than by binding him to you with the chains of matrimony? And besides, Jacques Rousselot wasn't just a good chef, he was also rather good-looking. And a widow of thirty, her appetites kept alive both by the compliments of her customers and the rich fare provided by her cook, must in the silence of the night, once the receipts have been counted, feel very much alone.

In reality, this *poulet Célestine* may simply have been the final chord in a nuptial symphony that Rousselot had been working out on his piano (for that is what chefs call their stoves in their own private slang) for a long while; the final assault of a heroic campaign in which the young man's silky mustache, bright eyes, warm complexion, and well-turned calf had led the lady, without her even being aware of it, to a position from which it was difficult to retreat.

But either way it is not material.

History does not say whether they lived happily ever after and had lots of children, and perhaps the contrary would be preferable. Stories with excessively neat morals have an air of immorality. The Restaurant du Cercle vanished in 1900 when the neighborhood was rebuilt. From 1860 to 1900, that's four decades. Long enough for a recipe to become both a legend and a classic at the same time.

In the long list of chicken recipes it seems to me that *poulet Célestine* deserves a place apart. Haloed with tenderness, it nevertheless remains of the earth. It is only in stories that one can live on love and spring water—unless it's a myth that people with bad digestions have disseminated. Hearty appetites go with love as mourning becomes Electra.

You could make a maxim of it: "Appetite feeds on love."

Poulet Célestine

1 chicken
  ¼ lb butter
¼ lb mushrooms
  1 large, ripe tomato
1 cup white wine
  ½ cup meat juice

1 liqueur glass brandy
  salt and pepper
cayenne
  parsley
1 small clove garlic

Cut up the uncooked bird (which must be a young and very tender one). Brown the pieces in butter.

Add the mushroom caps and the tomato (peeled and seeded) cut into big dice. Sauté for 5 minutes over a good heat.

Pour in the white wine, the meat juice, and the brandy. Salt and pepper. Add a pinch of cayenne and cook for 15 minutes.

Remove the chicken pieces and keep hot on a dish. Skim the fat off the sauce. Reduce it. Sprinkle it with chopped parsley and a little very finely chopped garlic.

Pour over the meat and serve.

MEAT

Hippolyte Mailly: Rossini

A great wine with the Rossini, if the sole will be content with just a pleasant dry white one. A Pomerol (Bordeaux) such as Château Pétrus seems a good choice, I think.

Tournedos Rossini

(Fillet of Beef with Foie Gras and Truffles)

In their *Journal*, the Goncourts report that the great composer wept only three times in his life, and that one of these occasions was when by some black chance he dropped a turkey stuffed with truffles into the Lac de Garde. Does that not suggest true *gourmandise*, raised to its epicurean apogee?

Joseph Méry, the noted journalist and man of letters, tells of a certain dinner at Rossini's at which an extraordinary macaroni was provided. And indeed there is no cause for astonishment that this man of the world, for whom the resonances of taste and smell were also music, should have given his name to a dish: the symbolic *tournedos Rossini*.

Symbolic from various points of view.

First of all, in its simplicity, which in no way excludes richness. The fillet, as we all know, is the most expensive cut of meat there is, and the *tournedos* is the most expensive part of the fillet, the *ne plus ultra*, the quintessence of the fillet itself. The true *tournedos* is in fact the "eye" of the fillet, with all the outside trimmed away, cut into slices whose thickness makes up for their small diameter. It can be laid down as a general rule that a true *tournedos* can never be more than

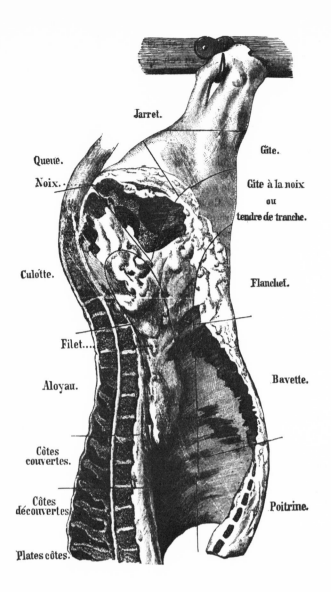

Jarret.

Queue.

Noix..

Culotte.

Filet...

Aloyau.

Côtes
couvertes.

Côtes
découvertes

Plates côtes.

Gîte.

Gîte à la noix
ou
tendre de tranche.

Flanchet.

Bavette.

Poitrine.

2½ to 3 inches in diameter. And to this "eye" of the fillet are added two other somewhat rare, very costly, yet simple ingredients: *foie gras* and truffle. Two products of French soil. Two eminently French constituents of all French "banquet cooking." But here caught in the freshness of their primal state, *au naturel*.

If he had been a poet, or a painter, or a novelist, or a sculptor, rather than a musician, I wonder whether Rossini would have "harmonized" his epicurean *tournedos* in exactly the same celestially bland way. Perhaps not. There is a kind of music in everything, certainly in every great dish. And the harmony of tenderest beef, *foie gras*, and aromatic truffle in the *tournedos Rossini* combines strings and brass in a composition at once dazzling and infinitely refined.

It is a symbolic dish too in that it is a permanent touchstone. Perfectly codified at the moment of its composition, the *tournedos Rossini* is nevertheless one of the most ill-treated recipes in the world. It is a costly dish, and whether it is from a misplaced desire to avoid ostentation or from a less pure desire to defraud us, chefs tend to impoverish it with *foie gras en purée*, out of cans, and mere scrapings of truffle skin. That's when it isn't worse still—though here we have gone beyond absurdity into the realm of deliberate fraud—as in a certain "encyclopedia of French cooking" that offers a recipe for the Rossini with pieces of bacon and tomatoes.

No, this symbol of a whole style of cooking as rich as the overtures to *Semiramide* or *William Tell*, this fanfare of flavors whose combination of opulence and rusticity is so sublimely patrician in effect, must never be sullied by additions or substitutions: away all ersatzes, all barbarians, all misers, all corner-cutters!

And lastly, is it not also symbolic that the season for fresh *foie gras* should also be that of the truffle? That the late autumn and early winter beef, still succulent from rich summer pastures, should be the best of the year? All the ingredients seem to have been fated from eternity to combine for the satisfaction of a robust appetite on some snapping cold winter holiday.

A rich dish and a rare one. Even if it were to mean paying tribute to it only once in one's life as a true lover of good food, it is still worth not bastardizing it with niggardliness and subsequent regrets. A lot of truffles and a fat slice of *foie gras*. And a great wine to go with it. Your thoughts turn to a Bordeaux, naturally. Perhaps a fragrant Pomerol, or one of those old reds from Graves, their subtle wisdom already proved by time. Though there is another wine that might form a perfect link between a *foie gras* from the Landes and a truffle from Périgord: an old Cahors.

Ah yes, if you are lucky enough to have a bottle or two still in your cellar, don't hesitate a moment. Rossini himself would have approved.

But before we leave the composer of *William Tell*, that intrepid eater and witty appraiser of everything to do with the table, I should just like to remind you that in a catalogue of unpublished works drawn up by himself and including

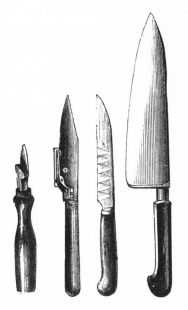

"56 semi-comic pieces for the piano" you can find two series listed as follows:

FOUR HORS D'OEUVRES
1. Radishes   2. Anchovies
3. Gherkins   4. Butter

FOUR DESSERTS
1. Dried figs   2. Almonds
3. Hazelnuts   4. Raisins

Ah, how delightful such a musico-epicurean collaboration seems on the part of the man who, in a final apotheosis, married his cook.

Tournedos Rossini

1 average-sized truffle
  1 wineglass Madeira
6 slices of bread
  ½ lb butter
6 thick slices of fresh foie gras *weighing about 3 oz each*

salt and pepper
  flour
6 tournedos weighing between 4 and 6 oz each
  strongly flavored veal stock

Wash and scrub the truffle. Put it into a small pan with the Madeira and simmer it gently with the lid on for 30 minutes.

Cut six slices of bread the same size as the *tournedos*. Fry them in 2 tablespoons of butter until they are golden. Keep them warm in a cloth.

Season the slices of *foie gras* very lightly with salt and pepper; then dust them very lightly with flour. Sauté them very quickly in 2 tablespoons of butter.

Season the *tournedos* with salt and pepper. Sauté both sides in 3 tablespoons of butter, over a moderate heat. Remove them from the pan when still very rare and put them on a warm plate.

Pour a little stock into the *tournedos* pan to deglaze it; then add the Madeira broth from the truffle. Allow to simmer for a few minutes. At the last moment add the remaining butter and whisk. Then add any blood that has run out of the *tournedos* onto the plate.

Arrange the pieces of fried bread on a warm dish. Place a *tournedos* on each, then a slice of *foie gras* and a slice of truffle on top of that. Pour the sauce over and serve.

NOTE: All these operations, and in particular the cooking of the *tournedos*, the *foie gras*, and the fried bread, should be done at the same time so that nothing has to wait too long.

There is a wine from the Sarthe
called Jasnières. It's a white
wine which will do quite
well, if you have no champagne.
If you prefer a red there's no
problem: a Bourgueil of
the current year.

Potée Sarthoise

(Meat and Vegetable Stew)

Once the first cooking vessel had been invented, this was
probably the first dish cooked in it.

First came the pot.

And the contents of the pot—which is what *potée* means
quite simply—would have been anything boilable and edible
that the caveman, whether nomadic or settled, could procure
in one way or another to put in it.

Over the centuries the *potée* may have been gradually
refined and perfected, may have taken its place in the culinary
hierarchy, risen to the rank of a great regional dish, but it
remains for all that simply one of the foundations of cooking
itself, the first dish cooked with water, the second great culinary advance, after the invention of fire had led to that first
great advance: grilled meat.

But let us leave prehistory behind us. The *potée* eventually became a sturdy farm girl; and though she sometimes
goes up to Paris for a visit, she still always wears her great
clogs.

She has the robust appetite of the peasant. She rises early
and knows the value of patience: she simmers all morning

in the hearth thinking of the men she's going to have to feed when they get in from the fields. Nothing lines the stomach better than a bowl of soup and a hunk of bread: so the *potée* is a soup. Nothing wins a heart or a stomach sooner than a dishful of steaming hot vegetables: so the *potée* contains cabbage, carrots, turnips, and potatoes. Nothing enchants an eager nose more easily than the aroma of cooked pork: so the *potée* provides it with the fragrance of bacon. For two pins, out of sheer love of humanity and dedication to duty, the womanly *potée* would turn herself into wine. And when the master pours a glass of red wine into his bowl and drinks it down mingled with the broth, it is still the *potée* whose aroma he is imbibing, whose richness he is drawing sustenance from, and whose rump he will pat with absent-minded hand in a moment or two, letting her know how much he appreciates such a good, hard-working girl.

In other words, trying to codify the recipe of the *potée*

278

would be a pretty chancy business. Though a chef may try to play fast and loose with her, it's never going to get him very far. He will always remain somehow an amateur: a Jean Gabin turned farmer, as it were. It is always the same with stars when they try to play secondary roles. They try too hard, they do too much, and the result is confused and bogus.

And there is nothing more unappealing than a bogus *potée*.

But just as there are rich landowners and poor tenant farmers, just as there are fertile plains and poor and arid plateaus, so the *potée* can either count its pennies or display a pair of plump calves; it always holds a mirror up to the soil that has produced it. The pasture, the pig-sty, the poultry run, and the kitchen garden are its very being. What they are it is: sometimes opulent, sometimes decidedly frugal. But never sham. And never proud either. A divine simplicity!

And you might draw up a map of agricultural France just from her provinces' varied *potées*.

In Berry, they make a *potée* with knuckle of ham, sausage, and red beans cooked with red wine.

In Auvergne, with the heart of a white cabbage, carrots, turnips, leeks, potatoes, and a pig's head. And they throw in a handful of lentils.

In Burgundy, you will find bacon in it, the knee and shin of a pig, the vegetables mentioned above, and a clove of garlic.

In Brittany, they add some desalted breast of pork and a smoked sausage to new cabbage and potatoes.

In Champagne, every vegetable available goes in with pig shin and pickled pork.

The *hochepot* of Flanders is a super-*potée*. Apart from top rib, neck of mutton, and shoulder of veal, you must also add a pig's ear and some pickled pork, together with all the usual vegetables plus juniper berries and a spiked onion. Some cooks also add *chipolatas*.

In the Morvan, they use beef again (top rib), shin of pork, and cervelat sausage. And they prefer kale to cabbage.

In the Landes, their *garbure*, when all is said and done, is just another *potée*. It is a cabbage soup to which are added butter beans and stringbeans, a piece of fat meat (goose or pork, or both), plus a pig's tail.

In Lorraine, they use green cabbage, carrots, turnips, leeks, fat bacon, knuckle, and rind of ham. Sometimes a fillet of roast pork too.

In Alsace, you must add celery, smoked ham, and garlic sausage.

In Savoy, the cervelat is a prime ingredient.

In Artois, over and above the pig's head you must put in some mutton breast and a chitterling sausage; the cabbage should be the green not the white sort; the beans white not red; and there should be celery and a clove of garlic.

But the most complete, the richest *potée* of all seems to me to be the one a late and lamented friend invited me to sample one particularly red-letter day, and which, in honor of both day and dish, we drank with champagne.

Potée Sarthoise

2 lbs top ribs of beef
  salt and pepper
1 onion spiked with a clove
  bouquet garni
1 pistachio-flavored sausage weighing 1 lb
  2 smoked sausages
½ lb salted ham

1 large green cabbage
  6 carrots
3 turnips
  celery stalks
1 rabbit
  6 potatoes

Put the beef into cold water to cover and bring to a boil. Add salt and pepper, the spiked onion, and the *bouquet garni*. Skim. Allow to cook for 15 minutes.

Add the pork (sausages and ham). Cook for another 20 minutes.

Blanch the cabbage in boiling water for 10 minutes.

Put the cabbage into the pot. Also the carrots, the halved turnips, the celery, and the back and thighs of the rabbit. Cook for another 40 minutes.

Add the potatoes. Cook for another 20 minutes. Skim off any excess fat and serve in a big warmed soup bowl.

C. Magini: Still-life

Illustration for Zola's *Le Ventre de Paris*

The wine I would most like to
see served with such a meal
is a little Burgundy from
the Côte de Beaune.

Navarin Printanier (Mutton Stew)

The *navarin* is indissolubly associated with the spring.

To those inclined to think of it as a quickly produced stop-gap, I should like to quote Romain Coolus's lines:

> I opine that a well-made *navarin*
> May well be signed by Savarin
> And its honest unctuosity . . .

It is that unctuosity which makes the *navarin* not merely a charming but a divine dish. Yes, I am weighing my words. For there exists in the heart of this mutton stew a spark of celestial suavity that makes it into something far more than a mere stew.

An element bestowed upon it not by its name—for who would dare to find a connection between the victory of the Anglo-Franco-Russian fleet over the Turko-Egyptian fleet on October 20, 1827, off the Peloponnese?—but simply by that springlike and gentle grace of which it is both the reflection and the very bouquet.

It must have existed before that October 20, I am certain,

even though I cannot find it in any book of reference. And in that case *navarin* would derive from what? From *navet*? From the turnip? Why not?

An old song comes to my mind:

Capped with green and swathed in white . . .
 Here is the spring!

Yes, yes, and in the moonlight, in the avenue of some extraordinary garden, I imagine the dance, not of the elves but of the kitchen garden divinities, freed from their vegetable skins and become the ballerinas of an epicurean minuet that would include the tiny round carrot, the *petit pois* already swelling with sweetness, the white Nantes turnips peeled into white globes, the onions wearing white clown masks, the new potatoes with firm yet melting flesh (if they still exist), the green beans as delicate as thistledown.

They are the springtime *navarin*'s pages, and the *navarin* is, as it were, the spell of eternal spring.

Can you say now that it is just a typical concierge's stew, born in some dingy lodge, swaddled in neighborhood gossip and overpowering smells? Certainly not. But a simple dish all the same, a dish smelling of morning dew, the breath of the earth quieted by its evening watering, and the slightly treacherous but disturbing and sweet smell of buds. "Simple pleasures," Oscar Wilde said, "are the last refuge of complicated minds." So we shall go for the recipe of the perfect *navarin*, not to a country cook who would seem to have been created for it, but to a great chef.

At a certain point in the recipe one is instructed to change saucepans. This change of saucepan, or let us say rather "vessel," was judged by Escoffier to be one of the secrets of the

dish. Why change at that particular moment of the operation? So that the meat may leave behind its unpleasant grease, its lowly color, so that it may draw in air and become lighter. It is, as it were, a change of step, the beginning of another figure in the *navarin* ballet.

And now, what meat should we use? Shoulder, breast, neck, and chump ends in equal proportions. But if you wish to go a step further, then you may increase the proportion of shoulder to a third, add a third of neck and breast mixed, and another third of best cutlets, well trimmed. And then you will have a great dish, worthy of being signed Savarin.

Navarin Printanier

1¾ lbs shoulder of mutton
1 onion
1 carrot
salt and pepper
3½ tbs butter
pinch of sugar
1 tbs flour
2 small cloves garlic
3 tomatoes

bouquet garni
12 white onions
12 turnips
20 small carrots
20 very small new potatoes
20 thin slices fat bacon
1 cup small fresh green peas
2 oz fresh stringbeans
parsley and chervil

Cut the mutton into pieces, and brown it with the onion, carrot, quartered, and salt and pepper, in a skillet in a little warm butter or smoking fat.

When the meat is well browned, drain off some of the fat. Sprinkle the meat with a very little sugar and shake over a hot flame for a minute to let it caramelize. Add a generous tablespoon of flour browned separately in a medium oven. Mix in well and cook until golden. Crush the garlic and sprinkle over the meat. Pour in water to just cover the meat. Lastly, add the tomatoes, peeled and seeded, and a *bouquet garni*. Bring to a boil then allow to cook gently, in the oven, with the lid on, for 1 hour.

When the hour is up, remove the meat from the pan. Inspect the pieces, removing any bones or fragments of easily detachable skin, *and place in a second skillet*.

Brown and glaze the onions. Stew the turnips, scooped out into little balls, the carrots, also rounded, and the new potatoes in butter for 15 minutes.

Add all these vegetables to the pan containing the meat, along with the scalded and browned slices of bacon.

Skim the fat off the original broth, strain it, then pour it into the second pan. Check the seasoning. If the sauce is too thick, thin it with a little warm water. Bring to a boil and then place in a slow oven for 25 minutes.

At the end of that time add the peas, and stringbeans cut into 1½-inch lengths. Cook for another 30 minutes.

Arrange in a pieplate. Sprinkle with chopped parsley and chervil. Serve.

MENU

Salade d'asperges
(*Asparagus salad*)
*Ris de veau Clamart
Fromage blanc
(Cream cheese)*

A Mercurey (Burgundy) will
do very well with the
sweetbreads, but a good hard
cider would be admirable too.

Ris de Veau Clamart

(Calf's Sweetbreads with Small Green Peas)

The vocabulary of the kitchen has its own, somewhat fanciful, geography. Florence means spinach, Portugal tomatoes, Flanders endives, Crécy carrots, and Clamart *petit pois*.

The *petit pois* too is an ambassador of spring. A Paris street cry under Louis XIV went:

> Buy your green peas for Lent
> Peas as sweet as any cream.

Already there was the snob obligation to eat them before anyone else.

Vernal, and therefore ephemeral, the green pea is naturally a delicate vegetable. The very freshness of its soul seems to rise in the vapor from a dish of fresh *petits pois*—of an almost unsubstantial green, the green of spring buds.

And that quality of freshness is what the housewife should seek above all in her peas. If she is not lucky enough to be able to pick them herself, then she must at least buy them still in their pods. And those pods must be bright green, shiny, and smooth. Yellowish and fibrous pods contain only hard and floury peas.

Mentha Saracenica.

If they cannot be shucked immediately, then those precious pods must be placed somewhere cool. And if the shucked peas can't be cooked immediately, then keep them wrapped up in a cloth.

They don't take long to cook. Put them in a covered pan with some melted butter plus a spoonful of water and your fresh green peas will be cooked in a quarter of an hour. This swift transition from garden to saucepan and thence to the table ensures that your peas will be digestible even by those suffering from complaints of stomach or liver. Though that's just an extra, thrown in for good measure.

A Clamart garnish is thus one of the mouth-watering joys of its season. It goes well with many meats, from young pigeons to veal scallops, but its harmony with calves' sweetbreads most enchants my personal sense of poetry.

Calves' sweetbreads have a bad reputation among dieticians. They are always forbidding you offal or advising you against it. I wouldn't be surprised if it were held in equal disfavor by gourmets too, considering the torments that chefs tend to put it through.

Those young ruminants whose dull eyes follow the express trains from the lush meadows where they graze, do they know they are harboring under their throats those luxurious glands to which every chef with the slightest pretensions dreams of contributing some new dressing and perhaps his name?

They say calves' sweetbreads, but they are thinking truffles, *foie gras*, port, *béchamel*. And the resultant dish is yet another pedantically luxurious compilation, an unbalanced amalgamation of flavors and aromas.

Whereas the true balance, the true blooming, the true sublimity (the word is not too strong) of this offal is to be found in the *ris de veau Clamart*, a dish at once superb and calm as one connoisseur put it, a dish of bourgeois and classic solidity, a dish rendered only too rare by the folly of the age.

For there are fashions in food too. One cannot picture a *ris de veau Clamart* appearing on official or aristocratic tables. It requires a setting more solidly familial than particularly well-to-do, a conversation without raised voices, and a bottle carefully selected from the cellar's special shelf. Not a great

wine, but a well-thought-out wine. Perhaps your mind may wander in the direction of certain white Bordeaux, less sweet than sappy, or to those Gaillacs that are allowed to become almost dry nowadays, but that still succeed in coming close to the richness of yesteryear. Or a Mercurey from Burgundy, or even hard cider, would go well.

A last trait in the green peas' social behavior. They get along well with almost any herb, seasoning, or spice. But they like sweet reason in these matters. They won't stand for excess. Which is why they particularly appreciate the smooth and caressing savory. You may also salute them with a little thyme, fennel, mint, and many another, but do, I beg of you, observe restraint. Don't overwhelm them with these favors. They get on well with cream too. And they insist on very fresh butter, with a nutty taste. This little peasant who has come up to the big town in his clogs—sorry, in his pod— nevertheless has sensibilities the equal of any aesthete's.

Ris de Veau Clamart

4 calves' sweetbreads
12 slices fat bacon
12 small calves' tongues
5 carrots
5 onions
fat for browning

bouillon
salt and pepper
fresh, new green peas
butter
chervil

Clean the sweetbreads by soaking them for a long time in cold water. Then poach them for 4 minutes and refresh with cold water.

Trim the sweetbreads carefully but leave the skin on. Press them between two boards or plates with a weight on top for 1 or 2 hours in order to break the fibers.

Spike the sweetbreads with slivers of fat bacon and slivers of tongue. Place them on a bed of carrots cut into slices and sliced onions browned in fat. Pour some bouillon over them and put them in the oven. Baste while they cook, which will take from 25 to 35 minutes according to size. The tops of the sweetbreads should become golden. Salt and pepper.

Cook the peas in butter and a little water. Add more butter and a little chopped chervil.

Place the sweetbreads on a serving dish, skim the fat off the broth, reduce it, then pour it over the sweetbreads. Surround them with the peas and serve.

And a Beaujolais of course!

Boeuf à la Ficelle

(Boiled Beef and Vegetables)

Of its origin I cannot be quite sure, but of its uplifting effect on the spirit I am totally certain. And its place in the poetic heraldry of the palate is perfectly precise, perfectly substantiated. The currents of human uncertainty lead perhaps to the *boeuf à la mode* or the *poularde Souvarow*, but everything to do with the *boeuf à la ficelle* is purest certainty. And I imagine its strings as being perfect conductors of the altruistic currents that flow outward from the table and its fellowship.

Is the *boeuf à la ficelle* a Parisian street arab, born in one of the meat markets between La Villette and the Halle aux Vins, or one of those brats you see along the rue de Garet in Lyons, a near relation to onion soup and fresh Beaujolais?

At all events it is clear that it was born under the sign of Taurus, and at nine in the morning: the hour of the workingman's breakfast.

The hour of noisy bistro back rooms, of waitresses dodging the hands aimed at their rumps and not yet worn out by the loud laughter. That hour fragrant with the tartness of new wines. The hour of bulging biceps beneath rolled-up shirtsleeves, of sawdust between the bulbous table legs, of laced coffee and croissants eaten at the counter—food of the fainthearted and the slug-a-bed. The frank, the openhearted hour of the true philosophers who lack words, hunters after stews, gigolos in search of chitterling sausage, wooers of pickled pork, lovers of boiled brisket, friends of all carafes and pitchers.

And note that your *boeuf à la ficelle* is a bold dish, always welcome, and equally at home either at luncheon or at dinner.

But since it was indisputably created for the working-man's breakfast, let us choose it as such, as we would choose a good friend. Let it not be best fillet but of a firmer, tastier cut. And served very simply, without any garnish, with nothing but an enormous pot of Dijon mustard, whose thick, bright yellow is almost a nourishment in itself.

At this point it occurs to me that one day I must celebrate such mustard as befits it, treating it as the true ambrosia of the gods of appetite. Not with a study, as Dumas did, for what do I care whether the Greeks and Romans already knew it, in the form of seed, and that they honored their stews with it under the frightful name of *sinapis*, or that Dijon became its elective capital among us as a result of a recipe devised by Palladius, or that John XXII finally created the post of First Mustard Bearer to serve him this condiment he called the golden key to appetite. No! Not a study, but a song of praise, a paean, under the protection of St. Bornibus!

And this hosanna to the patron saint of all mustard-makers would be inseparable from certain dishes among which the *boeuf à la ficelle* must undoubtedly figure as the leader, the *duce*.

And long may his advances make my mouth water.

Though I am by no means averse to its being served, in the course of some classic repast, with its logical accompaniment: the vegetables from the pot and coarse salt. I am merely amused to hear that Madame la marquise, in her excessively delicate way, has it served with little sautéed potatoes or green beans. It is a matter of indifference to me to be told that in such and such a tavern where I have just enjoyed the dish the *ficelle*, or string, hasn't been changed for decades, either from carelessness or thrift. It invites us to haul up our catch; that's all that matters.

And we obey so many less savory invitations without affectation or fussiness.

And since the reading of a restaurant menu is the customer's first course, as it were, so that the eye is allowed to satisfy itself before the stomach, I love particularly to read, on a slate, at the far end of a slightly murky room, clear in the light from a hatch through which the fragrant breath of the kitchen floats, those chalked-up words:

Today: *Boeuf à la ficelle*.

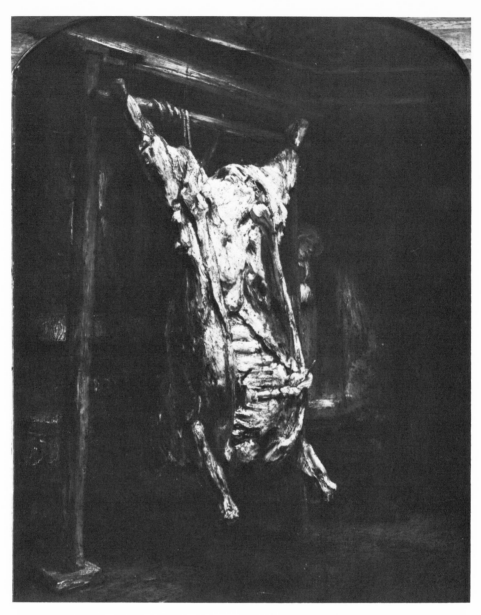

Rembrandt: The Slaughtered Ox

Boeuf à la Ficelle

1 slice of beef per person
2 qts stock made with leeks, carrots,
turnips, and herbs

boiled potatoes
coarse salt
mustard

Cut slabs of beef (sirloin or fillet) three-quarters of an inch thick. Tie them with string, leaving a long tail with a noose at the end.

Prepare the stock with leeks, carrots, turnips, and some herbs cooked in water, or even better, in chicken bouillon. Bring the stock to a boil; then lower the pieces of beef into it, with the nooses around a length of wood placed across the top of the pot. Allow the stock to come back to a boil and cook the meat for 5 to 8 minutes according to its thickness and your taste. The inside should be rare but hot.

Serve with the vegetables from the pot and boiled potatoes, plus coarse salt and mustard.

MENU

Saucisson, radis, olives noires et vertes
(Salami, radishes, black and green olives)
*Steack au poivre
Salade de haricots verts
(Stringbean salad)
Tarte aux pommes
(Apple tart)

Steack au Poivre (Pepper Steak)

Mr. Dreser, a New Yorker, after the most lengthy and costly investigation, has succeeded in codifying the requirements for a perfect steak.

It must weigh one and three-quarter pounds (I assume that Mr. Dreser is talking about a steak for two), and it must come from an animal—preferably a bull—that was four years old.

The carcass must have been hung for six weeks, partly at room temperature, partly in a cold room. The steak should be two to three inches thick. It should be removed from the refrigerator ten hours before it is cooked and each side should be warmed by exposure to warm air for a minute and a half.

Cooking should take eight minutes: four minutes per side five inches away from the red-hot charcoal.

Lastly, at the moment when this perfect steak is served, its internal temperature should be approximately 210° F.

This insistence on detail will doubtless make French readers smile, especially since some of those details tell such a very transatlantic story. I am thinking particularly of the bits about cold rooms and refrigerators. In France we have not yet

One wine, the same for either recipe, young and light. For such a generosity of pepper will kill your wine. But that is no reason to suggest—as a young pupil from a catering school once did at the Best *Sommelier* Competition at which I was one of the judges—for serving nothing with your *steack au poivre* but a glass of water.

No, let us say a Beaujolais-Villages, let us say a wine from the Côtes de Ventoux, let us even say one of those local wines that don't even have any official right to a name. Such a wine will go with the stringbean salad (which will serve as a vegetable, since there is no vegetable that really goes with *steack au poivre*, except perhaps—and on second thought definitely— boiled turnips).

And if you want to give your guests something more elegant in the way of wine, then keep it for the apple tart. It can be a Vouvray, say, or an Anjou.

become accustomed—fortunately—to the necessity for freezing and deep-freezing everything, and the best meat comes not from an anonymous four-year-old bull but from a Charolais bullock, its flesh perfectly marbled, killed the day before yesterday.

But at least Mr. Dreser's attention to detail indicates a certain respect for grilled steak that cannot fail to touch our hearts. Who was it that said the average Frenchman seems to eat nothing but *bifteck* and French fries? It seems to me that our American friends have nothing to learn from us in this particular matter. And besides I'm not at all sure that our preference for the steak is really so universal as it is claimed to be abroad. Easy to buy, quick to prepare, I agree that it is often met with on working-class tables. But as one moves up the social scale consideration of taste takes over, and the roast, the *entrecôte*, the rib of beef become predominant. When they are not passed by in favor of stewed or braised dishes.

And if the steak still triumphs in the restaurant it is in a form that is becoming ever more and more popular: the *steack au poivre*.

I wish some enlightened connoisseur, following Mr. Dreser's lead, would draw up a canon for the perfect *steack au poivre*. It would certainly spare us a great many arguments with restaurant chefs—all of whom have their own recipe and all of whom threaten apoplexy if you suggest changing even a comma of it.

To begin with, there is the conflict between the supporters of the peppercorn and the supporters of pepper essence. This latter group, though numerically inferior, nevertheless constitutes an active and vociferous minority on this one point: that crunching peppercorns is unpleasant and that only their flavor should infuse the sauce with its vigorous—but not excessive—bite.

So they simmer their sauce separately with a little bag of peppercorns that can be removed before the dish is served. Shall I be held up to public obloquy by the opposing faction, I wonder, if I confess to a preference for this method?

Then there are those in favor of alcohol and flambéeing and those against. Here, I feel, we are approaching the main problem. Flambéeing is one of the favorite procedures of the

chef taken as a species—always ready to indulge in anything a little showy, a little excessive, always inclined to throw in a little pinch of arrogance and self-display.

Alcohol, in the kitchen, is like Aesop's language, both the best and worst of adjuncts. And far too often, because it is abused, the worst. The home cook, thrifty as befits the good housewife, employs it with taste and discretion. The chef, on the whole, does the reverse. There are exceptions, but the rule seems to have been accepted that spirits should be employed in making a *steack au poivre*. Here again the majority is wrong: a *steack au poivre* has no need whatever of alcohol.

I once read in a book by some would-be arbiter of the table the odd statement that "this late-fall or winter dish is particularly appreciated by the gentlemen."

I am almost inclined to add, as someone once did apropos of Burgundy, "when it is the ladies who are drinking it."

For I have noticed over and over again in restaurants that it is women above all who seem to enjoy this dish, which is in no way a winter dish, and is indeed particularly welcome during the summer, since its spiciness will often revive an appetite flagging from the heat.

So without wishing to seem pernickety, I remain intransigent in this matter: the perfect *steack au poivre*—in my book—comes from a good bullock, lies thick in the pan, is rare, warmhearted, and covered in a sauce highly seasoned with an infusion of peppercorns but containing no jot of alcohol.

However, since no taste can be foreign to the nature of the gastronome—or of him who considers himself one—I shall give you the other recipe too, and you can choose for yourselves.

Oh, and one more thing: there are also the proponents of green pepper.

Steack au Poivre (1)

1 sirloin steak (½ lb) per person
  oil and butter
A cup white wine
  A cup bouillon

25 peppercorns
  heavy cream
salt

Oil your hands and thoroughly knead the meat. Fry it in half butter and half oil.

Meanwhile you must have boiled the peppercorns (in a cheesecloth bag if you like) in the wine and bouillon until the liquid has been reduced by three-quarters.

Keep the meat warm. Pour the peppery liquid (bag removed or peppercorns strained out) into the frying pan so that it deglazes any brown left by the meat. Then add the cream, all at once, whisking as you do so. Check the seasoning and serve the steaks with the sauce poured over them.

Steack au Poivre (2)

1 sirloin steak (½ lb) per person
  oil and butter
A cup white wine

peppercorns
  salt

Heat oil and butter in equal quantities in your frying pan.

Roughly crush 10 or more peppercorns. Roll the meat in them. Fry it. Remove it from the pan and keep it hot.

Stir the white wine around in the pan. Add a few pieces of butter and whisk. Pour over the meat.

I would suggest a Burgundy
with the côte de veau Foyot.
Something fruity but relatively
light from the Côte de
Beaune would be excellent.
Perhaps one of the Santenays.

Côte de Veau Foyot

(Baked Veal Chops with Cheese Topping)

Since 1937, at the far end of the rue de Tournon, opposite
the Sénat, a tiny little square (does it even have a name?) has
offered the passer-by little more than the shade of its three
wan-looking trees. Not even a plaque to tell him—as he certainly ought to be told: "Here the Restaurant Foyot lived and
died."

1937! Even then it was already almost a hundred years
old, and beneath its aging but noble moldings, redolent with
wisdom and an unobtrusive dignity, epicurean politicians,
lawyers, and judges waved contented forks at one another.

On the evening of April 4, 1894, its name emerged from
the history of cooking into history pure and simple when an
anarchist bomb deposited on one of its windowsills went off
and injured Laurent Tailhade. The poet and pamphleteer was
dining there with his friend Julia Mialke, and we know that
the explosion cost him an eye. Shortly before the incident he
had penned an "apologia for direct action." Fate moves in a
mysterious way.

But the fact remains that Laurent Tailhade must have
been fundamentally a good fellow, for he was a lover of good

food, and of all his considerable works, so utterly forgotten today, it is perhaps his *Petit Bréviaire de la gourmandise* that will outlast all the rest, celebrating as it does those diversions of the palate "that are at once the first need of our nature and the finest ornament of our civilizations."

But back to Foyot himself: chef to Louis-Philippe, put out of work by the Revolution of 1848, he lost very little time in opening his own establishment on the corner of the rue de Tournon and the rue de Vaugirard. Indeed, he bought the whole building, which had originally been built around the middle of the eighteenth century, was at first baptized "Au signe de Saint-Exupère," and then renamed, after Marie-Antoinette's brother had stayed there in 1777, "Hôtel de L'Empereur Joseph II."

A contemporary tells us that Foyot's meals were rather expensive for those days. But to eat one's dinner at the restaurant of a former master chef from the Tuileries kitchens was certainly worth the expense. And besides, over the public room there were also private rooms that were a great attraction for lovers of intimate dinners.

Within five years Foyot had become a very rich man. He bought himself a château at Igny—just outside Paris, near Paliseau—and sold his business for half a million francs. There is a story that his first concern was to have the largest oak on his new estate felled and made into a coffin. Once finished, it was placed on permanent display—open to show its pink satin padding—between two candelabras in the billiard room.

But, alas, idleness puts weight on a man. Ten years later, at the time of his death, Foyot was so fat that all ideas of inserting him into his oaken coffin had to be abandoned. A larger coffin was brought in from Versailles.

It is a curious fact that between 1854 and 1937 four great chefs in succession took over the management of Foyot's without for a moment thinking of changing its name. Modesty or good business sense? Had Foyot really left such a deep impression upon epicurean memories? We must suppose so. And yet his immediate successor, M. Lesserteur, lost no time in adding to the restaurant's fame. For during the siege of Paris it was he, together with the manager of the Restaurant Voisin, who bought up the animals of the zoo, so that it was

Explosion at the Restaurant Foyot

in his restaurant, as in that of his competitor on the Right Bank, that Parisians were able to eat bear and elephant.

From Lesserteur to Siroteau, from Siroteau to Léopold Mourier, from Mourier to Lavernoile, the Foyot star continued to rise. Everyone who was anyone in Paris came to sample the renowned *côte de veau Foyot*, the *pigeons Foyot*, the sheep's feet, and the *pommes de terre Ernestine*.

In 1910 the prices at Foyot's were the highest in Paris. But what food! What service! That excellent fellow M. Marange, whose bistro La Fontaine de Mars was one of the capital's most authentic establishments of the kind, as well as the temple of a simple and mouth-watering cuisine and good Cahors wine, first rose to the rank of *maître d'hôtel* there. He used to speak of it in later days with an enthusiasm that went beyond the ordinary rose-colored nostalgia of youthful memories. It was there that he learned a whole philosophy of living and eating that for all its being part of a bygone age is still conjured up for us, as alive as ever, in the name Foyot.

Côte de Veau Foyot

2 onions
  4 shallots
5 oz butter
  ½ cup dry white wine
½ cup bouillon
  cayenne

salt and pepper
  6 veal chops (about ½ lb each)
1 egg
  2 tbs oil
¼ lb Parmesan
  2 oz breadcrumbs

Chop the onions and shallots and brown in some of the butter. Pour on the white wine and bouillon. Add a dash of cayenne. Bring to a boil.

Salt and pepper the chops. Beat the egg with salt, pepper, and the oil. Dip one side of each chop in this mixture.

Pour the cooked onions and shallots into an ovenproof casserole. Place the chops on top, coated side upward. Sprinkle with the grated Parmesan and the breadcrumbs. Place a pat of butter on each cutlet and brown in the oven.

When they have browned, cover them with buttered greaseproof paper, then with a lid, and cook for 1½ hours.

NOTE: The chops may be served covered with *sauce Périgueux* and ringed with tomatoes stuffed with risotto.

And Belgian beer. Or a red
Alsace wine (Pinot).

Choucroute (Sauerkraut)

Choucroute is inseparable from beer. And anyone who tries
to tell you differently is in grave error.

Beer is a great hope opening up. Beer is a girlfriend who'll
never let you down. Beer is an epic scaled down to the dimension of the everyday, of the ordinary, of the humble.
Think of Manet's "*Bon bock*," the creamy head on the golden
glass, the rakishly tilted boater; beer is that traditional week-
end adventure on the Seine, a Renoir picnic on the grass.

And how different the afternoon stein is from the evening one. Or how different a beer is depending on where it's
drunk. So that the glass on the boulevards, the glass in Montparnasse, is never comparable with, say, the last bock of the
day, drunk at the counter before turning in, on the slopes of
Montmartre or Les Ternes.

Sauerkraut creates a thirst. Beer quenches that thirst. The
tippler therefore needs both to buttress his pleasure, one on
either side. I think of Monselet's verses:

"And why not? I ask. Well steeped,
With peppercorns blackly blinking.

For many a thirsting throat
It's been a spur to drinking.
Happy when hike is done, or shoot,
He who is served a blond *choucroute*
A maze of tresses wan and fine
Their vapors scenting all the inn,
Attended by that golden virgin,
Their cool blond sister the stein."

Though at this point we must reproach the poet for apparently giving his approval to the culinary error that consists in allowing the peppercorns and juniper berries to remain in the finished dish. Much better to have tied them in a cheesecloth bag and removed them before bringing your sauerkraut to the table.

Sauerkraut is not merely the vegetable that is served with —or may be served with—duck, pheasant, partridge, and even toad-in-the-hole. When married with due ceremony to its fit mate the pig, that king of beasts in some people's view and Monselet's "beloved angel," then the *choucroute* is a dish on its own, the perfect example of a dish that is a whole meal, a dish that is in itself a village feast.

And the more varied the meats served with it, the more irresistible the challenge to the appetite. A *choucroute paysanne* is what they tend to call it, and I remember one that was served up to me once on the flanks of whose golden mountain, lined up as for a last parade, there were smoked bacon, ham, pickled pork, pork chops, frankfurters, smoked sausage, blood sausage, and white sausage. And on the side, a pyramid of steamed potatoes and a tureen of puréed peas.

Where does our French *choucroute* come from? Almost certainly from Central Europe. At any rate, Central Europe always seems to have a smell of cabbage hanging over it, sometimes to a quite nauseating extent. So presumably sauerkraut came into Alsace via Germany. I know a Transylvanian recipe in which you add rice, paprika, and cream to the dish. I know a recipe from Prague in which you add the beef from a *pot-au-feu*. And I recall yet another, eaten in Berlin, that was served up with a knuckle of boiled salt pork and puréed peas.

Though not one of those recipes would deign to be seen

Chou poly.

except in the company of its lawful companion, a glass of golden beer.

But here is a question: Are there *crus* for sauerkraut, in the sense that we talk about the *cru*, or locality and vintage, of a wine? There are for milk and butter. For example, the cooperative dairy in Echiré (Deux-Sèvres) that produces the best butter in the world—the butter that Alexandre Dumaine always used when he was still active in Saulieu—is perpetually testing the milk it uses, and will accept only that from carefully selected herds, in order to make sure that its butter will have a very specific delicacy and taste. And the results obtained are above all due to the land the cattle are kept on. So that we can definitely say that there are *crus* for dairy produce so that the expert can recognize a butter from Brittany, or Normandy, or the Charente, solely by its taste. But are there such *crus* for sauerkraut?

A reader wrote in to ask me this question, and although I have certain very clear-cut opinions about *choucroute* I decided I really didn't have sufficient technical knowledge to answer it myself. So I wrote to my friend Léon Beyer, a vintner and gastronome who lives in Alsace.

Here are the main points of his reply, which I feel sure will be of interest to my readers:

"I do think that there are a number of sauerkraut *crus* in Alsace, since you ask. They may be differentiated according to the following criteria:

"(a) How the cabbage is grown: the variety sown; source of the seed; climate; nature of the soil; method of cultivation; time of harvesting.

"(b) The way it is made. Either privately, by the peasant for his private use (when it is far superior and more hygienic if well made), though this practice is tending to disappear since the maintenance of a sauerkraut barrel requires constant attention and meticulous cleanliness; or else in a factory. This latter produces very noticeable variations in quality according to the particular method and the ingredients employed.

"(c) How it is cooked and served. The variations at this stage are even more apparent. But I can tell you nothing on this aspect that you don't know. In my house we cook the sauerkraut for from sixty to ninety minutes, adding one or two

Chou creſpe.

glasses of very dry white Alsatian wine during the process, even though the finished product should be accompanied by a good beer. The sauerkraut should be crisp and not have been transformed into a sort of purée swimming in water by hours and hours of cooking. Personally I don't like it reheated. It is far, far superior and far more pleasing to the eye when new, which is to say at the beginning of the season. With age it begins to turn yellow in the barrel and acquire a much stronger taste."

So there you are! I am delighted of course to have such confirmation of my own position, which is that a *choucroute* should be yellow-green, crisp, and without an atom of grease. Moreover M. Beyer's notes also give a hint of why it is rarely good in restaurants, where it has either been reheated or else kept hot on the side of the stove.

And yet if ever a dish conjured up images of a restaurant, and more particularly of the brasserie, then it is the *choucroute garnie* above all!

Such brasseries, curiously enough, always seem to mushroom near railroad stations, as though *choucroute* were a dish connected at some hidden level with that world of iron and steam. Unless it is those other typical brasserie dishes that are the cause: the onion soup, the pickled herrings, the eggs in aspic, and the plates of cold cuts? Whatever the truth of the matter, it is clear that however much we have succeeded in modernizing the bistro, in neonizing our restaurants, nothing has been able to impinge on this particular style of brasserie: the dim waiters with their shuffling feet, that slightly sharp smell of beer, sauerkraut, and sawdust, the banquettes with their dark patina acquired from acquaintance with the seamy side of so many lives, and even down to those ladies quietly waiting, always so modest, beaming, and blooming, of an age that guarantees experience, and whose visible flesh seems to have borrowed its pink tints from the pork butcher's window.

It is in such places that your *choucroute* assumes its deepest meaning, and it is there that it ought to be—and sometimes is—at its best, smoking like incense in the company of a well-filled corporation, a solitary courtesan, an impatient couple, a penniless philosopher, a well-colored meerschaum, a late city edition, a none-too-wealthy sybarite, a hobo on the spree, and

Chou commun.

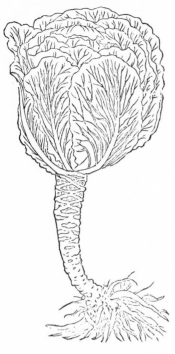

Chou cabu.

a sprinkling of those people apparently fated always to be "just passing."

I am also delighted that M. Beyer concludes his answer: "Generally speaking, I imagine it's the same with sauerkraut as with any regional dish: there are numerous ways of preparing and serving it, and all correct. But there are certain rules that oughtn't to be broken—as they are, for example, by that heresy the so-called *choucroute au champagne.*"

For that fool's gold they called *choucroute au champagne* did succeed in becoming the rage for a while in our capital's less reputable Alsatian brasseries.

A *choucroute* should be characterized above all by sheer abundance. Since it is the whole meal, it must be filling and fortifying. You shouldn't be able to finish it. There should be not only as much properly crisp, blond sauerkraut as you can eat, but also steamed potatoes. And a variety of meat.

Choucroute

4⅓ lbs sauerkraut
4 small Toulouse sausages
¾ lb lean bacon (not sliced)
goose fat
1 cooking apple
bouquet garni

juniper berries
¾ cup dry white wine
1 thick slice cooked ham per person
3 or 4 potatoes per person
4 small blood sausages

Wash the sauerkraut in two lots of water. Drain and shake dry. Then press with a cloth and spread out to dry still more.

Prick the sausages and blanch with the bacon for 3 minutes in boiling water (having started them in cold, as for onions). Drain.

Grease a cast-iron casserole with goose fat. Arrange a few slices of peeled apple on the bottom and cover with ⅓ of the sauerkraut. Place the blanched sausages on top with a small *bouquet garni* and some juniper ber-ries in a cheesecloth bag. Add a second layer of sauerkraut, then the bacon cut into 4 pieces. Finish off with the remainder of the sauerkraut.

Pour on the wine. Bring to a boil; then put in the oven for 2 hours—at the most.

Ten minutes before serving add the ham to the casserole.

Steam the potatoes and serve on the side.

Broil the blood sausages separately and add them to the dish just before you bring it to the table.

And I'm sticking to my guns: beer! Nothing at all with the asparagus. And the beer will do very well for the cheese fingers as well.

Tête de Veau en Tortue

(Calf's Head with Turtle Sauce)

London, the world's largest market for edible turtles, has a great relish for its turtle soup, in which, beyond all question, real turtle meat is an ingredient.

But how much turtle soup in the world generally is in fact no more than a meat stock with a specific flavoring of herbs?

For it is the "turtle" herbs—basil, bayleaf, sweet marjoram, thyme, myrtle, sage, rosemary, and parsley—that give turtle soup—even real turtle soup—its flavor. And because of this they have taken its name. And then, because the flavor after all is theirs, they have passed on that name to a sauce that can equally well accompany either the edible turtle or many other dishes including the calf's head, and which is in fact a Madeira sauce.

So we have come full circle. And it will easily be understood that there is no green Atlantic turtle, not even any terrapin in the *tête de veau en tortue*.

In which case we must assume that the British turtle soup is an ancient dish indeed, since the *tête de veau en tortue* is for its part a French dish that goes back a long, long way.

Les meilleures Viandes ne font pas
toûjours fervies les premiéres.

De la Tête de Veau, l'œil & les Oreilles en font les plus friants morceaux.

c'eft Viande de Gentilhomme, car il
y a à manger pour lui & fes Chiens.

But since no man is a prophet in his own country, the French are unaware of the fact. And indeed it was in Liége that I first discovered this amazing gastronomical construction. In that city, set solidly in its own jelly, it decorates the windows of almost all the *charcuteries* worthy of the name. In London too it is prized by lovers of good food. In Paris, until a short time ago, there was only a single restaurant that served it. (That one, I note in passing, is named L'Auberge Anglaise.) Now there is a second restaurant. You will find *tête de veau en tortue* on the menu of the Archestrate.

Those who dispute that the *tête de veau en tortue* is so named because of the herbs that are common to it and to the English turtle soup offer two alternative derivations.

"The *tortue*," one writer on cooking tells us—though he is a fellow I regard with grave suspicion, if only because of his opinions about champagne, which he will allow as a fit accompaniment to almost nothing, and to which he prefers the mediocre Arbois—"was once the little hemispherical copper cauldron in which all dishes described as *en tortue* were cooked."

"*En tortue*," the *Dictionnaire de l'Académie des Gastronomes* says on the other hand, "may be explained by the dome-shaped presentation—reminding one somewhat of the turtle's shell—of the dishes prepared in accordance with the method bearing that name."

So what are we to believe?

Myself, I intend to stick to the herb-and-Madeira-flavored sauce whose merits, many long years ago, were already being expounded by Carême.

And I would also qualify this dish as being medieval. Arbitrarily perhaps. Simply because for me it evokes an image of a medieval castle, of tall, Gothic-backed seats, a heavy oaken table dappled with multi-colored, enameled gleams from stained-glass windows. A troubadour in scarlet velvet, accompanying himself on a viol, is singing a Burgundian love song and hoping that his lady will throw him a smile. Clanging armor sets the flags of the neighboring room ashiver: "Madame, I have killed three wolves and fain would eat . . ."

A great scurrying and bustling in the kitchens. Kitchens like those in the Palais des Ducs, in Dijon, where, Curnonsky says, Charles the Bold had them built inside fireplaces.

It is not a grand banquet. It won't include the flaming peacock that my friend Christian Guy assures us, in his *Histoire de la cuisine*, is such an abominable dish.

What a lucky fellow to have actually tasted it, though! Apparently, somewhere down in the southwest there is a farm that raises peacocks specifically for culinary purposes. But perhaps it's just one of those legends?

Never mind. As I was saying, this is not a formal banquet. There are eight soups on the table. And those huge round slices of bread that serve as plates, that are distributed after the meal, still dripping with gravy, to the household servants. But the goblets are all made of gold, glowing in the cold darkness that is mitigated only by the tongues of flame that flicker from the whole beech trunk burning in the hearth.

The viol has fallen silent. The great hounds with their lean and dappled flanks have curled up at their master's feet. The first dishes are brought in. The moment for the *tête de veau en tortue* is almost upon us. Here it comes. Raising one imperious finger, the baron orders his squire to pour him . . . What? Mead? Or barley wine?

For this is the crucial question: What does one drink with this dish that is so unlike any other? This dish that has become such a rarity? This dish from the depths of the past?

As a matter of public responsibility, I have attempted to at least limit the problem to certain areas, even though I cannot claim to have solved it. Wine? Very well, wine. Red? Perhaps. A fairly fruity Beaujolais, "warm," even though served chilled? Why not? But then the defenders of a light Bordeaux rise to put forward their claims.

And then there is the baron's barley wine.

So why not beer? Yes, why not?

Tête de Veau en Tortue

4 tbs flour
  4 tbs vinegar
salt
  1 onion spiked with cloves
bouquet garni
  ½ calf's head with tongue and brain
1 slice lemon
  12 small balls of ground veal
24 pitted green olives
  12 mushrooms
6 crayfish

butter
  pepper
6 eggs
  oil for frying
12 cockscombs
  12 cocks' kidneys
1½ cups turtle sauce
  1 small truffle
1 large gherkin
  6 pieces fried bread

● TURTLE SAUCE

herbs (see recipe)
  bouillon
butter
  flour

½ cup tomato purée
  Madeira
salt and pepper

Mix the flour into 3 quarts of water. Add the vinegar, salt, onion, and a *bouquet garni*, and bring to a boil. Lower into it the tongue and the half head wrapped in a cloth. Cook gently for 45 minutes.

Remove the tongue and put it on one side in a little of the broth. Continue cooking the head for another 45 minutes.

Steep the brain for six hours in cold water, renewing the water periodically. Scald the brain, place in cold water, bring to a boil and boil 10 minutes, removing any scum. Wash by pouring cold water over it. Drain and rub with a slice of lemon.

Simmer the veal balls for 10 minutes. Drain them. Simmer the olives for 8 minutes. Simmer the mushrooms and save the broth.

Gut the crayfish. Turn back the claws and stick one point of each into the end of the curled-up tail. Sauté them in butter over a hot flame. Add the mushrooms. Salt and pepper.

Fry the eggs in oil. Poach the cockscombs and kidneys in some salty water with flour mixed into it.

Make the turtle sauce:

Infuse ¼ teaspoon each of sage, basil, sweet marjoram, thyme, crushed bayleaf, rosemary, and a few sprigs of parsley in ¼ cup of bouillon for 15 minutes in a covered pan. Strain off the infusion.

Make a blond *roux* with butter, flour, and bouillon. Mix into it the infusion of herbs, the tomato purée, ½ cup Madeira, the broth from the mushrooms, salt, and pepper. Reduce to ¼ cup; then strain. Adjust seasoning.

Into this sauce put the veal balls, the olives, the cockscombs and kidneys, the mushrooms, and the sliced truffle. Simmer very gently for 10 minutes. Just before using it add ¼ cup of Madeira.

Remove the calf's head from its cloth and drain it. Trim and cut into pieces. Skin the tongue and slice it. Cut the brain into thick slices.

Arrange the pieces of the head and the slices of tongue in a hot dish, then scatter slices of gherkin over them. Then pour on half the sauce. Decorate with the pieces of brain and the fried eggs alternating with crayfish and pieces of fried bread. Serve the remainder of the sauce on the side.

Martin Drolling: Kitchen Interior

A regional wine, full-bodied
and full-flavored: a
Cahors.

Cassoulet

(Meat and White-Bean Casserole)

Seven towns disputed the honor of Homer's birth. How many
lay claim to the *cassoulet?* For Prosper Montagné's formula
describing this household god of the Languedoc as a culinary
trinity has long since been outmoded. Though God the
Father may still be the *cassoulet* of Castelnaudary, God the
Son that of Carcassonne, and the Holy Ghost that of Toulouse, where does that leave the *cassoulet* of Chalabre, and
that other, deliciously rustic, from Castannau? And the *cassoulet* from Quercy?

If you are prepared to admit that each chef has the right
to his own method, every cook to her own little secret, then
you must imagine *cassoulets* receding to infinity, all different
yet all akin through their marriage with the bean—heavenly
vision or nightmare according to your mood.

But even with the bean we haven't hit bedrock. Although
the first *cassoulet* may not be as old as the globe itself, it is
certainly as old as cooking; consequently, it probably didn't
contain any beans. Beans are newcomers to the society of stews
and casserole dishes. However, that the *cassoulet* is a dish of
the Languedoc few would deny. Yet even here a doubt creeps

in. Though it may be deeply linked to the very soil of Languedoc, are we sure that the original recipe didn't come from the Moors of Spain?

In which case its ancestor would be the mutton stew made with beans that the Saracens introduced to the inhabitants of the Carcassé about 720.

And since there were no kidney beans, then it must have been some other sort of bean. (What today we wrongly call *haricot de mouton* should rightfully be called *halicot*—from the Old French verb *halicoter*, "to slice.")

Butter beans were later supplanted by kidney beans. The kidney bean became the soul of the *cassoulet*. But even then, just any old kidney bean won't do, you know. One purist, Senator Jean Durand, insisted that they must be from either Mazères or Lavelanet. Without going quite so far, let us say that they must at any rate be white beans.

I first made my literary acquaintance with the *cassoulet* in Anatole France. Do you remember how he takes us, in *Histoire comique*, into a little tavern, on the rue Vavin, called Chez Clémence? And there we found cooking a *cassoulet* from Castelnaudary. Cooking! What am I saying? It was infinitely slowly simmering! And had been for twenty years: "Mère Clémence adds some goose occasionally, or some bacon from time to time, and every now and then some more beans or sausage, but it is still the same *cassoulet*. The foundation remains, and it is that antique and precious foundation that lends the dish a quality comparable to those very particular amber tones that characterize the flesh tints of the old Venetian masters."

It took World War I to extinguish the flame beneath Mère Clémence's *cassole*, and so to kill off that joyous twenty-year-old *cassoulet* in the very prime of its life, one year before its majority.

And notice that word *cassole*. Because *cassole* it must be: no true *cassoulet* can be made other than in an earthenware casserole unglazed on the outside. Indeed, it is this very *cassole*, reddish, porous, holding the heat so well, becoming worn in by use like an old pipe, that gave the dish its name. A century ago all the *cassoles* in Castelnaudary were made of clay from Issel, a neighboring village, and the linguists are quite categorical about the matter: *cassoulet* is a corruption of *cassole d'Issel.* The container gave its name to the contents.

The seniority of the Castelnaudary *cassoulet* is thus proved and confirmed by the local *Canson d'el cassoulet,* whose refrain, roughly translated, states quite clearly:

Every place has its favorite dishes
And boasts of its special delights:
La Grasse has its plump partridges,
Villasavarry its luscious melons,
Limoux its sparkling *blanquette,*
Albi gilds its pastry rings.
All towns have some crowning glory,
But Castelnaudary alone has the *cassoulet.*

It only remains, eschewing all parochial squabbles, to define the main contestants, to differentiate their accompaniment to the beans.

Cassoulet de Castelnaudary: pork rind, salted goose, pork, a small pure pork sausage, not too fat and grilled beforehand on one side only (the other side, decorating the top of the dish, gets baked in the oven).

Cassoulet de Carcassonne: pork rind, small amount of preserved goose, small amount of pork, a half leg of lamb, and (in season) red-legged partridges. Or, more simply, country sausage.

Cassoulet de Toulouse: pork rind, pork, a good Toulouse sausage, and a great deal of preserved goose.

And there you have the Big Three. As for the others . . . There are just too many! And even when you think you've finished, there is even a *cassoulet à la bière!* And a fish *cassoulet* in which the goose is replaced by dried cod. And why not? In the United States they have their Boston baked beans, which is simply a Massachusetts *cassoulet.*

The *cassoulet* is a prime example of the dish that is the meal. I can't recall exactly who it was who wrote of it: "I often honor my friends with a *cassoulet* from the kitchens of Boiyssou, Castelnaudary's master cook, an unctuous *cassoulet* exhaling the soul of the bean and the very perfection of cooked sausage," but I do remember a certain tobacco shop in a tiny Languedoc village whose door handle, five or six times during the year, would be removed and whose customers would be met with a closed door and a curt note on it reading: "Closed on account of *cassoulet*." Nor would it ever have occurred to anyone to protest. Quite the contrary. Everyone envied the proprietor and his friends. The responsibility a *cassoulet* imposes is in proportion to the pleasure it bestows.

Cassoulet

3 lbs dry white beans (marrow or navy)
    ½ lb bacon
10 oz fresh pork rind
    2 boned pig's feet
fennel
    salt and pepper
5 onions
    3 carrots
5 tbs goose fat
    8 cloves garlic
1 tbs flour
    2 qts bouillon

bouquet garni
    6 tomatoes
pinch of saffron
    2 legs of preserved goose
1 garlic sausage
    1 boned leg of mutton weighing about
    2¼ lbs
2 cups dry white wine
    spices
soft breadcrumbs
    parsley

Soak the beans in the casserole for 24 hours along with the bacon, the pork rind, and the pig's feet in warm water flavored with the fennel.

Put your casserole over the heat and blanch the contents. Take out the blanched bacon, pork rind, and pig's feet. Change the water, and cook the beans for 45 minutes with salt and pepper; then drain them.

Chop the onions. Dice the blanched bacon. Slice the carrots and brown all of them in the goose fat. Add five cloves of garlic finely chopped, and the flour. Stir. Add the bouillon gradually, still stirring, and bring to a boil. Add a generous *bouquet garni*, then the peeled and seeded tomatoes, and allow to cook and reduce, skimming from time to time. When the sauce has been reduced by half, strain it, skim off the fat, and keep both fat and sauce warm. Add a pinch of saffron.

Brown the goose legs in their own fat on a moderate heat, together with the little garlic sausage. Cook 45 minutes. Skim off fat, put it aside, and keep the goose warm.

Use the fat skimmed from the sauce and the goose to brown the boned leg of mutton, which you have spiked with two cloves of

garlic. Cook for 45 minutes, but when it is half cooked pour on the dry white wine. Add the pork rind and the pig's feet. Complete the cooking; then keep warm.

Rub the earthenware dish with the remaining garlic. Put the goose legs at the bottom of it and cover them with a layer of beans lightly sprinkled with spices (paprika, *quatre épices*, etc.). Pour over the broth the goose was cooked in, making sure it is not fatty. Slice the lamb and add to the dish, covering likewise with beans. Pour in half the sauce. Put in the sausage thickly sliced, the pork rind, and the pig's feet, finishing off with the remainder of the beans. Then pour in the broth from the lamb and the remainder of the sauce.

Bring to a boil quickly. After it has boiled for 5 minutes remove the dish from the heat, sprinkle with soft breadcrumbs and chopped parsley, then place in the oven uncovered. Allow to simmer for 1 hour, breaking the surface two or three times with a wooden spoon. Serve in the dish it has been cooked in and, as I read in a poetic recipe once, let the well-browned dish be the color of ripe harvests.

Grandville: "Excuse me, sir, but I was told that I'd always be sure of finding you at this time."

MENU

Huîtres plates
(Raw oysters)
*Gigot à la sept heures
Salade de pissenlit au lard
(Dandelion and bacon
salad)
Granité à la liqueur
(Liqueur water ice)

With the oysters, a Chablis;
with the lamb, a rugged
red, such as a Cornas from the
Ardèche, or a Hermitage
(both Côtes du Rhône wines).

Gigot à la Sept Heures

(Seven-Hour Leg of Lamb)

The leg of lamb is, above all, a symbol. The symbol of the family, of the warm hearth, and of the good middle-class appetite. And a symbol too of prosperity and peace; claims Francis Amunategui, referring to "this beautiful cut of meat that has affinities with the gourd and the mandolin."

Let us put ourselves for a moment in the leg of lamb's place. What do we see surrounding us? The smiling faces of a family circle that may not be applauding our advent with loud cries, but are certainly quivering with delighted anticipation and metaphorically sharpening the teeth. The notion has been put into verse:

At dinner, when the leg of lamb arrives,
We feel its kindly spell cast out all gloom,
And at the sight the dullest appetite revives.

The leg of lamb is about to perish, but at least it is not going to do so surrounded by hypocritically weeping would-be heirs.

> Garlic-scented, respectable upon its bed
> Of happy beans . . .

It caters to all and to each, well bred, conscientious, anxious to please, for

> The essence of this joint when cooked
> According to the rules
> Is that it satisfies the tastes
> Of all the different schools.

One is almost tempted—thinking of Bernardin de Saint Pierre's melon, created segmented in order to be consumed by a family in slices—to write that the leg of lamb was specifically created for the family festive table.

It is much less welcome in a restaurant, already carved by a chef into lonely portions.

It is a detail—the most important one—the perfect subject for a still life even though it is still so much alive.

> Your flesh is perfection. In pastures green
> You browsed on flowers alone.
> Oh, legs of lamb, idealized and rosy clay.

For the poet, quite carried away by his own enthusiasm, would apparently have us believe that it is the legs of lamb that browse rather than the sheep. But it is a pretty picture all the same: a cook looking rather like a paniered Bo-Peep leading a cohort of plump, merry, playful legs of lamb through green pastures.

The leg of lamb is gentle, too, for

> . . . as the Doctor asked with great solemnity
> To whom has this joint done any injury?
> Even the full stomach can eat it without harm.

Moreover, our French term *gigot*—used also of course by the Scots—comes from the word *gigue*, or "jig." And hence is closely related to the *gigolette*, France's jig-loving good-time girl.

Which information somehow lends the leg of lamb's bourgeois simplicity a slightly less respectable tinge, an almost bohemian, rakish air. One begins to envisage it as being consumed not solely around happy family tables but also under tavern arbors, by couples out on a spree: a love of twenty has a healthy appetite and is better sustained by good pink lamb than by the delicate flesh of squabs. A poet of the last century hinted as much:

> *Gigot*, accept my heart-felt tribute.
> Dining with marquise or baronne,
> Often for you I have disdained
> The infinite delicacy of capon.

Though what he perhaps ought also to admit is that he tended likewise to disdain that marquise in favor of the *gigolette*, a girl who needs good solid food to stoke up her laughter and give zest to her kisses.

In short, the leg of lamb possesses the particular quality

of being at home anywhere: it will do honor to even the most formal of banquets—when served *en croûte* as Thuilier, the master from Les Baux, used to prepare it—and yet is at home even in the plate of cold cuts served up as a sad midnight meal in a brasserie somewhere, when joy is on the wane and fast the rosy glow is fading.

At home everywhere, yes without a doubt, and yet everywhere imbued with that first all-powerful image one has of it: its old family-retainer air, its middle-class solidity. And sometimes, enjoying a leg of lamb by chance, without thinking, leads to remorse at having left the straight and narrow where the true *gigot*, the family leg of lamb, reigns supreme, when . . .

> a servant trusted and true
> Bears in on its dish that succulent burden,
> Virtue's eternal, seventh-day guerdon.

To love the garlic-rubbed, perfectly roasted leg of lamb *à la française* is not necessarily to disdain the boiled leg of lamb with its mint sauce that Kipling thought of as so essential to the British Sunday. Or that favorite dish of Alexandre Dumas, which he may have invented—the *gigot à la sept heures*, which, like *lièvre à la royale* and certain *daubes* from Provence, is eaten with a spoon.

Gigot à la Sept Heures

¼ lb fat bacon
  ¼ lb lean ham
1 leg of lamb
  garlic
5 oz pork rind

2 large onions
  salt and pepper
bayleaf
  3 cups water
2 cups white wine

Cut the fat bacon and the ham into small strips. Lard the joint with them; then spike it with garlic.

Cover the bottom of an earthenware casserole with pork rind. Add the onions sliced into rings. Lay the joint on top, salt and pepper it, add a bayleaf and pour in the water and 1 cup of the white wine. Cover the casserole with a plate, concave side uppermost. Stick the plate to the edges of the casserole with paper or a flour and water paste. Pour the other cup of white wine into the plate and cook, in a slow oven, for 7 hours, or until very tender. Test it after about 4 hours. If the wine in the plate evaporates, pour in more.

MENU

*Saucisson beurre
(Butter sausage)*
**Miroton
Camembert
Pruneaux au vin rouge
(Prunes stewed in red
wine)*

Serve the same wine used to
cook the prunes.
A Cahors, for example.

Miroton (Leftover Meat with Onions)

The origin of the word is obscure. According to Robert's
dictionary, it was first used in 1691, which certainly invali-
dates the story sometimes put forward that it derives from the
song *"Malbrough s'en va-t-en guerre,"* which dates at the
very earliest from the battle of Malplaquet (1709), but more
probably from the Duke's death in 1722. So the refrain:

> *Malbrough s'en va-t-en guerre
> Mironton, mironton, mirontaine . . .*

has no connection with the *miroton.* Other than the fact that
one often meets menus on which the dish is erroneously described as *boeuf mironton* instead of *miroton.*

The *Larousse gastronomique* provides this definition of
the *miroton:* "a sort of stew made with cooked meats and
flavored with onions."

And Favre's dictionary goes into slightly greater detail,
adding that the *miroton* is the art of dressing up leftovers, that
the leftover meats were either roasted or boiled originally, and
that there is also a pudding christened with the same name: the
miroton de pommes—which is a *macédoine* of candied fruits

mixed into an apple compote and flavored with maraschino.

But let us leave these linguistic researches and come to the *miroton* as it is generally known today, the *miroton* in its quintessential form, the *miroton* of the typical concierge that is in fact a whole art in itself: that of dressing up the leftovers of the *pot-au-feu*.

It is desirable, in the home, to have an acceptable, even a delectable use for such leftovers. The simplest of all is the *salade bouchère* (the boiled beef cut up into small dice and put into a salad along with hard-boiled eggs, potatoes, tomatoes, and chopped parsley). Or there is the *hachis Parmentier*, in which the cold meat is minced, covered with a thick layer of mashed potatoes, and browned in the oven. Or there is the *miroton*.

So there is no doubt that it is a family dish, a thrifty housewife's dish. It has even been called a concierge's dish, perhaps because Balzac (in *Le Cousin Pons*) has his main character's concierge, Mme Cibot, a former oyster-opener at the Cadran Bleu, simmer a certain odorous stew of this kind. "It was made," Balzac tells us, "of leftovers of boiled beef bought from a cooked-meat merchant who dealt to some extent in secondhand goods, and fricasséed in butter with thinly sliced onions, until the butter was soaked up by meat and onion rings alike, so that this lodge-keeper's dish presented the appearance of a fried dish." And Balzac adds that the dish was "lovingly confected."

And that more or less covers it, I think. I am not ashamed to have a concierge's taste in this matter. I regard the *miroton* as being not merely a great French dish, but also a gastronomically acceptable dish. For gastronomy, I resolutely hold, does not necessarily imply richness of ingredients and preparation, and sometimes there is more truth in a concierge's *miroton* than in the inane extrapolations of bogus great chefs.

I remember that I used to visit an old great-aunt who lived out by the Porte Saint-Denis, that illustrious neighborhood where, tucked away behind its main street, the boulevard Saint-Denis itself, there lay so many dark little streets harboring hordes of modest Parisian people and families. A dark corridor, a dark staircase, a dark apartment, for the sun was only a very rare visitor in that inner court where the hammer

Vuillard: The Cook

of some artisan beat out a slower tempo than the one forced on us today. And in the entrance, in her by no means vast den, a half-crippled old concierge was always simmering vague dishes whose odors pursued me for a long while after my visit was over. Their exhalations emerged from her gloomy room, advanced to assault the sinister staircase, and met the other odors seeping downward from the floors above—stew conflicting with *civet*, cabbage soup colliding with jam, but perennially triumphant, soaring above this invisible ballet of smells, always and forever the old concierge's odorous *miroton*.

And at the heart of that memory is the deification it implies of the onion, that poor man's truffle, his prime resource, the treasured flavoring of his greatest culinary triumphs. The butter melts, but never boils; it soaks into both vegetable and meat; it melts into them as they melt into it: almost a purée, to be eaten with a spoon after having been slowly reduced to edible gold on the top of the stove or the oven. It is a kind of cooking consisting above all of patience. I forget exactly which old woman it was who said to me one day, describing how long it took to cook a rabbit stew, a *gibelotte:* "As long as it takes for one foot, monsieur!" She meant one foot of one of the socks she was knitting. Though she knitted quickly, I admit, chewing over the cud of her memories meanwhile. She remembered the Commune, for example. And her first *gibelotte* of all, I believe, was made with a cat!

I realize, of course, that some may dismiss the *miroton* as merely a dish of no more than literary interest. And see my delight in it as the result of cheap "salt of the earth" sentimentality. But they would be wrong! In an age when concierges no longer know how to fill their office—and in which they are moreover no longer needed in the vertical concentration camps that apartment buildings have become—I am not simply yearning for the past, for my youth, or for another way of life. But I do say that the *miroton* ought to be kept alive as a living witness of such a past, and that it has a better right to figure on our great menus than that idiocy the *truite aux amandes* or that nothingness the domesticated quail.

For though Balzac may have made Sylvain Pons a gastronome, one can nevertheless sense that he is only half mocking at the cooking of the concierge Mme Cibot. Because Pons was

familiar with such rather common dishes, born in the janitors'
lodges of Paris on days when potluck had proved somewhat
thin.

Does that mean that the *miroton* is a Parisian dish?

I would be prepared to swear to it, despite the oniony
fragrance that constitutes its chief merit and might lead one to
associate it more with Lyons.

Raymond Dumay, in a charming work on French gastronomy, has outlined the geographical regions where the
shallot, garlic, and the onion respectively hold sway. The
onion undoubtedly originated in the north, just as garlic
spread from the Mediterranean basin and the shallot from

Aquitaine. And just as the southern limit of the onion and the northern limit of garlic are easily definable as they now stand, so the advance of the onion through the land, first reaching Paris, then the Rhône Valley and the Massif Central via Lyons, is equally clear.

"The onion rolled steadily forward, a dietetic steamroller, remorselessly pushing down from north to south, and only a rampart of olive trees cheated it of an absolute victory," Raymond Dumay writes. So be it! But I also think there are further nuances to be added on the subject. For example that garlic is a rustic, peasant flavoring, while the onion is a city-dweller.

The onion brings a little of the country into town-dwellers' cooking. It assuages their territorial imperative! Herbs have their season, they sing of spring! The onion is an all-year-rounder, but in winter, above all, it is a little of the earth's springtime preserved in its fleshy bulb. A symbol. With the onion the city can take a country trip with every meal.

A poor man's dish, the *miroton?*

Yes indeed, but let us take another look at Balzac's text, all the same: the beef (the *bouilli*) is bought from the cooked meat seller—in this case a secondhand meat seller—a trade that scarcely exists any more today. Though admittedly the butcher does sometimes sell boiled beef to housewives who haven't the time to put a piece of meat in a pot, and at every street corner we see those rotating chickens—factory-made and commercialized fowl—that are the symbol of our gastronomic decadence. All right, so it's a poor man's dish. And yet Mme Cibot cooks it with butter. With butter! And she isn't stingy with it either. It is with margarine, every molten drop measured from a pipette, that a concierge of Mme Cibot's stamp would feed Balzac's poor Schmucke today!

So you begin to see that the *miroton* can be something more than a slatternly shrew's makeshift. A well-considered dish, a lovingly cherished dish, a great dish!

And one mustn't be niggardly with either the onions or the butter. You must have well-cooked beef that was originally started—needless to say—in cold water. The meat should be of good quality but nevertheless a cut with a bit of taste to it, not fat because the fat in the dish is the added butter.

Top round springs to mind immediately. But there are other cuts that would do nicely: rump and chuck, for example. And also sirloin. Why not? The cooking process should be long, slow, and, as it were, miserly. But there must be an abundance of the onions upon whose imparted fragrance the dish depends. And served in this way, coated and sliced, the poverty-stricken *bouilli* throws off its plebeian livery and acquires a monk-like serenity whose neutral tints only serve to conceal an intense and underlying emotion, a sensual and inner ecstasy.

The dictionary of the Académie des Gastronomes, in a wry aside, remarks apropos of this simple and somewhat homely dish that it has given rise to the expression *père miroton*, which means a placid, uncomplicated sort of old man. It isn't slang, mark you. Simply a popular expression derived from a dish that has always been a dish of the people. Though personally I have much more often heard the expression *frère miroton*. You see! I said there was a monk-like serenity about it! It is a dish that dresses always in rough homespun, as it were. But homespun doesn't always conceal asceticism—as Rabelais is our witness! For many centuries, love of eating, that sin of virtuous monks (again a quotation from Balzac) was common in monasteries. And one might say too that the old-style concierges' lodges resembled dark cloisters in their way. Cloisters whose incense was perhaps the aroma of a religiously simmered *miroton!*

Miroton

6 tbs finely chopped onion
¼ lb butter
1 tbs flour
2 tbs wine vinegar
2 tbs white wine

bouillon
cold boiled beef
breadcrumbs
melted butter
parsley

Sauté the finely chopped onion in the butter. Sprinkle the flour over it and stir till the onion is nicely golden.

Add the wine vinegar and white wine. Then add bouillon and bring quickly to a boil.

Put a layer of this sauce in a flat, ovenproof dish. Arrange thinly cut slices of cold boiled beef, overlapping, on top. Pour over the rest of the sauce. Sprinkle with breadcrumbs.

Pour melted butter over the top and put in a medium oven.

Allow to cook and brown slowly, without burning.

Serve sprinkled with chopped parsley.

Gustave Doré: Gargantua As a Baby

If possible, hard cider. If you
insist on wine, then let
it be a light red of the region, or
a very light wine from the
Côtes de Bordeaux.

Tripes à la Mode de Caen

(Casserole of Tripe)

"*Gaudebillaux* are fat tripes from *coiraux*. *Coiraux* are cows
or steer fattened by manger-feeding and in *guimaux* meadows.
Guimaux meadows are meadows that bear two crops of grass
a year. Of such well-fattened cattle they had ordered 367,014
killed for salting on Shrove Tuesday, so that in the spring
there should be beef of that season aplenty at the beginning of
every meal and so with its saltiness set them up well for the
enjoyment of their wine. The abundance of the tripe there-
from you may imagine, and of such savor was it that one and
all licked their fingers at the thought. But the very devil of it,
they being only four, was the impossibility of preserving it all
for long, since it would have gone bad, which seemed unfit-
ting indeed. Hence they concluded that all must be gorman-
dized without a jot being wasted. And to this end they sent
out for all the citizens of Sinais, of Seuillé, of La Roche Cler-
maud, of Vaugaudray, without forgetting Le Coudray, Mont-
pensier, Le Gué de Vède and other neighboring towns, all
good drinkers, good companions, and fine skittle-players to
boot. . . . After dinner all went in a body out to Saulsaie,
and there on the thick grass did they dance to the sound of the

joyful flutes and sweet bagpipes so beautifully that it was heavenly pastime to see them so revel there."

Ah, how right he was, our Rabelais. A feast of *tripes à la mode de Caen* is indeed junketing and revelry, brotherhood in merriment and best friendship. They have tripe of sorts elsewhere too, and sometimes of the very best! But it's not the same thing. The feet and tripes of Marseilles are like exiles, captive ambassadors swaddled in garlic and saffron finery that makes them merely ridiculous! The *tripous* of Aveyron are like expatriates suffering from degeneracy. They still give you the illusion of what they used to be; they are hypocritically decked out in former merits; they are trying their best to make you believe they are happy having gone native, but their smiles just make you feel sorry for them, because you can sense the effort of it all. They don't belong here! The *gras double* of Lyons? Now, that is admittedly different; it has kept its self-respect somehow. And better still, it has taken on a local color by adapting itself to the golden onion; it has become naturalized. Yet how are we to forget that its origins were elsewhere: those *guimaux* meadows in the north so dear to Gargantua and Pantagruel!

And then only a short distance from the cradle of the tripes supreme there is another dish of them to be found, another Normandy dish, the *tripes de la Ferté Macé* cooked in small rolls. They have inspired at least one poet. And yet? Sickly, twisted with envy, annihilated by their own immodesty, they don't even really exist. Let us stick to the real tripe, the tripe of Rabelais, *les tripes à la mode de Caen* (and district).

Yes, and district, for how can I forget the *tripes* of that honest Léopold at Boulon (on the road from Caen to Thury-Harcourt, where a country farm stood in for an inn. Léopold had just won first prize in the *Tripière d'Or* competition. We turned up to celebrate that happy distinction with him. The menu: tripe, then tripe again, and I truly think that if those three great Normandy cheeses (Camembert, Livarot, Pont l'Evêque) had not appeared with their rival temptations we should still be there eating the tripes so succulently simmered by Mme Léopold, and all washed down with a cider such as you don't find any more. What a meal! Mme Bovary's wedding feast, in a word! And, moreover, Flaubert was there at table with us. For it would be impossible to sit down to such a feast, in Normandy, without the living presence of his memory.

The *Tripière d'Or*, as with many other institutions of the same kind, is no longer a serious or important affair, merely an occasion for a few good souls to rub against one another (it sounds slightly different in Latin, I believe). But in those days it had only just come into being, at the instigation of a rather eccentric chef and poetaster who was driven by the thought of tripe into a long recipe in shaky octosyllables:

At your request, dear Jeanneton,
I write in order to give you
The recipe for *tripes à la mode*.
To cook them in the correct fashion,
To perfection, according to the code.

And so on. Presumably you will be grateful to me for sparing you the rest!

In Paris, well-cooked tripe is rare. Perhaps it's because perfection of ingredients and cooking just isn't enough, and they also need a certain atmosphere. You don't eat tripe just anywhere or anyhow, and even less with just anyone. First of all, you need a suitable partner—or partners—to enter into your communion of tripe with you. You need plenty of time and plenty of appetite. And a certain intellectual comfort too.

Chez Pharamond (though only in the evening; at midday there is too much of a crush), the approach of the little individual heaters on which the *tripière* takes its traditional stand already goes a long way to creating the right ambiance. You know that your tripe, in just a moment now, is about to speak to you. Then the dishes you will be eating from, well warmed also, follow the heater itself rather as the first limousine follows the motorcyclists on the occasion of some state visit. And now, here comes the sovereign himself. Cheer, good people! All you gourmets, cheer!

You need plenty of potatoes with your tripe, to perform the office of bread and soak up the sauce, that *fondu* of offal with its characteristic sweet fragrance: pure juice, the juice not solely of the beast itself, of its digestive organs, but also of those twice-bearing meadows and their nourishing, life-giving grass. And the juice of Normandy's fat earth and its fruits too —its apples, pears, cream, and cheese.

And then, but only then, the eater who is really an eater will cry with Rabelais: "The kingdom for good tripe!"

Tripes à la Mode de Caen

11 to 13 lbs ready-to-cook tripe
3 carrots
10 onions
2 oz parsley sprigs
1 sprig thyme
2 bayleaves
1 garlic clove

salt and pepper
spices
2 ready-to-cook calf's feet, split in half
½ cup Calvados
2 cups hard cider
potatoes

Cut the tripe into pieces two inches square. Cut the carrots into quarters, slice the onions into rings, and tie up two *bouquets garnis*, made of the parsley sprigs, thyme, bayleaves, and garlic.

Spread a layer of tripe squares in your earthenware casserole. Salt lightly, pepper well, and add some spices. Add a third of the carrots and onions, a *bouquet garni*, and two half calf's feet (bought already scalded). Put in another layer of tripe, then another layer of carrots, onions, the second *bouquet garni*, and seasoning, plus another two halves of calf's feet, finishing off with a third layer of tripe.

Pour in the Calvados and cider.

Cover. Seal the lid on with flour and water and cook very gently, if possible in a baker's oven, for 10 hours or so.

When cooked, remove the *bouquets garnis*, the carrots, and the bones of the feet.

Serve on a table stove.

With the tripe serve steamed whole potatoes.

MENU

*Oeufs à la Toupinel
*Daube de boeuf en gelée
 Salade de mâche
 (*Lamb's-lettuce salad*)
*Sorbet

The same wine you used to cook the beef. A Burgundy in other words. Perhaps a Mercurey or a Santenay from one of the less noble years, light and discreet.

Daube de Boeuf en Gelée

(Cold, Jellied Casserole of Beef)

"You have a chef of the very first order! This is something that you can never find in any hostelry, not even the best, a *daube de boeuf* in which the jelly doesn't taste of glue, in which the beef has soaked in the flavor of the carrots; it is admirable. Allow me to ask for a little more."

Those were the words of M. de Norpois at the table of the narrator's parents in Proust's *A l'ombre des jeunes filles en fleur*. The cold beef with carrots had just made its entry, laid "by the Michelangelo of our kitchen upon enormous crystalline blocks of jelly like transparent quartz," Proust adds.

The Michelangelo is none other than Françoise, the family's old cook. But "since she attached an extreme importance to the intrinsic quality of the raw materials that were to be used in the fabrication of her creation, she always went herself to Les Halles to see that she was given the best pieces of rump steak, of shin of veal, of calves' feet, just as Michelangelo spent his eight months in the quarries of Carrara selecting the most perfect blocks of marble for the monument of Julius II."

And later, when the ambassador's compliments are conveyed to her, with the question: "But, Françoise, how do you explain it, the fact that no one can make jelly as good as yours?" Françoise, while appearing to assure them naïvely that she "doesn't know where her talent can be coming from," does give her explanation: "Chefs cook it in too much of a hurry and also not all together. The beef has to be like a sponge, so it soaks up the juice to the very last drop. Though there was one of those cafés where I did think they cooked quite well. I don't say it was quite my jelly, but it was done very gently, and the soufflés were really creamy too."

For the narrator's parents had sent Françoise to perfect her art in various great kitchens. And when they ask her which restaurant it is that has found such favor in her eyes—for it isn't Henry's (in the Place Gaillon), or Weber's, or the Cirro—it becomes apparent in the end that the establishment she is talking about with such a perfectly blended mixture of pride and kindly condescension is none other than . . . the Café Anglais!

I like this pride of Françoise's, the just pride of the good cook who knows her worth. Though in fact the *boeuf en gelée* is by no means a typical woman's dish. There is something in the *gelée*, something Proust was very much aware of, that requires an artist's touch, something much more masculine in essence. Nevertheless, the *gelée* apart, the loving patience required for a good *boeuf à la mode* is something that ought to touch the heart of—and be within the talents of—any good housewife-cook.

And also, let us not mince matters, the ingredients are modest enough for most households to encompass. Beef—and not the costliest cuts either!—bacon, lard, onions, a calf's foot. It is a still life much more suited to the farmyard kitchen than that of Lucullus. Yet when the beef is finished and on its serving plate, what a change is there! A construction *à la Carême*. And when one at last tastes it, then all previous impressions are as nothing, everything is different, as though belonging to a wholly different world of sensation. One was talking in terms of the kitchen, but now one finds one should be talking in terms of music, of poetry. The beef itself is a background of brass from which the variations of the jelly, the harmonious meditation of the strings, the distant and

The kitchen of Marcel Proust's Aunt Léonie at Illiers

The Café Anglais,
Boulevard des Italiens

parsley-sprinkled tune of the distant flute, the tart note of the triangle, the infinitely skilled piano of the supporting vegetables can all develop. Shall we perhaps hear the little phrase, that famous *petite phrase de Vinteuil*, leitmotif of Swann's love, as we crush a morsel of that magical jelly against our tongue? The *miroton* hums a popular ballad, the *boeuf à la mode en gelée* sings like Mozart, and sometimes even like Bach.

When cold, of course.

I shall be accused of repeating myself, but it must be repeated. Even if only in order to set at ease the minds of all those good chefs who no longer dare admit, in front of their peers, that almost all cooking is better cold than hot—more delicate, and more difficult.

Yet it is too often a hot *boeuf à la mode* that we are offered in restaurants. It seems to take an absolute heat wave to make chefs resign themselves to the *gelée*. And then we see

340

arriving on our plate a dismal slab of rubber, dry and fibrous, soddenly heaped with carrots that are plainly not what they should be (they should have given their all to the beef and given up their very existence in the process).

M. de Norpois was right. Even in the very greatest restaurants the jelly and its beef lack the class, the harmony that is the result of talent, certainly, but also of esteem. The *boeuf à la mode en gelée* is simply not rated high enough! However, here is a more domestic recipe: the *daube* of beef in jelly.

Daube de Boeuf en Gelée

9 oz sliced fat bacon
  pepper and salt
powdered thyme
  bayleaf
parsley
  3 lbs beef (⅓ chuck, ⅓ top round,
  ⅓ rump)
spices
  ¼ cup brandy
½ bottle red Burgundy
  2 shallots

¼ lb fresh pork rind
  1 calf's foot
½ lb lean breast bacon
  4 large onions
4 garlic cloves
  4 carrots
3½ tbs butter
  bouquet garni
bouillon
  thin slices of bacon

Pepper and salt the bacon slices, roll them in a little powdered thyme and crushed bayleaf, then in parsley. Let them stand for 1 hour.

Cut the beef into pieces of about 3½ ounces each. Lard them with the prepared bacon slices, working with the grain.

Sprinkle with salt, pepper, and spices. Place in an earthenware terrine with the brandy and Burgundy, the shallots, minced, and some parsley. Marinate for 2 hours.

Put the pork rinds and calf's foot into cold water. Bring to a boil, and boil for 5 minutes. Refresh with cold water and cut the rind into small squares. Break the bones from the calf's foot and set aside.

Cut the breast bacon into large dice and scald it.

Cut up the onions.

Grate the garlic.

Slice the carrots.

Drain and dry the pieces of meat.

Heat the butter in a skillet till it sizzles. Brown the pieces of meat in it 5 or 6 pieces at a time.

In a large earthenware, top-of-the-stove casserole with a cover, arrange the bones from the calf's foot, then a third of the meat, carrots, onion, and garlic, half the pork rind and pieces of bacon. Add salt and spices. Then a second layer of meat, more spices, pork rind, salt and pepper, a *bouquet garni*, and the last layer of meat.

Pour in the marinade and stock that isn't too salty. Cover with a layer of bacon slices.

Put the cover on and seal it with a paste of flour and water.

Place on top of stove and bring to a boil. Then place in the oven and cook at a low heat for 6 hours.

Remove the cover. Skim off any fat and remove the *bouquet garni*. Allow to cool in the casserole.

MENU

Bouillon
*Pot-au-feu
  Pommes au four à la gelée
    de groseilles
  (Baked apples with
    red-currant jelly)

A modest Bordeaux, a wine
from the Premières Côtes,
light and lively.

Pot-au-Feu

(Beef Simmered with Vegetables)

The truth is that for a long time this dish led a double life.

In the working-class home it was quite simply boiled beef, a boiling process that produced at the same time a broth, meat, and vegetables. Not to mention the leftovers, for it was from the leftovers of the boiled beef that the worker's wife created those two wonders of French cooking the *miroton* and the *hachis Parmentier*.

Higher up the social scale (in the world of middle-class dinners, cooks, and suppers), it was simply the basis for a stock, soon to become a consommé. No Germiny without the *pot-au-feu* first. And if the Germiny is a "great" soup, then it owes its eminence in a way to the humble *pot-au-feu* that made it possible.

But today things are different. For one thing, no one has time to make a *pot-au-feu* at home any more, and for another our gourmets have rediscovered the virtue of culinary simplicity. The *pot-au-feu* has become one and indivisible again. And it dares to speak its name. For it is cherished by the connoisseurs, welcomed in the best society, and treated with great consideration wherever it goes.

"In the hierarchy of pure foods, that good fellow the dish of boiled beef occupies no summit but is rather a foundation for all the others," a descendant of Brillat-Savarin wrote. And not only a descendant but a follower of the great professor, who treated the *bouilli*, or boiled beef, in these disdainful terms: "We may divide those who eat *bouilli* into four categories:

"1. The slaves of tradition who eat it because their parents did, who are merely continuing the practice out of an imbecility of will, and who live in expectation, moreover, of being similarly imitated by their own young.

"2. The impatient, who abhor even a moment's inactivity at table so much that they have contracted the habit of hurling themselves forthwith upon the first edible matter that presents itself (*materiam subjectam*).

"3. The absent-minded, who, not having received the sacred fire from heaven, regard mealtimes as a kind of forced labor, look upon everything actually edible as of absolutely equal value, and sit up to the table like a gaping oyster in its bed.

"4. The ogres, who have been endowed with an appetite so vast that they feel obliged to conceal its extent, and therefore make haste to introduce a first victim to their ravening stomach as quickly as may be, hoping thus to appease the gastric fire raging within and to provide a foundation for the diverse further consignments they intend to dispatch as soon as they can to the same destination."

From all of which it is clear that it did not even occur to Brillat-Savarin that it is possible actually to enjoy a *pot-au-feu*, or that this dish can be considered a gourmet's delight in the same way as a *foie gras*, truffles, or those game terrines that his mother, the beautiful Aurore, used to prepare "as one praises God." And he was in error. In grave error!

But we will pardon him, all the same, in consideration of his *osmazôme* theory—which is such a help and a spur when one is trying to codify the recipe for the best *pot-au-feu*.

This *osmazôme* of which Brillat-Savarin announced the discovery was a superlatively savory constituent of meat that is soluble in cold water—and thus to be distinguished from the *extractable* constituent which is soluble only in boiling water.

And it is this *osmazôme*, he assures us, that lends its quality to the best stock and forms, when browned by heating, the crusty juice of meat. In short, it is *osmazôme* that makes your truly superior broth.

In practical culinary terms this may be expressed in the following pair of alternatives:

    (a) If you want good broth start the meat in cold water;

    (b) If you want better meat, then start it in hot water.

It will be observed from my recipe that these two propositions may in fact be synthesized, thus totally annihilating the assertion by the author of *La Physiologie du goût* that "*le bouilli* is merely meat minus its juices."

Because of its base extraction (which it had even come to believe in itself) and perhaps out of shyness as well, the *pot-au-feu* appeared at one time only on the menus of the very humblest bistros. It had developed an inferiority complex.

But during recent years things have changed, and now the *pot-au-feu* is all the rage. A little pinch of snobbery seems to suit it very well, and so we find it surrounded by a variety of mustards and pickles, and the elegant salt mill with its sea salt that decorates the tables of young, rather affected ladies who know that a knowledge of just how far to go slumming is the number-one social grace these days.

And immediately all the phony bistro-owners have rushed to retrieve the *pot-au-feu* from the back-number cupboard. They chalk up its name with pride now; they are only too pleased to be seen in its company. And they dress it up.

It has become the poor man's *Dodin-Bouffant!*

And in case you haven't heard about the *pot-au-feu Dodin-Bouffant* I shall give you an account of it here. It is to be found in Marcel Rouff's novel *Vie et Mort de Dodin-Bouffant* and is a sumptuously barbaric recipe invented wholly by that writer-gastronome.

The prince of some country or other has received Dodin and friends at his court. Fancying himself as a gastronomist, he serves them a lot of those complicated and absurd dishes that ought to kill chefs in the making but alas never do. So Dodin-Bouffant invites this rather grandiosely inclined ruler to a meal in his turn. The menu consists of a single dish: *pot-au-feu*. And Rouff has amused himself by inventing, under cover of that contemptuous name, a sort of picaresque or episodic dish in which over and above the piece of beef itself there is also a big pork and veal sausage, a capon, shin of veal rubbed with mint and mother of thyme, and goose liver cooked in Chambertin.

One day I wrote somewhere that we needed a Maecenas to remove such a magnificent dish from the realm of the literary imagination and bring it, via the kitchens of Croesus, within the grasp of a circle of privileged gourmets. And my wish was granted. At Prunier's. Though I'm afraid I have to put it on record that the Dodin-Bouffant is better on paper than in reality.

Much better! On paper one is carried away by the rich sauce of adjectives; they make the episode into a fine anthology piece, one that could well serve—and a great deal better than some that are used—as a set piece for an exam, if those responsible for such things weren't so exclusively concerned with the literary fads of the moment. But at a second reading? Or, to be more exact, when you have eventually laid the mirage that the words have conjured up, pierced that flavorsome literary mist—well, there isn't much left of this culinary monument, I'm afraid.

Even those thick slices of *foie gras* so pointlessly cooked in Chambertin only succeed in giving it an air of *nouveau riche* vulgarity!

No, let us rehabilitate the *pot-au-feu* by all means, but the genuine article please, the *pot-au-feu* that springs from the soil, the natural *pot-au-feu*, our fathers' *bouilli*. Looking to experience and experiment merely to provide slight changes that will make it even better still.

Pot-au-Feu

1 lb boned and rolled top ribs
  coarse salt
1 lb top round
  2 large onions spiked with cloves
bouquet garni
  5 or 6 leeks
5 carrots

5 turnips
  1 stalk celery
pepper
  marrow bones
potatoes
  croutons
grated cheese

Place the boned and rolled top ribs in cold water to cover.

Add a handful of the coarse salt. Bring to a boil and skim.

Add the top round, the spiked onions, and the *bouquet garni*. Bring to a boil again and skim again.

Add the leeks tied in a bundle, the carrots, whole, the turnips, and the celery. Cook for three hours at a slow simmer.

Test the meat for tenderness with a fork.

Check the seasoning. Pepper. Add 1 or more marrow bones rubbed with coarse salt and cook for another 30 minutes.

Boil or steam 10 or more potatoes.

Serve the meat surrounded by the potatoes, the carrots, the turnips, and the separated leeks. Also the marrow bones.

Strain the broth. Reduce it if necessary. Serve it with fried croutons and grated cheese on the side.

Sebastian Stosskopf: Winter

A wine from central France,
young and sturdy: a Marcillac
would be appropriate.
Unless you happen to have
a Cahors. Or a Côtes du Rhône
from an unexceptional year.

Poitrine d'Agneau Farcie

(Stuffed Breast of Lamb)

It's a strange thing! If you say, for example, stuffed salmon
or stuffed pigeon, then people will immediately start thinking
about what *sort* of stuffing? They will wonder whether it is
to be a cooked one or simply a stuffing *ménagère*, whether it
is to have truffle in it or to be enriched with *foie gras*. Or
what prestigious brandy will be used to flavor it.

But when you say stuffed breast, whether it be calf's,
sheep's, or lamb's, there is no hesitation whatever over such
questions. Everyone knows that the stuffing will be a good
bonne femme stuffing, a truly rustic recipe, and in a sense
a whole way of life!

A stuffed rabbit may find its way to either of these two
cookery poles, into the good old countrywoman's pot or the
chef's tinned copper pan. But the breast, no!

One thinks of the remark of the poet Joseph Delteil: "The
great sin in cookery is indulgence, sentimentality, flowery
rhetoric." Stuffed fillets of sole are purest rhetoric, hare stuffed
with *foie gras* and truffles is wild indulgence, and perhaps
sentimentality too.

Writing of the stuffed chicken—which I was forgetting—

Delteil also says: "Success lies in the stuffing itself; it should be made with simple ingredients, those nearest to hand." Should it, indeed? That is something a Carême would never subscribe to, despite all his genius, even though Carême nevertheless remains Carême. But the others! Their stuffings are follies, pyramids, squarings of the circle. Whereas the stuffing for stuffed breast should be made of love, pure love.

Let us now take a look at the geographical distribution of various stuffings. Stuffed sole is entirely the product of city kitchens, of chefs, of great households. Rich stuffings are the products of rich districts, of privileged areas. Find me a recipe for stuffed breast that doesn't originate in a poor district.

Whether we are talking of calf's breast, or sheep's breast, or breast of lamb, the geogastronomic map of France is categorical: they are dishes from the Rouergue, from the Auvergne, from areas perpetually battered by their climates and unremittingly jounced by their geological development.

Nor are they makeshift meals. No, they are feast-day dishes. What we think of as their simplicity is looked upon when they are at home as extravagance. They are the child's Christmas orange, as it were. You may smile perhaps. Children today, even poor ones, are crammed with good things until their Christmas becomes a competition between superfluities. In the old days, in "our" mountains, the Christmas orange was the richest gift of all. And useful! And blessed of God! Give us this day our daily bread, our stuffed breast on Sundays, and our orange from the Three Wise Men!

What I am trying to say is that we must never lose sight of the fact that this stuffing is an act of grace, that the piece of meat in its braising pan is bearing witness to a modest but stable prosperity that has no need or wish to dazzle the eye.

And *foie gras*, or truffles, elsewhere natural and simple products of their own regions, would here be just so much artificial dazzlement.

In the Auvergne, it is calf's breast. And they call it *falette*. In Rouergue, it is lamb's or sheep's breast from the Causses. The stuffings are the same. They combine bread (or flour), which is sacred; herbs, which are a medicament; onion, which is a god to so many peoples that it must possess extraordinary

merits—and does, in fact, possess them; egg, which is the beginning of the chicken, and therefore of everything; bacon, which is one of the household gods. Simplicity itself, in fact. Every one of the ingredients is at hand on the farm, with the exception of salt, and that is why salt was for so long the measure of wealth. For it is possible to do without pepper and spices when one possesses the secret of the herbs. And sugar, after all, is merely a substitute; paleolithic man ate only the true sugars, those of the bees and fruit.

Which leads me to a certain stuffing from Aveyron (Rouergue) into which they put raisins. Raisins in such a context are simply a form of sugar. Genuine sugar. The childhood of sugar in the childhood of cooking. Prunes could be used in exactly the same classic and ancestral way. It is a return to the beginnings. To that wise, traditional cooking in an age when sugar was no more than one more spice or flavoring among all the rest.

This mixture of sugar and salt is typical of French cooking before the Italian invasion of Catherine de Médicis' chefs. In the Loire Valley, the cradle of France and her monarchy, you will still find certain sweet-sour dishes made with prunes that have mostly been driven out elsewhere toward the north, into Flanders, Britain, and Brittany.

What a pleasure it is, in someone like Guy Nouyrigat of the gravelly, singsong accent and patient, benevolent voice, to encounter an abiding love for these dishes that speak so eloquently of the long history of our race.

So I shall give you Guy Nouyrigat's recipe for breast of lamb with raisin stuffing.

But I repeat, it could also be a prune stuffing.

And it could be breast of mutton. Or veal! It doesn't matter. What does matter is your faith. And the knowledge as you eat the result that it is the sap and the sweat, the faith and the toil of twenty generations of peasant women in a country of poor peasants.

So let us have no common bowl of creamed potatoes to accompany it, but instead an *aligot*. The *aligot* is, in a way, the *fondue* of the Auvergne. It is fresh Cheddar-like cheese melted in the same way they melt the *vacherin de Fribourg* in Switzerland. But the *aligot* is also a dish of poor peasants. So to the cheese there is added a proportion of potato, the truffle of the have-nots. And the result is an admirable drapery of dripping gold as it is drawn up with a wooden spatula from the casserole it has been cooked in and cut with scissors.

Could anything be better than such a breast of lamb with *aligot?* Taste it and you will never ask again.

Poitrine d'Agneau Farcie

1 lb lean pork
  ¾ lb ham or bacon fat
3 oz breadcrumbs
  milk
2 oz parsley
  3 eggs
½ lb raisins
  salt

pepper
  nutmeg
3 to 4 lbs breast of lamb
  coarse salt
½ lb onions
  1 garlic clove
lard

Chop the pork and ham or bacon fat with the breadcrumbs, which have been soaked in milk and then dried. Mince the parsley and mix in.

Add the eggs and mix well.

Add the raisins, which have been well soaked in warm water and drained.

Add salt, pepper, and a pinch of nutmeg.

Bone (or have boned by your butcher) a whole breast of lamb weighing between 3 and 4 pounds. Lift the skin without breaking it, and remove a layer of fat.

Sew the two edges together (skin side outside) and one end, so as to make a bag.

Put the stuffing inside it, without filling it too full. Sew up the other end.

Pierce two or three times with a fork on each side.

Brown in a medium oven for 45 minutes. Sprinkle with coarse salt.

Chop the onions and brown them with the crushed garlic in lard in a metal casserole. Put the breast in on top. Cover the casserole and cook in a medium oven for another 45 minutes.

MENU

*Goujons à la cascamèche
*Blanquette de veau
 Compote de fruits
 (Stewed mixed fruit)

And for wine a Côtes du Rhône *primeur*.

Blanquette de Veau

(Veal and Onions in Cream Sauce)

Blanquette equals *blanchette*. So it means something not only white but also diminutive. There is something virginal in the word, and something naïve and timid too.

I remember a theoretician, a man deeply imbued with Pavlovian theory, once explaining to me how profoundly the color of a dish conditions our appetites. We all know, of course, that the bold green of watercress is the perfect foil to rare leg of lamb, while the tender green of lettuce "coaxes" the similarly tender pink of York ham. But my theoretician went much further than that. He assured me that a green dish rejoices the eye quite as much as the stomach, that a blue dish predisposes us to nausea, and that a white dish stifles the appetite at birth.

How then are we to explain the attraction—for me as for so many others—of this *blanquette de veau* that by its very name, and certainly by its aspect, quite contrary to that theory, makes the mouth water?

For the *blanquette* is very white indeed, and its name comes from that whiteness.

And this despite the fact that the same word is used to

OIGNON.

designate a kind of beer, lamb's lettuce, a variety of early pear, and a species of long-stalked fig, not to mention the *blanquette de Limoux*, which is a light but golden wine.

In the kitchen, when we say "a *blanc*" we mean a clear veal or poultry broth, or a *court-bouillon* whitened with flour, and the *blanquette* is a white dish in both these senses.

It is a dish that may be made of chicken, lamb, or kid, but that was initially, it seems to me, made of veal. And of that particular veal that was once termed "white" also, because the calf had been killed while still suckling at its mother's breast, even before it had made its first attempt, with clumsy, un-learned tongue, to tear off the taller grass spears in the field or pull at wisps of hay in the manger.

I imagine the first *blanquette* being made from one of those Pontoise calves whose praises La Reynière was still sing-ing in the eighteenth century. The farmers of Pontoise did not make butter from their milk, but used it instead to feed their calves, whose white, short-fibered, delicate flesh then became the highly prized delight of wealthy Parisian gourmets. Nor did they even stop there, those Pontoise farmers, since in the Larousse of 1877, under *veau*, we find the following: "The calves of Pontoise are especially famous, the succulence of their flesh being due to the cream and biscuits on which they have been fed."

Nowadays we do still find a few milk-fed calves being raised around Brive and Saint-Gaudens. But even they are tending to disappear, alas, to melt away into the herd of grass-eating, red-fleshed calves, artificially fattened with chemical additives, that is now becoming "our daily herd." It is perhaps for the *blanquette* that we shall chew our bitterest cud of regret on that last day of healthy human appetites in this insane world where we shall all soon be living on pills.

In their *Dictionnaire de gastronomie joviale*, Derys and Curnonsky observed that the *blanquette* may be an "appalling 'anything goes' used to disguise the more unspeakable cuts and trimmings." Though they add that a good *blanquette* is an appetizer and an antipyretic. And certainly it cures us of that true fever of impatience we feel when appetite is clamoring for its due delight and satisfaction.

The origin of the *blanquette* remains uncertain. This well-behaved young miss, this virgin maid is not prudish or straitlaced. Indeed, by dint of consorting with onions (also white) in the kitchens of restaurants for coach and hansom cab drivers (ancestors of today's truck-driver diners) she has acquired a certain acidity. She has a sharp tongue in her head, the little baggage! She is a coquette too, wears the white, stiff-starched apron of Molière's soubrettes, and despite her country accent would not disgrace the boards of the Comédie Française; for although we sometimes tend to forget it, those boards were once laid on simple trestles, down by the Pont-Neuf.

Yes, it is the onions—plenty of onions!—that give the *blanquette* that underlying sprightliness not quite concealed by its rich and unctuous cream. The richness of that sauce, enfolding its treasure of equally virginal meat, may take us in for a moment and enable the dish to insinuate its way onto the highest of high tables. But Rogue Onion is hidden inside. He prompts the guest as soon as the first mouthful has been taken. He hisses the right line to the forgetful diner's tongue—a sharp, pointed, triumphantly comic line. And the *blanquette*, thanks to him, thanks to the onions, becomes once more what she should be, a dish for the jolly low-life rather than high society—a true bistro meal.

"I could light my pipe from the embers of your nose." So a Bacchic poet once said to the hansom-cab driver of the Belle Epoque. And that is the image I associate with a "real" *blanquette*, superbly simmered in the yard-square kitchen of a stop-off for hansom drivers. At the door, her straw hat pierced with holes for her ears, Cocotte is happy in her dream of oats. Inside, her master asks for another half pint from Marguerite or Jeannette, the waitress with her easy laugh and ever-ready palm. The menu on the slate proclaims: "Today: *blanquette de veau à l'ancienne*."

Why "old style"? I must confess I've never been able to find much difference between the two recipes, which both, in any case, have so many variants. Let's not bother over that! What is really important is the quality of the veal and the quantity of the onions. And above all, none of your button mushrooms!

Blanquette de Veau

2 lbs milk-fed veal (⅓ gristle; ⅓ top ribs;
⅓ shoulder)
  5 oz butter
salt and pepper
  2 carrots
1 onion spiked with cloves
  1 tbs flour

white stock
  1 bouquet garni
36 small white onions
  3 egg yolks
3 tbs heavy cream
    nutmeg
juice of 1 lemon

The veal *must* be milk-fed. Cut it into large cubes.

Lay the cubed meat in an earthenware casserole. Pour boiling vinegary water over it, and let it stand for 5 minutes with the cover on. Drain.

Melt half the butter in a cast-iron casserole. Add the slightly salted and well-peppered cubes of veal, together with the carrots, quartered, and the onion. Sauté on a low heat, stirring occasionally, for 15 minutes.

Sprinkle with the flour. Stir in well, taking care not to let the flour brown at all; then moisten with slightly salted white stock. Bring to a boil, still stirring. Add the *bouquet garni.* Allow to cook, just at boiling point, for 2 hours.

Scald the onions, drain, and sauté in the rest of the butter in a covered skillet till cooked. They must remain quite white.

When the *blanquette* is cooked, remove the meat cubes with a strainer and set aside on a very hot dish. Add the onions to them.

Remove carrots, spiked onion, and *bouquet garni* from the veal broth; then reduce it, stirring all the time with a spatula. If the sauce becomes too thick, add milk.

Mix the egg yolks and 3 tablespoons of white stock in a bowl with the cream. Add nutmeg. Add a ladle of the cooked sauce, whisking quickly, followed by the lemon juice.

Pour this mixture into the sauce and work in with a whisk. The sauce must not boil from then on. Strain over the veal and onions.

LA FESTE AV FRANCOIS

Les Tauernier et bons garsons   Auec la bouteille et la tronche de jambon
font la feste aux bons Jambons   Nous auons reduit l'espagnole a la raison
Il ne se voit point de Jambons mechant   80
comme il se voit beau coup de Jeans

Boisseuin fug petit pont au
chaudron

auec Priuilege

For wine, a Pouilly-Fumé.

Jambon en Saupiquet

(Ham in Vinegar-Cream Sauce)

The *Répertoire de la cuisine* by Th. Gringoire and L. Saulnier (referred to by chefs as *Gringoire and Saulnier*, so authoritative is it generally considered) gives two recipes for *sauce zingara*, and it will soon become apparent that it is not an irrelevance to reproduce both of them here:

(a) A tomato-flavored demi-glace sauce. Permissible additions: chopped mushrooms, truffles, ham and tongue, dash of cayenne, drops of Madeira.

(b) Chop shallots finely. Moisten with vinegar. Reduce. Add brown meat juice, plus breadcrumbs browned in butter. Cook five minutes. Finish off with chopped parsley and lemon juice.

And now to the pages of history.

The first mention of both word and thing, to my knowledge at least, occurs in the *Nouveau Cuisinier royal et bourgeois* of 1713, which mentions young rabbits *à la saingaraz*, and gives this recipe: "Lard your young rabbits fittingly, then roast them. After, you must have beaten slices of ham and brown them with a little bacon and flour; then add a bouquet of herbs and good meat juice, not salted, and cook all together. Add also a little vinegar and bind this sauce with a little bread sauce. Cut your rabbits in four and set on a dish. Pour the sauce over, together with the slices of ham, and serve hot with all grease skimmed off."

Note to begin with: vinegar, bread sauce, meat juice. The main elements of *zingara B*, plus the ham from *zingara A*.

In 1750, in an edition of the *Dons de Comus*, we find a recipe for *jambon au cingarat:* "Cut rounds of ham very thin, brown them in a pan with melted bacon fat. Serve them with a little water, vinegar, and crushed pepper." This is to some extent the ham from the young rabbits *à la saingaraz* served on its own. But then in 1808 we find Viard's *Cuisinier impérial* telling us how to make veal cutlets *à la Saint-Garat:* "You must grate a little bacon, warm it, then season slices of tongue with pepper and nutmeg and sauté them in this fat. Spike veal cutlets with these slices of tongue when they have cooled, then brown in butter. Then, having garnished a pan with the trimmings of the tongue and the bacon pieces it was cooked in, plus a little bayleaf, basil, and slices of ham, sliced carrots, and chopped onions, lay in the cutlets. Moisten with consommé. Cook gently for two hours. Remove the cutlets. Strain the sauce. Complete it with an addition of *sauce espagnole* and tomato sauce. Serve." A recipe that includes two elements of *zingara A:* tongue and tomato. But that's not the end!

In 1830, the *Cuisinier Durand* gives a recipe for *jambon à la cingara* as follows: "Cut slices of ham rather thick, cook them in a frying pan with oil or lard till brown on both sides, then place in a baking dish with two glasses of cold water and a dash of vinegar. In the same pan used before, brown a little flour, moisten this *roux* with the liquid from the baking dish, stir, and halt boiling as soon as bubbling begins. Toss in the ham slices, boil for just a moment, and serve. Love apples (tomatoes) may be mixed into the sauce."

But the quest continues. In the *Dictionnaire général de la cuisine française* (1839) we find recipes for partridges *à la singarat*, chicken *à la singarat*, and chicken fillets *à la singarat*. All contain tongue in a *demi-glace* sauce. While Plumerey, in his *Art de la cuisine française au XIXe*, 1843 edition, offers cutlets of veal *à la singara* (cutlets and slices of Bayonne ham

sautéed in butter, covered in a *demi-espagnole sauce*, then finished off with a little butter, cayenne, and lemon juice).

Though, oddly enough, in the 1844 edition, Plumerey speaks of a ham *à la Saint-Gara*, which is simply the recipe from the *Dons de Comus* with the vinegar replaced by lemon juice. And the spelling also differs—both from that in the *Dons de Comus* (*cingarat*) and also from that in Plumerey's first edition (*singara*).

Perhaps it is time to look a little more closely at this matter of the spelling. It is not until 1876, in the *Cuisine classique* by Dubois and Bernard, that we first find (applied to their chicken stomach *à la zingara*) the spelling we use today. Until then we have had successively: *saingaraz, saingara, cingarat, cingara, gingara, Saint-Garat, Saint-Gara, singarat,* and *singara.*

There was, it is true, a Saint-Garat family (one representative of which was a friend of Robespierre), but I rather doubt that any of its members could have inspired the creator of our rabbits *à la saingaraz* as early as 1713. And I also have my doubts about the theory of the term's origin put forward by that very erudite and shrewd culinographer Alfred Guérot. According to him, certain nomadic tribes from Hindustan, by name the Tzengaris, were at some past time welcomed into Italy, where the Italians promptly turned them into *zingari* (singular *zingaro*). And the Italian cooks who accompanied Catherine and Marie de Médicis into France—bringing their recipes with them—included this *sauce zingara* in their baggage. In which case the *sauce zingara* is Italian.

But, look here, you may be saying, there's nothing about *zingara* in this recipe of yours. It says *saupiquet* at the top of it. Aren't you wandering a little? Not at all. But again, I must explain that there are two *saupiquets*.

Firstly *lièvre en saupiquet Provençal* (and that *sau* tells the French scholar that there is salt involved), and secondly *jambon en saupiquet* from the Morvan in the province of Nivernais. So what is the Morvan *saupiquet*? It is ham in a sauce of vinegar-tinctured cream. And the *saupiquet* (in Spanish *salpicar*) is a medieval sauce whose recipe we find given by Taillevent in his *Viandier:* toasted bread soaked in stock, onions browned with bacon, spice, red wine, vinegar.

The *saupiquet* therefore existed before the *saingaraz* of 1713, yet certainly resembles it. Or, if you prefer, the *sauce zingara* existed in Italy, the *sauce saupiquet* in France, and they were quite similar. And it is, I suppose, possible if not certain that the arrival of the Italian cooks in France might have caused—at least at court and in the cookbooks—the names *saupiquet, saingarat, Saint-Garat*, and so forth, to be changed to *zingara*.

What I do know is that in one of the oldest cookbooks dating from classical times, that of Apicius, we find the recipe for a sauce that is called neither *saupiquet* nor *zingara*, but whose sweet-sour contents inevitably evoke the *saupiquet* of the Morvan.

Let us therefore leave to more dedicated researchers the task of determining whether those Tzengaris did in fact come into Italy—and when—bringing with them a name for the unnamed recipe of Apicius, and thus, indirectly and many centuries later, revolutionizing all our cookbooks.

And let us simply sing the praises of the *jambon en saupiquet* from the Morvan.

The Drouillet brothers, who have devoted a very charming little work to the gastronomy of the Nivernais, quote the remark that "sauces can be a confidence trick." By which they mean to imply that the *saupiquet* is not just some vaguely vinegary sauce that comes from everywhere and nowhere, but a dish in itself, and a "national" dish. For Curnonsky himself has written: "The *saupiquet grosso modo jambon à la crème* is to the Nivernais what *garbure* is to the Béarn, *beurre-blanc* to Anjou, *cassoulet* to the Languedoc, and *bouillabaisse* to Provence."

And he also called it: "One of those dishes that are worth a whole banquet and sum of centuries of experience." I used to know a chef named Lhoste, who had a gift for sauces but a penchant for excess. Instead of a brown *roux* he used a strongly spiced *sauce piquante* as a basis. Which was perhaps going too far.

And I know the chef Belin, who has a gift for sauces but a penchant for complications. He adds—when making a *sau-*

piquet he entitles "Montbardois"—fresh button mushrooms and tomato, then finishes it off with *petits pois*. Which is perhaps too somnolent.

The recipe I give is more classic—and possibly more peasantish. But I like to imagine it is the very same one that delighted those food-loving counts of Nevers back in the fifteenth century.

Jambon en Saupiquet

Slices of salted country ham
  1 qt milk
lard
  1 tbs flour
bouillon
  1 cup dry white wine (Pouilly)
5 shallots
vinegar
  2 peppercorns
2 juniper berries
  1 cup heavy cream
sweet butter
  parsley

Have thick slices cut from a leg of salted ham. Soak them in the milk to remove the salt; then drain and sponge dry.

Brown them in 2 tablespoons of lard in a frying pan.

In another pan make a *roux* of lard and flour. Moisten with the bouillon, then add the white wine.

Steam the chopped shallots in vinegar with the crushed peppercorns and the juniper berries. Cook for 10 minutes.

Mix the shallots into the *roux*.

Strain through a fine sieve. Add the fresh cream and pats of sweet butter. Pour over the slices of ham.

Reheat without allowing to boil. Sprinkle with chopped parsley. Serve.

MENU

Pamplemousse au crabe
(*Grapefruit stuffed with crabmeat*)
**Côtes de mouton Champvallon*
Fourme d'Ambert
(*Cheddar-type cheese*)

Wine: Châteauneuf-du-Pape.

Côtes de Mouton Champvallon

(Ribs of Mutton with Onions and Potatoes)

Marguerite de Valois, the celebrated Reine Margot, episodic wife of Henri IV, once turned her thoughts at the court of France to "the sole sun of her soul, her beauteous heart," Harlay de Champvallon. He was a seductive courtier indeed, handsome, young, and cultured. But that, I'm afraid, is all I know about him. And furthermore, despite those inflamed epistles Margot sent to him from Nérac, the beauteous Champvallon must have been swiftly replaced by a successor. For we know that Henri II's daughter went through men almost as quickly as our good king Henri IV did through women. As opponents in the game of "cuckold the other," they were perfectly matched.

So that the handsome Champvallon (Margot's fancy-man as someone today would doubtless vulgarly call him) has left but little mark on history. And I hope for the sake of his golden memory that he was somehow involved in this recipe for mutton ribs Champvallon.

But hope I must perforce be content with. There is not the slightest shred of evidence anywhere that could justify such a supposition.

Le Boucher.

Ie ſuis Boucher des plus adroits,
Pour bien habiller vne beſte
Depuis les pieds iuſques à la teſte,
Et ſçay fort bien les bons endroits.

Moreover, gentlemen of the gourmet jury, the story of mutton ribs Champvallon is going to be rather short, because it is a dish that has no history. Or, to be more exact, because no one seems to know its history, as though it were suddenly born quite out of the blue one day, between courses. Worse still, we are not even quite sure how to spell it. Like the *Larousse gastronomique*, and Queen Margot's beautiful boy, I write Champvallon with two *l*'s. But the *Répertoire de la cuisine* allows its mysterious Champvalon only a single *l*. Surely that's of no importance, you may say. But I can't agree with you, I'm afraid. As I eat a dish, I also like to savor an anecdote or two, and dip my bread in that delicious sauce of gossip that laps its past. Such garnishes can often throw fresh light, not only on the details of the recipe itself but even on the way of tasting it, of appreciating it.

Take this recipe, for example. To start with, the rib chops used are mutton. Yes, mutton, even though chops are usually lamb, which is certainly a tenderer meat but also less strongly flavored. So that in restaurants a great deal of hearty mutton is only too often christened lamb, which at least allows the customer to feel there is a certain elegance to his meal. Well, it may be that grilled or fried chops should indeed be of genuine lamb, but it is mutton, good mature mutton that you need for the makings of our Champvallon.

And another thing: lamb and mutton, even down to their legs, are in France generally served rare. In this case, no. I would not go so far as to describe the meat as boiled, but it is certainly cooked very thoroughly in its own juice. It is reminiscent of English cooking. But then English cooking is really only our own cooking from way back before the Renaissance, as I have had occasion to point out elsewhere. All meat in those days was boiled before being roasted. And though the process is reversed in this case, the facts are not altered—quite the contrary. Ribs of mutton Champvallon is almost Irish stew. A Frenchified Irish stew, one might say, if Irish stew had not been a French recipe in the first place! Nothing, as you see, is simple. The difference between Irish stew and our Champvallon lies mainly in the fact that in the former the mutton is stewed uncooked, whereas in the latter it is first sealed in a frying pan, browned in short.

The Champvallon, curiously enough, is a rather rare dish
in our restaurants. There are a number of "forgotten" dishes
like that. Today's chefs are no longer familiar with them and
never think to look them up in publications of the past in order to delight our palates. Not that I really think the Champvallon, under this name at least, is by any means an old dish. In
fact, I imagine it's more likely to date from the end of the
nineteenth century than from its beginning. Arbitrarily, I
must admit. To find out, one would have to work one's way
back through time, searching through the great cookbooks for
the moment of its literary birth. (Which is precisely what
Jean Desmur has done. He has discovered that the Champvallon in question was a late-nineteenth-century chef. I almost
feel it's a pity though. We oughtn't to poke around too much
perhaps; it rubs the poetry off things. I prefer to see this dish
striding toward me with a sword at its side, eyes brimming
with the slightly vulgar joy of a young, handsome lad picked
out by love, just as Harlay de Champvallon once was. A
swashbuckling rogue who swashed his way into the arms—and
between the sheets—of a *déclassée* queen. A dish without nobility, I must admit, but entertaining, like some bourgeois
eccentric in a Labiche comedy who might well be called
Champvallon.)

For my own part, I made its acquaintance very late in
life. Thanks to my friend Georges, who from his bar in
Château Frontenac finally made his way to Vichy and achieved
fame and fortune with his Rotonde du Lac and his Grillade.

One evening last year I happened to reminisce with him about this ribs of mutton Champvallon, which he had once served, with a flourish, as his "dish of the day" for habitués and friends:

"Oh, it's years since I made those! They're good though! I tell you what, come for lunch tomorrow. I'll have some ready then."

And next day I found it fresh as ever, the slightly "guttersnipe" attraction of this dish, its gruff courtesy, its "thrifty housewife" streak. And now that I have tried to define its quality, I realize that the great tragedy of the ribs of mutton Champvallon is really a very simple one: it is a dish more suited to the home than to the restaurant, and it is not made any more in the home because it takes too long.

It is a dish that must have retreated now to the haven of middle-class provincial homes, a dish for small market towns, lurking behind the rusticated masonry of some private house bearing a prosperous lawyer's brass plate. No one is expected for dinner today, there will be no one in but the family, and the mistress of the house said this morning to her old cook—who saw her born: "Marie, why don't you do us the Champvallon today, the master loves it so!"

Côtes de Mouton Champvallon

6 mutton rib chops
¼ lb butter
salt and pepper
6 onions

2 cups stock
parsley
12 potatoes

Brown both sides of the chops in some of the butter. Salt and pepper them.

Arrange the chops flat, tight against one another, in an earthenware casserole rubbed with garlic.

Lightly brown the thinly sliced onions in the remaining butter.

Pour the stock over the onions. Boil for 5 minutes; then pour over the chops. Add a sprig of parsley. Bring to a boil. Cover and cook in a moderate oven for 30 minutes.

Peel, wash, and dry the potatoes and cut them into round slices. Arrange over the meat. Salt lightly, and pepper. Bring to a boil again. Cover and put back in the oven for another 20 minutes.

Remove casserole lid. Cook another 20 minutes in the oven, basting often with the broth that has formed, and which should have been completely absorbed by the time cooking is complete. Sprinkle with parsley. Serve in the casserole.

Derain: Kitchen Table

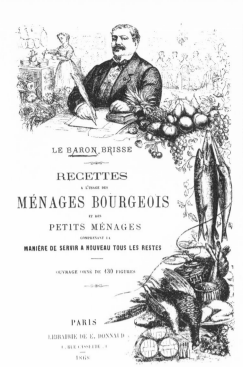

A red Bordeaux would do well with both beef and sauce. I would suggest a Saint-Emilion. Château Cheval-Blanc, for example.

Côte de Boeuf Béarnaise

(Roast Ribs of Beef with Béarnaise Sauce)

I like this definition of the public-relations director, that very typical product of our age: "A person who knows nothing about a product and is paid to see that it is talked about by a lot of other people who know even less about it."

And as an illustration of its truth I offer the story of the gentleman who, some years ago, as publicity for the launching of a brand of *béarnaise* sauce in tubes, thought up the idea of celebrating its anniversary.

A big lunch (it is a well-fed profession) was held in Saint-Germain and a great quantity of glossy paper was doled out explaining to the uninitiated that this oil sauce was created at the Pavillon Henri IV in Saint-Germain, in 1830, and that it was in honor of its birthplace that it was called *béarnaise*—after that king's birthplace.

And the whole story, needless to say, was untrue.

Untrue because the *béarnaise* is not made with oil but with butter.

Untrue because it existed long before 1830.

So I'm afraid our public-relations man was caught red-handed, as it were. Though there are others who legitimately

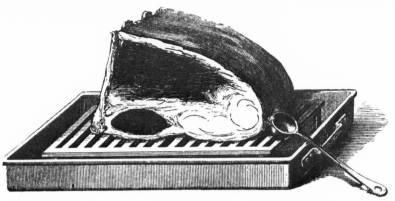

claim that the name *béarnaise* is an indication that the sauce must originally have been made with oil. That seems to me fair enough. But of course it means accepting, *ipso facto*, that it is much older than 1830 and created on the spot, in the Béarn itself, where butter is scarce and oil highly prized.

The error of the gentleman in question—an error emphasized by the dictionary of the Académie des Gastronomes—derives from an excessive reliance upon the observations of one Baron Brisse, who first offered the information that the sauce in question was created in 1830 in Saint-Germain. And given that, the obvious connection between Pavillon Henri IV and *béarnaise* was bound to occur to someone.

Alas for both the Baron and the public-relations man he misled, we find the *sauce béarnaise*, under that name, in culinary works that appeared before that date. In particular, in J. B. Andot's *La Cuisine de la campagne et de la ville*, which came out in 1818.

In fact, this Baron Brisse—whose rosy face the caricaturists of the age seemed to like to draw crowned with roses against a background of truffles and *foie gras*—was little more than a slightly fantastical glutton whose vast appetite was rivaled only by his imagination. An amusing enough fellow nevertheless, and someone you'd always be glad to meet at table. When he retired to the country, in 1872, it was to take up residence under the roof of a celebrated innkeeper named Gigout, where he continued to receive his friends at dinner. His last invitation proved fatal. The arriving guests found him dead in his room. They stood silent for a while. Then Monselet said: "I think we'd better go down and dine now. He always hated his food overcooked!"

Was the *sauce béarnaise* really made with oil when it first saw the light of day? I myself don't believe it. And never shall. It is too delicate, too subtle, too sensitive in its preparation. And besides, since it is basically a hollandaise with the addition of a reduced herbal infusion (and who ever saw a hollandaise sauce made with oil?), it may fairly be supposed that the name *béarnaise* derives solely from that infusion, whose rather lively aroma conjures up the hot south rather than the north, the zest for life of the king from Béarn rather than the insipidity of a Louis-Philippe.

And this vivacity, this eagerness, make the *béarnaise* the very feather in the cap (though a gilded feather not a white one) of the thick slice of rare meat. The *chateaubriand*, but even more the slice of red roast rib surrounded by its *pommes soufflées*. And then the hint of watercress green from the herbs in the sauce. A very moving still life indeed. A palette in three major tones. A dish for those with hearty appetites!

The *béarnaise* sauce has two derivatives:

Sauce Valois: This consists in the addition to an ordinary *béarnaise*, at the very end of its preparation, of two tablespoons of meat glaze (it can be bought in concentrated form in delicacy shops) and is used particularly as an accompaniment to mutton.

Sauce Choron: This is made by replacing the chopped herbs in a *béarnaise* sauce with very much reduced warm tomato purée (one-quarter cup to one cup of *béarnaise*). Served with a *tournedos* it results in the *tournedos Choron* (for whom it was invented). It can be served with all broiled meat, and also with broiled fish. Choron was a chef at the former Restaurant Voisin.

Côte de Boeuf Béarnaise

4 tbs dry white wine
  4 tbs wine vinegar
pepper
  2 tbs shallots
tarragon

chervil
  salt
2 large egg yolks
  14 tbs butter
cayenne

Put the white wine and vinegar into a saucepan with a generous pinch of pepper, the chopped shallots, a sprig of tarragon and two of chervil (both roughly chopped). Bring to a boil with the lid off. Let stand to infuse. Reduce by half and crush through a strainer. Replace in the rinsed pan.

When the infusion is cold, place it over very moderate heat or boiling water and add a pinch of salt and the egg yolks. Blend with a wooden spatula. Add a piece of butter. Work in well. Continue the process until all the butter has been added in small pieces. Then add a pinch of cayenne and a few pinches of chopped chervil and tarragon.

N O T E : This sauce should have the consistency of a thick mayonnaise.

For the wine, a young Fleurie.

Pieds de Porc
à la Sainte-Ménehould

(Pigs' Feet in Breadcrumbs)

Sainte-Ménehould: chief town of the *arrondissement* of Marne, on the Aisne. Population 5,583. Known as *Méne-hildiens*. Former fortress. Military graveyard. Precision tools.

The *Petit Larousse* is succinct indeed. It omits to mention that this small town, though less well known than Rheims or Epernay, is the gastronomic capital of the province of Champagne.

The low town, rebuilt in the eighteenth century, has retained its character. As well as the former post house where Louis XVI was recognized on June 21, 1791, before being arrested a little farther on, his mouth full. The Republic has turned this historic house into a police station.

The arrest at Varennes, work of the postmaster Drouet, perhaps changed the course of history. It certainly changed the course of the postmaster's. And it is noteworthy that his subsequent adventures brought him back to Sainte-Ménehould, briefly, as the subprefect.

Is it, I wonder, because of that pillar in Sainte-Ménehould's church, the one with the capital carved into an oak, and the peasant leading his pigs there to eat the acorns, that the town's cooks have been so successful with pigs' feet? And does the Hôtel Bazinet still exist? If it does, then you must certainly stop there and lunch in their kitchen! A historic kitchen, reconstructed as a replica of the one where Victor Hugo and Alexandre Dumas stopped to sample these same pigs' feet *à la Sainte-Ménehould*, cooked in accordance with a recipe jealously guarded by the Bazinet family since 1820.

But Sainte-Ménehould, the true capital of Champagne for all lovers of the table, even though it is still neglected by many gastronomes, has many other delicacies to offer, and in old recipe books I have unearthed skate *à la Sainte-Ménehould*, and also calves' feet, calf's head, oxtail, and neck of mutton, all *à la Sainte-Ménehould*.

And among all the recipes there is a link: breadcrumbs. The fish, as well as the offal and meat, after being cooked (by braising mostly), are sprinkled with or rolled in breadcrumbs, and then finished off under the broiler.

As we know, all parts of the pig are good! And **Monselet** was particularly fond of praising its feet, which he claimed would have reconciled Socrates with Xanthippe (and who is to say he was wrong?) if cooked *à la Sainte-Ménehould*. Though he seems to have been under the impression that there are truffles in the recipe, which is certainly not true.

The pig's foot is admittedly not an aristocratic form of nourishment. But there is something comforting all the same in its very vulgarity. For it is by no means a poor man's dish either, despite its rather modest cost. I mean that economic necessity never inspires anyone with a desire to dine off a pig's foot if he is the sort who can be content with a chunk of bread and a slice of Brie or head cheese, for example. There is a sort of refinement in the foot's modesty. A promise of the exquisite dish it can become, for example, when boned, wrapped in a piece of caul, enriched with meat, with *foie gras*, with truffle. In that guise it enters the top shelf of the *Entrées* section. It was just such a pig's foot that M. Trompette, Léon Gambetta's cook, chose to use for stuffing a simple wild rabbit, thus achieving for it, under the resounding name of *lapin Trompette*, a brief hour of epicurean glory!

But back to the pig's foot pure and simple, to the pig's foot prepared according to the time-honored recipe of Sainte-

Pieter Brueghel the Younger: Autumn

Ménehould. You will find it on the menus of bistros, but it doesn't seem to enjoy much of a vogue. You will also find it—sometimes—on the menus of rather more elegant establishments, as though to salve some hidden remorse of the chef.

And do you know, if I made a list of my friends and a list of my enemies, and you went around asking all the people mentioned how they feel about pigs' feet, I'm pretty sure all the people on the friends' list would be in favor of them and all the others against.

And one more thing: an old and amusing country tradition from Lorraine. When a pig was killed, the young girl of the house would send a pig's foot decorated with ribbons and bayleaves to her suitor as a symbol of his victory. Or, if she wished to reject him, she would send the pig's tail with a pickle. But are these ribbons, these love favors, the origin of the bandages around the pig's foot *à la Sainte-Ménehould*, or did the ribbons originate with the recipe?

Alas, I lack the space here to go into the philosophy of the pig's foot considered as a good conductor of the nostalgic elements of instinctive sympathy.

For the moment, however, let us content ourselves with deciding what to serve with it.

Chefs are laziness personified, and their benumbed imaginations never manage to get beyond the French fries that they christen *pommes Pont-Neuf* in an effort to evade the fact that they are simply French fries. A purée seems to me to be better advised. But why of potatoes? There are also, after all, the purée of onions, of split peas, of kidney beans, of stringbeans, of celery, of lentils. And I know not how many more.

But since the pig's foot is not served on crystal but on the thick crockery of the roadside bistro, let us suit the rest of the meal to the same honest and friendly setting by serving a purée of kidney beans.

It was, after all, with a red and revolutionary cap on its head that the town of Sainte-Ménehould entered history.

Pieds de Porc à la Sainte-Ménehould

6 pigs' feet
½ bottle white wine
pickling brine
6 carrots
6 onions
parsley
1 leek

thyme
1 bayleaf
1 whole clove
3½ oz butter
pepper
grated breadcrumbs

Bind each foot tightly with wide tape. Fasten in place with string.

Put half a bottle of dry white wine into a saucepan with a little pickling brine, carrots and onions, sliced, parsley, leek, thyme, bayleaf, clove, and enough water so that the pigs' feet can be left to simmer for 24 hours.

After this time allow them to cool in the broth; then unbind them and let them stand for another 24 hours.

Dip each foot in melted butter. Pepper them and roll in the breadcrumbs.

Reheat gently under the broiler.

VEGETABLES

Les Halles, Paris

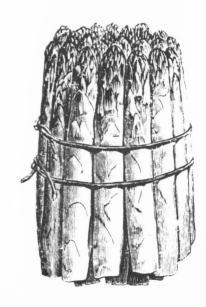

And as I say, wine even with the asparagus, even with the salad. But an "easy" wine. Let us say a rosé, full-bodied enough to hold its own against the seasoned steak: a Tavel (from the Côtes du Rhône), for example.

Asperges à la Fontenelle

(Asparagus with Butter and Egg)

Everyone should believe in fairies.

There are no fairies, admittedly, to watch over the cradle of the beet or carrot. Or if there are then they are second-class fairies, or beginner fairies who have been assigned to the commoner regions of the garden on probation. But the fairy that reigns over the asparagus, over its birth, its life, its form, and its color, must hold the most senior, the most elevated of all ranks in the fairy hierarchy.

I imagined her in my childhood as proud and stately in a pastel dress, smiling as spring, with a diadem of dewdrops and a fresh asparagus shoot as a scepter.

And one should never be untrue to one's childhood.

"It's so pretty, an asparagus shoot," Monselet said, "and so gay. It's as though spring has sent in its visiting card on a plate."

A friend of mine, a poet and a gourmet, said to me one day—with his mouth full—that the asparagus shoot is profoundly linked to the first lilacs, to the first cuckoo, to the awakening of the vine. The awakening of the vine, I must say, leaves me cold. It doesn't really awaken, in my sense and to my

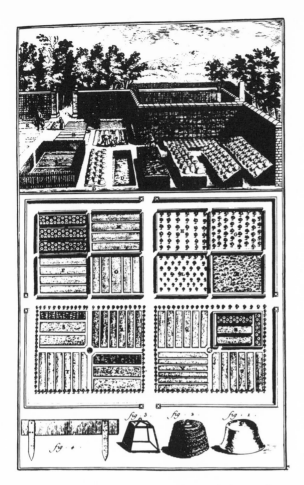

senses, until it reaches my glass—or perhaps in the barrel, if I am invited to sample the new wine. But in the market, it's true, you do see the asparagus side by side with the common lilac, and together, for several weeks, they transform the stalls into scented gardens.

For the asparagus is essentially one of those sensitive and delicate natures whose shimmering beauty is fleeting only. The fairies who watch over the green Lauris asparagus and the pink Argenteuil asparagus have still not found the secret that Ninon de Lenclos, that seventeenth-century charmer, or Diane de Poitiers, favorite of Henri II, used so successfully to keep themselves young. How else to explain the fact that once their brief season is over there is nothing left of these delicate shoots but frightful, withered things, a sort of vegetable kindling, its skin faded and graying. Or else the canned ones, which are to asparagus what the woman emerging from cosmetic surgery is to true beauty.

Let us enjoy this fleeting gift while we may.

Shall we eat it with oil and vinegar, with butter, or clothed in that *sauce mousseline* that so rarely attains the desired sublimity?

Le Bovier de Fontenelle liked them *en vinaigrette*. One of his dinner guests, the Abbé de Voisenon, preferred them *à la crème*. So orders had been given that half should be prepared one way, half the other. But as they gossiped of this and that, suddenly the Abbé felt unwell and collapsed. Whereupon Fontenelle scurried toward the kitchen: "All *vinaigrette*, Marie! All *vinaigrette!*"

However, the recipe for *asperges à la Fontenelle*, invented since then by some admirer of the author of *Entretiens sur la pluralité des mondes*, employs melted butter. And the asparagus itself plays the role of sippet. It is dipped first in the melted butter, then in a boiled egg. Try it, and you will forgive Fontenelle his callousness to the poor Abbé.

I once met a thin and gloomy man who claimed to be a gastronomical expert. He lived for edicts and embargoes. He wanted to ban all wine from my table while asparagus was being served. Poor man! Even a *vinaigrette* should not have to drown in tasteless water. A wine as rosy as the fingers of the dawn, a white wine as light as the sun's early beams, or even, if your sauce is the *mousseline*, a warmer wine, a gentle Sauternais—any of these is a fitting escort to asparagus.

There is a Confrérie de l'Asperge. At one of its meetings the servants of this tender vegetable were served the following repast: Asparagus with ham (the asparagus warm with slices of smoked ham and a *vinaigrette* made with egg yolk on the side); *croustade Héloïse* (pie crust filled with asparagus stewed in a *sauce américaine*); rib of veal *aux asperges*.

Asperges à la Fontenelle

2 lbs asparagus
1 egg per person

8 tbs melted butter
pepper

Choose fairly large shoots of asparagus. Peel them (after washing them and trimming the cut end). Wash again in cold water and shake dry. Tie in small bundles and cook in boiling salted water (12 minutes at the most). Drain and serve on a warm cloth.

Cook the boiled eggs at the same time.

Serve them in eggcups.

Melt the butter in a saucepan over water. Strain it through muslin into a sauceboat. Pepper lightly.

Each person will have butter in an individual bowl so that he or she can first dip each asparagus shoot into it and then into the boiled egg.

Detail from *Les Très Riches Heures du Duc de Berry*

Truffe en Feuilleté

(Truffle in Puff Pastry)

"To speak the word *truffe* is to pronounce a word of note indeed," Brillat-Savarin tells us in his *Physiologie du goût*.

"This egregious 'tuberculum,'" he went on, "is not merely delicious to the sense of taste but also elevates a potency the exercise of which is accompanied by the sweetest of the other pleasures."

Ah, with what delicate gallantry the culinary sage expressed himself!

And even though in practice the truffle may prove less aphrodisiac than was supposed, the legend still remains, and the careful circumlocutions of the old master.

Tuberculum? Yes, perhaps. Or fungus? We don't exactly know. Even the truffle's origin is unknown. It is found—but no one seems sure where it comes from, or how. Some centuries ago a Spanish priest tried to persuade the world there was something diabolical in it. A sort of mandrake in fact.

The tale of the supernatural genius who makes a fortune selling "truffle seed" is part of French folklore. In fact, the truffle seeds only legends—but those generously. In Périgord the old women still tell the story of the good fairy, trapped

into temporary poverty, fed on potatoes by the region's poorest family, and rewarding her benefactors by causing their field to sprout a whole crop of black potatoes. Truffles! And indeed all through central France the word *truffe* is also a nickname for the potato, and a *truffade* is a sort of potato *pâté*.

The Romans knew the truffle, but theirs came from Libya and was reddish in color; or else from Greece, in which case it was white with a hint of the garlic about it. Even today, in Italy, the white Piedmont truffle is cherished far too lovingly for me to risk any denigratory comment. But it is not at all the same thing as what the French think of as *the* truffle.

Périgord is our pride and our joy on account of the truffle. In that long interregnum, when the truffle was not, from the age of the Roman taste for them to the epicurean fanfares that greeted their reintroduction in the early eighteenth century, what became of the dormant deposits that were later to boost this French province to such an elevated position of fragrant and truffled fame?

"In about 1780 truffles were still rare in Paris," Brillat-Savarin goes on to say. "They were only to be found—and then only in very small quantities—at the Hôtel des Américains and the Hôtel de Provence, and a truffled turkey was an object of the very greatest luxury, to be seen only on the tables of the very greatest lords and kept women. In 1825, at the time of writing," he then adds, "the glory of the truffle is at its apogee."

So that in less than half a century (and even then we really oughtn't to count the dismal Revolution years), this troglodytic and secretive "tuberculum" had become first a prime delicacy on the nation's table, then the firmest pillar of its culinary art.

Reality can sometimes outdo fiction.

On winter mornings they let loose the sows, "whose black snouts go searching beneath the ground for that little, dull-skinned, bulbous copy of themselves." Dogs may also be given the task of hunting it out, and it is not for nothing that their quivering noses are often referred to as truffles in France. But there are also men, truffle-diviners, who can tell merely from an inspection of the terrain whether the earth in a certain spot has come under the magic spell or not.

The fragrance of the truffle spreads itself abroad with the November frosts. It is mysterious and many-sided. Some have found a hint of the earth itself in it, the robust smell of green oak trees, the heady aroma of the laurel, of the mastic tree, of thyme. Dissolved and held in a spirit, the scent of the truffle is such that sometimes a mere sniff can make the head spin.

This pungent power is more particularly appreciated by certain very delicate palates. An enthusiast has written: "I find this aroma of the truffle even preferable to the truffle itself, whether scenting a good Dauphiné turkey cock, or a Languedoc guinea fowl, whether marbling a blond galantine, or dappling the cream of a *ragoût*."

But in that I cannot follow. The "vegetable" upon which Colette dreamed of conferring the title "Black Princess" deserves—nay, demands!—to be loved for herself. The lover who makes do with the beloved's perfume is less delicate in his appetites than impotent. Mere aromas are too insubstantial. My zeal, my love, my appetite require more palpable satisfactions.

To consider the truffle merely a flavoring, a kind of herb or spice, is merely a way of excusing niggardliness in its use because of its great cost.

And in a fresh *foie gras*, moreover, if the dish has been well prepared, the truffle will always prove unnecessary, since the two flavors, both so subtle, conflict—and also intertwine, I must agree, but to each other's detriment.

To regard the truffle as an accompaniment, an escort, is a great improvement. The fowl lavishly larded with truffle slices ("I have left blue kisses on your white, white skin," as they sang in 1900), and for that reason termed "*demi-deuil*" or "half-mourning"; or the pheasant Souvarow, drawing after it the beads of a rich necklace of truffles are both highly recommended dishes.

And better, much better a truffle feast but once a year—at exactly the right moment—than those merely trufflish scrapings scattered over fancy banquet dishes in the vain hope of creating a munificent illusion.

Truffe en Feuilleté

6 truffles of 5 oz each
¼ lb butter
salt and pepper

1 lb puff pastry
¼ lb fine sausage meat
1 egg

Scrub the truffles under the faucet. Dry them.

Melt the butter in a heavy-bottomed saucepan. Put in the truffles, then a little salt and pepper. Cover. Cook gently for 20 minutes. Allow to cool.

Roll out the pastry as thinly as possible. Cut six squares from it.

Wrap each truffle in sausage meat, then in a pastry square. Seal the edges of the pastry with water. Brush with beaten egg. Bake in a hot oven for 20 minutes.

La Pomme de Terre.

A menu of the purest La Villette style. And one that requires generous libations of a young, cool, light red wine. A Beaujolais would do admirably. But why, I wonder, does the Bourgueil with its raspberry fragrance come to my mind instead? Perhaps because the meal is one of such traditional serenity and moderation, like the Loire country itself.

Pommes Soufflées (Puffed Potatoes)

No one is a great man to his valet. Are there any great kings to their cooks?

Louis-Philippe of Orléans, for example—representing the regicide branch of the family—who has gone down in popular memory as the king with the pear-shaped head, is said to have eaten like a prosperous shopkeeper, which is to say he did not eat well. He has left us one immortal, though not particularly gastronomical, remark: "Salad is a boon to the insides."

And it can also be marked up to his credit that he was the first mortal to eat *pommes soufflées.* Which might have served to bestow a little honor on his reign.

But when all is said and done, the miracle of *pommes soufflées* was really a railroad accident.

I once read somewhere about the pronouncement that the historian Adolphe Thiers made on the subject of the railroad when it was in its infancy. "This invention," he informed the world categorically, "has no future." Gavarni's remark in 1852, quoted in the Goncourts' *Journal:* "The railroad? Less important in itself than the fact that man's lust for speed has now been multiplied tenfold." But M. Thiers ought at least to have recognized, since it had produced *pommes soufflées*, that the railroad had a present. I'm afraid, however, that our little Thiers, like the fat king, didn't really know much about food either.

The Paris–St.-Germain line is generally thought to have been France's first railroad. Wrongly. There were sections open between Lyons and St.-Etienne, and between Beaucaire and Alès, before that, and the inhabitants of Beaucaire were the proud possessors of the very first railroad station, opened in 1833. It wasn't till four years later, on August 26, 1837, that the Paris–St.-Germain line, built by the engineer Flachat, was officially opened. A line that afforded the Parisians so much entertainment, as dear Gaston Derys put it, "in those days of Pamela hats, nankeen trousers, and Gardes Nationaux."

Under a constitutional monarchy as under a republic— and vice versa—"official opening" inevitably also means "banquet." And so, at St.-Germain, a royal chef was putting the last touches to a menu of which the *pièce de résistance* was to be a *fillet aux pommes frites*.

He had his timetable. At the exactly calculated moment he plunged his thinly sliced potatoes into the crackling fat. Then he waited. The inaugural train did not appear.

"Sister Anne, sister Anne, do you see no one on the road? Is there no plume of smoke above the green carpet of the forest? Above the Seine all blue in the heat? Above the château built by Francis the First? Above Le Nôtre's terrace?"

So he might have questioned some scullery maid standing by. Or he might have thrust his larding spike through his body, like Vatel himself. But he did nothing of the sort. Wisely and calmly, despite his irritation at this untoward delay, he withdrew his still unfried French fries from their boiling bath and set them to drain.

And when at last Louis-Philippe and his spouse (for that was how the French court talked at the time) did finally appear, to a shaky fanfare from a local brass band, the chef plunged his potatoes back into the fat.

And the miracle took place! The pieces of potato swelled into delicate, tasty, golden bubbles, at once crisp and smooth on the tongue.

So the legend goes—and if you take my advice you will go along with it.

Although it must be added, all the same, that if you want your *pommes soufflées* to work you must never cut them up as you would ordinary French fries.

Pommes soufflées are the potato made into poetry.

Pommes soufflées are an all-or-nothing dish. They leave no room for mediocrity. It is possible to encounter deplorable creamed potatoes, shameful French fries, but there can happily never be such a thing as bad *pommes soufflées*, since if you cook them badly they simply won't be *pommes soufflées* at all.

However, the plump opulence of the *pomme soufflée* is not only a perilous precondition of its very existence; it is also what gives it the right to accompany the very best meat, those cuts that equal the potatoes in their individual opulence of texture and taste: rib of beef, thick *entrecôte*, and the marbled sirloin. One cannot imagine a simple rump steak bartering its traditional French fries for the intimidating luxury of *pommes soufflées*.

Parmentier

The domain of the *pommes soufflée* is also that of the finest meat: La Villette, the meat district of Paris, where people really know their beef. Here beef is enthroned, and the *pomme soufflée* is its pale gold scepter, swollen with pride. You go to places like La Villetouse, to Chez Dagorno, or the Cochon d'Or, or the Comète des Abattoirs, or L'Horloge, or Le Boeuf Couronné. And there you will rub shoulders with the slaughtermen in their white smocks, the dealers in their blue smocks, and you will enter into communion with their immoderate passion for rare meat and *pommes soufflées*.

A health to all railroads! And even to that pear-shaped Louis-Philippe!

Pommes Soufflées

Select potatoes that are yellow-fleshed and as large as possible. Peel them. Cut them into slices an eighth of an inch thick and dry them thoroughly in a cloth.

Have your fat not too hot. Throw in the slices of potato (not more than twenty at a time, depending on the size of the pan). Wait for a few minutes. Then turn up the heat while stirring with a slotted spoon. The potatoes will be starting to swell. Remove them and allow them to drain in a wire basket.

Heat the fat to its maximum temperature. Immerse the potatoes in it again. They will swell. As soon as they are golden and crisp drain them, salt them lightly, and serve immediately.

NOTE: Failure is the result of the fat's being either too hot or not hot enough. The steps must be carefully adhered to: moderate heat at first, gradual increase, then very hot indeed. Moreover, once the potatoes have cooked it is possible to place them in the fat a third time (especially if you've cut them thicker) to make sure they are well cooked, since once they have swollen and become crisp there is no risk of their collapsing again.

MENU

Huîtres
(Oysters)

**Timbale de macaroni
    financière*

*Anguillette de boeuf en
    gelée*
(Rolled beef in aspic)

Saint-Honoré
(Cream-puff cake)

You might continue drinking the white wine served with the oysters as an accompaniment to the *timbale* too, in which case it should be a dry but nevertheless mellow Graves (Bordeaux). Another approach would be to serve a red wine with the *timbale* that would also go with the *anguillette*; this could also be a Graves, but red of course. Lastly, such a meal could be accompanied by champagne throughout.

Timbale de Macaroni Financière

(Macaroni in Pastry Shell with Mushroom-Truffle Sauce)

My story, gourmets of the jury, will be brief.

Because the *timbale milanaise à la sauce financière* doesn't have a story—not of any kind.

It is a dish that dates back to the days when cooks still had time to cook. A dish you never meet in these bustling days, either in private houses or on menus. An eminently upper-middle-class dish, both in conception and in its richness: a solid not an ostentatious richness. A comfortable, gilt-edged dish, a dish to sit down to after signing a satisfying contract.

A dish, moreover, with a rather complicated recipe. A recipe as copious as the thing itself, and without any genuine verve, I'm afraid. You could not even call it a classic. Comparable, you might say, to those authors on the second shelf who nevertheless figure automatically in any anthology. We have grown accustomed to them.

And during the last century people were accustomed to it for many decades, this *timbale* that may be *milanaise* or may be *financière*, or may be both, and that the mistress of the house ordered her caterer to bring in on important occasions. It was the crowning glory of her dinner—so she thought; but

the secondary-school superintendent, the local poet, the railroad company director, the surgeon who had just operated on a celebrity, the almost-famous soprano, they would all meet it again the very next day at the dinner being given by the Prefect, or by the President of the Court. How many white wedding dresses, how many First Communion muslins, I wonder, have been splashed with its tomato sauce? How many noble white beards have left the table still bearing the stains temporarily concealed by embroidered napkins?

And I also wonder whether all those notaries who were supposed to have run off with their clients' funds did not really disappear to Belgium simply in order to escape the inevitable *timbales* at all those middle-class receptions.

But today, when the dreaded *timbale* is no more than a memory, it would be delightful just once, on some day of happy chance, to see it appearing at one's dinner table.

Dear, old-fashioned *timbale*, round as the belly of a wealthy investor; glazed and golden, as though beneath a layer of Victorian varnish; anachronistic as honesty, of which nothing remained afterward for the staff downstairs in the kitchen but that delicious bottom crust, soaked with richness, like a *baba*.

Timbale de Macaroni Financière

•SAUCE FINANCIÈRE

¾ lb mushrooms
  ¼ lb butter
2 cups Spanish sauce
  1 liqueur glass Madeira
salt and pepper
  2 truffles

½ lb macaroni
  2½ oz Gruyère
2½ oz Parmesan
  5 tbs tomato purée
2 oz cooked ham

6 oz cockscombs and kidneys
  bouillon
1 tbs flour
  juice of ½ lemon
1 piece calf's sweetbread

2 oz cooked tongue
  ¼ lb butter
pepper
  pastry (either puff paste or flaky)
egg yolk

Clean the mushrooms and wash them quickly in water. Put a third of them (the smallest ones) to one side. Heat 2 tablespoons of the butter and sauté the other two-thirds of the mushrooms in it after drying them well. Pour the Spanish sauce on them (the same amount of stock strengthened with a bouillon cube may be substituted). Reduce slightly; then take off the stove and add the Madeira. Without returning to the stove, add 4 tablespoons of butter in small pieces, shaking the pan as you do it. Add salt and pepper. Put through a fine strainer.

Sauté the small mushrooms you put aside with the thinly sliced truffles in the rest of the butter.

Cook the cockscombs and kidneys in some stock to which you have added a spoonful of flour and the juice of half a lemon (unless you are using canned combs and kidneys already prepared).

Braise the blanched piece of calf's sweetbread and cut it into slices.

Add the small mushrooms, the sliced truffles, the sliced sweetbread, and the cockscombs and kidneys to the strained Madeira sauce. Adjust the seasoning, and keep the sauce hot.

Cook the macaroni in boiling salted water for about 15 minutes. Drain well. Replace in pan and place over heat in order to dry it off still further. Add the grated Gruyère and Parmesan, then the tomato purée.

Slice the ham and tongue thinly. Add them to the macaroni. Then stir in the butter piece by piece. Add pepper.

Line the bottom and sides of a buttered pie plate with the pastry. Prick the bottom with a fork. Cover the pastry with white paper; then fill with fruit pits, dry beans, or even well-washed small pebbles. Do the same on the bottom of another pie plate to make a cover for the pastry shell. Bake in a hot oven. Empty out the beans or pits and turn the *timbale* and its cover out of their pans. Brush both *timbale* and lid with egg yolk; then replace them in the oven for a moment till they are golden in color.

Fill the *timbale* with alternate layers of the macaroni and the hot *sauce financière*. Finish with a layer of sauce. Put on the pastry lid and serve on a hot folded napkin.

And of course a Cornas (a red
wine from the Ardèche)
throughout the meal.

Caillettes

(Pig Organs with Spinach and Herbs)

The *caillette* comes from the Ardèche.

It is a dish that could have come only from a poor district,
and as my grandfather used to say: "Art and poverty go together."

Of its kind the *caillette* is undoubtedly a work of art. Its
ingredients and its smell combine, in fact, to produce an epit-
ome of the Vivarais I have always loved, with its murmurous
valleys, its dry plateaus, its sequestered villages whose inhabitants still believe a host of myths that are undoubtedly
just as valid as the substitutes they are being offered.

Yes, the *caillette* comes from the Ardèche. But it is rather
amusing, now I come to think of it, that this humble dish, this
"pork butcher's hors d'oeuvre" as a chef in a restaurant would
classify it, is also claimed by our rich neighbor the Dauphiné,
across the river. A chef, born in Valence-sur-Rhône, though
recognizing that the *caillette* is highly prized in the Ardèche,
claims it for his bank of the river and offers us the recipe for
it used in Chabeuil. Well, I'm sorry, but no, really no! I have
been to Chabeuil. I have been into several of the pork butchers
there and bought the things they sell under the name of

Antoine Raspal:
Provençal Kitchen

caillette, and they're not the same thing at all. Any more than the *caillettes* from Valence, for which the same chef also gives the recipe.

And I find a childhood refrain rising to my lips:

Oh, hail and snow, please keep away
With frost and folk from the Dauphiné.

The so-called *caillettes* in the Dauphiné, the *caillettes* from the "Imperial" shore are much richer: in them it is the pork that dominates. With us it is the herbs.

I have even seen an Ardèche housewife putting in lungs! But that's because she has never clambered like a goat climbing over fallen rock, early in the morning, up to her uncle Edouard's almond tree, a *caillette* in her knapsack with a good hunk of bread and the necessary bottle. If she had, ah what a feast she would have thought it, up there in the sun and the wind, her *caillette!*

Why, for two pins I would give you here and now the sonnet I wrote at sixteen:

Crussol, proud crag, against the setting sun . . .

For it was among the ruins of the Château de Crussol that a cousin gave me a *caillette* made by her mother, offering it with that shy impulsiveness only sixteen-year-olds can command, and the words: "It has the summer singing in it!" By which she meant that apart from the chicory, the strawberry spinach, and the various wild mountain herbs, this particular *caillette* had as one of its ingredients—poppies.

Caillettes made with poppies. Those, in Dauphiné, they don't have!

The strawberry spinach, blite—a medieval herb—is a typical vegetable of this region, with its thick leaves, its powerful, fleshy taste of the earth. It is also an ingredient, along with the New Zealand spinach, of a sort of *caillette* made in the lower Vivarais called a *pouytrolle*. But strawberry spinach on its own is not enough, any more than just spinach. The true *caillette* must also contain at least some of those herbs that are picked on the way back from guarding the goats, herbs that often have no names, or at least no names that one knows, and whose secrets only the very old village women know. There must be white dead nettles (but only the very tips: even the frugal can be choosy), and I have also seen radish tops included, if they weren't being kept for the soup.

In Paris, the chef of the L'Enclos de Ninon makes excellent *caillettes*, following a recipe provided by the owners, the Teissier brothers, who hail from Les Vans. But why is it that when Monsieur the Pig is killed there, in Les Vans, not far from La Vignasse, the farmhouse of Daudet's ancestors, and the visiting Teissiers bring back some of the freshly made *caillettes*, they are even better?

It pleases me that Alphonse Daudet is not the Provençal people believe him to be, but a genuine Vivarois:

> My uncle had an orchard where
> In March the birds flew down to eat
> And spring provided all the fare.

And these *caillettes*, flavored with the heart and soul of the country, stored in an earthenware crock, in lard, against the winter ahead, they too are fare provided by the spring, with spring's accent and spring's moderation, the garlic in them the merest hint at the heart, no more.

Caillettes

1 head strawberry spinach
  1 handful of spinach
1 handful of aromatic herbs, nettles, and so forth
  2 stalks celery
½ lb pig's liver
  ¼ lb pig's heart
1 lb pig's throat

2 garlic cloves
  salt and pepper
quatre épices
  basil
thyme
  ½ lb pork caul
½ lb lard

Wash and roughly chop the strawberry spinach, spinach, herbs, and celery. Blanch for 15 minutes in boiling salted water. Drain. Refresh with cold water. Drain again.

Now chop all these vegetables very finely. Wring in a cloth to squeeze out any remaining water, and hang up to wait till next day.

Cut up the liver, heart, and throat of the pig in large pieces; then chop finely with the garlic. Mix the chopped meats and vegetables together. Add salt, pepper, *quatre épices*, basil, and thyme. Form into balls of about half a pound each.

Wrap each ball (*caillette*) in a piece of the caul. Grease a baking dish with some of the lard. Arrange the *caillettes* on it, tight against one another. Spread the rest of the lard on top. Bake in a medium oven for 25 minutes.

N O T E : *Caillettes* can be eaten either hot or cold. But believe me, it is cold that they are at their best, as an hors d'oeuvre.

MENU

Jambon cru de Savoie
(*Raw ham, Savoy*)
*Gratin de cèpes farcis
Tarte aux pruneaux
(*Prune tart*)

Dr. Ramain, who proclaimed himself "an independent gastronomer," recommended a Château Chalon with this miraculously subtle dish. But if you want to serve only one wine, then an old Hermitage will go perfectly with both the ham and the *gratin*— even with the prune tart.

Gratin de Cèpes Farcis

(Stuffed Mushrooms with Breadcrumb and Cheese Topping)

Some definitions, at least, are accurate: *gratin* (the crust produced on a dish during cooking) comes from *gratter*, to scratch, because one does in fact have to scratch at the browned part to loosen it from the rest of the dish. But in gastronomy extrapolation has always been the rage. *Gratin* denotes "any dish generally sprinkled with breadcrumbs or cheese whose surface becomes crusted in the heat of the oven."

At that rate onion soup is a *gratin*.

And so is a baked apple.

Which enables the dictionary of the Académie des Gastronomes to go on: "The *gratins*, whether savory or sweet, are among the most delicate dishes."

I'm not so sure in a great many cases!

It is true that our pontiffs add: "Possibly they are somewhat too filling." But even that isn't necessarily true.

One thing in any case is certain: the language of the people has endorsed the superiority of the *gratin* by enshrining it in several slang phrases. A *gratin* is something that is absolutely first class. A *type du gratin* is a wealthy member of society, and Maxim's is a restaurant *pour le gratin*.

Which doesn't mean that you will necessarily find any on Maxim's menu.

The *gratins* are legion.

There are *gratins* of shellfish (lobster, crayfish tails, prawns) and of fish (turbot, brill, carp).

There are the vegetable *gratins* (spinach, pumpkin, eggplant, Jerusalem artichokes, macaroni, and of course potato).

The potato *gratin* takes many forms. The process of baking—even when not carried out in the home but in the village baker's oven, oddly enough—leads every cook to develop an empirical notion of what such a *gratin* should be. For the perfect color of it, the redolent russets and browns of it when fresh from the oven is an undoubted treat for the eye, that emissary of the palate. Sometimes, here and there, the gratin is *burned* slightly. Those twisted, dried flakes, those black tips or ridges mingling with the expanses of old ivory, the tints of old wood, give the *gratin* not just a particular aroma but a sort of gastronomic guarantee: it was high time! But ah, the warmth of that only-just-salvaged savor, ah the enthusiasm we feel at this gastronomic rescue operation! For that slightly burned taste is, in short, the cinders of hellfire only just avoided. And it tastes all the better for that near escape, still just perceptible on the tongue, persistent yet fleeting, a constant reminder of the dark background to life's joys.

Yes, the *gratin* takes many forms. Every family has its recipe, or better still its tradition. And its phraseology. Here they refer to it quite simply as baked potatoes. There as potatoes *boulangères*. There again as potatoes *au gratin*. And then, by extension, the potato is also *au gratin* in a sense when it is gilded in the frying pan. And so we get potatoes Lyonnaise, woven with golden onion strips, potatoes Anna, and the version of the dish from Périgord, rich land of truffles, potatoes *sarladaises*. All these *gratins* are the spiritual offspring of clearly recognizable parents: the father is the *gratin* of Savoy, the mother the *gratin* of the Dauphiné.

Taste may lead us to grant one or other of these the supremacy. The *gratin* children, scattered across the country, are clear enough proof of the laws of heredity, of the possibility of taking after one's father, or one's mother, or both equally. But I don't think there is any room for discussion as to seniority: the *gratin* of Savoy is the older of the parents.

When Christopher Columbus brought back from America "a sort of yam resembling a carrot" and which we now know as the potato, this new vegetable took the most roundabout route it could find into France. Even then, of course, there were the Pyrenees. And so from Spain the potato first made its way to Genoa, thence through Italy up into Savoy and Germany. Oddly, we find that during the sixteenth century the potato was known in Savoy as the *cartouffle*—obviously a near relation to the German *kartoffel*. And eventually, descending the foothills on the far side of the Alps, these *cartouffles* from Savoy, cooked *au gratin* by the mountain dwellers there, arrived in the Dauphiné. There the less rugged climate civilized the *gratin* of the mountain heights to some degree—feminized it. Papa *gratin* had found a wife, and from then on little baby *gratins* were sent out to colonize the rest of the culinary world.

Perhaps it would be as well to give these happily married recipes?

You slice up the potatoes, which must have been carefully peeled and be of a kind that will not disintegrate in the cooking. Wipe them with a cloth, salt and pepper them, then lay them in an earthenware dish that can be placed on top of the stove and has been rubbed with a clove of garlic and buttered. Over the last layer of potato slices pour a good 2 cups of stock (to 2 pounds of potatoes). Sprinkle with grated cheese, add a few pieces of butter and start it off on top of the stove. Once it has heated through, place it in the oven for about 45 minutes.

So much for the Savoy *gratin* (in which it is permissible to increase the cheese content by sprinkling it between layers too. A matter of personal taste).

In the Dauphiné *gratin* the stock is replaced by a mixture of boiled milk and two eggs. You can add a little nutmeg too.

Better to advise a *gratin de cèpes farcis* such as I was treated to by the good Dr. Paul Ramain, the eminent myco-gastronomist from the Savoy, after a long fungus-gathering walk through the autumn countryside of his home, the Douvaine.

Gratin de Cèpes Farcis

12 large mushrooms
  5 oz pheasant meat
2 oz lean bacon
  2 chicken livers
1 shallot
  6 fresh walnuts
tarragon leaves
  ⅓ cup butter

walnut oil
  white bread
milk
  1 egg yolk
salt and pepper
  curry powder
2½ oz grated Parmesan

Your mushrooms should be the best possible, regular in size and firm. Wipe them with a wet cloth, trim them, and pull the caps away from the stalks. Place the caps, not overlapping, in a big, heavy frying pan, concave side downward, and steam them over a moderate heat for 8 minutes. Turn them over with a spatula and place them in a warm oven for 5 minutes. Drain and allow to cool.

Chop up the upper, edible part of the stalks together with the raw pheasant meat, the bacon, the trimmed chicken livers, the shallot, the peeled fresh walnuts, and the tarragon. Brown this stuffing quickly in some of the butter, melted, and some of the walnut oil. Bind with a little white bread soaked in milk. Remove from heat to add the egg yolk, salt, pepper, and a dash of curry.

Brush the tops of the mushrooms with walnut oil. Lightly salt and pepper them. Fill each one with the stuffing heaped up into a dome; then arrange them in an ovenproof earthenware dish greased with a little of the melted butter and walnut oil.

Sprinkle with crumbled white bread and grated Parmesan. Pour the rest of the melted butter over them and bake in a moderate oven for 30 minutes.

NOTE: Duck or guinea-fowl meat may be used instead of pheasant. Gruyère or that amazing cheese from the Savoy, Beaufort, may be used instead of Parmesan. A little garlic may be added to the shallot.

In Lyons we would choose
a single wine: a Chénas
or a Brouilly of the last vintage
served well chilled. But
the scallops could be
accompanied by a white Graves
(Haut-Brion) and the rest of
the meal by a red
Haut-Brion.

Cardons à la Moelle

(Thistle and Beef Marrow)

The cardoon is close kin to the artichoke. It is quite simply an edible thistle, as its name implies, since the French for the various common or garden thistles is *chardon* and the name for the edible thistle is *cardon*, both quite obviously from the same root—linguistically speaking of course. And if the ordinary thistle is the food of the donkey, the artichoke (yet another of the thistle family) that of man, then I am very much inclined to claim that the cardoon is the food of the gods!

The cardoon was known before the artichoke, or so at least it would seem. Theophrastus gives Sicily as its country of origin and tells us that the peasants there scraped its leaves into salty water to make a stew of them. A picture which hardly seems to fit in with the version of Athenaeus, who assures us that the *carduus* or *cinara* was very much sought after in Rome and was a dish to be found only on the tables of the rich. It was imported from Carthage and Cordova (where, according to Pliny, a single small plot of this luxury vegetable could bring in an annual income of 6,000 sesterces).

And let us also note, in passing, that *cinara* is derived from *cinis* (ash), either because of the cardoon's grayish color or

406

Abraham Bosse: Taste

because ashes had proved to be the best fertilizer for it. Later the word became corrupted to *cynara* on account of the dentate form of its leaves and the analogy drawn with the teeth of the dog. A few years back someone put on the market an apéritif based on an extract of artichoke. It was named Cynar—and was totally disgusting.

But let us return to our cardoons.

This modest plant has allowed the artichoke to upstage it in modern times. The artichoke is such a showy creature. It puffs out its plump belly and wears its legend like a decoration in its buttonhole: Catherine de Médicis, finally successful in her struggle for the crown of France, enjoying its delights too enthusiastically and "thinking she would burst with an indigestion of artichoke bottoms"; Ronsard turning it into a rondeau; the Paris street vendors singing its name in their street cries and celebrating its fame as an aphrodisiac. So that eventually the artichoke felt it just couldn't go on having anything as lowering as a "bottom" and decided to change the word to "heart"—though the original word (*cul*) was in fact more accurate and never shocked our grandmothers.

Meanwhile, discreet in the background, the cardoon makes no attempt to compete.

It has the gourmets on its side.

And as proof of that, it is in Lyons that this vegetable is most grown and cooked.

Is the so-called Lyons variety the best, as Paul Bocuse maintains from behind his three Michelin stars? The cardoons of Tours were equally renowned in the last century. But it doesn't greatly matter. When the cardoon has reached its full height it is tied and placed in a trench in order to blanch its stalks and make them more tender. A process that has been referred to as "wrapping the cardoons in their autumn mufflers."

Only the central ribs or stalks of the leaves are used. A six-and-a-half-pound plant will provide between one and three-quarter and two pounds of usable stalk.

After the preliminary preparation of the cardoons, there remains only the decision as to which of the many different recipes they should be used in. It is Lyons that has, over the years, evolved my favorite: the *cardons à la moelle*.

The *cardon à la moelle*, if you should ever by happy chance (and it won't be often) meet it in Paris, will be a kind of postcard sent to you from the south. One of those postcards on which you find on one side, along with the signature of a friend and the words "Wonderful trip, wish you were here," the unspoken implication: "Ha ha, I'm here and you're not!" and on the other side, either in black and white or color, a landscape in which every house, every stone, every tree, is—if it is a country landscape—reflects a regret: your own regret at being forced to gaze at them secondhand.

A postcard from Lyons, in the life of a gourmet, is always something incomparable, something rare, something moving, and also a spur to the appetite. In this dish of cardoons cooked with marrow you should see, running like a sort of watermark, the Saône under the bridge at Collonges, the road suddenly turning into the narrow path leading to the other bank, the poor-looking little square and the vast, welcoming gate of the Auberge. A sudden delight in life, a ballet of white jackets beyond flowery window boxes, a gentle, blond smile of welcome (from Mme Paul Bocuse), then life itself exploding, dear Paul himself, that adventuring musketeer of the table, that sly-tongued and infinitely aristocratic host.

All that in a simple dish of vegetables? Yes indeed!

But let me pass the pen on to Paul himself for the recipe:

Cardons à la Moelle

cardoons
  lemon
3 tbs flour
  1½ tsp salt

1 lb butter
1 qt very strong beef bouillon
beef marrow
  Emmenthaler cheese

Remove and discard any tough or tired leaves from the cardoons. Then remove all the tender stalks, one by one, till there are none left. Cut them up into 3-inch sections, beginning from the bottom. Don't use the last section at the top, leafy end.

Peel the cut-up sections in order to remove all the threads. Rub them with a slice of lemon and, as soon as you have done so, throw them into a pan of water with some lemon juice in it.

Prepare a *blanc*. That is: to 2 quarts of water in a saucepan add 2 tablespoons of flour mixed with the cold juice of half a lemon. Add the salt. Bring to a boil, stirring all the time. Throw in the drained cardoons, and then add ½ pound plus 2 tablespoons of butter in pieces. Simmer with the lid on for 2 hours.

Heat the remaining butter in a saucepan. Add 1 tablespoon of flour and cook quickly to a russet color, stirring constantly.

Pour the cold bouillon into this *roux* and cook for 20 minutes.

Carefully drain the pieces of cardoon. Mix them into the sauce.

Arrange in a *gratin* dish.

Poach your beef marrow in salted boiling water for 10 minutes. Drain it and cut it into large slices. Lay these slices over the cardoons. Sprinkle with the grated cheese and bake in the oven for 40 minutes.

Just the one wine: Champagne.
Or a Pinot Chardonnay.

Timbale de Riz Roy Soleil

(Rice in Cream Sauce, Sun King)

I imagine that if you asked a hundred Americans which came first on their continent, rice or the potato, very few would know that the potato is a native there, and therefore countless thousands of years the senior of rice, which came from the Orient by way of Europe.

Similarly, in the mind of the average Frenchman, rice is still thought of as exotic, whereas the potato is looked upon as being utterly "at home" in France.

But of course he is mistaken. Rice was being cultivated in France, and eaten (imported from Spain or Italy) long before Columbus's sailors brought back the potato from Mexico.

It was sailors again, probably Spaniards, who took rice to America. So that for a brief period the Old and New Worlds were sending their respective products to and fro across the Atlantic as though it were a tennis net.

The exchange was not an equal one. Quantitatively we were the winners: we owe the Americas the tomato, kidney beans, the turkey, the potato, and tobacco. They owe us the vine and rice. But qualitatively we have no reason to boast of the bargain, since rice, dietetically and gastronomically, is out of all proportion superior to the potato.

This fact is reflected even in the poetry surrounding the two products. Rice has a legend. Not the potato. Rice has given birth to proverbs. There is a civilization based on rice, whereas it is difficult to imagine the potato inspiring anything whatever noble, or beautiful, or great. It is, as the working class has instinctively felt, simply a humble "spud." What can you expect of a spud except that it shall be a spud? And to be christened "Spud" is to be consigned to the ranks of the homely for life.

But rice can be romantic. "Love is like a young rice plant," says one Madagascan proverb. "If it is transplanted it will grow elsewhere." And another goes: "Grief is like a store of rice in a loft: it shrinks a little every day, and in the end there is nothing left."

And its first fruits are celebrated today much as they were by the Greeks during their Thargelia, for rice is a bringer of happiness. Hence the custom of bombarding newlyweds with it.

Potatoes, on the other hand, are thrown only at bad performers, along with rotten tomatoes. There's a difference!

Rice is beyond any doubt an ancient form of nourishment for the French.

Quiqueran de Beaujeu, in his *Provence louée* (1614) notes: "On fast days they eat rice cooked in milk of almonds with much sugar. The rest of the year, when it is permitted to eat flesh, it is employed in the confection of a thousand sorts of sauces."

And in all the old cookbooks rice has a place of honor, whereas they all ignore the potato completely.

It was in one such ancient cookbook that I found this recipe for a *timbale de riz*. It dates from the early eighteenth century. For which good reason I have christened it *timbale de riz Roy Soleil*.

Recipes of those days, beginning with the very first cookbook in time, the famous *Viandier* by Taillevent, are often elliptical and a little vague. But how mouth-watering sometimes too.

And here I must begin a digression.

Alas, Brillat-Savarin's well-known remark about the happiness that the discovery of a new dish brings to mankind has

inspired too many chefs to inflict the most unseemly dishes upon us in the name of "creation." It is not enough for a dish to be new. It must also be good. And harmonious. The creator must have been brushed by the wing of genius for an instant.

And as we all know, genius is not to be found on every street corner. So too often the creations of our chefs are merely approximations, pedantic compilations, misshapen constructions produced by a wrongheaded confusion between symphony and cacophony, originality and eccentricity.

Even though the solution to their problem is right in front of their noses.

All they need to do is to *re-create!* To search out the forgotten dishes of the past and interpret them for our age.

When I discovered this rather complicated *timbale de riz* from the reign of Louis XIV, and in no more than sketch form as it were, I conceived the idea of entrusting a great restaurateur with the task of realizing it, and of making it into a virtually new dish.

Which was how René Lasserre came to develop and produce this small wonder of a great cuisine.

Let us forget the present, the harshness and the indelicacy of the age, and all its threats. Let us imagine ourselves attending the French Regent's *petit souper*. The gardens of the Palais Royal are murmuring below us, and a few distant violins are playing among the trees with the spring breeze. The furniture, though not yet Louis XV, is no longer Louis XIV. The mirrors reflect the thickening waist of the king's mistress, who eats too much, but also her still admirable bosom. Cardinal Dubois is there, half priest (look at my cassock), half clown (look at my face), and his sallies provide constant amusement for the company of *roués*. Does Louis-Philippe know that he is to be the last civilized offspring of the Orléans line? For the moment he is silent, almost moved: the dish that the footmen are bringing in is one he worked out himself with his master of the kitchen. He knows what is in store.

He knows that Lully has been brought to life again, and that a veritable ballet of flavors and fragrances is about to begin, its aerial figures and *entrechats* unfurling on the guests' plates in a coating of tender ivory, in a velvet sauce of innocent wantonness. He knows that every detail of the dance has been perfectly rehearsed, from the eager entry of the sweetbread, on through the mushrooms *sur les pointes,* and the *jeté-battus* of the artichoke hearts. Smiling, he pierces a creamy morsel with his golden fork. He remarks to his mistress: "Cockscomb!" She bursts into rather coarse laughter, but aristocratically coarse: she knows well enough, as does her lover and master, the reputation—the erroneous reputation—of cockscombs. And that it is in any case too late for them.

And already she might reply, before Brillat-Savarin: "The pleasures of the table are there to console us for the loss of the others."

Timbale de Riz Roy Soleil

6 oz long-grain rice
 2 pieces calf's sweetbread
salt and pepper
 butter
2½ oz caps of large mushrooms
 6 artichoke hearts

2 oz truffles
 ¼ lb cockscombs
½ lb caps of small mushrooms
 scant 2 cups champagne
1 cup chicken velouté *sauce*
 2¼ cups heavy cream

Cook the rice by the pilaff method.

Blanch the pieces of sweetbread for 10 minutes. Remove the skin, veins, and so forth, and cut into dice. Season with salt and pepper. Seal, then cook in butter. Sauté the large, well-washed mushroom caps in butter. Check the seasoning.

Sauté the diced artichoke hearts in butter. Salt and pepper them.

Chop the truffles into small dice.

Blanch the cockscombs.

Brown caps of the small mushrooms in a skillet. Salt and pepper. When they are just beginning to turn color pour the champagne into the pan and stir it around. Reduce by half.

Add the chicken *velouté* sauce and half the cream. Cook very slowly, without boiling, for 10 minutes.

Mix all the other ingredients into this sauce very gently. Bring briefly to a boil. Add the remaining cream. Check the seasoning.

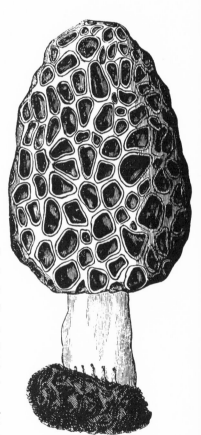

MENU

*Pieds de porc à la
  Sainte-Ménehould
*Morilles à la crème
*Melon de Schéhérazade

A white Arbois should do
splendidly.

Morilles à la Crème

(Creamed Morel Mushrooms)

The good Dr. Ramain, whose *Mycogastronomie* has become
the authoritative work on the subject, was accustomed to
shrug his shoulders when anyone in his presence referred to
the poisonous properties of wild fungi. "In all Europe," he
would say, "there are no more than four main lethal species,
all very easy to recognize, and thirty-two species that are
mildly but not seriously toxic!" And he had himself counted
1,877 non-toxic wild fungi—350 of them edible and of gastronomic value—in France alone!

In short, France—happy country!—has more species of
fungi to delight its palate than it has cheeses. Which is saying
a lot.

All the same, though, a mere three or four of those varieties are sufficient for my gastronomic happiness: the *chante-
relle*, the edible agaric, the *cèpe*, and above all the morel.
Together with the truffle—but is the truffle in fact a fungus?

And if I had to narrow down the choice to one, then I
feel sure I should sacrifice all but the last—the morel, the admirable, the perfumed, the tender morel.

Academician Jean-Louis Vaudoyer distinguished between

two different kinds of truffle-eaters: those who think truffles are good because they are costly and those who think they are costly because they are good. The same might be said where morels are concerned. They are certainly both costly and rare.

For we must be careful not to confuse it with the *gyromitre*, an ascomycetes fungus that Larousse tells us it is wiser not to consume and that is nevertheless offered more or less everywhere, in dried form, under the name of *morille*.

Though also an ascomycetes, the morel, with its sponge-like honeycombed top and its short, thick stalk, is nevertheless quite distinct as a species. It appears in spring on banks and in hedges, near elms and ashes, and is without peer in the fragrance it can impart when freshly picked.

Alexandre Dumas said that the morel stimulates the appetite, fortifies and refreshes the stomach, and is of great help in the concoction of sauces. He also recounts an anecdote from the life of St. Pardoux that there is no space to repeat here but which seems to prove that it takes divine intervention—in the form of punishment—to render this particular fungus harmful.

All labor deserves a wage, no doubt; but also you mustn't expect anything for nothing. La Fontaine's fable makes that clear, and like the plowman's children we must work and take pains before we can enjoy our morels as we should: they are full of grit and very difficult to clean! "Double, double, toil and . . ." No, perhaps that's rather unflattering: to reader and morel alike. But all the same, unlike all the other mushrooms, which should only be rinsed, the morel requires an abundance of running water so that each fold of that little vegetable brain can be soused and cleaned beneath it.

Which reminds me of a story: In a very great Paris restaurant I asked specifically before ordering their morels whether they had been properly cleaned. I was assured that they had. Alas! My teeth crunched a Sahara every time they met, making not only enjoyment of the dish but even consumption of it impossible. A little later the owner of the restaurant, inspecting his tables, came over toward me. I pretended to doze:

"Asleep, my dear sir?"

"Alas yes, the sandman emptied his bag into my morels!"

Were there more morels in the past? Probably. Progress is killing them off. At all events the morels that we scarcely ever see on restaurant menus any more, and even then mostly in omelettes or as a garnish, once occupied a great deal of space in cookbooks. In *Portable Dictionary for the Kitchen, the Pantry, and the Distillery*, published anonymously by Lottin le jeune, in 1770, with a royal license issued in 1765, I find *morilles à l'italienne* (with parsley, dash of garlic, Welsh onion, olive oil, served on fried bread); *morilles au lard* (on skewers alternating with pieces of bacon); *morilles en ragoût*, *à la crème*, and *au gras*; *morilles* in soups, *morilles en croûtes* (covered in a *coulis à la reine*); *morilles farcies* (stuffed with white meat of chicken); *morilles frites* (fried in lard and served with mutton gravy); *morilles* served in *vol au vent* cases, and so forth.

For my own part, a dish of *morilles à la crème* is the answer to all my dreams.

I can think of nothing at once so potent and so delicate.

And though my modesty must suffer in the admission, I feel bound to add that I myself, once upon a time, was a past master in the preparation of *morilles à la crème*. The fact was well known. My friends were never backward about inviting themselves up to my little seventh-floor terrace apartment to savor my version of a dish that was becoming an obsession:

"Yes, we'll come, but you must cook us your *morilles à la crème!*"

The great Frédéric at the Tour d'Argent had his famous duck, Escoffier his *pêche Melba*, Duglèré his sole. And I had my *morilles à la crème*. I used every saucepan in the place, I dirtied every dish, the day was not long enough for the task, the drop of cognac never suave enough, the cream never thick enough for that alchemical process that moreover was utterly forbidden to all spectators. Closeted with just my genius (too little, alas, in the event) and of course my morels, I labored.

Hugo "talking to God" and Balzac sweating with inspiration had no more superb an air than I. I was Molière on his trestle stage and Rostand crowing to the morning in my pride. I was thinking, therefore I was cooking. I was even prepared

to prophesy a little: they were due to arrive; already I could hear the murmur of their entrance line: "Well, where are they, these morels of yours?"

Thank heaven at least that the morel season is a short one. Yet even so I felt that spring was already on its way, that nature was already quivering with returning life again as soon as autumn was upon us, and as the song goes—more or less:

A springtime without morels,
Why that's just not spring!

Well, one must always be able to laugh at oneself, and I give you permission to join in if you want to: perhaps the subtlety of that dish of mine was simply a flattering joke invented by my famished friends. He who flatters the cook never goes hungry, the proverb says. Or ought to say, even if it doesn't. Well now it does, because we've invented it. Enough.

In order to escape my daily morel I was eventually forced to move out. Perhaps that terrace had something to do with the friendship my guests felt for me. Certainly they came to see me less often in my new ground-floor apartment. Morels are like the great love of one's life: they don't last.

Morilles à la Crème

1 lb fresh morels
¼ lb butter
juice of ¼ lemon
salt and pepper

2 tbs brandy
¼ cup flour
2 cups heavy cream

Wash the morels thoroughly under running water, opening up the cells in order to drive the sand out. Shake dry.

Melt butter in a saucepan. Add the morels with half the lemon juice, a pinch of salt, and one mill twist of pepper. Bring to a boil, tossing from time to time.

Cover and steam for 10 minutes.

Drain the morels.

Reduce the liquid they have been cooked in, adding the brandy. Set aside.

Melt the remaining butter and mix the

sifted flour into it. Stir with a wooden spoon and cook for 3 minutes, but gently, so that the flour doesn't brown.

When this white *roux* is cold, add the cream and allow to thicken, stirring constantly with a whisk. Add some of the liquid from the morels to thin the sauce. Salt and pepper. Strain.

Put the sauce back in a saucepan, check the seasoning, add the morels and warm slowly without allowing to boil.

418

MENU

Quiche Lorraine
Rôti de porc froid
(Cold roast pork)
*Salade de lentilles
Fromage blanc aux fines
  herbes
(Cream cheese with
  herbs)

White wine or red? As you please. A very good case could be made for an Auvergne wine such as a Corent (which can be a rosé). Personally, I feel a Chinon has an even stronger claim.

Salade de Lentilles *(Lentil Salad)*

First let us destroy the legend: it was not for a dish of lentils that Esau sold his birthright but for the sustenance it represented at a moment when he was dying of hunger. Genesis is quite clear on the matter: "And Esau said to Jacob, Feed me, I pray thee, with that same red pottage; for I am faint!" So that it was for food that he sold his birthright. And that food just happened to be lentils.

The lentils in question were the common red Egyptian lentils, which are much less tasty than our lentils from the Puy district.

However, it does seem to me that we are just a little unjust to this vegetable which, though it may not be worth a birthright—valueless today in any case—certainly merits the gourmet's consideration.

It is said to be common. It brings with it a whiff of the boarding school, of the barracks, not to say of prison. Women reject it on the grounds of their figures. Abbé Boeuf, when giving a commentary on the Holy Scriptures to his fellow students at the Lycée Henri IV, and coming to Esau and Jacob's bargain, refuted it in these terms: "Moreover, how is it possible to believe that he was idiotic enough to sacrifice so enviable a privilege for a few spoonfuls of so insipid and uncouth a vegetable?"

Uncouth! Now the cat is out of the bag. In Greece, the rich had banished lentils from their tables, and one of Aristophanes' characters says of a man who has recently become rich: "Oh, he doesn't eat lentils any more, you know." In Rome, the refinement of manners relegated lentils to plebeian kitchens, and when Martial serves this vegetable from the banks of the Nile to his friends it is not without expressing a certain disdain. The Middle Ages and the Renaissance were both prejudiced against it, and Platina of Cremona considered it to be "the worst of all vegetables."

Given all these precedents, how could any modern middle-class woman not look upon the lentil as unworthy of her palate?

Yet the true gastronomer will revel in them, and at any stage of his meal before dessert—from lentil soup through to lentil salad.

The ordinary family *soupe aux lentilles* is usually made simply of the water the lentils have been boiled in, enriched to some extent with cream and fried croutons. But when we move on to *potage de lentilles*, or better still, *crème de lentilles*, then the dish is edging its way up past the salt, as it were, and is to be found in the pages of the very greatest cookbooks. For example, in his *Gastronomie pratique*, Ali-Bab gives us a cream of lentils in which half a pound of lentils is joined by half a cup of fresh cream, a measure of veal stock, and a partridge!

Pickled or salt pork with lentils is of course a universally accepted classic. And indeed, in any list of happy culinary marriages and blissful gastronomic unions, after the pigeon and *petits pois*, the pike and *beurre blanc*, the duck and spring turnips, room must be found for pork and lentils. The lentil in one form and one form only: that grown in the Puy district. Pork in almost all its forms, from sausage to roast, from salted or pickled cuts to knuckle, from tongue to tail. And it is a marriage that merits the tribute of a *bouquet garni*, a sprig of parsley, and a big spiked onion.

Some Parisian restaurants serve pickled pork and lentils

Trappist monks in the kitchen: their tastiest foods include lentils

as one of their *plats du jour*. And they are often amazed at its popularity. Whereupon, because of the very fact that it is popular they proceed, very wrongly, to disdain and neglect it. And soon the pork is too salty; the lentils haven't been picked over and they swim insipidly in an excess of water. As for the butter—for butter there must be—one is reminded of André Gide's somewhat stingy cousin who remarked as she buttered her bread: "If the corners want some, let them come closer!"

The truth is, that when you buy your piece of pork it is fifty to one that the butcher will say to you: "It's only slightly salted, so you need only wash it and put it on to cook." And it's just not true. Remember the saying of those who know about these matters, the specialists in fish salting: "Preserving salt is one thing, cooking salt is another." So you must desalt your piece of pickled pork at least overnight, and in a cool place, so that there is no fermentation. Better to have to salt the water when you start cooking it than to use any of the preserving salt. And you must take care over the cooking. Put the joint in cold water with the *bouquet garni*, the spiked onion, the parsley, a carrot cut into roundels, and then as soon as it begins to boil skim off any froth. Then add the lentils, which must also have been soaked, but only for a few hours (they mustn't begin to sprout). When it is cooked, remove the meat, strain the broth, and drain the lentils very carefully. Then remove the herbs and flavorings and put the lentils into a pan in the oven or over low heat so the rest of the water evaporates. Then, and not till then, stir in a good piece of fresh butter, sprinkle the lentils with a little chopped parsley, and arrange them around the pork.

Very few chefs treat this dish with the respect it demands. I wish they would reread their elders (and betters). In Viard's *Cuisinier impérial* (1806) there is a recipe for duck with lentil purée that I will pass on to you without changing a word:

"You prepare your duck as for the so-called *canard à la poêle;* you place a lining of bacon slices in the bottom of a saucepan, then the duck, then a few slices of round of veal, two carrots, three onions, two cloves, a bayleaf, a little thyme, a bunch of parsley and scallions, after which cover over the duck with more bacon slices and pour on a ladleful of stock. If your duck be tender, then three-quarters of an hour will suffice for its cooking; if it be tough, then leave it longer over the heat; when the time comes to serve it, then take it up from the pan, drain it, untruss it, and set it upon a good dish. Then cover it with a purée of lentils. Excepting if your duck be nicely plump and white, then you may put the purée beneath it."

And now for the *salade de lentilles*, which is certainly more than just an *hors d'oeuvre* and in the right hands can be a *chef d'oeuvre*.

Salade de Lentilles

1 lb lentils
  coarse salt
2 onions spiked with cloves
  2 carrots
1 garlic clove

bouquet garni
  1 tsp strong prepared mustard
olive oil
  2½ oz lean bacon
parsley

Soak the lentils overnight.

Drain them.

Put them in cold water together with a sufficient quantity of coarse salt, the spiked onions, carrots, crushed garlic, and a *bouquet garni.*

Bring to a boil and continue to cook at a very gentle boil.

Drain. Remove the carrots, onions, garlic, and *bouquet garni.*

Leave the pan on the corner of your stove for a few minutes so that as much water as possible will evaporate.

Mix the mustard into some olive oil.

Pour this onto the lentils while they are still hot. Mix in well.

Cut the bacon into small pieces and crisp them in a frying pan. Drain them. Add them to the lentils.

Sprinkle with chopped parsley.

DESSERTS

Sologne stands midway
between the district of Sancerre
and the Touraine, both wine
countries. A white
Sancerre won't mar your
veal; but a Bourgueil would
be even better, and
with the cheese, as well. But
a sparkling Vouvray will
be magical with the tart.

Tarte Tatin

(Apple or Pear Upside-down Tart)

It has figured on the menu at Maxim's for decades now. It has
won its spurs. Or rather, if I may so express it, it has acquired
the assurance of a beautiful, and just slightly flirtatious woman.
But preserving a great fund of simplicity that can still surprise
—to say the least—the uninitiated. As they enjoy it they may
even think to themselves that perhaps it isn't quite at home at
Maxim's. They obviously don't know that it was born in a
country inn, and that it came to Paris in clogs.

I don't know how it happened, but about ten years ago
the *tarte Tatin* suddenly became all the rage. It is the inevitable
complement to the minks one sees in all those *bistroquets* that
Paris Society (which one can't help thinking of sometimes as
enemy number one of society) will suddenly seize upon and
besiege until they become quite untenable, and in which a meal
eventually starts to cost twice what it would in one of the great
restaurants. And in such places you will hear the diners going
into ecstasies over their "upside-down tart" (the other name
for the *tarte Tatin*). And on one occasion I even heard a be-
diamonded parrot assure someone that she had known the
Monsieur Tatin in question.

In fact, this delicious tart (delicious when made simply, as it was born) is our only legacy from two old maids who at one time—when this century was still only a few years old—ran their family hotel, the Hôtel Tatin, in Lamotte-Beuvron.

In Lamotte-Beuvron, the Hôtel Tatin still exists, opposite the railroad station. Its proprietress may well be the best cook in the world. But of course it's not the same thing at all. And because I never knew the Demoiselles Tatin, because I don't even have two first names to put to the memory of their anonymous faces, I would never dare to ask for the distinguished tart in her dining room.

Distinguished less because of its present fame than in itself. It is distinguished in its very conception, for it is a true representation of the cookery of the Orléanais region, which according to Curnonsky is "pure, noble, and simple, like the lines of that province's very landscape, like the French they speak there, like the light from its skies." In fact, Lamotte-Beuvron, together with Salbris, is the hunting center of the Sologne, that slightly sad but very taking region, the fief of Maurice Genevoix's novel *Raboliot*, where the gleaming ponds in the autumn mists are traps set for our imagination. Charles d'Orléans himself, that perfect, gentle knight and poet, wrote of the hunts of the Saulongnois and the Beausserons for autumn partridges and hares. Yes, it has always been hunting country, and this *tarte Tatin* is above all a contribution to the warrior's—I mean the hunter's—repose. After the chase across the autumn stubble, it is the logical end to the traditional fortifying, restorative evening repast. It is the feminine note in a meal for men, eaten in the slightly stuffy and smelly atmosphere exhaled by game bags, by boots, by damp jackets hanging to dry in the great hearth. Talk and drink are flowing with equal generosity. Any dish venturing to enter the menu with tiny mincing steps at such a moment could only be a disaster: a *tartelette*, for example, garlanded with delicious little strawberries. The diners would not dare to eat it, for fear of hurting it with their big boots, their coarse tongues, their big appetites. Whereas this *tarte Tatin* is a country girl who's seen a thing or two. An innkeeper's daughter, accommodating, not averse to a jest. One or two glasses of wine won't scare her away, or even a glass or two of marc brandy. But careful all the same, she's not just a nobody! She has a sharp side to her tongue as well, even though she's all dimpled sweetness at the moment. She can laugh a merry laugh and take a joke, but you mustn't assume she's a nobody. Her nest will be nicely feathered, you may be sure, like all those of honest innkeepers' daughters.

In truth, dear unknown ladies I refer to as old maids, dear Mesdemoiselles Tatin, you who were also young once, as we all were, this tart is perhaps the first and now eternal smile of your girlish spring.

Tarte Tatin

¾ lb butter
¼ lb powdered sugar
2 lbs Pippin apples

½ lb flour
1 egg
1 pinch salt

Butter the bottom of a tin-lined copper skillet, 2 to 2½ inches deep, generously (using 3½ ounces of the butter); then sprinkle in a layer of half the powdered sugar.

Peel the apples, dry them with a cloth, and cut them into thick slices, even just into quarters. Pack the pieces into the bottom of the skillet so that it is completely covered. Sprinkle the remainder of the sugar on top. Melt 2 tablespoons of butter and pour over the top. Cook over high heat for 20 minutes or so. The sugar should become caramelized but remain a pale brown.

While the apples are cooking make your pastry. Pile the flour on your pastry board. Make a well in the center and put into it the egg, the salt, and the remaining butter softened over water. Mix together. If necessary, add a little water in order to achieve a soft pastry that you can roll out very thinly.

Having rolled it out, place it on top of the skillet, tucking the edges down inside. Place in a medium oven for 30 minutes.

To serve, turn your *tarte Tatin* out on its serving dish. Serve warm but not hot.

NOTE: You can make it with other kinds of apples or with pears.

Jean Béraud: Inside a Pâtisserie, 1889

MENU

Crudités et cochonnailles
(Raw vegetables and cold
pork)
Entrecôte marchand de
vin
(Rib steak with red-wine
sauce)
**Baba au rhum à la*
Chantilly

Nothing to drink with the *baba*, unless perhaps a glass of cool water as a foil to the rum. Before? Simple! A light red, a Beaujolais-Villages, will see you nicely through both courses.

Baba au Rhum à la Chantilly

(Yeast Cake with Nuts and Raisins)

The *baba* of our sweet-toothed childhood, that big gilded corporation full of rum and crested on occasion with vanilla-flavored cream, the *baba*, that sponge soaked with dreams and fragrant sweetness, so jolly sitting there in the window of the bakery, came to us from Poland! But it received its naturalization papers very quickly!

"It is generally accepted," the *Larousse gastronomique* tells us, "that the invention of this cake must be attributed to the Polish king Stanislas Leczinski, though certain authors dispute it."

Very well. Let us accept that Louis XV's father-in-law, in exile at Nancy, did no more than introduce an already existing Polish confection to France. The cake in question was perhaps the *kugelhopf* (which had been made in Lemberg since 1609), which the exiled king amused himself with by dousing with some spirit or other and setting fire to as though it were a plum pudding. And since he was an enthusiastic reader of *The Arabian Nights*, he named this delicious volcano of his the Ali Baba.

"In the homes of the good king's descendants," Carême

tells us, referring to the same Stanislas, "when *babas* are served they are always accompanied with a sauceboat containing a mixture of sweetened Malaga wine and a sixth part of distilled tansy water."

Carême also writes: "We know from Mme la Comtesse Risleff, *née* Comtesse Potoka and a relation of the Leczinski family, that the true Polish *baba* should be made with rye flour and Hungarian wine."

The *baba* was first introduced to Paris early in the nineteenth century, by the pastrycook Sthorer, who had seen it being made at Lunéville when the Polish court moved there from Nancy. Indeed it was his Ali Baba that guaranteed the success of the shop he opened on the rue Montorgueil (a street also honored by the presence of a number of famous restaurants, among them the celebrated Rocher de Cancale of Balzacian memory, and also the houses of Lesage—whose young hares stuffed with Périgord truffles were a delicacy of some renown—and of Perrier, Rouget's pupil, whose *timbales de macaroni* and *gâteaux de riz* were the pride of an establishment unique in Paris). Sthorer developed the practice of making his *babas* in advance and brushing them with the necessary

liquid as they were sent out. Later on he devised the method of immersing them in a rum syrup.

At about the same time, in Bordeaux, another sweetmeat known as a *fribourg* was being invented that was a very close relation to the *baba* from Lorraine. And in Paris, Julien the master pastrycook was creating his *Brillat-Savarin*. As the *baba* lost its Ali, so the *savarin* lost its Brillat, but nevertheless achieved a brilliant career running parallel to that of its cousin, which in fact it rather resembles.

"The true color of the *baba*," Carême also writes, "should be reddish. It is a male pastry and the judgment of it in the baking not easy."

A male pastry! The way these things are put! But of course it is indubitably true. The world of cakes and pastry is visibly inhabited by males and females. A woman the meringue, oh and infinitely so! And a good honest housewife the apple pie; a pretty young thing, not to mention the *religieuse*, the strawberry tartlet. Eclairs, on the other hand, are self-evidently masculine; the *moka* is not merely male but a lord to boot; and the *baba* is a kind old uncle.

"No babas?"
"There aren't any left,
an English lady has just eaten
the last two dozen."

— Pas de babas?
— Il n'y en a plus, une dame anglaise vient
de manger les deux dernières douzaines.

Baba au Rhum à la Chantilly

1 oz fresh yeast
1½ cups milk
2 lbs flour
10 oz powdered sugar
pinch of salt
¼ lb Smyrna raisins
¼ lb chopped almonds

6 eggs
½ lb butter
breadcrumbs
1 cup water
rum
whipped cream

Mix the yeast very gradually into the warmed milk in a big bowl. Add half the flour. Mix in well. Cover the bowl with a cloth and leave it in a warm place for 3 hours for the dough to rise.

Mix into the risen dough 3½ ounces of sugar, the salt, the raisins, the chopped almonds, and—one by one—the eggs.

Melt half the butter and when it is barely warm mix that in too, followed finally by the remainder of the flour. (Do not stick too rigorously to the amount of flour indicated; be guided by the consistency of the dough, which should be like a very thick batter, just able to flow.) Then beat this batter well with a wooden spoon until it comes away from the spoon. Put back into a warm place for another 2 hours.

Lightly butter your individual charlotte molds. Sprinkle the breadcrumbs onto the butter. Fill the molds three-quarters full with batter. Allow to rise for another 2 hours. Then place in a hot oven and bake for about an hour. They will be done when a knitting needle or skewer comes out clean.

Dissolve the rest of the sugar in the water and bring momentarily to the boil. Skim if necessary. Allow to cool.

Turn out the *babas* when they are still hot, dip them in the cold syrup, then drain them on a wire rack. Later, pour a generous quantity of rum over them.

Serve with lightly sweetened, vanilla-flavored whipped cream.

432

For an important *soufflé* an important menu. The one above ought to delight a Lucullus invited to the table of a Lucullus, I feel. Needless to say, champagne would do very well throughout the meal. The same one—extra dry—that was used to pour over the fruit. But if you are in a Pelion on Ossa mood, then a great Burgundy with the larks (Meursault-Charmes, say), a great Bordeaux with the *soufflé de truffes* (Château Haut-Brion), and Pol Roger for the melon.

Melon de Schéhérazade

(Melon Filled with Fruits and Liqueurs)

The literature of the melon is abundant. It is a fruit, more-over, that has even been set to music, and I remember an old friend of my family—a dandy of a bygone age whose moiré waistcoats and ivory-topped cane I much admired—often singing couplets like these:

> "Oh, my friends, this is the moment
>   To gather round me and be silent.
> As an aid to our digestions
> We'll ponder that oldest of all old questions:
> To give our hearts to melons is it wrong,
> Whether they be round or whether they be long?"

I listened with astonishment. I had never seen any long melons—or, if you prefer, any watermelons. My allegiance was still exclusively to the cantaloupe—brought back from Armenia to one of the popes at his country palace called Cantaluppi and then brought on from Italy into France by Charles VIII—and with the melons of Cavaillon, because they were beloved by Alexandre Dumas.

Had the father of the *Three Musketeers* not sent his works to the municipal council of that tiny town in the Vaucluse on the understanding that they would send him twelve of their melons in yearly exchange?

This fruit, round as the sun, capable of being either abominably nasty or celestially delicious, need never go into eclipse over our dinner table. By which I simply mean that we can serve it as an hors d'oeuvre, as a soup, as a vegetable, and as dessert.

Round as the sun, I said. But the sun is much more reliable than the melon. As the old dandy's song had it:

> Though on the tongue its melting sphere
> Can be with heavenly sweetness graced,
> Sometimes of the pumpkin sere
> It has the faded tint and taste.

As for the watermelon, its traitorous mask can sometimes conceal a heart of colocynth. As another philosopher observed in a bitter quatrain:

> Friends nowadays, I do protest,
> Are much like melons to my mind:
> Fifty you will have to test,
> Ere one that's good you'll find.

But I shall suppose here that you, with your skilled and delicate thumb, have found *the* melon, all sugar and honey, scented as a bee's sweet soul, plump and bursting with life. And that you are hesitating as to how you should serve it. Well, remember that your melon came from the East, and that it still retains an innate sympathy with the luxuries and dappled daydreams of eastern palaces and subtle sultans' palates.

I have no information at all about who Lucette Darbelle was. I imagine her as a nineteenth-century actress, a charmer who has left no trace of herself behind—besides her name—except for this one very feminine recipe for Scheherazade's melon.

To that pretty and coquettish woman it conjured up

434

Larry: Scheherazade

"all the sensual luxury of an Arabian Nights world." And you must admit that even though Lucette Darbelle left nothing else behind her, this recipe alone ought to guarantee her immortality.

Melon de Schéhérazade

1 large Persian melon
  salt
2 slices of pineapple
  2 peaches
1 banana
  18 raspberries
18 wild strawberries

3½ tbs of sugar
  ¼ bottle champagne
2 liqueur glasses crème de menthe
  1 liqueur glass maraschino
1 liqueur glass kirsch
  butter

Make a fairly large opening at the top of a good, well-ripened melon, retaining the piece you remove. Scoop out the flesh of the fruit with a melon scoop to make small balls. Lightly salt the inside of the melon and stand it on a plate, open side down, to drain the water from it.

In a salad bowl mix the balls of melon with the pineapple slices, diced, the peaches and banana, sliced, and the raspberries and strawberries. Sprinkle with the sugar and steep for 1 hour.

Mix the champagne and liqueurs together. Add them to the juice given out by the sugared fruit.

Turn the melon cut side up. Fill it with the fruit. Pour the mixture of alcohol and fruit juices in on top.

Butter the edge of the piece you removed and press it firmly back into place. Stand the melon in crushed ice for 2 hours before serving.

It is probably as well to make the menu as a whole a festive one, thereby establishing once and for all that the surprise omelet is a special treat. But not too heavy a meal, nevertheless. I think the one given above fits the bill.

The wines can be simple enough: a Muscadet, a light Bordeaux, a champagne. Or champagne throughout. And best of all, Dom Pérignon.

Omelette Surprise Brésilienne

(Omelet Filled with Ice Cream)

Being a physician need not make one any the less a man—or even, on occasion, a gourmet. For it was apparently a doctor of medicine, Benjamin de Rumford, a remarkable contributor to the theory of heat, who gave this nickname to a flambéed omelet filled with ice cream. "RUMFORD (Sir Benjamin Thompson, Count of), American chemist and physician, born at Woburn (Mass.), 1753–1814, author of research papers on heat and light," my *Petit Larousse illustré* tells me.

But others assure us that the invention of this combination of heat and cold is much more ancient, and that it originated first in China. And why not? Thousands of years intervened between the first blooming of that Celestial art of cooking and the first tottering steps of our own, and there is nothing new under the sun—or almost nothing anyway.

One thing is certain: the designation *à la norvégienne* came later, suggested no doubt by an association of ideas linking the ice cream inside the omelet and the northerly—and therefore snowy—geographical situation of a country that is in practice outstanding for its frugality, and whose favorite dessert is in fact a sort of cake, somewhat like a *savarin*,

Renoir: At the End of the Lunch

stuffed with butter cream, and caramelized on the outside—the *Kransekake*.

Be that as it may, the Norwegian omelet has indubitably given rise to a whole series of "surprise" omelets that correspond in some sense to a certain epicurean state of soul.

The child and the demiurge are coupled in its womb.

But as for surprise, there is in fact none at all. We know from its first flickering appearance that its swelling and flaming flanks conceal that impossibility, a vanilla-flavored snowdrift. But the game has to be played. For the sake of the children perhaps, but much more often for the sake of that eternal child-woman to whom this dessert is truly dedicated.

It is not a family sort of dessert (the housewife, quite wrongly, usually considers it far too complicated), but rather a restaurant treat, and as such perfectly calculated to please its public. Dedicated to pleasing it in fact.

Because it takes some time to prepare, it is generally offered on menus as a dish for two. Men don't actually like it, though. So it isn't the pudding of the married, the official couple, but rather that of the couple in the making, of the lover who is willing, out of his great love, to share with *her*. How many ducks *à l'orange* (another dish for two) and Norwegian omelets must have been ordered in such circumstances, by ardent wooers who have in fact enjoyed neither dish? The man will eat his share of the duck all the same. One has to keep one's strength up, after all! But he will just sit and toy with a minute portion of the omelet, having thankfully watched the omniscient maître d', despite the lady's birdlike cries and mock indignation, slide the vast majority of it onto her plate.

Whereupon she will eat it all. Pink with pleasure.

And then lick her lips like a kitten.

It is true that it is to a large extent just air—an illusion. But perhaps that is part of its glamor; the very reason that has made her dream of it all week, as she sat at home, eating everyday meals with her parents.

And then there are those gourmet couples, drawn into friendship by their shared tastes and appetites, who have fallen into the habit of going out on "good food" sprees together, like four musketeers ready to spur one another on to greater epicurean feats—as if they needed any urging.

They have all tucked into the *foie gras* with equal masterliness, liquidated the *poularde à la crème*, and moved on to the cheese. The ladies take only "the merest morsel" to go with the Corton '47. They are keeping a space for the surprise omelet.

And they are not about to forgo it either. They have been looking forward to it ever since the dinner was first arranged. They will light the last Roman candles of their appetites at its blue flames, and the resulting heat will flush their cheeks with strange carmine patches, the tints of two laboring digestions.

"And the ice cream, you see, helps the stomach digest," they will explain with their mouths full, as though feeling they ought to apologize for such enthusiasm over this really rather dull dish.

Or, if you prefer, over this poetically dull dish, with its aura of small-town romanticism.

"We shall meet again at your wedding breakfast," the *omelette norvégienne* seems to whisper to the young lady whose flushed and syrupy greed has made her look good enough to eat herself.

And to the others, to those greedy-lipped matrons already panting up the foothills of obesity, in tones more honeyed still: "There, you see? Do you remember the wedding? And here I still am. Faithful as ever. Love fades, you see, but I remain."

Superficially all fire, cold as egotism inside, is this not in fact the wicked fairy among desserts? I have often wondered.

The classic Norwegian omelet has a base made of sponge cake, vanilla ice cream for the filling, and a liqueur flavoring. Obviously the flavor of the ice cream and the liqueur can be varied. However, the Parisian restaurateur Papa Olivier has given me the following recipe for an *omelette surprise brésilienne*, made with coffee, that I feel is one of the best. Moreover it is perfectly simple and within the capacity of any housewife to make. So here it is: a Brazilian-Norwegian omelette.

Comme on l'écoute!...

Omelette Surprise Brésilienne

8 small slices sponge cake
  8 egg whites
4 tbs sugar
  4 tsp coffee essence

8 scoops of coffee ice cream
  1 tbs sliced almonds
powdered sugar
  9 tbs rum

Select a large, ovenproof serving dish. Arrange the slices of cake on it with their sides touching.

Beat the egg whites till they are very stiff. Beat in the sugar and coffee essence.

Quickly place a scoop of ice cream on each slice of cake, then cover all of them with the whisked egg whites, using a silver knife to completely cover the cake. Sprinkle the sliced almonds and a little powdered sugar on top.

Place the dish under your broiler for 5 minutes at the most. Warm the rum in a pan. Pour it over the "omelet." Ignite and serve.

MENU

Toasts de caviar
(*Caviar on toast*)
Côte de boeuf à la moelle
(*Ribs of beef with marrow*)
**Crêpes Suzette*

Only champagne really goes with such a dessert. Choose a really good one. And if you want my specific advice, then Pol Roger.

Crêpes Suzette

(Pancakes with Orange Butter)

In France, between Candlemas and the middle of Lent, there appears above the icy horizon the pale gold circle of a vernal moon: the pancake. The pancake, like a saint's halo, and flavored with the orange blossom's odor of sanctity.

There was a time, on the second of February every year, when people and clergy walked together in procession, lit wax candles in their hands, through all the churches in the land. Hence the name of Candlemas. Though that ceremony, dating back certainly to the sixth century, may well have derived originally from the solemn festivities of Ceres and the pagan Lupercal.

Not that it is of great importance one way or the other. But all gourmets will agree that the pancake is a charming folk tradition. To children, pancakes present the possibility of future happiness and prosperity. Even today, when the coin they symbolized, the bright *louis d'or*, no longer exists, we still toss our pancakes and wish for wealth. And during my childhood it was a tradition that the first pancake of every year was wrapped in paper and placed on top of Grandmother's big kitchen dresser—where it certainly contributed to the prosperity of the mice.

The custom originates, I am told, in Burgundy.

But I have found many variants of it in G. Bidault de l'Isle's monumental *Vieux Dictons de nos campagnes.*

In the Yonne, for example, at Champlost, successful pancakes meant the wheat ears would fill out; at Toucy they kept illness at bay. Around Ligny-le-Châtel people pressed them against their faces before eating them, thereby guaranteeing that they would not be stung by insects during the coming harvest.

In olden days the village children used to go from farm to farm, candles clutched in their hands, collecting ingredients for pancakes and wax to make a big candle for dedication to the Virgin on the day of her Purification.

In the Gâtinais, not content with eating pancakes themselves, the villagers also used to feed them to their hens in order to ensure that they laid well.

We also know that on Candlemas 1812 (just before he left on his Russian campaign), Napoleon insisted on making pancakes at Malmaison—which he still visited now and then, despite his divorce from Josephine.

The Emperor, a firm believer in omens, tossed four pancakes successfully (which meant four battles won). But the fifth, to his utter mortification, he missed. And he remained gloomy throughout the remainder of the evening. The day Moscow went up in flames, all those months later, he said to Ney: "There is my fifth pancake!"

There are hundreds of recipes for pancakes. But their workaday, family origins argue overwhelmingly in favor of the simplest of them all, the pancake our grandmothers made, in every memory inevitably the best: flour, milk, eggs, a discreet flavoring of orange blossom with its hint of rum.

There is no filled, or flambéed, or fruit-flavored *crêpe* that can ever equal that humble pancake our mouths watered over so as children. But it is nice, just occasionally, to vary it with the subtleties of the *haute cuisine*, the researches of an experienced chef. As with the *crêpe Suzette*.

The *crêpe Suzette*, moreover, is a dish set apart by the fact that for foreigners, and particularly for Americans, it somehow seems to symbolize all the suavity, all the elegance they expect in French cooking. If a Paris restaurateur puts *crêpes Suzette* on his menu he will certainly not sell any except to Anglo-Saxon tourists. But he will sell as many portions as he has tourists at his tables. Because for them, gastronomically, the *crêpe Suzette* is Napoleon's tomb, the Eiffel Tower, and the Casino de Paris all rolled into one.

And it appears on more menus in New York than in Paris!

Why this enthusiasm? Why such infatuation? No one knows. It is just a gastronomical fact. And only a few years ago the wire services informed us of the death of a self-styled "French chef" who had made his fortune in the United

States and who was the "creator" of the *crêpe Suzette*. Or so he had told everyone. And built up great transatlantic fame on a lie.

Because this Henri Charpentier had been in the United States since 1905, when he was twenty-three. And according to his own account of the matter: "It was seven years earlier, in 1898, that I created the *crêpe Suzette* for the Prince of Wales, on the terrace of the Café de Paris in Monte Carlo."

But those dates alone, of course, tell us that it would have been quite impossible for this "chef"—unknown to the Société des Cuisiniers—to have created this dessert. Because at the time he claimed to have done so he was, by his own admission, only sixteen. And at that age he couldn't have been anything more than an apprentice; whereas only a much older man, a *maître d'hôtel*, could conceivably have been waiting upon so very eminent a guest.

And yet, at bottom, his anecdote is perhaps quite true. And the young Charpentier could perfectly well have been present on the occasion.

The future Edward VII has been, or is about to be, made happy. He finds this new dessert delicious; and his companion is even more enthusiastic.

"What do you call this dessert?" the august guest demands to know.

"Well . . . it, er, has no name, Your Highness."

"Aha! Very well, then, it shall be *crêpes Suzette*," the Prince announces, deferring with one regal hand to his pretty companion.

Another version has it that the *crêpe Suzette* was created by Dugnol, *maître d'hôtel* in the renowned Restaurant Bignon on the avenue de l'Opéra. But that story is no more authenticated than the other, and not nearly so charming.

So let us accept pretty Suzette and her Royal Friend as the official godparents.

After which, it must now be said that ninety-nine times out of a hundred the *crêpes Suzette* that are served in restaurants aren't anything of the kind. And the recipes you usually read aren't the real recipe either: *crêpes Suzette* aren't flavored with oranges but with mandarins (tangerines). And this detail, this clue, limits the possible scene of the crime, if I may so put it, since the mandarin in those days was hardly ever seen—or heard of—farther north than the Côte d'Azur. And another thing: *crêpes Suzette* aren't *flambéed*.

Pancakes generally, whether *flambéed* or just flavored, are yet one more proof of the lack of imagination prevalent among restaurant chefs. Two, perhaps three kinds of spirit, a few liqueurs, always the same ones, when there are dozens there waiting to help us vary our aromas, our scents. And that reminds me of a recipe thought up by the novelist Henri Duvernois, whose charming books are no longer remembered, I'm afraid. But this recipe called for chestnut flour with a spoonful of cocoa added to it. Then you just carried on with your pancake recipe as you would normally, but you could also fill the pancakes, when you'd cooked them, with fresh cream, flavored with orange zest and a cacao liqueur.

Crêpes Suzette

½ lb flour
  3 eggs
2 cups milk
  2 mandarins (or tangerines)

2 tbs Curaçao
  5 tbs oil
3½ tbs powdered sugar
  3½ tbs butter

Put the flour into an earthenware casserole. Mound it and make a well in the middle. Break the eggs into the well. Mix them into the flour with a wooden spatula; then add the milk, little by little. Lastly, add the juice of one mandarin, 1 tablespoon of the Curaçao and the oil. Let this batter settle for several hours.

Work the juice of the other mandarin, its grated zest, the other tablespoon of Curaçao, and the powdered sugar into the butter.

Heat a heavy skillet or griddle (if possible one kept solely for *crêpe*-making, and never washed, but merely wiped with clean paper after each use). Beat the batter again. Drop a small ladleful of it into the pan and tilt the pan so the batter spreads and the pancake is very thin. Cook the pancakes one by one, keeping them warm on a plate till you have used all the batter.

When all the pancakes are cooked put them back one by one into the pan. Fill each one with a little of the worked butter. Fold them in four and serve very hot.

Sebastian Stosskopf: The Five Senses

One doesn't drink anything with the peaches, but there is nothing to stop you from serving champagne after them. For this menu, a glass of vodka with the salmon, and with the lamb a Bordeaux (say, a Haut-Brion), which will go with the Roquefort as well.

Pêche Melba *(Peach Melba)*

Saturnin was Louis XVIII's gardener and grew peaches for him. One day, the story goes, Saturnin said to his son: "Son, carry these fine peaches to the King." So the child arranged the fruit carefully in a basket and dutifully set off to carry them to His Majesty.

When he beheld them, those nonpareils among peaches, Louis XVIII—being particularly partial to that fruit—wished to show his appreciation to the child. He beckoned him over, had him sit down, and applied himself to the largest of the fruit while the boy watched. And with what pleasure!

Saturnin's son was shrewd and a joker.

"Child," the King said, "I like the look of you. Here, take this second peach and eat it yourself."

"Gladly, sire," the delighted urchin replied, and producing a clumsy-looking knife from his pocket, began very delicately peeling the fruit.

"Unhappy boy," Louis XVIII cried, putting out a gouty, swollen hand to restrain the tiny, childish one, "don't you know, you little idiot, that one never peels a peach?"

"Yes, sire," the boy answered. "But, you see, I dropped

Nelly Melba

my basket on the way, picking blackberries, and the peaches rolled out into some muck!"

That anecdote is no less moral for being almost certainly apocryphal.

But to facts: the peach came to us from China, by way of Persia. And it is written in the book of Chinnoug-king that a peach eaten at the right moment will preserve the body from dissolution until the end of the world.

And it is true that there is something Oriental in the peach, something at once opulent and mysterious, a patrician richness, an aura of ceremonial that is in some way foreign, almost Byzantine.

And if the peach needs a poet, then it is not Ronsard or Verlaine, but Hugo, who celebrated it thus:

This fruit seduces all men's eyes
And all their senses gratifies;
Its velvet cool our touch can teach
How roses may be blent with lilies;
This golden form could well be Phyllis . . .
Were it not a tender peach.

This gift from the mysterious East, painted by Jean-Baptiste Chardin cheek by jowl with the proletarian walnut—which also came to us from Asia, but long before—is most often eaten uncooked. But it will accommodate itself to more complicated approaches, and Clemenceau, in the evening of his days, used to eat a peach in syrup daily, in the season.

Incomparably the best way of serving it, however, is the one that was devised for Nellie Melba.

This celebrated singer, who had come to Europe from Australia to delight the Old World with the beauties of her silver voice, had many recipes dedicated to her, among them *les ris de veau Melba,* a dish of braised calf's sweetbreads coated in a sauce made of butter, mustard, and lemon juice, and served with asparagus tips and mushroom purée.

And it was in 1892 or 1893, in London, during the years when Escoffier ruled supreme over the kitchens of the Hotel Savoy, that he created the *pêche Melba.* He had heard that the famous soprano "adored" ice cream, but that she did not dare to eat it very often for fear of the effect on her vocal cords. He therefore began to muse on the possibility of a dessert in which the ice cream would be merely one element in a whole that would take the chill off it slightly. The previous evening he had attended Covent Garden and applauded Nellie Melba in *Lohengrin,* and this gave him the inspiration of serving up his creation next day, at a dinner she was giving, in a silver dish encircled by the wings of an ice swan. The peaches themselves lay beneath a veil of spun sugar, and everyone went into ecstasies over both the dessert itself and the symbolism: the *pêche Melba* was born.

Pêche Melba

6 peaches
sugar syrup
6 scoops vanilla ice cream

raspberry jam
kirsch

Peel the peaches carefully. Make sufficient sugar and water syrup in a saucepan to poach the peaches in. The syrup should be cooked until it forms a thread.

Poach the peaches in the syrup, but do not let them become soft. Leave them in the syrup to cool.

Place each of the scoops of vanilla ice cream in an individual serving dish. Then place a drained and carefully pitted peach on top of each scoop of ice cream.

Mix some thick raspberry jam (if you have whole, preserved raspberries, which are better, drain them and mash them) with a little kirsch. Coat the peaches with one or two spoonfuls of this mixture.

The first thing one thinks of after glancing at such a menu is champagne. But why not serve vodka with the fish, a red Burgundy with the partridge, and a Tokay with the *soufflé*?

Soufflé Rothschild

(Soufflé with Candied Fruits and Liqueur)

The *soufflé?* That flavored cylinder of nothingness.

Air. Thin air!

Perfume the wind for me and doubtless its caress will delight me even more, but without in any way modifying the transitoriness of its presence or the speed of its passing. And even the perfume will vanish with it.

On this subject I find myself in total agreement for once with the dictionary of the Académie des Gastronomes: "Particularly ephemeral and somewhat empty satisfaction."

And so true is that comment, to be found under *soufflé,* that no one even knows who invented this dish. Or when it was invented. The *soufflé* was not, and then suddenly, one fine evening, it was. And that is the sum of our knowledge.

And even now, now that it *is,* it continues to be not, since it will have ceased to be tomorrow. What do I mean, tomorrow? In five minutes! The chef brings it in. As puffed up himself with pride and gratified vanity as his creation. He sets it down. He leaves. And the *soufflé* has gone before he has, dwindling on our plates: a fragment of nothingness momentarily materialized and even now disintegrating again.

And even its flavor, hard on the chef's retreating heels, has vanished too. At the very moment when our quivering nostrils were transmitting the ironical, elusive savor of that ephemeral delicacy to our palates.

What point then in itemizing these dishes? In listing them on a menu? In making them one's claim to fame? Let us simply take the word of elementary cookbooks that there are two kinds (or even three, if you count the *soufflés glacés*, but I really don't think we should): the *soufflés de cuisine* and the *soufflés d'entremets*. In other words, *soufflés* that are main dishes in themselves, in which you put salt, and *soufflés* that are puddings, in which you put sugar.

And that's it. Unless we make a separate category for *soufflés* made with shellfish, in which the flesh of some crustacean is incorporated in the form of diced meat, thereby at last conferring upon the *soufflé* a spuriously tangible existence.

I can already hear the counterblasts: that I am a dull and earthbound creature; that the entire charm of this edible zephyr resides in its delicacy; that the most delicate of ingredients become more sublimely rarefied still when used in it; that a truffle *soufflé* is the very last word in gustatory refinement; and that Epicurus himself is said to have contented himself with sucking the stone of the olive that was in the lark, that was in the quail, that was in the partridge, that was in the pheasant that was cooked inside the cabbage. And I believe it! But I am not Epicurus—and mistrustful of legends —so I prefer the olive and the lark, just as I prefer the truffle itself to a mere shadow of it on my olfactory nerves.

So I rather tend to smile at this notion of the volatile essences of ingredients attaining their perfection in the *soufflé*. I remember when three of us—René Lasserre, Albert Simonin, and I—decided to have a "slang" dinner. It was to start with "Pigalle pimps with their good ladies in a *soufflé*." In other words, mackerels in white wine and cod *soufflés*, since *maquereau* also means a pimp and *morue* (cod) is one of the names they give to streetwalkers in Paris.

"But of course I shall serve turbot *soufflés* instead," Lasserre said. "They're more delicate."

I demurred. Less out of a concern for authenticity than

because I have always professed that the cod (whether on the sidewalk or the dining table) has been criminally underestimated. And in fact those *soufflés* were a wonder (for *soufflés* that is, of course) and we were all ecstatic about them. And the best of it was that the rather strong taste of the cod turned out to be more volatile and more perceptible (if not actually recognizable) than that of the turbot.

But, you will ask, if you are so opposed to *soufflés* why include one among these recipes?

And my answer is: for the sake of the ladies.

They recognize in the *soufflé*, as though in a mirror, their own fragile and delicately fabricated beauty, the precarious glamor of social poise, the vanity of their superficial essence. They revel in it. They are intoxicated by it, by its perfume, by its flimsy showiness: it emerges from such and such a celebrated kitchen the way a dress does from Dior's workshops, with a signature—that irreplaceable, unfathomable something. The little dressmaker in Montmartre who copies the dress, *exactly*, can never give it that extra something that is in fact a pure illusion. The bistro in Belleville or the cook in Montparnasse who slaves away in order to turn out the same *soufflé* as the Tour d'Argent or Maxim's are amazed when they fail for exactly the same reasons. Their *soufflés* lack that little something that is everything, that doesn't exist, that will win the heart of a woman—and sometimes a man's—but makes the wise man merely smile.

At the heart of the *soufflé* lies nothingness itself, and its perfumed soul is light, as light as a vow of love.

And needless to say it is the recipe for a dessert *soufflé* that I intend to give you. Because at least the *soufflé* at this point in the meal does have an excuse for existing: after the cheese, a gourmet once observed, with much justice, any man worthy of the name has finished his meal.

And so the dessert *soufflé* is not a dish for the gastronome. It is a *divertissement*. And from the ranks of the dessert *soufflés* I have selected for you the *soufflé Rothschild*.

It is the very embodiment of empty display, the *ne plus ultra* of culinary fancy, while at the same time concealing in its depths, spangling the sweet and fragmented kaleidoscope of candied fruits, the mystery of Danziger Goldwasser.

Yet how many chefs, I wonder, have even heard of it?

Soufflé Rothschild

½ cup milk
   5 tbs plus 1 tsp sugar
salt
   3½ tbs flour
1 vanilla bean (or 1 tsp vanilla)
   4 egg yolks
2 tbs butter

6 egg whites
   4 tbs mixed candied fruits (cherries, angelica, pineapple, orange peel, citron, lemon peel)
Danziger Goldwasser
   12 large strawberries

Boil the ½ cup of milk with the sugar and a pinch of salt. Sift the flour, mix it with a little extra cold milk and add it to the hot milk. Add the vanilla bean and cook for 3 minutes. Remove the vanilla bean.

Remove from the heat. Whisking lightly, quickly add the egg yolks, 1 tablespoon plus 1 teaspoon butter, and the stiffly beaten egg whites.

Dice the candied fruit very finely and soak in some Danziger Goldwasser with plenty of gold spangles in it.

Mix the *soufflé* mixture and the fruit together.

Use the remaining butter to butter a *soufflé* dish, dust with sugar, and fill with the mixture. Smooth the surface. Place in the oven and bake at a moderate heat for about 30 minutes. Just before serving arrange the strawberries on top of the *soufflé*.

Only a champagne *nature* or
a Mumm Crémant de Cramant
is a truly fit companion for this
springtime banquet.

Fraises et Framboises Chantilly

(Strawberries and Raspberries with Whipped Cream)

Strawberries and raspberries are among the few fruits that did not come to us from Asia. The cradle of the strawberry was probably the Alps, where it grew wild. As for the raspberry cane, that came from the same place, and its name in French is of course a contraction of *fraisier du bois* (wild strawberry plant). So the two fruits are sisters.

For a long time, moreover, the only strawberries we had were wild ones. And personally I don't really feel that cultivation has produced any improvement. The idea of wild strawberries evokes for me the little sixteenth-century village girls who used to pick them on the edges of the woods and then bring them into town, nestling in little bark containers, to sell in the streets, where they were particularly enjoyed by the ladies, who ate them with cream and sugar.

Strawberries and cream. Is it an association of colors? Is it because the flavors marry so perfectly? Whatever the reason, the red of the strawberry and the pallor of rich cream have been united since all eternity both on our tables and in poets' imagery. And like Ronsard, we compare La Reine Margot's complexion (or another's, for our mistress is always, after all, our queen)

458

An English-style tea at the Prince of Conti's

. . . to the dye of a reddening pink
Or strawberry sunk in milky deeps
When through the mantling cream it peeps.

Before embracing the earth with its spreading stalks and its benefits (the image is that of the naturalist Bernardin de Saint-Pierre and typically a little extravagant), the wild strawberry plant dots it, in spring, with the tiny white rosettes which are the Legion of Honor buttons at the edge of our woods. The cultivated strawberry, the "ordinary" strawberry as I think of it, that big lump of a strawberry, evokes no more romantic image than a comfortable, a long-married garden bed. But the little wild strawberry is altogether gayer and more piquant! The wild strawberry hovers on the lips of a young shopgirl in a novel by Paul de Kock.

Nor is the strawberry allied to the raspberry solely in song:

Ah, les fraises et les framboises,
Le bon vin qu'nous avons bu . . .

Its stern purple is the ideal foil for the strawberry's bright red, more temperate, more assured, and richer too. J. K. Huysmans paid homage to the alliance of monk's sackcloth and cardinal's purple by spreading raspberry jelly on slices of buttered gingerbread; and our intention here is to consecrate the virginal alliance of strawberries, raspberries, and cream to the budding spring.

But the seventeenth century was to bring to cream a new mode, a new sublimity by making it suddenly and magically aerial—the miracle of *crème Chantilly*.

Chantilly was at that time the residence of the Condés. They received the King there as befits a king. And though history does not tell us who ran their kitchens, we do know that the major-domo of food was that Vatel, of whom we have spoken before. (The widespread assumption that Vatel was a cook is erroneous. Yet many restaurant owners still call their establishments Au Petit Vatel, or Au Grand Vatel.) And we know, from the famous letter written by Mme de Sévigné to her daughter, all the details of the poor fellow's death, on April 23, 1671.

To impale oneself on one's sword on the grounds that no fish has been delivered is the act not of a chef but rather of a manic-depressive major-domo. But here is the letter of the *Grand Siècle*'s Gossip-in-Chief:

Paris, Sunday April 26, 1671

It is Sunday; this letter will not leave until Wednesday, but then this isn't a letter but simply an account, just passed on to me by Moreuil for your benefit, of all that happened at Chantilly concerning Vatel. I wrote to you on Friday that he had stabbed himself: here is the matter in detail.

The king arrived on Thursday evening: hunt, lanterns, moonlight, walk in the gardens, collation in a spot carpeted with jonquils, everything as perfect as could be wished. They supped: there were one or two tables left without roast meat because of several unexpected guests. This made a great impression on Vatel; several times he said: "I am dishonored. This is an affront I can never bear." To Gourville he said: "My head is swimming; I haven't slept for twelve nights; help me give orders." Gourville reassured him as much as he

N° 3. — 1ʳᵉ Année.
Dimanche 9 Juillet 1905.

BRILLAT - SAVARIN

LE NUMÉRO : 5 Centimes

La CUISINE des Familles

ALEX. DUMAS PÈRE

CHARLES MONSELET

RECUEIL HEBDOMADAIRE
de Recettes d'Actualité très clairement expliquées
très faciles à exécuter
Rédactrice en chef : Mᵐᵉ JEANNE SAVARIN

LA MORT DE VATEL

could. But the roast that had been short, not at the king's table but at the furthest possible remove, remained in his head. Gourville told Monsieur le Prince of it, and Monsieur le Prince even went up to his room and said: "Vatel, everything has gone very well, nothing could have been finer than the king's supper."

Vatel said: "Monseigneur, your kindness is the finishing stroke: I know that there was no roast for two tables." "Not at all," Monsieur le Prince said, "you mustn't get worked up, everything has gone off very well."

Night fell: the fireworks were not a success because of the low cloud: the display had cost sixteen thousand francs. At four o'clock, Vatel was on his rounds, everywhere at once, and found everyone asleep. He met a small fishmonger who had only two baskets of fish for him; he asked him: "Is that all you have?" The man answered: "Yes, monsieur." He didn't realize that Vatel had sent for fish to every port on the coast. He waited a little while; the other fishmongers didn't come; his head began to spin. He thought there was not going to be any more fresh fish; he found Gourville and said to him: "Monsieur, I shan't survive this further affront; I have too much honor and reputation to lose." Gourville tried to laugh him out of it. Vatel went up to his room, lodged his sword against the door, and pushed it through his body, *though not until his third try, because he had given himself two wounds that had not proved mortal first; then he fell dead. Meanwhile fresh fish was pouring in from all sides; they went looking for Vatel to find out what to do with it; they went up to his room; they knocked, then broke down the door; they found him in a pool of his own blood; they ran to Monsieur le Prince, who was in despair. Monsieur le Duc wept: his whole journey to Burgundy depended upon Vatel, Monsieur le Prince informed the king very sadly: they say that it was all because he was so concerned with his honor, in his way; he was highly praised, some blamed and some praised his courage. The king said that he had been putting off coming to Chantilly for five years because he understood what an embarrassment his household and presence was. He told Monsieur le Prince that he must have only two tables and not burden himself with all the rest. He swore that he would not permit Monsieur le Prince to go on as he had been doing; but it was too late for poor Vatel. Meanwhile Gourville was trying to make up for Vatel's loss; he succeeded; they dined very well, they were served a collation, then supper, they walked, they played, they hunted; everything was heavy with the scent of jonquils, everyone was enchanted. Yesterday, Saturday, they did the same, and in the evening the king went to Liancourt, where he had ordered a midnight supper; he is to stay there today. That is all that Moreuil has told me to pass on to you. So there you must allow me to draw breath, for I know no more.*

Fraises et Framboises Chantilly

wild strawberries
* raspberries*
brandy

pinch of pepper
* heavy whipping cream*
powdered sugar

Pick over an equal quantity of raspberries and wild strawberries. They should not be washed.

Put them in a big bowl with a few spoonfuls of brandy and a pinch of pepper. Let them steep.

Whip your cream in a cool place 1 hour before you will be using it. Fold a sufficient quantity of powdered sugar into the whipped cream (bearing in mind that no sugar has been added to the fruit). Stir the strawberries and raspberries in their bowl. Top with the *crème Chantilly*. Serve.

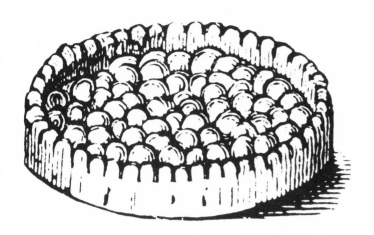

MENU

*Terrine d'anguilles
*Poulet Célestine
*Tarte Bourdaloue

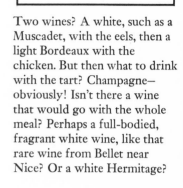

Two wines? A white, such as a Muscadet, with the eels, then a light Bordeaux with the chicken. But then what to drink with the tart? Champagne—obviously! Isn't there a wine that would go with the whole meal? Perhaps a full-bodied, fragrant white wine, like that rare wine from Bellet near Nice? Or a white Hermitage?

Tarte Bourdaloue

(Pear-Apricot Cream Tart)

Louis Bourdaloue, born in Bourges in 1632, began preaching in 1666. His startling success led him in 1669 to Paris, where he delivered more sermons to the Court than any other preacher. And it was in Paris that he died in 1704.

He did not preach exclusively to the Court; he was also to be seen and heard at a little chapel dedicated to the Virgin of Loretto on the rue Coquenard (now the rue Lamartine). Later on, and a little farther on too, the church of Notre-Dame de Lorette was to be built in this neighborhood and to remain—indirectly through his love of good food—indissolubly linked with the name of the celebrated preacher.

Let us try to sort out legend from reality.

A plan of Paris in the reign of François I shows us how much still lay outside the city gates in the sixteenth century: Saint-Martin, Saint-Denis, Montmartre, and the Marais des Porcherons. The Clos Montmartre was all orchards as yet. So would this chapel, built in 1645, have included in its Sunday congregations the peasants who lived nearby? Probably. In any case, there is no difficulty in accepting that a *fouacier*

should have set up a temporary stall nearby and sold his products to those leaving the building after Mass.

A *fouacier?* Larousse explains that this was the name given to one who baked and sold *fouaces* (from the Latin *focus*, meaning hearth), which were a sort of thick biscuit cooked in an oven or in the embers of a wood fire.

Of this primitive *fouace* we can still find in the south of France those more refined and brioche-like descendants the *fouasses* and *fougasses*. But the *fouace* remains the forefather of all our pastry.

Later on, as the neighborhood began to become more populous, the original vendor's successors built a more permanent stall and eventually a little shop.

So you can see the inevitable legend already. Bourdaloue, it goes, preached so often in this church that he came to live with the *fouacier*. Moreover Esprit Fléchier is supposed to have preached there too, and the two rivals in eloquence, each in his own chapel, engaged in admirable duels of rhetoric. Possibly. What is certain is that one of the first *fouacier*'s successors erased his own name from the shop sign and replaced it with that of Bourdaloue. But when? And who was he?

J. H. Favre, in his *Dictionnaire universel de cuisine* of 1883, gives a recipe created by M. Fasquelle of the rue Bourdaloue, Paris. And I imagine that it was from the street and not from the man that this pastrycook took the name of his establishment.

For how could Bourdaloue have lived in a neighborhood that wasn't built until one hundred fifty years later, under Louis-Philippe?

The present proprietor of Bourdaloue (whose name, significantly enough, is M. Fouassier) is the successor of a M. Coquelin. And that M. Coquelin, having been apprenticed when young to a M. Briam, bought his establishment from him in 1889 for one franc!

And according to M. Fouassier, it was Briam who created the *tarte Bourdaloue*. But perhaps the recipe had actually been passed on by his predecessor Fasquelle?

At all events it is not the only recipe dedicated to the famous preacher. In Gringoire and Saulnier's *Répertoire de la cuisine* I find a *potage Bourdaloue* (consommé with tomato, purée of green asparagus, and carrots); a *velouté Bourdaloue* (cream of rice with purée of chicken, white beans, tomato, and green asparagus); apricots, bananas, nectarines, peaches, pears, and clingstone peaches *Bourdaloue* (hot

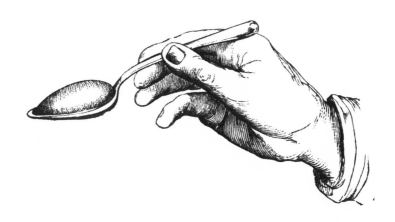

entremets made with these fruits, frangipane, and crushed macaroons); a *bombe Bourdaloue* (anisette and vanilla with candied violets). Not to mention Fasquelle's *gâteau à la Bourdaloue* (filberts, flour, butter, sugar, and eggs) and a few more still.

But the best known is still the *tarte Bourdaloue*, the recipe of which probably goes back to our M. Briam (in the workshops of the present establishment there are still copper dishes with his name stamped on them). M. Fouassier still sells scores of them every day. It is ordered by people from every branch of society, and I have even read somewhere that De Gaulle had them served at his Elysée blow-outs.

So I went along to the shop and asked M. Fouassier for the recipe. And here it is:

Tarte Bourdaloue

puff pastry
  ¼ lb sugar
3 egg yolks
  salt
4 tbs flour
  liqueur glass kirsch

1 cup milk
  scant 2 tbs butter
8 pears
  sugar syrup
¼ lb sugar
  ¼ lb apricots

Make some puff pastry, very light, with sweet butter. Let it stand.

Beat the sugar into the egg yolks. Add a pinch of salt, the flour, and kirsch.

Boil the milk and add it to the egg-yolk mixture. Pour the mixture back into a saucepan and bring to a boil, stirring constantly. When this custard has thickened pour it into an earthenware dish.

Spread the butter over the top of the custard to prevent a skin from forming. Let it cool. This is your *crème pâtissière*.

Peel the pears and cut them in two lengthwise. Remove the cores. Poach them in sugar syrup.

Cook the apricots and sugar together for 1 hour, or until they become a syrupy purée. Clarify and strain this apricot purée.

Roll out the pastry, line a pie plate with it and bake the shell.

Spread a layer of your *crème pâtissière* on the bottom of the baked shell. Arrange the poached pear halves on top. Coat them with the apricot purée.

A light Burgundy from the
Côte de Beaune to start with.
A Sauternes or Barsac with the
pithiviers. If you don't want to
go as far as the prestigious
Château d'Yquem, why not a
Château Climens or a Château
Doisy-Daëne, which may be a
second-class growth officially
but is nevertheless excellent.
Drink it well chilled.

Pithiviers (Almond-Rum Pastry)

Pithiviers: chief town of the *arrondissement* of Loiret, on the
river Oeuf, tributary of the Essonne. Population: 9,122. Inhabitants known as *pithivériens*. Sixteenth-century château.
Lark pies, cakes known as *pithiviers*.

The dictionary is too terse by half. It ought also to say
that Pithiviers grew up around a church built over the tomb
of Salomon III, king of Brittany in the ninth century. St.
Gregory, the bishop of Armenia, also died here, and his relics
attracted numerous pilgrimages. And lastly, having been introduced from Arabia by the Moors, saffron penetrated as
far as Pithiviers, and after the Moors were finally defeated at
Poitiers the saffron industry became established on the river
Oeuf and flourished there in the Middle Ages.

We know that the Sybarites—according to Virgil anyway—used to drink saffron before putting on their saffron
wreaths and hurling themselves into their orgies.

However, it is many a long day now since saffron ceased
to be anything more than just another—not much used—spice;
and nowadays its role as "fun thing" and orgy-inducer seems
to have been taken over by marijuana.

The fact remains, however, that Pithiviers wasted no time in setting itself up as a good-food center. Its lark pies have been famous ever since the well-known story of Charles IX and the Huguenots (see the section on *Terrine de Canard Madeleine Decure*) earned Margeolet, known as Provenchère, a pastrycook on the rue de Cygne, a royal patent that remained in the family for three centuries. It is also the center of the famous Gâtinais honeycombs, and the home of a cheese called *Pithiviers au foin*. Lastly, it was a part of the country celebrated for its filberts, and it was possibly some kind of hazelnut pastry that was the forerunner of the present *pithiviers* made with almonds.

And that is about the sum of what I know about this very pleasant cake, a pastry that also has the distinction of being much revered by wine lovers and wine experts. For sugary dishes generally tend to ruin the taste of good wine, but the presence of the almonds in the *pithiviers* makes it one of the rare desserts that can be eaten with, for example, a great Sauternes.

And it would certainly deserve a place among the hundred glories of French cooking for that reason alone.

It also has a sort of aura about it that I can only describe as a quintessence of Sundayness. It is the cake that one goes to buy at the famous pastry shop after Mass. There is still a smell of incense floating around the good wife and mother that mingles, as she enters it, with the sugary fragrance of the shop. The young lady serving in the shop, her hands red but her face of a distinguished pallor, is herself all sugar. She gives the children a piece of candy, pretending not to let their mother see it.

A sly look from the little boy. She has crescents of sweat under the arms of her cream-colored bodice, and somewhat hairy legs, the young lady in the shop. But her chest is plump as a juicy *baba*, and her lips as bright as her strawberry tarts.

"Here, you may carry it. But be careful. Hold it level. And don't dawdle. Come on now!"

These walks home from Mass, in provincial towns, are the same from one end of the country to the other. The cakes vary sometimes of course; but I suspect that the *pithiviers* is the one that recurs most often. Granny and Auntie Chiffon are so fond of it for one thing! And of course they won't turn up their noses at a small glass (a little drop as they simperingly put it) of some precious, syrupy wine, amber-colored, clear, and sweet as the baby Jesus himself.

Yes, it ought really to be a communion wine, so that it could be drunk to the honor of the Lord. For it is almost a communion cake they are drinking it with, this *pithiviers* from which a whiff of bitter almonds sometimes escapes. A whiff of cyanide? Well, you never know in provincial families. . . . But at least the skeleton in the cupboard has the consolation that—pastry for pastry—to be poisoned with a *pithiviers* at least has a certain class!

Pithiviers

¼ lb almonds
  ¼ lb powdered sugar
2 eggs
  3½ tbs melted butter

6 tbs Demerara rum
  puff pastry
granulated sugar

Grind the almonds. Mix them in a bowl with the sugar. Add 1 egg and beat the mixture.

Add the melted butter and rum. Set aside to cool.

Make some very light puff pastry. Roll it out to a thickness of a little less than one-quarter inch and cut out a circle 8½ inches in diameter. Roll out the pastry again and cut out another circle twice as thick and slightly larger.

On this larger circle spread the almond mixture, leaving 1½ inches all around the edge. Wet this edge. Put the smaller circle of pastry on top, press down well around the edge. Then slash the edge of the larger bottom all around and fold it up to make a good seal. Brush with some of the other beaten egg. Cut a decoration in the center with the tip of your knife. Bake in a hot oven.

Sprinkle with granulated sugar when you remove it from the oven. Put it back for 30 seconds. Take it out again and let it stand until cool.

First the wine used to make the
meurette, a red, that will go
perfectly with the cold lamb.
Then a glass of Banyuls or
Frontignan, well chilled.

Raisiné de Courtenay

(Pear, Quince, and Grape Preserve)

All the culinographers from Alexandre Dumas to Prosper
Montagné are in agreement that the best *raisiné* is made in
Burgundy. Which hasn't prevented either Reboul or the
Larousse gastronomique from giving us the recipe for the
Mediterranean *raisiné*.

For my part, this most splendid of jams is a childhood
memory and remains essentially a product of the Vivarais in
my mind—and would wherever its birthplace was—simply
because my godmother was incomparable in its confection,
making her *raisiné* as her mother had taught her in her birthplace "over Aubenas way."

The Vivarais is a buffer state. The dialect is soft and
singing on the tongue like Provençal, and yet in the north of
the region they share the harsh life of the peasants in the
Auvergne. And lastly, via the Rhône Valley there come
whiffs of both Marseilles and Lyons, and from farther off
still the savors of Burgundy. Was that *raisiné* from Aubenas
a child of the mistral or a son of the glorious Burgundian
dukes? But the truth is that any wine-growing region can
have its *raisiné*. And the jam or fruit preserve was born, in

our country, with Nostradamus teaching us "the fashion and manner of making all liquid preserves with sugar, honey, and with boiled wine."

It is not without justice that comparisons are drawn between the culinary science and alchemy. Alchemy is one of the sources.

Nostradamus had studied first in Avignon, then in Montpellier, before returning to practice his profession at Salon-de-Provence (he was born in 1503 at Saint-Rémy). Then the rumor of his amazing predictions filtered up to the Court, to which Catherine de Médicis and Charles IX thereupon summoned him. Meanwhile, however, back in Provence, he had read the books of Baptiste de Cavagioles, author of a work entitled *Manière de faire toutes confitures*. For it was from Italy, in fact, that we acquired the still infant art of making candies, jams, fruit cheeses, candied fruits, ice cream, and sherbet. And the first result of the acquisition was the book by Nostradamus that appeared in Lyons in 1555.

This *Confiturier français* is the first complete work on the subject. Nostradamus does not conceal the fact that he knows his Cavagioles, but he assures us that he has also acquired a personal knowledge of the methods of Toulouse, Bordeaux, and La Rochelle, "in short of the whole country of Guyenne and the Languedoc and the whole of Provence, from the Dauphiné to the Lyonnais." He is thus able to describe "the most sovereign recipes" in his work and teach the reader how to "preserve little lemons and oranges whole, make quince marmalade, pine-nut cake, spun sugar, syrups, preserved pears, Spanish *turrón* (*touron d'Hespaigne*), marzipan tart, and jelly both costly and difficult to make."

My dear godmother had never read Nostradamus, and her grandmother knew nothing more of him probably than a few vague and anonymous prophecies, but the whole of that lower Ardèche region, bordering on both the Languedoc and Provence, still retains the tradition of the admirable all-fruits preserve in which melon and green tomato so deliciously cohabit.

Moreover, those were days when from May to November, all along the Rhône, the fragrance of jams and preserves was a constant presence in all "the best houses." It was an

ardéchois, Olivier de Serres, who in giving his advice and recipes assured "the young lady reader" that "she will delight in these, continuing the proof of her mind's subtlety."

Like a proper young lady of one of the best houses, my godmother must have learned this "occupation suitable for young ladies" (preserve-making) from the very wellspring, from the oral tradition that goes back through the centuries to Nostradamus and Olivier de Serres themselves. It was they who had inspired the lawyer Tourton of Annonay who, in about 1700, made all the entries in his family's Household Book himself, and later on the Mme Seignobos who codified the recipe for pickled walnuts for the earliest home-economics classes late in the nineteenth century.

The grape jelly of the Basse-Ardèche is also a *raisiné*, though at La Louvesc the jelly made with bilberries was very popular; and I also remember a preserve made of figs in which pieces of watermelon rind, almonds, and walnuts seemed to be held prisoners in a black and sugary juice—voluntary, delighted, dreamy prisoners.

The *raisiné* seems to be disappearing now, in these days when no one has any time. And besides, why go to all that bother making sweet things that our factories can offer us ready-made, ready digested too, almost, with their horribly eye-catching and sometimes noxious colors? The murderer is there on your table, and his death's-head chemical grin, dripping with beet sugar, looks to you like a friendly smile. So much the worse for you!

In an old issue of *Cuisine des familles* I came across a defense of the *raisiné* written by an anonymous Burgundian who was already, even then, rejecting and condemning the *raisiné* sold in Paris "in the preparation of which apples, beet, and pumpkin are used."

This correspondent also remarked that the *raisiné* made in the southernmost region of France is made with grapes that are too sweet and should, therefore, be picked before they are quite ripe; whereas in the north, on the contrary, the grapes must be left until they are as ripe as it is possible to get them. In conclusion he extolled the middle-of-the-road perfection represented by the Burgundian grape, grown on *pineau* vines, as used in the *raisiné* of Courtenay. I don't quite know why, but this little village once had the reputation of being the home of the best *raisiné* of all.

So here is the recipe of the *raisiné de Courtenay*.

It makes a magical dessert served in iced crystal goblets with little individual brioches and a glass of sweet wine.

Raisiné de Courtenay

white grape must
  pears

quinces
  golden rum

Take a quantity of white grape must after the first pressing. Boil in a tin-lined copper kettle over low heat for at least 8 hours until it has been reduced by three-quarters.

Peel some pears and quinces (1 quince to every 3 pears) and cut them in quarters. Remove seeds and cores. Add them to the reduced must and continue to cook.

When the pears and quinces can be easily pierced with a knife the *raisiné* is cooked. Put into sterilized jars and lay paper dampened with the rum directly onto the surface of the cooled *raisiné*. Then tie a second piece of paper over the jar.

476

With the duckling, a Burgundy from the Côte de Beaune. A good year, but not too old. With the rice we shall serve champagne. A Pol Roger, for example.

Riz à l'Impératrice

(Rice with Candied Fruit and Kirsch)

I have been unable to discover the origin of this dessert anywhere. There have of course been a great many empresses in other countries, but if one keeps to France alone then the choice is restricted. The empress in question could be Josephine, Marie-Louise, or Eugénie. It may be supposed that the *riz à l'Impératrice* must date back before the Second Empire, in which case it must be either Josephine or Marie-Louise. The former was the more food-loving of the two, the one more likely to have a dish dedicated to her. But the second, plaintive and plump, must, being Viennese, have had a sweet tooth. So what is the answer?

There exists a stable companion, one might say, to the *riz à l'Impératrice* mentioned in a number of works. This is the *riz à l'Impériale*. The most noticeable difference between them is that the first is flavored with kirsch and the second with maraschino. Which provides evidence in favor of neither theory really. Napoleon's campaigns took him as far as the Adriatic coast, and there is plenty of kirsch in Austria. Perhaps Josephine would have preferred the rum of her native Antilles?

The truth is we just don't know.

Perhaps some attentive and curious reader will find the thread (of spun sugar) that will enable us to find our way back to the origin of this *entremets*—which I include here less from any personal affection for it than because it represents a sort of tradition. The tradition of the set piece. Carême, we know, actually studied architecture in order to improve the construction of his desserts. And indeed the illustrations in his cookbooks are very much like architects' plans or blueprints; a fact that rather tends to cut my appetite, so far does it all seem from "the nature of things." Constructive cooking I'm all for, but constructivism in the kitchen, no.

All the same, who would deny the fluted riches of the *riz à l'Impératrice* a place on Big Rock Candy Mountain? It makes one think of the cake that Proust's Gilberte used to offer to her little friends on Thursdays, that "architectural" *gâteau.* "In order to proceed to the destruction of this Nine-vite confection," the narrator tells us, "Gilberte inquired if I were hungry or not, while extracting for me a whole slice of her collapsing monument glistening and studded with scarlet fruits, in the Oriental taste."

Brought to such a peak of perfection, a pastry is no longer merely a pastry, a dessert is more than just a dessert. All things considered, such pomp and circumstance must indubitably date back to the First Empire, and there can hardly be any connection with the gloomy and pitiful Eugénie.

Since I have no more to say about the dish, I ought by rights to pass directly to the recipe. But allow me, I beg, to put in another word here on the subject of rice. Partly because it can never be repeated often enough that it is a magical form of nourishment and—albeit Asiatic in origin—far, far more French than the potato. But also, alas, because the French have not yet learned how to cook it.

As further proof of this I instance Favre's *Dictionnaire de cuisine*, in which he writes: "The Indians and Chinese, cooks less highly educated than ourselves, regard as a profanation the French way of cooking rice—which is always to over-cook it. A practice that has been admirably crystallized in that popular expression to be found in all the routine cook-books: boil some rice till it bursts. Whereas that is precisely the capital error in the preparation of rice, which should remain intact, whole."

Having said that, and said it well, Favre goes on to give his recipes, and the first of all blandly begins: "Boil some rice till it bursts. . . ." Which goes to show that no man is a prophet in his own works!

The *riz à l'Impératrice* is enriched with candied fruits.

I don't know why a basket of candied fruits makes me think of a Gothic stained-glass window. Same bright and simple patchwork of colors, as it were, lit up from inside. Same slight mystery. Our childhood kaleidoscopes offered similar treats to our eyes, an almost physical, sensual treat that you felt you could taste. Whenever they appeared, those familiar yet also—thanks to the confectioner (oh, Nostradamus!)—somehow foreign fruits, I gazed spellbound at the transparent cherry, the big golden apricot, the Reine-Claude plum that

La marchande de gâteaux.

Le tir.

was now Claudia and an Empress, and that green orange, the kumquat. My favorite.

Rice from the East, then, vanilla so difficult of impregnation from the Indies, and candied fruits brought down from the Middle Ages along the cathedral-builders' canals, these are the materials you need to construct this dessert monument so forgotten today—and that a Creole woman, wanton, bold, frivolous, for a while adored by a little egocentric general, christened in a moment's gay abandon.

Riz à l'Impératrice

½ lb long-grain rice
10 oz powdered sugar
1½ cups heavy cream
1 vanilla bean

½ lb mixed candied fruit
kirsch
2 egg whites
sweet almond oil

Cook the rice for 20 minutes in boiling water. Drain. Put it into a slow oven just long enough to evaporate any remaining water.

Put the rice back on the top of the stove and add the sugar, cream, and vanilla bean. Cook gently for 45 minutes. Remove the vanilla bean.

Cut the candied fruit into small dice.

Soak the dice for 2 hours in kirsch.

Drain off the kirsch. Add the fruit to the rice. Mix together well.

Beat the egg whites until stiff and fold them into the rice.

Wipe the inside of a decorative pudding mold. Oil it lightly with sweet almond oil; then pour in the rice. Refrigerate for several hours.

The wine used in the cooking of the *pochouse* can be served with the cheese as well. And even, at a pinch, with the fritters. But it would be better to drink nothing with those and then to finish the meal with a glass of medium-dry sherry.

Beignets d'Ananas

(Pineapple Fritters)

It was during his second voyage that Columbus found this fruit being cultivated by the Indians of tropical America, for whom its main virtue, incidentally, was as a medicine.

Until the eighteenth century pineapple-eating was mostly confined to the Antilles, where the young Françoise d'Aubigné discovered it with astonished wonder. History does not recount whether it was she, later on (when she had become both Madame de Maintenon and Madame Louis XIV), who induced her aging master to taste it. Legend has it at all events that the King—by then very much a declining sun—omitted in his ignorance to cut the rind off the fruit, and lay about him as a result with a tongue no less sharp than the fruit's own spiny leaves.

The truth, however, is that the first pineapples ever to reach maturity in France, in 1733, were enjoyed by Louis XV. They were produced by the greenhouses at Choisy-le-Roi.

For the pineapple this was the beginning of a notable gastronomic career, while the scientists began vying with one another to discover its numerous beneficent and medicinal properties.

482

So that no one today is likely to dispute the title of King of Fruits bestowed upon it, as early as the seventeenth century, by Father du Tertre: "The flesh of the pineapple dissolves in water and is so tasty that you may find in it the fragrance of the peach, of the apple, of the quince, and of the pear. I may with just cause term it the King of Fruits because it is both the most beautiful and the best of all fruits on this earth. It is no doubt for this reason that the King of Kings has placed a crown upon its head as the essential mark of its royalty."

But a pineapple cultivated under glass by the Duchess of Cleveland's gardener was presented to Charles II as early as 1672, and there is a painting commemorating that extraordinary gift.

Like all children, I was for a long while under the impression that pineapples came into this world sliced and rindless and grew inside cans. It is, alas, only too common an error, and the grownups who continue to use nothing but canned pineapple—an incomparably mediocre product!—show no sign of any greater awareness. When fresh, moreover, the pineapple should never be cut in horizontal circles but in vertical slices cut with the grain. The taste is then totally different and much better. Lastly, though of American origin, the pineapple has now been acclimatized in Asia and Africa, and the best on the French market are those from the Azores.

In his history of the Indies, Hernandez de Oviedo (who says that the fruit's name originates in the Caribbean, where *nana* means "perfume of perfumes") praises its delicate and delicious taste, which he claims resembles those of the melon,

the strawberry, the raspberry, and the pippin apple all at the same time.

Alexandre Dumas, in his *Grand Dictionnaire de cuisine*, informs us that the really ripe pineapple takes on a bluish tinge and that its aroma resembles that of the raspberry. Its taste is sweet, and its juice, he adds, is much like that of Malmsey wine.

Peach, apple, quince, pear, raspberry, strawberry, melon . . . Why don't we just say it tastes above all of pineapple! And that we're quite happy with that.

La Reynière calls it "the most distinguished of the fruits we see served on our tables." It appears only at banquets, he says, because it can only be grown under glass and with considerable effort. And he also singles out a certain confectioner, M. Bourdeau, who made pineapple *pastilles* "that capture the fragrance of this fruit in a most conspicuous manner."

The pineapple is one of those fruits that can hold their own admirably in savory dishes and was immediately adopted —despite being several centuries behindhand—as an addition to the list of sweet-and-sour dishes of the Gothic cuisine. Did duck with pineapple originate in China, for example? It may have. But it seems more likely that it was created by Chinese cooks in the United States.

It is true of the pineapple as of all fruits that they are best eaten *au naturel*—which in this case means simply cutting it in vertical slices, as I have already said. One day I asked Joseph Delteil for his idea of a truly bizarre dish, and he answered: "The *pêche Melba!* A peach from the tree, how good that is!" A pineapple from the tree, or at any rate from the plant, perfectly ripe and simply pared, cored, and sliced is quite incomparable. It is scarcely necessary to scent it with a hint of alcohol, and above all not with kirsch. I become quite crimson with fury when I find those three horrible words at the bottom of a restaurant menu: *ananas au kirsch*.

It is a well-known fact that people who run restaurants haven't got much inside their heads, and certainly not imagination. But they must be able to think a bit, surely! Are there cherries in the Antilles? Did the cherry tree come to us from America? Whereas rum, by essence and definition, is now and always has been the ancestral companion of the pineapple!

A simple quarter of fresh pineapple flavored with dark

rum (very little, just an aromatic hint as a foil to the fruit's own fragrance) is a choice dessert indeed, and one for which I would willingly sacrifice all the pineapple's other incarnations: *ananas Fontanges* (buried beneath pistachio-flavored Italian meringue); *ananas à la Ninon* (mixed with wild strawberries and *crème Chantilly*); *ananas à la piémontaise* (on croquettes of vanilla-flavored polenta); *ananas à l'andalouse* (on a mound of rice covered in thick fruit syrup); *ananas favorite* (wrapped in frangipane), and so forth. Nevertheless, the recipe I have chosen is pineapple fritters.

Fritters are a childhood treat, and the child that always lives on inside us, no matter how old we may live to be, likes to see its memories and its dreams brought to life again in them. The fritter is more than a dessert; it is a reward! Holidays, whether they rate church bells or not, all have their fritter to buttress them, the traditional ritual of folklore that melts the heart with tender recollections. Every province, every village has its fritter, often made with fruit, sometimes just of batter, like the *bugnes* of Lyons. There are the "little pillows" of Montpellier; the *choch'creupés* of Lorraine; the fritters with a cream cheese filling from Champagne; *Mam' Goz* fritters from Brittany, which are made with potatoes and jam; sour milk fritters from the Bourbonnais; Berry *beugnons*; Vendée *tourtisseaux*; Béarn *crespets*; Roussillon *bunyetes*; mush fritters from the Franche Comté; vine tendril fritters from Provence; the *fritelles* of Corsica . . .

And to all those fritters dating back so many centuries, dredged in our wire baskets from the hot and smoking deep of time itself, let us add the pineapple fritter.

Beignets d'Ananas

1 fresh pineapple
apricot jam
fritter batter

fat for deep-fat frying
vanilla-flavored sugar
raspberry jam

Cut your fresh pineapple into round slices (just this once), and let them steep several hours in dark rum.

Spread 1 slice pineapple with a thick layer of apricot jam and place another slice on top to form a fruit sandwich. Continue until all the slices are used.

Dip these sandwiches in a light fritter batter (made with beer) and drop them into deep boiling fat. Take them out again as soon as they are golden. Drain and dry on absorbent paper.

Sprinkle with vanilla-flavored sugar. Serve with raspberry jam on the side.

Boulevard des Italiens

Sorbets *(Sherbets)*

No menu before World War I—or at least no menu for a dinner of any importance—would have been complete without an entry, after the fish and entrées, just before the roast, reading *sorbet*, or *granité*, or else *punch à la romaine* or *spoom*.

Each is a variant of the other.

The French believe *spoom* to be an English word, so presumably it is a distortion of "spume." It is a sherbet or water ice made with wine or fruit juice and given a particular frothiness by the addition of Italian meringue (beaten and sweetened egg white).

Punch à la romaine is a sherbet made with white wine, champagne, or orange or lemon juice, also mixed with Italian meringue but with a little rum added also, just before serving.

A *granité* (from the Italian *granita*) is a water ice made so that tiny crystals form in it. It is served sprinkled with flavored sugar.

Since the word *sorbet* also comes from the Italian *sorbetto*, one might easily conclude that its origins, as well as those of its derivatives—the *spoom*, the *punch à la romaine*, and the *granité*—need be sought for no further. But in fact the word *sorbetto* is itself derived from the Turkish word *sherbet*, "drinks." And it was the Chinese who first taught the Arabs how to make their sherbets.

During the Crusades, in the course of a truce, Saladin served Richard Coeur-de-Lion sherbets made from the snows of Lebanon. Perhaps that was the origin of the English "spoom"? Perhaps not—especially since there are those who say that the British "spoom" is entirely a figment of the French imagination—but what is certain is that it was the Arabs who introduced the Italians to the water ice and the Italians who brought it to France. Signor Procopio of the Café Procope initiated his customers into its cool delights; and later, when the Italian ice-cream makers had conquered the boulevards, Frascati and Tortoni made it fashionable. To such an extent that the churn used for making ice cream in general was named a *sorbetière*.

To return to our menu, however—the sherbet or water ice is a sensible way of making a break between courses. Not only does it clean the palate, but the chill slows down the digestion and revives the appetite.

And like so many other things that were once fashionable, it is now returning to favor again. I recall a recent lunch at the Tour d'Argent during which Claude Terrail served us a different sherbet after each course, the last of them, flavored with garden mint, a somewhat bizarre confection, but all carefully thought out, so that they related not merely to the dish they followed but also to the one they preceded. Personally—unless it is some sort of a banquet I am attending, consisting of a lot of dishes chosen more for visual and prestige reasons than for serious gastronomical motives—I am not over-fond of the *sorbet de milieu* (a phrase modeled on what was once termed the *coup de milieu**). But as a dessert your sherbet is a more sensible way of concluding a meal than even ice cream, since it makes less demands on the digestion (the sherbet being made solely of water, whereas ice

---

* The *coup de milieu* originated in Bordeaux. It consisted originally in the sudden appearance, in the middle of a banquet, of a young and sprightly village maiden whose task it was to pour out a glass of rum for each guest. The effect, they say, was magical.

cream—at least properly made ice cream—contains cream). The sherbet perfumes the palate, refreshes the mouth, and caresses the imagination.

For there is still an Oriental element lingering in it: it is a seraglio sweet with the power to evoke potentates' palaces, where contented digestions were lulled by the tinkling and tingling music to which beautiful dancing girls kept time.

You will say that it takes a lot of imagination to get all that out of a water ice. Indeed, indeed! And that is one thing your true epicure must never lack, since every dish is for him a springboard toward dreams less materialistic than people are often willing to allow.

Spoom au Vin de Muscat (Muscat Wine Sherbet)

2½ cups sugar
  ¾ cup water
2 lemons

1 orange
  2 cups Muscat wine
2 egg whites

Make a syrup with 2 cups plus 3 tablespoons of the sugar and the water. Let cool. Add to it the juice of the lemons and the orange. Strain and add the wine. Pour it into your ice trays and leave in the freezer compartment of your refrigerator.

Put the remaining sugar in a small saucepan and add just enough water to dissolve it. Heat over water until you have a syrup.

Having beaten the whites of egg to a froth, pour the boiling syrup into them and keep on whisking until the whole is completely cold. The result is what is called Italian meringue.

Gently mix this meringue into the first, frozen mixture. Serve in chilled glasses.

Granité au Citron (Lemon Water Ice)

3 lemons
  2 or 3 pieces lump sugar

10 oz granulated sugar
  1¼ cups water

Rub the rind of a lemon with two or three lumps of sugar. Put these lumps with the rest of the sugar in an earthenware casserole together with the juice of the three lemons and the water. Stir with a silver spoon till the sugar has dissolved. Strain through muslin and place in the ice-cube tray in the refrigerator.

From time to time pull the frozen edges away from the sides of the tray. In about 3 hours the *granité* should have formed. Beat it lightly with a whisk. Serve in goblets topped with a light sprinkling of granulated sugar.

Sorbet au Kümmel (Kümmel Sherbet)

9 oz sugar
  2 cups water
½ clove
  1 twist of lemon peel

1 twist of orange peel
  2 egg whites
1 cup kümmel

Put 5¼ ounces of the sugar in a saucepan with the water and add the half clove and the twists of peel. Make a fairly thin syrup. Put into refrigerator.

With the remaining sugar and the whites of egg make an Italian meringue as in the *spoom* recipe.

Gently combine the meringue, the cooled syrup, and half the kümmel. Replace in the refrigerator for a short while. Serve in chilled glasses after dividing the rest of the kümmel equally on top of the sherbet in each glass.

Pousse-Café

So there we are! A delicious meal!

In a restaurant this would be the moment for coffee—supposing their coffee is good!

Well, let us suppose it is, then: real mocha prepared *à la chaussette*—which does not, happily, mean literally "in a sock," but in an earthenware coffeepot kept warm in simmering water with the coffee dripping in drop by rich drop. (And above all don't forget that tiny pinch of salt on the freshly ground coffee that brings out its flavor!)

Good digestion inclines us to indulgence. So do not waste time judging your dismal contemporaries. Discuss instead the dish you have just eaten. Now is the time for those happy conversations I evoked before we began our hors d'oeuvre.

And the moment, too, for those forgotten handmaids, the liqueurs!

No one drinks liqueurs any more in France. The elixirs our grandmothers made have been driven out by mere unmysterious brand names. Marie Brizard is no longer an old lady who lives in Bordeaux; she is a corporation. And as for

Mme Amphoux, so dear to the heart of Balzac, who has even heard of her today?

So let us say, if you prefer, that it is the moment for *eaux-de-vie*. I won't say brandy; that limits it too much.

And even here our personal tastes may become the matter for enjoyable controversy: has the brandy of Armagnac become again today what once it was? Should good cognac be served at room temperature? How many pounds of raspberries to make a quart of the best liqueur? Is the grape brandy of Bugey superior to that of Burgundy? . . . And I have another suggestion for you, too: personally, after my coffee, I choose an old Scotch whisky, straight. And I drink it chilled!

And then, to our hundred glories of French cooking, and to a glory of Scottish distillation, I would also add another from Havana: a cigar.

Comfortably settled, stomach filled but free (the vital difference between gastronomy and gluttony), mind alert, I am ready to match your every shaft. And the conversation is bound to be a brilliant one (with you here there can be no doubt of that!) as is only fitting after such a flavorsome meal. The ladies, of course, will have no share in it, since, following the good old custom, we have retired without them to the smoking room.

We shall join them again later. For the moment though, let us talk of them, since it is they who are the true gourmet's dessert. For that is the real difference between a dish and a woman: the former one can discuss as one enjoys it, but the latter one can talk of only when she is not present.

INDICES

Names

Amunategui, Francis, 194–5, 321
Aux Lyonnais (*bistro*), 70–4

Bécard, Dr., 199–200
Beyer, Léon, 308–10
Bignon, Restaurant, 182, 446
Blanchard, Célestine, 268–70
Bocuse, Paul, 66, 408–9
Bolloré, Gwen-Aël, 46
Brillat-Savarin, Anthelme, 66, **99**,
    140, 158, 160, 201, 206, 207–8,
    215, 228, 254, 344–5, 387–9, 412

Cadran Bleu, Le (restaurant), 100
Café Anglais, 88, 107, 110, 182
Café de Paris (Biarritz), 226
Carême, 36, 90, 101, 181, 183, 187,
    215, 221, 313, 429–31
Chapelle, Vincent de la, 26, 88
Charpentier, Henri, 446
Chevet, 88–90
Choron (chef), 373
Copains, Les (restaurant), 118–19
Coralie, 78–9

Cubat, Pierre, 107–10
Curnonsky, 49, 66, 90, 130, 217,
    252, 313, 355, 363, 426

Derys, Gaston, 19, 355, 392
Doyen, Antoine-Nicolas, 94–5,
    155
Duglèré, 88, 107, 110
Dugnol, 446
Dumaine, Alexandre, 137, 247, 308
Dumay, Raymond, 329–30
Dunan, 229–30

Escoffier, 50, 181, 284, 451

Favre, Joseph, 174–5, 465
Fouassier, 465–7
Foyot, Restaurant, 299–302
Fraisse, Pierre, 49–50

Goncourt, Edmond and Jules de,
    58, 95, 101, 109–10, 195–7, 233,
    264, 273

Grimod de La Reynière, Alexandre, 99, 129, 208–10, 225, 226, 484

Lachman, Thérèse (La Païva), 108–10
Lallemand, Roger, 217–18
Langlais, 99–101
Laporte, Pierre, 227
Laporte, Robert, 227
Lasserre's (restaurant), 118–19
Lasserre, René, 255–6, 413, 454
Le Bègue, Charles-Gabriel, Comte de Germiny, 35–8
Ledoyen (restaurant), 94–5, 195

Maincave, Jules, 255
Maire, Restaurant, 194–7
Maison Dorée (restaurant), 182
Maxim's, 148, 402–3, 425, 456
Melba, Nellie, 451
Mirabeau, 58
Monselet, 305–6, 372, 376, 383
Montagné, Prosper, 181, 317, 185, 473

Nignon, Edouard, 181–4
Nouyrigat, Guy, 115, 153, 351–2

Oliver, Raymond, 212, 218, 233
Olivier, Pierre, 153, 440

Pansey, Henrion de, 254
Père Lathuile (restaurant), 195, 231–3
Peter's Restaurant, 49
Pointaire, 184
Potel et Chabot (catering firm), 182

Ramain, Paul, 405, 415
Restaurant du Cercle, 268–70
Rocher de Cancale, Le (restaurant), 99–100
Rousselot, Jacques, 268–70

Saguet, Mère (cabaret-restaurant), 261–5
Sarrassat, Lucien, 66

Tendret, Lucien, 158
Tour d'Argent (restaurant), 61, 243, 257–60, 456

Vaudoyer, Jean-Louis, 11
Vieux Paris (restaurant), 54
Violet, Daniel, 72
Violet, Daniel (son), 72
Voisin, Chez (restaurant), 182, 300, 373

Recipes

Page numbers in italic type indicate actual recipes

Aïoli de morue, 137–40, *140*
Almond-rum pastry, *57*, 225, 240, 469–72, *472*
Andouillette, 166–8
Anguilles, terrine d', 117–19, *120*, 463

APPETIZERS
  beuchelle tourangelle, 184
  blond chicken-liver cake, 160
  blood sausage, Auvergne style, 180
  boudin à l'Auvergnate, 180
  cheese tarts, 152
  foie gras, 156
  fricandeaux, 176
  gâteau de foies blonds de volailles, 160
  goose-liver pâté, 156
  gougères bourguignonnes, 152
  ham, parsleyed, 149
  jambon persillé, 149
  kidneys, sweetbreads, and mushrooms, 184

  little pies of Pézenas, 169
  meatballs, larded, 176
  meat pies, 172
  parsleyed ham, 149
  pâté of jellied duck, 164
  petits pâtés de Pézenas, 169
  terrine de canard Madeleine Decure, 164
Asparagus with butter and egg, 173, 383–5, *385*
Asperges à la Fontenelle, 173, 383–5, *385*

Baba au rhum à la Chantilly, *53*, 157, 211, 429–31, *432*
Beef béarnaise, 371–3, *373*
Beef, boiled, and vegetables, 291–3, *294*
Beef, cold, jellied casserole of, 337–41, *341*
Beef, fillet of, with foie gras and truffles, 273–6, *276*

BEEF RECIPES
   boeuf à la ficelle, 294
   boiled, and vegetables, 294, 347
   cold, jellied casserole of, 341
   côte de boeuf béarnaise, 373
   daube de boeuf en gelée, 341
   fillet, with foie gras and truffles, 276
   leftover, with onions, 331
   in meat and vegetable stew, 280
   in miroton, 331
   pepper steak, 298
   pot-au-feu, 347
   in potée Sarthoise, 280
   roast ribs, with béarnaise sauce, 373
   steack au poivre, 298
   tournedos Rossini, 276
Beef simmered with vegetables, 343–7, *347*
Beuchelle tourangelle, 181–4, *184*
Beurre blanc, *127*
Beignets d'ananas, 483–5, *485*
Bisque de homard, 26–7, *27*
Blanquette de veau, 353–6, *357*
Blood sausage, Auvergne style, 177–80, *180*
Blue trout, 129–30, *131*
Boeuf à la ficelle, 291–3, *294*
Boiled beef and vegetables, 291–3, *294*
Boudin à l'Auvergnate, 177–80, *180*
Brochet au beurre blanc, 125–7, *127*
Buntings, European, 57, 225–7, *227*
Butter-shallot-vinegar sauce, for fish, *127*

Caillettes, 398–401, *401*
Calf's head with turtle sauce, 311–14, *315*
Calf's sweetbreads with small green peas, 33, 287–9, *290*
Caneton aux navets, 250–3, *253*, 477
Caneton Tour d'Argent, 257–60, *260*

Cardons à la moelle, 406–9, *409*
Cassoulet, 317–20, *320*
Cheese tarts, 133, 150–1, *152*, 469
Chicken and mushrooms, 267–70, *270*, 463
Chicken, grilled, 261–5, *265*, 469
Chicken in the pot, 245–8, *249*
Chicken-liver cake, blond, 157–60, *160*
Chicken Marengo, 228–30, *230*
CHICKEN RECIPES
   Célestine, 270
   coq au vin, 239
   grilled, 265
   Marengo, 230
   and mushrooms, 270
   in the pot, 249
   with potatoes and artichokes, 234
   poule au pot, 249
   poulet à la crapaudine, *265*
   poulet Marengo, 230
   poulet père Lathuile, 234
   poussin Viroflay, 256
   rooster in wine, 239
   squab-chicken with spinach, 256
Chicken with potatoes and artichokes, 231–4, *234*
Chitterling sausage, 166–8
Choucroute, 305–10, *310*
Cod with garlic mayonnaise, 137–40, *140*
Cod with potatoes and eggs, 112–15, *115*
Coq au vin, 235–8, *239*
Coquilles Saint-Jacques à la nage, 69–75, *75*, 161, 169, 225, 359, 406
Côte de boeuf béarnaise, 371–3, *373*
Côte de veau Foyot, 117, 299–302, *303*
Côtes de mouton Champvallon, 125, 365–9, *369*
Cotriade, 103–6, *106*
Crayfish (freshwater), 63–6, *68*
Crêpes Suzette, 257, 411, 442–6, *447*

Daube de boeuf en gelée, 337–41, *341*

DESSERT RECIPES

almond-rum pastry, 472

baba au rhum à la Chantilly, 432

beignets d'ananas, 485

crêpes Suzette, 447

fraises et framboises Chantilly, 462

granité au citron, 490

kümmel sherbet, 490

lemon water ice, 490

melon de Schéhérazade, 436

melon filled with fruits and liqueurs, 436

muscat wine sherbet, 490

omelet filled with ice cream, 441

omelette surprise brésilienne, 441

pancakes with orange butter, 447

peach Melba, 452

pear-apricot cream tart, 467

pear, quince, and grape preserve, 476

pêche Melba, 452

pineapple fritters, 485

pithiviers, 472

raisiné de Courtenay, 476

rice with candied fruit and kirsch, 481

riz à l'Impératrice, 481

sherbets, 490

sorbet au kümmel, 490

sorbets, 490

soufflé Rothschild, 457

soufflé with candied fruits and liqueur, 457

spoom au vin de muscat, 490

strawberries and raspberries with whipped cream, 462

tarte Bourdaloue, 467

tarte Tatin, 427

upside-down tart, apple or pear, 427

yeast cake with nuts and raisins, 432

Deviled sauce, *265*

Dindon farci, 206–10, *210*

Duck, pâté of jellied, 161–4, *164*

DUCK RECIPES

caneton aux navets, 253

caneton Tour d'Argent, 260

duckling with new turnips, 253

duckling, Tour d'Argent, 260

pâté of jellied duck, *164*

terrine de canard Madeleine Decure, *164*

Duckling, Tour d'Argent, 257–60, *260*

Duckling with new turnips, 251–3, *253*, 477

Écrevisses à la nage, 63–6, *68*

Eel, baked, 117–19, *120*, 463

EGG RECIPES

oeufs en meurette, 193

oeufs pochés à la sauce béchamelle, 188

oeufs à la Toupinel, 197

omelet, Mother Poulard's, 203

omelets, variations, 200–2

omelette de la Mère Poulard, 203

poached, in baked potatoes, 197

poached, in béchamel sauce, 188

poached, with meurette sauce, 193

Escargots à la suçarelle, 77–9, *79*

Estofinado, 112–15, *115*

Fillet of beef with foie gras and truffles, 273–6, *276*

FISH RECIPES

aïoli de morue, 140

blue trout, 131

brochet au beurre blanc, 127

cod with garlic mayonnaise, 140

cod with potatoes and eggs, 115

cotriade, 106

eel, baked, 120

estofinado, 115

fish stew, 135

fisherman's stew, 106

fried freshwater fish, 123

friture, 123

FISH RECIPES (*cont.*)

goujons à la cascamèche, 144
gudgeons, marinated, 144
merlan frit, 86
pike with shallot-vinegar-butter sauce, 127
pochouse, 135
salmon trout with green sauce, 96
sole Cubat, 111
sole filet with shellfish and mushrooms, 102
sole normande, 102
sole with mushroom sauce, 111
stockfish, 115
terrine d'anguilles, 120
truite au bleu, 131
truite de mer sauce verte, 96
turbot soufflé au champagne, 91
turbot, stuffed, braised in champagne, 91
whiting, fried, 86
Fish stew, 133–5, *135*, 482
Fisherman's stew, 103–6, *106*
Foie gras, 153–6, *156*
Fraises et framboises Chantilly, 93, 141, 458–62, *462*
Freshwater fish, fried, 121–3, *123*
Fricandeaux, 173–6, *176*
Friture, 121–3, *123*

GAME RECIPES

European buntings, 227
hare in cream sauce, 219
jellied rabbit, 240
lapin en gelée, 240
lièvre à la Duchambais, 219
ortolans à la Robert Laporte, 227
partridges, young, with vegetables, 223
perdreaux en chartreuse, 223
pheasant, ragout of, 215
salmis de faisan à la Laguipière, 215
Garlic mayonnaise with cod, 137–40, *140*
Gâteau de foies blonds de volailles, 157–60, *160*

Gigot à la sept heures, 321–4, *324*
Goose-liver pâté, 153–6, *156*
Gougères bourguignonnes, 133, 150–1, *152*, 469
Goujons à la cascamèche, 141–4, *144*, 353
Granité au citron, *490*
Gratin de cèpes farcis, 403–5, *405*
Green sauce, *96*
Gudgeons, marinated, 141–4, *144*, 353

Ham, parsleyed, 146–9, *149*, 173, 191
Ham in vinegar-cream sauce, 359–64, *364*
Hare in cream sauce, 217–19, *219*
Hollandaise sauce, *55*
Homard à l'Américaine, 45–50, *51*, 53
Homard aux légumes, 53–5, *55*
Huîtres frites à la Villeroi, 57–62, *62*

Jambon persillé, 146–9, *149*, 173, 191
Jambon en saupiquet, 359–64, *364*
Jellied rabbit, 240–3, *243*

Kidneys, sweetbreads, and mushrooms, 181–4, *184*
Kümmel sherbet, *490*

Lamb, breast of, stuffed, 141, 349–52, *352*
Lamb, leg of, seven-hour, 321–4, *324*
Lapin en gelée, 240–3, *243*
Leftover meat with onions, 325–31, *331*
Lemon water ice, *490*
Lentil salad, 419–22, *422*
Lièvre à la Duchambais, 217–19, *219*
Little pies of Pézenas, 169–72, *172*
Lobster bisque, 26–7, *27*

Lobster with vegetables, 53–5, *55*

Lobster with wine, tomatoes, and herbs, 45–50, *51*, 53

Macaroni in pastry shell with mushroom-truffle sauce, 395–6, *397*

Meat and vegetable stew, 277–80, *280*

Meat and white-bean casserole, 317–20, *320*

Meat pies, 169–72, *172*

Meatballs, larded, 173–6, *176*

Melon filled with fruits and liqueurs, 39, 415, 433–6, *436*

Melon de Schéhérazade, 39, 415, 433–6, *436*

Merlan Colbert, 33, *86*

Merlan en colère, *86*

Merlan en lorgnette, *86*

Merlan frit, 33, 83–6, *86*

Miroton, 325–31, *331*

Mme Maigret's coq au vin blanc, 238, *239*

Morilles à la crème, 415–18, *418*

Muscat wine sherbet, *490*

Mushrooms, creamed morel, 415–18, *418*

Mushrooms, stuffed, with breadcrumb and cheese topping, 403–5, *405*

MUTTON RECIPES
  in casserole, with white beans, 320
  cassoulet, 320
  côtes de mouton Champvallon, 369
  navarin printanier, 285
  in pies of Pézenas, 172
  ribs, with onions and potatoes, 369
  stew, 285

Mutton ribs, with onions and potatoes, 125, 365–9, *369*

Mutton stew, 283–5, *285*

Navarin printanier, 283–5, *285*

Nettle soup, 29–32, *32*

Oeufs à la Toupinel, 194–7, *197*, 337

Oeufs en meurette, 146, 191–3, *193*, 473

Oeufs pochés à la sauce béchamelle, 185–8, *188*, 267

Omelet filled with ice cream, 133, 177, 437–40, *441*

Omelet, Mother Poulard's, 199–203, *203*

Omelets, variations, 200–2

Omelette de la Mère Poulard, 199–203, *203*

Omelette surprise brésilienne, 133, 177, 437–40, *441*

Onion soup, 17–20, *21*

Ortolans à la Robert Laporte, 57, 225–7, 227

Oxtail soup, 39–42, *42*

Oysters, fried, with sauce Villeroi, 57–62, *62*

Pancakes with orange butter, 257, 411, 442–6, *447*

Partridges, young, with vegetables, 221–3, *223*

Pâté of jellied duck, 161–4, *164*

Pâtés de Pézenas, 169–72, *172*

Peach Melba, 254, 449–51, *452*

Pear-apricot cream tart, 77, 463–7, *467*

Pear, quince, and grape preserve, 473–6, *476*

Pêche Melba, 254, 449–51, *452*

Pepper steak, 53, 295–8, *298*

Perdreaux en chartreuse, 221–3, *223*

Petits pâtés de Pézenas, les, 169–72, *172*

Pheasant, ragout of, 211–15, *215*

Pieds de porc à la Sainte Ménehould, 375–9, *379*, 415

Pies of Pézenas, 169–72, *172*

Pig organs with spinach and herbs, 398–401, *401*

Pigs' feet in breadcrumbs, 375–9, *379*, 415

Pike with shallot-vinegar-butter sauce, 125–7, *127*

Pineapple fritters, 483–5, *485*

Pithiviers, 57, 225, 240, 469–72, *472*

Poached eggs in baked potatoes, 194–7, *197*, 337

Poached eggs in béchamel sauce, 185–8, *188*, 267

Poached eggs with meurette sauce, 146, 191–3, *193*, 473

Pochouse, 133–5, *135*, 482

Poitrine d'agneau farcie, 141, 349–52, *352*

Pommes soufflées, 257, 371, 391–4, *394*

Potatoes, puffed, 257, 371, 391–4, *394*

Pot-au-feu, 343–7, *347*

Potage Germiny, 33–8, *38*, 257

Potage queue de boeuf, 39–42, *42*

Potée Sarthoise, 277–80, *280*

Poule au pot, 245–8, *249*

Poulet à la crapaudine, 261–5, *265*, 469

Poulet Célestine, 267–70, *270*, 463

Poulet Marengo, 228–30, *230*

Poulet père Lathuile, 231–4, *234*

Pousse-café, 491

Poussin Viroflay, 254–6, *256*

Rabbit, jellied, 240–3, *243*

Raisiné de Courtenay, 473–6, *476*

Raspberries, and strawberries, with whipped cream, 93, 141, 458–62, *462*

Rémoulade sauce, 75

Ribs of beef, roast, with béarnaise sauce, 371–3, *373*

Rice in cream sauce, Sun King, 411–14, *414*

Rice with candied fruit and kirsch, 477–81, *481*

Ris de veau Clamart, 33, 287–9, *290*

Riz à l'Impératrice, 477–81, *481*

Rooster in wine, 235–8, *239*

Salade de lentilles, 419–22, *422*

Salmis de faisan, 211–15, *215*

Salmon trout with green sauce, 93–6, *96*

Sauce Choron, *373*

Sauce diable, *265*

Sauce Duchambais, 217–18

Sauce Hollandaise, 55

Sauce rémoulade, 75

Sauce, turtle, *315*

Sauce Valois, *373*

Sauce verte, *96*

Sauce zingara, 359

Sauerkraut, 305–10, *310*

Sausage, blood, 177–80, *180*

Sausage, chitterling, 166–8

Scallops, 69–75, *75*, 161, 169, 225, 359, 406

Seven-hour leg of lamb, 321–4, *324*

SHELLFISH RECIPES

    coquilles Saint-Jacques à la nage, 75

    crayfish, 68

    écrevisses à la nage, 68

    escargots à la suçarelle, 79

    homard à l'Américaine, 51

    homard aux légumes, 55

    huîtres frites à la Villeroi, 62

    lobster with vegetables, 55

    lobster with wine, tomatoes, and herbs, 51

    oysters, fried, with sauce Villeroi, 62

    scallops, 75

    snails in sauce, 79

Sherbets, 166, 337, 487–9, *490*

Snails in sauce, 77–9, *79*

Sole Cubat, 107–10, *111*

Sole filet with shellfish and mushrooms, 39, 99–101, *102*

Sole normande, 39, 99–101, *102*

Sole with mushroom sauce, 107–10, *111*

Sorbet au kümmel, *490*

Sorbets, 166, 337, 487–9, *490*

Sorrel soup, cream of, 33–8, *38*, 257

Soufflé Rothschild, 453–7, *457*

Soufflé with candied fruits and liqueur, 453–7, *457*

SOUP RECIPES
  bisque de homard, 27
  cream of sorrel, 38
  d'orties, 32
  lobster bisque, 27
  nettle, 32
  onion, 21
  oxtail, 42
  au pistou, 25
  potage Germiny, 38
  queue de boeuf, 42
  vegetable with noodles and basil, 25
Soupe à l'oignon, 17–20, *21*
Soupe d'orties, 29–32, *32*
Soupe au pistou, 23–5, *25*
Spinach and herbs, with pig organs, 398–401, *401*
Spoom au vin de muscat, *490*
Squab-chicken with spinach, 254–6, *256*
Steack au poivre, 53, 295–8, *298*
Strawberries and raspberries with whipped cream, 93, 141, 458–62, *462*
Sweetbreads, calf's, with small green peas, 33, 287–9, *290*

Tarte Bourdaloue, 77, 463–7, *467*
Tarte Tatin, 194, 221, 425–7, *427*
Terrine d'anguilles, 117–19, *120*, 463
Terrine de canard Madeleine Decure, 161–4, *164*
Tête de veau en tortue, 311–14, *315*
Thistle and beef marrow, 406–9, *409*
Timbale de macaroni financière, 395–6, *397*
Timbale de riz Roy Soleil, 411–14, *414*
Tournedos Rossini, 273–6, *276*
Tripe, casserole, 50, 333–6, *336*
Tripes à la mode de Caen, 50, 333–6, *336*
Trout, blue, 129–30, *131*
Truffe en feuilleté, 387–90, *390*
Truffle in puff pastry, 387–90, *390*

Truite au bleu, 129–30, *131*
Truite de mer sauce verte, 93–6, *96*
Turbot soufflé au champagne, 87–90, *91*
Turbot, stuffed, braised in champagne, 87–90, *91*
Turkey, roast stuffed, 206–10, *210*
Turtle sauce, *315*

Upside-down tart (apple or pear), 194, 221, 425–7, *427*

Veal and onions in cream sauce, 353–6, *357*
Veal chops, baked, with cheese topping, 117, 299–302, *303*
VEAL RECIPES
  blanquette de veau, 357
  calf's head with turtle sauce, 315
  calf's sweetbreads with small green peas, 290
  chops, baked, with cheese topping, 303
  côte de veau Foyot, 303
  and onions in cream sauce, 357
  ris de veau Clamart, 290
  tête de veau en tortue, 315
VEGETABLE RECIPES
  asparagus with butter and egg, 385
  asperges à la Fontenelle, 385
  caillettes, 401
  cardons à la moelle, 409
  creamed morel mushrooms, 418
  gratin de cèpes farcis, 405
  lentil salad, 422
  macaroni in pastry shell with mushroom-truffle sauce, 397
  morilles à la crème, 418
  mushrooms, stuffed, with breadcrumb and cheese topping, 405
  pig organs with spinach and herbs, 401
  pommes soufflées, 394

VEGETABLE RECIPES (*cont.*)
  potato puffs, 394
  rice in cream sauce, Sun King, 414
  salade de lentilles, 422
  thistle and beef marrow, 409
  timbale de macaroni financière, 397
  timbale de riz Roy Soleil, 414
  truffe en feuilleté, 390
  truffle in puff pastry, 390

Vegetable soup with noodles and basil, 23–5, *25*
Villeroi sauce, *62*

Whiting, fried, 33, 83–6, *86*

Yeast cake with nuts and raisins, 53, 157, 211, 429–31, *432*